Little Green Men, Meowing Nuns and
Head-Hunting Panics

Little Green Men, Meowing Nuns and Head-Hunting Panics

A Study of Mass Psychogenic Illness and Social Delusion

ROBERT E. BARTHOLOMEW

Foreword by Erich Goode

McFarland & Company, Inc., Publishers

Jefferson, North Carolina, and London

Portions of Chapter 1 first appeared in Bartholomew, Robert and Erich Goode (2000). "Mass Delusions and Hysterias: Highlights from the Past Millennium." *Skeptical Inquirer* 24(3):20–28, and Bartholomew, Robert (1997). "Collective Delusions: A Skeptic's Guide." *Skeptical Inquirer* 31(3):29–33.

Parts of Chapter 7 were first published in Bartholomew, Robert (2000). "Rethinking the Dance Mania." *Skeptical Inquirer* 24(4):42–47.

A portion of Chapter 13 originally appeared in Bartholomew, Robert (1998). "Before Roswell: The Meaning Behind the Crashed UFO Myth." *Skeptical Inquirer* 22(3):29–30, 59.

Parts of Chapter 14 appeared in Bartholomew, Robert (1998). "The Martian Panic Sixty Years Later: What Have We Learned?" *The Skeptical Inquirer* 22(6):40–43.

All material from *The Skeptical Inquirer* is reproduced by permission of Barry Karr, Committee for the Scientific Investigation of the claims of the paranormal, P.O. Box 703, Amherst, NY 14226-0703.

A portion of Chapter 2 first appeared in Bartholomew, Robert and F. Sirois (1996). "Epidemic Hysteria in Schools: An International and Historical Overview." *Educational Studies* 22(3):285-311. It is reprinted with permission from Carfax Publishing Limited, Oxfordshire, England.

A portion of Chapter 3 is forthcoming in *Transcultural Psychiatry* and is reproduced by permission of Transcultural Psychiatry, 1033 Pine Avenue West, Montreal, Canada H3A 1A1.

On the cover: A Brooklyn factory worker has a fit of hysterics which spreads to others (*National Police Gazette*, 1886, courtesy Mary Evans Picture Library).

Library of Congress Cataloguing-in-Publication Data

Bartholomew, Robert E.
    Little green men, meowing nuns, and head-hunting panics :
a study of mass psychogenic illness and social delusion /
Robert E. Bartholomew ; foreword by Erich Goode.
        p.   cm.
    Includes bibliographical references and index.
    ISBN-13: 978-0-7864-0997-6 (softcover : 50# alkaline paper) ∞
    1. Hysteria (Social psychology)   2. Social psychology.
3. Panic. I. Title.
HM1033.B37   2001
302'.17 — dc21   2001018029

British Library cataloguing data are available

Manufactured in the United States of America

McFarland & Company, Inc., Publishers
  Box 611, Jefferson, North Carolina 28640
    www.mcfarlandpub.com

I dedicate this book to a handful of extraordinary people
who have encouraged me to clarify my
thoughts on this complex subject:

Keay Davidson, Wolfgang and Louise Jilek,
Robert J. Rickard, Simon Wessely,
and François Sirois.

Table of Contents

vii

Each believes easily what he fears and what he desires.
— La Fontaine

Foreword

The social sciences, Michel Foucault reminded us, are *discursive* disciplines. In the natural sciences, theories are overturned or absorbed by later developments. Newton's theories tell us exactly how and under what conditions physical bodies move; if his theories had failed to predict, they would have been of interest only to the antiquarian. In contrast, the work of writers such as Karl Marx or Sigmund Freud transcends the accumulation of empirical data. Their writings never quite go away, despite twists and turns in intellectual fad and fashion, because they supply "a paradigmatic set of terms, images, and concepts which organize thinking and experience about the past, present and future of society."[1] Marx and Freud, along with Foucault — as well as the best representatives of our craft — do not quite fail to predict because they do more than predict. They offer us a vision of how society is put together, how it works, and what its dynamics are. They organize our talk and thinking about the social world.

Rationality and irrationality represent two polar points on a continuum of images supposedly depicting human action. Over the centuries, fashion has dictated that intellectuals grasp one or the other pole.

The eighteenth century, described as the Age of Enlightenment, brought forth such rationalistic and utilitarian thinkers as Adam Smith, Jeremy Bentham, and Cesare Beccaria, who saw human action as dominated by reason. Self-interest, they argued, ultimately generated the greatest good for the greatest number.

By the turn of the nineteenth century, the tide had shifted, and Gustave LeBon's infamous *The Crowd* was published. LeBon broke with the basic assumptions of human rationality, arguing that assembled collectivities were stupid, suggestive, impulsive, intolerant, impetuous, and barbaric.

By the late 1960s and early 1970s, fashion in the social sciences had changed once again, and intellectuals came to see human action as controlled by reason and rationality. For the most part, crowds—far from the unreasoning, barbaric mobs LeBon depicted — usually act in ways that advance the interests of their members. Victims of disasters are not dominated by self-destructive hysteria, but meet upheaval with sensible, organized, altruistic practicality. Most social movements are not made of marginal misfits eager to follow any demagogue preaching an insane, apocalyptic message; instead they act in ways that maximize the achievement of specific, practical goals.

Yet what makes human behavior so fascinating is that it is so rarely entirely captured by a single discursive image. Sometimes human action is rational and sane, and sometimes it is not. Sometimes the means we select maximize the attainment of our goals, and sometimes they subvert them. Sometimes the formulations we devise to account for the material world are fairly accurate and empirically sound; sometimes tales, myths, and legends appeal far more than strictly factual accounts. Sometimes the threats out there — the "things that go bump in the night," the terror that comes lumbering out of the darkness— are real; sometimes forces conspire to make them simply *seem* real.

An entire intellectual generation has, for all practical purposes, ruled irrationalist tendencies out of existence. Yet they are there, and they need to be understood.

In this book, Robert Bartholomew bucks the tide of fashion and offers fascinating case studies of mass hysteria and delusions. Under what conditions do entire communities become terrorized by a nonexistent threat? Why do we see beasts and monsters lurking in the bushes, poised to attack us at the first opportunity? What do past episodes of collective delusion tell us about today's potential for such outbursts? At the dawning of the third millennium, are we really as immune from being terrorized by imaginary threats as we imagine?

Bartholomew reminds us that we are as much beast as angel, and that intellectual fad is utterly incapable of exiling our more fanciful, demonic tendencies to the dustbin of history.

Erich Goode
The State University of New York at Stony Brook

Preface

A boy stands on the platform of a country railway station. As the trains come and go, he notes their numbers in his notebook, along with their times of arrival and departure. And one day, reviewing his notes, he discerns a pattern; there are recurrences, frequencies, periodicities. And gradually he senses, beyond the isolated events he has been noting, the larger process... — Hilary Evans[1]

Mass psychogenic illness (MPI) is becoming increasingly recognized as a significant health and social problem that is more common than presently reported. For instance, in a recent study in the prestigious *New England Journal of Medicine*, the authors surmise (based on similar "war stories" from colleagues attending medical conferences) that the incidence of MPI outbreaks is greatly underreported.[2] Incidents are often a significant financial burden to responding emergency services, public health and environmental agencies, and the affected school or work site, which is often closed for days or weeks. Diagnoses often meet fierce resistance from victims, their families and community members, fostering an atmosphere of suspicion and mistrust that is reflected in the media, newly formed social movements and emotionally charged public forums.

Social delusions can produce similar results. When communities pursue imaginary bogeymen such as the "mad gasser" of Mattoon, the phantom slasher of Taipei, or midwestern cattle "mutilators," law enforcement agencies expend considerable time and resources to resolve such cases— and among their duties is keeping vigilante groups in check. Witch-hunts and rumor-induced panics about community evil-doers can endure for years and periodically recur, resulting in the persecution, imprisonment or even execution of innocent people, to say nothing of the ongoing emotional trauma that may persist long after the "successful" resolution of a particular episode.

In this book I offer a taxonomy or classification scheme for understanding episodes of mass psychogenic illness (MPI) and social delusions—something that is sorely needed given the confusion and misunderstanding which surround the topic. I identify four categories of MPI and five of social delusion, providing one or more case studies of each.

I began researching "mass hysteria" in 1986, and was initially baffled by the absence of a single comprehensive taxonomy. I quickly realized why. A literature survey identified 82 synonyms and no universally agreed upon definition. The interdisciplinary nature of the topic adds further confusion by prompting the use of diverse methods and assumptions in interpreting these behaviors. To make matters worse, it is evident that many episodes of social delusion are inappropriately labeled as forms of hysteria. Melanesian cargo "cults," medieval religious flagellants, the Dutch tulip "mania" of 1637, the communist infiltration "red scare" of 1919, the 1938 Martian invasion panic radio drama—each has been erroneously placed under the "mass hysteria" rubric. Ambiguously defined and conceptualized, terms such as "mass" or "epidemic" hysteria were and continue to be loosely employed to describe a variety of separate behaviors occurring across different cultures and time periods—behaviors having no association with hysteria as a clinical entity.

Media reports of mass psychogenic illness and social delusions offer fleeting glimpses of seemingly bizarre behaviors and beliefs with little understanding of the underlying social and psychological processes involved. Many outbreaks have a quasi-religious quality. It is as if an unseen force has seized control of the participants' minds. Viewers are hard-pressed to make sense of what they see, and to discern the larger pattern. Even in the scientific literature the context and meaning of episodes are downplayed, with psychogenic illness typically oversimplified as a relatively unproblematic cause and effect reaction to pent-up stress affecting innately susceptible females; social delusions are attributed to psychological abnormality, irrationality or ignorance.

It is my ultimate hope that this book will reduce or eliminate much of the present confusion and ambiguity that characterize the subject, in an effort to deepen understanding of these fascinating behaviors.

SECTION ONE

Broad Overview

Chapter 1

Mass Hysteria and Social Delusions: A Concise History

You can't depend on your judgment when your imagination is out of focus. — Mark Twain[1]

Hysteria and Mass Hysteria

There is a great deal of confusion about what is meant by the terms "mass hysteria" and "collective delusion." Let us begin by looking at individual hysteria, which involves the excitation, impairment, or loss of sensory or motor function — in addition to an array of psychogenic disturbances of these functions — with no apparent organic basis. Symptoms can include tremors, seizures, and the restriction of consciousness in dissociative reactions.[2] Sensory function pertains to the five senses, and motor function refers to impulses traveling on nerves or neurons that can cause muscles to contract. In other words, people experience symptoms that cannot be traced to any physical problem.[3]

The modern names for hysteria are "conversion disorder" and "dissociation disorder," terms widely used by mental health professionals such as psychiatrists, psychoanalysts, and psychologists. "Conversion disorder" refers to the converting of deep emotional conflicts and anxiety into physical complaints. A classic example is the army draftee deeply opposed to killing whose arm temporarily "freezes" when trying to fire a gun at the enemy. This is commonly referred to as "primary gain," which is derived by alleviating the anxiety generated from the internalized conflict. Primary gain is meeting a psychological need and providing a partial solution to an internal conflict. Hence, the soldier cannot pull the trigger, temporarily relieving his moral dilemma.[4] "Secondary gain" is an advantage that is derived by the manifestation of the unconscious conversion reaction. It can involve everything from interpersonal to social and material benefits (such

7

as affection from significant others) to public attention to compensation for suffering.[5] Secondary gain allows someone to avoid undesirable situations or outcomes, such as when a person's leg paralysis prevents his or her lover from breaking off a relationship. Primary and secondary gain are the two "benefits" derived from conversion disorder that in turn reinforce the symptoms.

Anxiety and Motor Hysteria

In relatively rare instances, hysteria can spread to groups. Episodes of "mass hysteria" are also known by such labels as "epidemic hysteria," "contagious hysteria" and "mass psychogenic illness." British psychiatrist Simon Wessely identified two types affecting groups: "anxiety hysteria" and "motor hysteria."[6]

Anxiety hysteria has a rapid onset and recovery time, usually lasting just a day. It is triggered by the sudden perception of a threatening agent, most commonly a strange odor or a rumor of tainted food. Symptoms are transient and benign, typically including headaches, dizziness, nausea, breathlessness and general weakness. Essentially, the symptoms result from an overwhelming stress reaction to sudden anxiety. Prior to the outbreak, there is rarely any preexisting group tension.

Under rare circumstances, anxiety hysteria can spread to communities. Symptoms in such cases appear to begin within cohesive, typically enclosed social units, but the imaginary harmful agent is at large within the communities in question, and anyone is viewed as a potential victim. Episodes often occur amid rumors and intense, credible media publicity involving the propagation of a false belief. Some episodes have involved rumors of the use of poison gas against ethnic minorities who distrust distant, central governments, including the Palestinian fear of the Israelis,[7] the Soviet Georgian suspicion of Moscow,[8] and ethnic Albanian mistrust of Serbs.[9]

In Auckland, New Zealand, in February 1973, fifty drums of the relatively harmless defoliant merphos were being unloaded at a wharf when someone noticed that several barrels were leaking, and a chemical-like smell permeated the air. After immediate requests for information on its toxicity, authorities were wrongly informed that merphos was extremely toxic. A state of emergency was declared and an evacuation ensued, after which at least 400 dock workers and nearby residents received treatment for various complaints including headache, breathing difficulty, and eye irritation.[10] During the 1980s, 400 people reported illness symptoms after intense media coverage about the contamination of a water supply in

Camelford, England. A subsequent investigation concluded that contrary to popular media claims, the incident posed no long-term harmful effects, and that anxiety triggered the symptoms.[11]

Mass motor hysteria develops more slowly than anxiety hysteria. It occurs amid an atmosphere of accumulating long-term group stress. It is prevalent in intolerable social situations such as strict school or religious settings where discipline is extreme. Symptoms include trancelike states, melodramatic acts of rebellion known as histrionics, and what physicians term "psychomotor agitation," whereby pent-up anxiety building over a long period results in disruptions to the nerves or neurons, sending messages to the muscles and triggering temporary bouts of twitching, spasms, and shaking. Symptoms appear gradually and usually take weeks or months to subside. An array of dissociative states characterizes many episodes.

Occasionally, motor hysteria spreads in epidemic form to a community. This was more common in previous centuries due to the prevalence of repressive political and social systems. A prominent historical example, related to the persecution of "witches," was the outbreak of demon possession that was mostly confined to women living in rural communities in southern France during the fourteenth and fifteenth centuries. Typical symptoms were crying, screaming, lewd sexual gestures, tremors, convulsions, and altered states of consciousness.[12] Modern reports are confined to subjects living in non–Western societies or indigenous peoples residing on reservations in the West, who experience a culturally camouflaged form of hysterical conversion. No known community cases were reported during the twentieth century among people living in mainstream Western society. Presumably, their acculturation provides them with various outlets with which to channel frustrations.[13]

Let us examine two modern cases of motor hysteria. The first occurred between October 1973 and June 1974, when anthropologist Stephen Frankel documented an episode of faintness, dizziness, confusion, temporary deafness and violence among about two dozen females between the ages of twelve and thirty.[14] Symptoms originated in persons most enculturated to Western values at an Australian nursing school. These nurses were the most acutely affected, exhibiting symptoms over twelve days versus just over four days for locals who were not nurses and had not been exposed to Western ways. The events occurred in the vicinity of Telefomin, Papua New Guinea, where tribesmen are infamous for their domination of women. Females are restricted to pastoral duties: gardening, animal husbandry, child care and food preparation. They must also adhere to rigid female-only taboos, and their sexual lives are strictly controlled. Marriages are pre-arranged, and there is little means of redress for abusive or demanding husbands. Females are also prohibited from quarreling with elders. The females internalize grievances. The episode occurred during a period of intergenerational conflict. Elders exerted strong pressure to conform with traditional values, while the younger generation was becoming acclimated to Western ways, mostly through contact with the European school system. Violent acts during the episode never resulted in serious injury and were characterized by considerable histrionics or melodramatic displays.

A similar episode of motor hysteria occurred over several months in 1972 at a remote, impoverished Canadian community of Cree and Ojibway descent.[15] Psychiatrists who went to the village interviewed thirteen residents between the ages of eleven and eighteen. They immediately noticed that life was very dreary, and those affected were not having much fun. They typically complained of fatigue, irritability, headaches, and nightmares prior to having hysterical fits, during which they would often try to run into the woods. Episodes coincided with their anger and depression over the social and cultural isolation in the poor village where there was little for them to do. Strict Christian discipline, scant privacy, and prearranged marriages were common, and the decision of parents was absolute. Histrionics and use of the sick role as attention-seeking devices were prominent. Several females intentionally halted breathing so as to attract attention by receiving artificial respiration. Episodes drew scores of neighbors and turned into big social gatherings with refreshments even being served. The fits subsided after the psychiatrists made several important changes. They put a stop to social functions surrounding incidents, improved family communication, and increased recreational and educational activities.

In both cases, traditional societies were undergoing rapid social change, placing extraordinary stress on certain groups that are low in the power hierarchy (e.g., females and adolescents). While desiring many Western values, they endured repressive and oppressive practices imposed by elders or husbands, whose wisdom cannot be questioned. Internalized anxiety fostered by this intolerable psychic conflict gradually built over weeks or months, culminating in trance states and maladaptive behavior. Females may not be innately susceptible per se, but they typically find themselves in positions of low power in indigenous cultures and subcultures. The display of unusual behavior was accepted with impunity since their illness status deflected the attribution of blame. Considerable community sympathy was engendered, which encouraged histrionics and role playing.

How are both motor and anxiety hysteria controlled? Remove the stressful agent (either real or perceived), and the symptoms go away. This may be easier said than done due to the emotionally charged nature of many outbreaks and the difficulty that is often encountered in convincing skeptical group members. In anxiety hysteria, the key is to persuade those affected that the "toxic" agent has either been eliminated or never existed. Episodes of motor hysteria are often interpreted by the affected group as confirming the presence of demonic forces. In such cases, it is essential to convince group members that the offending "spirits" have been eliminated or appeased.

It may seem difficult or impossible to tell whether an outbreak of illness symptoms is caused by hysteria or has a physical cause. Indeed, hysteria is often said to be able to mimic almost any illness.[16] Yet epidemic hysteria is not a diagnosis of exclusion that can never be confirmed with positive medical and environmental testing. It has several distinct characteristic features, the confluence of which almost certainly indicates the presence of psychogenic symptoms. These include the following:

no plausible organic basis
symptoms that are transient and benign
occurrence in a segregated group
presence of extraordinary stress
rapid onset and recovery; symptoms spread by sight or sound
dispersion down the age scale, beginning in older or high-status persons

By all means, test the air, food, and water supply. However, even before these tests come back, it is possible to make an accurate diagnosis based on these criteria.

Delusions and Collective Delusions

Based on a literature survey, most epidemic hysteria episodes occur within closed, tightly knit social settings: schools, factories, convents, and hospitals.[17] While there have been several reports of events that were labeled as community-wide mass hysterias in the social science literature during the twentieth century, most do not involve the spread of hysterical conversion and anxiety, and there is a complete absence of illness symptoms. These episodes involve the rapid spread of false beliefs and or the redefinition of ambiguous objects or events. They are most accurately described as collective delusions.[18] To use the word "hysteria" to describe such episodes is inaccurate and confusing. The infrequent cases that actually involve the spread of conversion symptoms should be referred to as "mass hysteria" or "epidemic hysteria."

When psychiatrists use the word "delusion," they use it to describe a persistent pathological belief associated with serious mental disturbance, typically psychosis. We will refer to the word "delusion" as it is used by social scientists such as sociologists and social psychologists, who employ it to describe the rapid, spontaneous, temporary spread of false beliefs within a particular population. The use of the word "delusion" should not be implied to suggest that those affected are experiencing psychological disturbance. "Delusion" refers to the socially constructed nature of the episode.[19]

History is replete with examples of group delusions, many of which may seem humorous to those outside the historical or cultural setting. In 1806 near Leeds, England, residents became terror stricken that the end of the world was imminent when a hen began laying eggs with the inscription "Christ Is Coming." Masses thronged to glimpse the miraculous bird — until discovering that the eggs had been inscribed with a corrosive ink and forced back into its body. In March 1993, excitement was created in Texas when the *Morning Times of Laredo* published a hoax account of a giant three hundred-pound earthworm undulating across Interstate 35. Many citizens in the vicinity of Laredo believed the story despite claims that the worm was an incredible seventy-nine feet long! Unfortunately, the outcomes of collective delusions are often more sinister. Historical examples are racial persecution under Nazism, mass suicide in certain sects, witch-hunts, communist-infiltration scares, and outrages that occurred during the Crusades. In fact, certain collective delusions, which in themselves are not indicative of individual mental illness, may have a much more deleterious effect than the delusional symptoms in schizophrenics.

There are four major types of collective delusions: immediate community threats, community flight panics, symbolic community scares, mass wish-fulfillment. All involve a rapid spread of false but plausible beliefs that gain credibility within a particular social and cultural context. They can be positive and take the form of wish-fulfillment, but they are usually negative and spread by fear. Rumors are an essential ingredient common to each category of delusion. As persons attempt to confirm or dismiss the accuracy of these unsubstantiated stories of perceived importance, everyday objects, events and circumstances that would ordinarily receive scant attention become the subject of extraordinary scrutiny. Ambiguous agents are soon redefined according to the emerging definition of the situation, creating a self-fulfilling prophesy. Many factors contribute to the spread of episodes. The mass media, low education levels, the fallibility of human perception, cultural folk beliefs and stereotypes, group conformity, and reinforcing actions by authority figures (e.g., politicians) or institutions of social control (e.g., military agencies) are some factors.

Immediate Community Threats

This category includes exaggerated feelings of danger within communities, where members of the affected population are concerned over what is believed to be an immediate personal threat. Episodes usually persist from a few weeks to several months and often recur periodically. Participants may express excitement and concern, but they do not panic and take flight. The underlying process of creating and spreading the delusion is the fallibility of human perception and the tendency for persons sharing similar beliefs in group settings to yield to the majority consensus.

An example of an immediate community threat occurred in New Jersey in 1909. Since at least the 1730s, stories of a bizarre creature have circulated among residents of the vast, desolate Pine Barrens region of central and southern New Jersey and adjacent eastern Pennsylvania. Occasional sightings of the "Jersey devil" were recorded until the turn of the twentieth century, when the creature seemed destined to fade into the annals of local folklore. But between January 16 and 23, 1909, the region was overwhelmed with reported sightings of the creature or its footprints.[20]

Descriptions varied, but it was often said to stand three to four feet tall with a head resembling a horse and sporting batlike wings. Others would say it was only as big as a dog. In their book *The Jersey Devil*, folklorists James McCloy and Ray Miller state that during the brief scare, most residents stayed behind locked doors, factories and schools closed, and posses searched for the elusive creature.[21] One of the first reported sightings occurred to Woodbury, New Jersey, policeman James Sackville, who was on patrol when he said he spotted a winged beast hopping like a bird and giving off a bloodcurdling screech, which then flew into the early morning darkness.[22] According to press reports, over 100 people in more than two dozen communities saw the devil.[23]

Another example of an immediate community threat were the mass sightings of imaginary rockets flying across Sweden in 1946. In conjunction with rare comet debris entering the atmosphere, rumors were circulating that remote-controlled German V-rockets, confiscated by the Soviets at the close of World War II, were being test-fired as a form of political intimidation or invasion prelude. The historical and political contexts were key factors in rendering the rumors plausible. The episode occurred amid a long history of Swedish mistrust of Russia that existed long before the formation of the Soviet Union. Invasion fears, border disputes, and spy scandals have preoccupied Swedes for centuries. Public statements reinforcing the rockets' existence were made by top Swedish military officials, politicians, scientists, police, and journalists. Convinced of their existence, many citizens began redefining comet spray that was sporadically streaking across the sky as enemy rockets. Some residents even claimed to distinguish tail fins or a fuselage. Of 997 reports investigated by the Swedish military, including nearly 100 "crashes" in remote areas, not a single shred of solid evidence confirming the rockets' existence was found, despite the military taking the extreme measure of draining some lakes.[24]

For a two-week period in 1956, residents in the vicinity of Taipei, Taiwan, lived in fear that they would be the next victims of a crazed villain who was prowling the streets and slashing people at random with a razor or similar weapon. At least 21 victims were reported during this period, mostly women and children of low income and education. Norman Jacobs of the University of Kansas[25] taught in Taipei at the time, and he surveyed local press coverage of the event. He concluded that those affected had redefined mundane slash marks, attributing them to a sinister slasher.

Rumors amplified by sensational press coverage treating the slasher's existence as real fomented the scare by altering the perceptual outlook of residents to include the reality of the daring, blade-wielding maniac. Police eventually concluded that the "slashings" had resulted from inadvertent, everyday contact in public places that ordinarily would have gone relatively unnoticed. One man told police in minute detail how he had been slashed by a man carrying a mysterious black bag. When a doctor determined that the wound was made by a blunt object and not a razor, the victim admitted that he could not recall exactly what had happened, but he assumed that he had been slashed "because of all the talk going around." In another example, it was not the supposed victim but doctors who were responsible for creating an incident. In this case, an elderly man with a wrist laceration sought medical treatment, but the attending physician grew suspicious and contacted police when the patient casually noted that a stranger had coincidentally touched him at about the same time he first noticed the bleeding. A thorough examination found that the "slash" was an old injury that had been re-opened after inadvertent scratching. In concluding that the episode was entirely psychological, the police announced the results of their investigation, determining that of the 21 slashing claims examined by their office, "five were innocent false reports, seven were self-inflicted cuts, eight were due to cuts other than razors, and one was a complete fantasy."

There are other historical examples of phantom slashers and stabbers. In Paris, France, near the turn of the twentieth century, numerous residents mistakenly reported being "pricked with a long hat pin or the like" until police determined that the episode was imaginary.[26] During a span of nine days in late November and early December 1938, residents in several communities in the vicinity of the northern English city of Halifax were terrorized by a razor-brandishing madman dubbed "the Halifax Slasher."[27] There were so many reports in so many locations, often several in a single night, that police speculated there may have been as many as three slashers:

> On reaching work ... a man discovered two slight cuts in his raincoat; he couldn't remember having been approached nor attacked, but thought he'd better notify the police anyhow. Half an hour later a volunteer watcher ("who said that, as husband and father, he was going to do all he could") chased a suspicious character over a wall.... 30 minutes or so onwards after a nervous boy claimed that he'd been clutched on the shoulder, a Hume Street patrol similarly failed to make anything of "a man up to no good ... lurking in the shadows."[28]

Sporadic reports were received as far away as Manchester and London. In a series of events remarkably similar to the Taipei slasher, by the time Scotland Yard became involved on November 30, the affair had peaked and the slasher seemed to be everywhere. In all, there were estimated to have been between 200 and 400 slasher reports. At the height of the scare, hundreds of vigilantes were patrolling the Halifax streets, and at least 80 citizens were deputized as acting constables.

One unfortunate man was nearly lynched by an angry mob of 200 after being mistakenly identified as the slasher. Police arrived at the last minute to rescue him after being cornered and pinned against a wall.[29] Another potentially disastrous incident involved Hilda Lodge, who claimed that she was slashed on November 25 when, in fact, she had scratched her face and arms with a broken vinegar bottle. While she later confessed, Clifford Edwards, in the wrong place at the wrong time, was nearly "dismembered by a frenzied mob" intent on finding her "attacker."[30] In a case from London, an elderly woman dashed into a nearby pharmacy for treatment of a slash wound after a man brushed against her and she noticed a scratch on her hand.

Another incident occurred in the early morning hours of November 28, when Mrs. Constance Wood was standing near the front gate of her home. Suddenly, a man in a raincoat ran by. She was knocked down and felt a sharp pain in her left arm. Assuming she had been slashed, she screamed for help, sparking a number of separate chases involving tall men who had the misfortune of having been in the area and wearing raincoats. When the *Yorkshire Evening Post* later interviewed Mrs. Wood, it became evident that she and her neighbors had been living in a state of semipara-noia for the week prior to the incident and were expecting an attack. As for her "slashing," the extent of the wounds consisted of two superficial lacerations (from where she apparently hit the ground) and a torn sweater.[31]

During the first week of December, reports declined dramatically as the press grew critical of the episode, which was being increasingly attrib-uted to "hysteria" and imagination. Fueling the skepticism was a series of "victims" who confessed to having slashed themselves for attention, includ-ing two separate incidents involving young women who were upset at their boyfriends.

In non–Western settings, immediate community threats are closely associated with cultural traditions, as in the case of head-hunting rumor-panics that have occurred for centuries in remote parts of Malaysia and Indonesia.[32] These episodes represent fears by "primitive" peoples of los-ing political control to a distant, central government. Head-hunting scares are characterized by sightings of headhunters or their alleged parapher-nalia. Just as the vast, ambiguous night sky is an excellent catalyst for spawning UFO sightings — and lakes are conducive to sea-serpent reports — the thickly vegetated Southeast Asian jungle is ideal for misperceiving headhunters lurking in the myriad of foliage. Villages are often paralyzed with fear, travel is severely restricted, sentries are posted, and schools closed for months. Most head-hunting scares coincide with the nearby construction of a government bridge or building, during which it is widely believed that one or more human heads are required to produce a strong, enduring foundation. The panics are a projection of tribal-state relations reflecting "ideological warfare between the administrators and the admin-istrated."[33]

During March 1937, the first Indonesian prime minister, Soetan Sjahrir, was living on the Moluccan island of Banda, where he described a head-hunting rumor-panic that swept through his village.[34] The episode coincided with rumors that a *tjoelik* (someone who engages in head-hunt-ing for the government) was operating in the area and searching for a head to be placed near a local jetty that was being rebuilt. According to rumor, government construction projects would soon crumble without such an offering. Sjahrir said that "people have been living in fear," were "talking and whispering about it everywhere,"[35] and after 7 P.M., the streets were nearly deserted. There were many reports of strange noises and sightings:

Every morning there are new stories, generally about footsteps or voices, or a house that was bombarded with stones, or an attack on somebody by a tjoelik with a noose, or a cowboy lasso. Naturally, the person who was attacked got away from the tjoelik in a nick of time![36]

Sjahrir described the scare as an example of "mass psychosis."

For several weeks in late 1979, a kidnapping rumor-panic suddenly broke out on the island of Borneo. At the time, anthropologist Richard Drake was studying the Mualang people living on the Belitang Hulu River in Kalimantan Barat, Indonesia.[37] Soon guards were posted throughout the village, rubber-tapping ceased, and a local school closed for insufficient attendance. A variety of ordinary events and circumstances, such as noises and rustling in the jungle, were defined as kidnapper-related activity. The scare was triggered by rumors that the government was constructing a bridge in the region and needed a body to place in the foundation for strength. The outbreak was related to periodic kidnapping and head-hunter scares in the region dating back to the seventeenth century, coinciding with real or rumored government construction projects and a local belief that such developments require a head or body to be laid in the foundation or on a special pillar nearby to make for an enduring structure.[38]

Between February and March 1975, reports circulated in Puerto Rico of a mysterious creature attacking domestic and farm animals, draining their blood, and scooping out chunks of their flesh. Residents claimed that they heard loud screeches and or flapping wings coinciding with the attacks. Academics and police examined the carcasses and blamed everything from humans to snakes to vampire bats. Locals referred to the attacker as "the Vampire of Moca." This incident may have been spurred by the better-known "cattle mutilation mystery."[39] In November 1995, similar attacks were reported on the island. Called *chupacabras*[40] or goat sucker, named after a bird of the Caprimulgidae family that purportedly steals goat's milk,[41] the bizarre being was described as a "bristly, bulge-eyed rat with the hind legs of a kangaroo, capable of escaping after its crimes in high-speed sprints."[42] It also exuded a sulfurlike stench. Stories said that the bodies of animals were discovered disemboweled and drained of blood. One member of a civil defense team in a small city in the affected area said he was spending half his time responding to chupacabra calls. Some people, he reported, were so distraught that they were treated at hospitals.[43] Interest in the creature ran so high in May 1996 that a *chupacabra* Web site received enough hits to be ranked in the top 5 percent of all Web sites.[44] By March 1996, goat-sucker stories had spread to the Hispanic community in Florida. By May, accounts of *chupacabra* attacks began to circulate in Mexico and, soon after, to the Mexican-American community in Arizona. The *chupacabra* flap ended abruptly in mid–1996.[45]

Community Flight Panics

A second type of delusion involves community flight panics, where inhabitants attempt to flee an imaginary threat. Most episodes last a few hours to several days or weeks, and they subside when it is realized that the harmful agent did not materialize. Examples include several mass flights from the city of London in response to prophesies of its destruction by a great flood in 1524, the Day of Judgment in 1736, and an earthquake in 1761.[46]

The latter episode occurred on February 8, 1761, when a minor earthquake struck London, damaging several chimneys. When another tremor occurred exactly one month later, March 8, the coincidence became the subject of widespread discussion. According to prominent British journalist Charles Mackay, a man named Bell then predicted that London would be destroyed in a third quake on April 5: "As the awful day approached, the excitement became intense, and great numbers of credulous people resorted to all the villages within a circuit of twenty miles, awaiting the doom of London."[47] People paid exorbitant fees to temporarily border with households in such places as Highgate, Hampstead, Islington, Blackheath, and Harrow. The poor stayed in London until two or three days before the predicted event when they left to camp in fields in the countryside. When the time arrived, nothing happened.

One of many modern examples involving apocalyptic prophesies and mass panic occurred in Adelaide, Australia, in the month leading up to January 19, 1976. Many people fled the city and some even sold their homes after "psychic" John Nash predicted that an earthquake and tidal wave would strike at midday. In examining the circumstances of the event, many of those who sold their homes or left to the hills for the day were first-generation Greeks and Italians. Both countries have a long history of devastating earthquakes, and the belief in clairvoyants is generally taken very seriously.[48]

On Halloween 1938, a live radio version of *The War of the Worlds* was produced by Orson Welles and broadcast across much of the United States by the CBS Mercury Theater. It depicted an invasion by Martians who were attacking with heat rays and poison gas. Princeton University psychologist Hadley Cantril concluded that an estimated 1.2 million listeners became excited, frightened or disturbed. However, a subsequent review of Cantril's findings by sociologists David Miller, William Sims Bainbridge, and others concluded that there was scant evidence of substantial or widespread panic.[49] For instance, Miller found little evidence of mobilization, an essential ingredient in a panic. Hence, it was a collective delusion and not a true panic. Cantril also exaggerated the extent of the mobilization, attributing much normal activity of the time to the "panic." In short, many listeners may have expressed concern, but they did not do anything in response, like try to flee, grab a gun for protection, or barricade themselves inside a house. Either way one views this episode, it qualifies as a collective delusion. If as Cantril originally asserted, many listeners were frightened and panicked, it is a mass delusion. Conversely, if we are to accept the more recent and likely assessments that the "panic" was primarily a media creation inadvertently fueled by Cantril's flawed study, then erroneous depictions of a mass panic that have been recounted in numerous books and articles for over six decades constitute an equally remarkable social delusion.

Symbolic Community Scares

These community scares typically endure in a waxing and waning fashion for years, encompassing entire countries and geographical regions. There is less of an immediate concern for safety and welfare, and more of a general long-term threat. They are primarily symbolic and rumor driven, consisting of fear over the exaggerated erosion of traditional values. These moral panics are characterized by self-fulfilling stereotypes of ethnic minorities and deviants who are wrongfully indicted for evil deeds, giving them much in common with the infamous European witch persecutions of 1400 to 1650. In *Collective Behavior*, Erich Goode aptly summarizes these events, noting that they originated from the disintegration of the Roman Catholic Church during the latter Middle Ages and early Renaissance. The feudal hierarchy was unraveling, and peasants were migrating to cities. Scientific rationalism's secular philosophy conflicted with church doctrine, and new religious denominations were being formed beyond the church's control. In an unconscious attempt to counteract secularism and reestablish traditional authority, the church-sponsored persecution of witches attempted to redefine moral boundaries, and church inquisitors focused on eradicating various deviants who were viewed as a threat.[50]

Two prominent moral panics have persisted for the past decade. Scores of Western communities with predominantly Judeo-Christian traditions have experienced ongoing concern about the existence of a network of satanic cults kidnapping and sacrificing children. These rumors coincide with the widespread perception of declining Western morality and traditional values. Under similar historical circumstances, subversion myths have appeared in which a particular alien group is believed to threaten the moral fabric of society. Common scapegoats include minority ethnic groups, Jews, Africans, communists, heretics, deviants, and the poor. Such myths flourish during periods of economic downturn and social unrest, and they are characterized by dramatic, plausible rumors containing meaningful, timely morals or messages reflecting popular fears. During oral transmission, local details are supplanted and a credible source is identified. Their function is primarily metaphorical. Victor notes that the contemporary Satanic cult scare coincides with the disintegration of traditional family structures, intensifying fears and the desire "to blame someone."[51] Unlike scares involving imminent danger, subversion myths present a more generalized threat to both people and a way of life.[52] Rumors and urban legends of satanic cults function as cautionary cultural metaphors about the inability of the weakened family to protect children.[53] A similar symbolic process drives child-molestation panics that have appeared periodically in certain regions for decades.[54]

Symbolic community scares often develop into immediate community threats that may endure for considerable periods of time. Two examples are the Italian well-poisoning scare and the New England witch-hunts. Both occurred in the 1600s.

Mackay described a poisoning scare that terrorized Milan, Italy, in 1630, coinciding with pestilence, plague, and a prediction that the devil would poison the city's water supply.[55] On one April morning, people awoke and became fearful upon finding "that all the doors in the principal streets of the city were marked with a curious daub, or spot." Soon there was alarm that the sign of the awaited poisoning was at hand. It was believed that corn and fruit had also been poisoned. Many people were executed. One elderly man was spotted wiping a stool before sitting on it and was accused of smearing poison on the seat. He was seized by an angry mob of women and pulled by the hair to a judge, but he died on the way. In another instance, a pharmacist who was found with several preparations containing unknown potions was accused of being in cahoots with the devil to poison the city. He protested his innocence, but he eventually confessed after prolonged torture on the rack, admitting to cooperating with the devil and foreigners in poisoning the city and anointing the doors. Under duress, he named several accomplices who were eventually arrested and tortured. They were all pronounced guilty and executed. Mackay states that "[t]he number of persons who confessed that they were employed by the Devil to distribute poison is almost incredible," noting that "day after day persons came voluntarily forward to accuse themselves."[56]

In 1692, Salem Village (now Danvers, Massachusetts) was the scene of a moral panic that spread throughout the region involving witchcraft accusations that led to trials, torture, imprisonment, and executions. At least 20 residents lost their lives. Social paranoia was such that two dogs were even accused and executed! All convictions were based on ambiguous spectral evidence. The witch mania began in December 1691, when eight girls living in the vicinity of Salem exhibited strange behavior: disordered speech, convulsive movements, and bizarre conduct. Explanations for the fits ranged from outright fakery to hysteria to ergot poisoning of the food supply. By February 1692, the affected girls had accused two elderly women and a Barbados servant of being witches, and they were arrested. Soon hundreds of residents were accused of witchcraft, and trials were held. In May 1693, the episode ended when Governor Phips ordered that all suspects be released.[57]

Mass Wish-Fulfillment

Episodes of wishful thinking involve similar processes that cause community threats and moral panics, except that the object of interest is esteemed and satisfies psychological needs. Cases typically persist from a few weeks or months and recur periodically in clusters. Examples include Virgin Mary "appearances,"[58] "moving" religious statues in Ireland,[59] widespread reports of fairies in England in the nineteenth century,[60] and reports of flying saucers worldwide since 1947.[61] These myths are supported by a spiritual void left by the ascendancy of rationalism and secular humanism. Within this context — and fostered by sensationalized documentaries, movies, and books—contemporary populations have been conditioned to scan the heavens for UFOs, which represent what psychoanalyst Carl Jung termed "technological angels."[62] These sightings serve as a projected Rorschach test of the collective psyche, underscoring the promise of rapid technological advancement during a period of spiritual decline.

Accounts of UFO occupants and fairies depict god-like beings capable of transcending natural laws and, thus, potentially elevating humans to an immortal realm. They reflect similar themes found in religion, mythology, and folklore throughout the world, camouflaged for contemporary acceptance.[63] Transcendence and magical or supernatural powers are an underlying theme in most wish-fulfillments. Education builds resistance, but it does not provide immunity to what philosopher Paul Kurtz terms "the transcendental temptation."[64] Even observations of imaginary or extinct creatures such as Bigfoot and the Tasmanian Tiger, once considered the sole domain of zoology, have undergone recent transformations with the emergence of a new motif among paranormal researchers that links extraterrestrial or paranormal themes with phantom animals.[65] The existence of such animals can be viewed as antiscientific symbols undermining secularism. Like claims of contact with UFOs or the Virgin Mary, evidence for the existence of Bigfoot and Tasmanian Tigers ultimately rests with eyewitness testimony, which is notoriously unreliable. It is interesting to note that the Native people living along the Pacific Northwest coast of North America regarded Bigfoot (or Sasquatch) as a supernatural being endowed with spirit power in their mythology. Only later was it reinterpreted by non–Native people as a primordial human being.[66] In recent decades, it has been reinterpreted again as a paranormal or extraterrestrial entity by non–Native North Americans.

At 11 A.M. on May 25, 1953, an estimated 150,000 people converged at a well in Rincorn, Puerto Rico, to observe the appearance of the Virgin Mary, which seven local children had predicted. Over the next six hours, a team of sociologists led by Melvin Tumin and Arnold Feldman[67] mingled in the crowd and conducted interviews. During this period, some people reported seeing colored rings encircling the sun and a silhouette of the Virgin Mary in the clouds, while others experienced healings and a general sense of well-being. But others saw or experienced nothing extraordinary. A media frenzy preceded the event, and the local mayor enthusiastically organized the visionaries to lead throngs of pilgrims in mass prayers and processions. Tumin and Feldman found that the majority of pilgrims believed in the authenticity of the children's claim, and they were seeking cures for either themselves or friends and relatives for conditions that physicians had deemed incurable. Various ambiguous objects in the immediate surroundings mirrored the hopeful, expectant state of mind of many participants at the time.

On June 24, 1947, Kenneth Arnold was piloting his private plane near the Cascade Mountains in Washington state when he saw what appeared to be nine glittering objects flying near Mount Rainier. He kept the rapidly moving objects in sight for about three minutes before they traveled south over Mount Adams and were lost to view.[68] Worried that he may have observed guided missiles from a foreign power, Arnold flew to Pendleton, Oregon, where he tried reporting what he saw to the FBI office there. Finding the office closed, he went to the *East Oregonian* newspaper. After listening to Arnold's story, a journalist at the paper named Bill Bequette produced a report for the Associated Press (AP). It is notable that at this point, Arnold had described crescent-shaped objects, referring only to their movement as "like a saucer would if you skipped it across the water."[69] However, the AP account describing Arnold's "saucers" appeared in over 150 newspapers.

The AP report that Bequette filed was the article from which the term "flying saucer" was created by headline writers on June 25 and 26, 1947.[70] Of key importance was Bequette's use of the term "saucer-like" in describing Arnold's sighting. Bequette's use of the word "saucer" provided a motif for the worldwide wave of flying-saucer sightings during the summer of 1947 and other waves since. There are a few scattered historical references to disc-shaped objects, but no consistent pattern emerges until 1947 and Arnold's sighting. There were only a handful of occasions prior to 1947 in which a witness actually used the word "saucer" to describe mysterious aerial objects. Hence, the global flying-saucer wave can be regarded as a media-generated delusion unique to the twentieth century.

From April 1968 to May 1971, more than 100,000 people reported Virgin Mary apparitions above a Coptic Orthodox Church at Zeitoun, Egypt. Descriptions varied between two main types: small, bright, short-lived lights nicknamed "doves" and more enduring, less intense, diffuse patches of glowing light.[71] Canadian neuropsychologist Michael Persinger of Laurentian University and his American colleague John Derr analyzed seismic activity in the region from 1958 to 1979. They found an unprecedented peak in earthquakes during 1969. Stating that "[t]he 'narrow' window of significant temporal relationship between luminous phenomena and earthquakes is within the classic time frame of more acceptable antecedents (e.g., microseismic activity) of imminent earthquake activity," Persinger and Derr speculate that observers were predisposed by their religious backgrounds and social expectations to interpret the seismic-triggered light displays as Virgin Mary-related.[72]

The Lure of Mass Delusions

Collective delusions possess a powerful seductive lure that continuously changes in a chameleonlike fashion to confirm our deepest fears or realize our greatest desires. Most Westerners can easily distinguish head-hunting scares as the products of myth and superstition. Yet polls suggest that many of these same people are likely to believe in the reality of flying saucers, ghosts, or psychic phenomena. The underlying themes of collective delusions remain constant. Circumstances surrounding the Adelaide earthquake panic of 1976 are virtually identical to the London earthquake panic of 1761. Modern-day child-molestation or satanic-cult fears resemble the persecution of various deviants and ethnic groups during the medieval European witch-hunts. Contemporary wish-fulfillments parallel transcendent elements that have been prominent fixtures in religious movements for millennia. Only the form changes to reflect the social and cultural context.

SECTION TWO

---

*Mass Hysteria
in Closed Settings*

Chapter 2

Epidemic Hysteria
in Schools

*The mind has great influence over the body, and maladies often
have their origin there.* — Molière[1]

Throughout history, a curious phenomenon has been reported in
which students in close, cohesive social units collectively exhibit a variety
of signs and symptoms that are judged to be bizarre by prevailing social
and cultural standards of normality for both the country and historical
era of occurrence. One hundred and sixteen cases have been recorded in
the scientific literature under an array of labels. The terms "mass hysteria" or "epidemic hysteria" are most frequently used to describe school
episodes since the turn of the twentieth century. Prior to that time, they
were typically referred to as "epidemic chorea," "psychic contagion," or
"psychic epidemics."

This article is intended to be of practical value for school administrators, teachers, parents, and health professionals who may be summoned
to intervene in such cases. It has theoretical and historical interest to
educators in general. It is not known whether episodes are rare or just
uncommonly reported in the scientific literature. A survey of approximately 1,900 schools in the Canadian province of Quebec during 1973
uncovered two cases, both which were previously unreported.[2] During the latter nineteenth century, school reports were common. They were
rare between 1910 and 1950, but they have increased steadily since. During the past two decades, there has been a marked increase in the number of reports in both Western and non–Western settings. Historically,
episodes of epidemic hysteria in school and nonschool settings have
appeared in clusters. This may reflect the prevailing medical zeitgeist or

The author is grateful to François Sirois for his co-authorship of this chapter.

psychiatric ideology on the recognition and interest afforded to the problem.[3]

In reviewing the reports, most researchers assume that outbreaks are a variant of individual "conversion hysteria," a term devised by Sigmund Freud to describe a well-documented disorder involving the converting of psychological conflict into involuntary physical symptoms without a corresponding organic basis. A classic example is the soldier who is opposed to killing experiencing temporary arm paralysis when attempting to fire a gun. "Epidemic hysteria" refers to the rapid spread of conversion hysteria and anxiety states within a particular cluster of students who are exposed to a common threat, either real or imagined. The association between conversion hysteria and epidemic hysteria is natural because the major symptoms of the latter are prominent features of collective episodes. This includes the frequent overlapping of other hysterical symptoms such as a histrionic personality, a sudden onset in an atmosphere of extreme psychosocial stress, and a preponderance of female participants. Symptoms are believed to enable victims to unconsciously avoid undesirable activities or situations and to simultaneously receive support and attention.

In recent years, several researchers have recommended the abandonment of the terms "mass hysteria" or "epidemic hysteria," believing it to be prejudicial toward females.[4] However, attempts to use more neutral terminology such as "mass psychogenic illness," "mass sociogenic illness," and "collective exaggerated emotions" to describe school outbreaks have not gained widespread acceptance. Other phrases such as "group mental disorder" possess undesirable, potentially stigmatizing connotations. Also, such labels may be inaccurate because attempts to identify abnormal personality correlates in victims versus nonvictims among affected students are inconclusive.[5] Unfortunately, considerable confusion persists over the ambiguous meaning of the word "hysteria," because it is used to describe no less than ten distinct behavioral patterns, including the histrionic personality, forms of psychosis, and psychogenic pain disorder.[6]

Defining Parameters and Terms

All known obtainable reports are reviewed (N=118) based on a search of MEDLINE, sociological abstracts, psychological abstracts, cross references, and reliable press accounts. A syndrome consists of signs and symptoms that, when occurring together, indicate the appearance of an illness or abnormal condition. Because epidemic hysteria is affected by social, cultural, and precipitating factors—and features distinct presentation patterns—"epidemic hysteria syndrome" most appropriately describes the process. We shall use the term "epidemic hysteria" for short. An episode is two or more students in a school setting exhibiting perceptions, sensations and or related beliefs that are of a psychogenic origin in the absence of an identifiable pathogenic agent. This definition encompasses groups of students outside school premises who participate in school-related activities such as a field trip, dance, concert, play, chorus, marching band, or sports event. Excluded from this definition are fainting, twitching, shaking, glossolalia, altered states of consciousness, and related phenomena originating in an organized, ritualized, or institutionalized manner, such as deliberately induced ecstatic states in school-related religious organizations. With the exception of a series of Malaysian press reports, primary sources are restricted to scientific journal accounts. Malaysian newspapers often dispatch reporters directly to the scene and provide timely, voluminous, and highly detailed press coverage, including interviews with affected students, physicians, psychiatrists, school officials and investigating government bodies. They also provide follow-up accounts when episodes recur or have ceased.

What may have been the first recorded episode of epidemic hysteria in an educational setting occurred in 1639 at a girls school in Lille, France, during a period of widespread belief in witchcraft. With great consternation, school founder Antoinette Bourgignon told her pupils that she had observed "little black angels" flying about their heads warning them "to beware of the devil, whose imps were hovering about them."[7] Each of the fifty students eventually confessed to being witches, eating the flesh of babies, and flying through the air on broomsticks. The students narrowly escaped burning at the stake when the activities of the headmistress, who escaped, became the focus of public scrutiny. Because Charles Mackay, an accomplished journalist of the period, did not provide further details, this report is provided for historical purposes only, and it is not included in our list of cases.

A Theoretical Overview

Contemporary explanations for the appearance of epidemic hysteria syndrome in schools fall within five broad theoretical traditions: psychoanalytic, sociological, social psychological, biological, and anthropological. These theories are not mutually exclusive and often share overlapping features. While each perspective emphasizes the influence of different mechanisms and processes in precipitating outbreaks, all converge on the pivotal role of extreme psychosocial stress.

Psychoanalytic theories are formulated upon observations of individual cases of conversion hysteria. It is assumed that the victim is reacting to a state of extreme psychological conflict by unconsciously converting the conflict into physical symptoms. Often the affected body parts are related to the specific conflict. Thus, in singular conversion, a soldier in psychological dissonance over the morality of combat may suffer temporary arm paralysis and be unable to discharge a weapon. Another classic example involves the witness to a traumatic event who subsequently experiences partial or complete blindness.[8]

Psychoanalytical perspectives have been used to explain why histrionics and play-acting are prominent among mass-hysteria victims and how they exacerbate outbreaks, especially in enduring episodes involving strict academic discipline. This includes the conscious, unconscious, or partially conscious utilization of the "sick role" to obtain sympathy or attention and to manipulate cherished or undesirable activities and situations. For example, an outbreak of spasmodic twitching at a Louisiana high school spread after symptoms in the first pupil enabled her to avoid dance classes and rekindle a boyfriend's waning affection. After observing the success of the initial case, six other female students obtained secondary gains over the ensuing weeks as a result of their newly acquired illness status.[9] Benaim et al. reported that Louise, the index case in an episode of falling among 16- and 17-year-old schoolgirls near London, admitted to faking "drop attacks" after becoming accustomed to the growing attention that she received from her initial genuine fainting spells.[10]

The term "secondary gains" is typically used by psychiatrists to refer to symptoms that are only unintentionally produced, while the feigning of symptoms is classified as malingering.[11] Histrionics produced during school outbreaks of epidemic hysteria often do not appear to be intentionally produced with the conscious intent of obtaining secondary benefits, but it appears that considerable feigning may occur to convince authority figures to take some immediate action to nullify the perceived threat. This is especially evident in persistent outbreaks where authorities are not perceived as having thoroughly investigated the potential triggering agent. One must remember that even if medical investigators are unable to detect the presence of a toxic gas or biological agent, those experiencing epidemic conversion symptoms and their parents are often convinced that the external agent exists but has not been identified.

A major sociological explanation is outlined by Smelser,[12] who contends that episodes occur within dysfunctional social orders. Rapid social and cultural changes are believed to produce a disequilibrium within the normal state of society. Smelser believes that five factors must be present to trigger episodes. First, there must be structural conduciveness, whereby the structure of society permits the emergence of mass behavior. Hence, a school episode of epidemic hysteria cannot transpire in a "primitive" society that does not have enclosed classrooms and an organized school system. Similarly, a stock-market crash cannot occur in communist societies that prohibit private entrepreneurship. The second determinant is structural strain, which is the existence of stress or conflict, such as an unfamiliar odor or poor student-teacher relations. Third is growth and spread of a generalized belief, whereby the "strain"—a false, irrational hysterical belief—is interpreted by the individual group members in a like manner. The strain must be ambiguous, generate extraordinary anxiety, and result in a redefinition of the situation that is attributed to the stressful agent. The strain is often exacerbated by precipitating factors, which are usually specific events that exaggerate the effects of the imaginary threat by "providing 'evidence' that something terrible is at work."[13]

For instance, in Seremban, Malaysia, a sudden electricity disruption was believed to confirm the presence of supernatural forces in the school.[14] Prior to the appearance of a mysterious gas at a Hong Kong school that affected over three hundred students, rumors of a recent toxic-gas scare at a nearby school were in circulation. Several teachers had discussed the incident with their pupils, some to the point of advising them what action to take if it should occur there.[15]

Mobilization for action and inadequate social control are Smelser's final two determinants. The former category considers how communication and leadership contribute to fostering a mass reaction. This is clearly evident in many episodes where symptoms begin in the older, high-status students and spread to the younger ones. Often, the first affected pupil is an influential group member. Social control is a counterdeterminant that is unable to impede or prevent outbreaks. An anxious look, indecision, confusion, or panic by teachers, administrators, medical personnel, or law-enforcement officials is counterproductive and fails to contain episodes. Smelser contends that his theory can explain the appearance of such diverse mass behaviors as panics, riots, crazes, and both norm- and value-oriented social movements.

There are two prominent social psychological perspectives: convergence and emergent-norm theories. The former position holds that students sharing similar predispositions, such as atypical personality traits, have the highest risk of exhibiting psychogenic symptoms following exposure to a stressful stimulus. This view remains unsubstantiated. Several investigators have attempted to differentiate affected versus unaffected pupils within the same group setting by administering standardized personality inventories. However, there is no consistent pattern. Some results indicate a tendency for affected pupils to score higher on scales for paranoia,[16] neuroticism,[17] and hysterical traits,[18] while others have found no such correlations.[19] Goldberg noted an association between absenteeism and being affected,[20] while Cole did not.[21] Small et al. identified a relationship between academic performance and being stricken,[22] but Goh found no association.[23] The death of a significant other during early childhood has been correlated with epidemic hysteria syndrome,[24] but this observation was not confirmed in another study by the same investigator.[25] While some researchers note that affected pupils possess below-average intelligence quotients,[26] opposite impressions were gained by others.[27]

The emergent-norm perspective rejects the notion that students become "hysterical" per se as a cathartic response to accumulating stress. This perspective focuses on the influence of sociocultural norms and unique contextual circumstances in structuring episodes.[28] Instead of emphasizing the role of stress per se, or pathological group processes, this focus is on the newly emerging definition of the situation from the viewpoint of those affected, creating what Thomas first described as a self-fulfilling prophesy.[29] In investigating an episode of epidemic hysteria in a Malaysian school, Lee and Ackerman emphasized the importance of examining stress "as a matter of definition in a specific sociocultural context rather than as an objective given from which predictions can be made," focusing attention on how victims versus those unaffected retrospectively interpret events.[30] This sociocultural approach examines how victims, observers, and the community explain the episode. Its focus is "analyzing the consequences of these interpretations."[31] Whether or not a particular student becomes affected is determined by such factors as physical and visual proximity, social and cultural beliefs, education level, personality traits (not necessarily abnormal), social and spatial distance from the threatening situation, and precipitating events. For instance, students with the strongest social ties with those already affected, or in close physical proximity to the perceived threat, should experience the highest stress levels because they are the most likely to observe the initial index case. The actions of authority figures such as teachers or administrators, either through calm reassurance or expressions of outward anxiety, can validate or defuse situations.

Kerckhoff observes that outbreaks are most likely to occur in settings where one or more dramatic illness cases (e.g., fainting, vomiting) or abnormal behavior (e.g., epileptic seizures, drug ingestion) appear.[32] The situation is ambiguous because during the initial incident, students are unaware of the cause. These initial dramatic events must be viewed as a direct threat to the remaining students, thus increasing group stress and associated physiological symptoms (e.g., heart palpitations, hyperventilation). The potential threat must be credible. For instance, if a student were to faint during a given school day, it would not ordinarily precipitate epidemic hysteria syndrome. Yet if this incident were to occur during the 1991 Middle East War and coincided with the presence of a strange odor, many of the young, naive schoolchildren might assume that they were the subject of an Iraqi poison-gas raid. In fact, a similar scenario was reported at a Rhode Island school during the Persian Gulf War.[33] Similar imaginary poison-gas attacks in the Israeli-occupied West Bank,[34] and in Soviet Georgia have also occurred.[35] In the two latter instances, political unrest, rumors, and speculative media reports engendered widespread, plausible beliefs that such attacks were a credible possibility. The episode in Soviet Georgia affected about four hundred adolescent females, who exhibited symptoms soon after a political rally that was dissipated by Russian troops dispensing toxic gas, including chloropicrin. As is typical in such cases, the transient, benign symptoms reflected the complaints of gas victims: burning eyes, abdominal pain, skin irritation, and dry throat.

Instead of representing abnormal responses to stress, it is arguable that pupils are conforming to group norms. Thus, upon seeing a classmate fall ill and noting a strange odor, some pupils might assume a connection, triggering immediate and acute conversion reactions.

Of course, what is credible and plausible to one group, culture, or time period may seem incredible to another. This is especially evident in certain non–Western countries where superstitious beliefs combined with low levels of formal education have contributed to what — by Western standards of normality — would appear bizarre. An extreme illustration of this point is an episode reported by Legendre.[36] He describes an incident that occurred in 1908 affecting twenty males at a school in Szechwan, China, in which the anxious students became convinced that their penises were shrinking. The episode subsided after several days. Before judging the mental stability or gullibility of these students, it is important to examine the sociocultural context. There is a common belief in certain regions of Asia that eating particular foods, or having contact with ghosts, can cause one's sex organs to rapidly shrink. It is a remarkable example of the power of the self-fulfilling prophesy that Asian men and women continue to experience epidemics of what they call *koro*, a contagious disease that causes their penises or breasts to shrink. Episodes last from a few days to several months and can affect thousands. Victims suffer intense anxiety (e.g., sweating, palpitations, insomnia), often taking the extreme measure of placing clamps or tying strings on the organ. Ignorance of human perceptual fallibility, combined with rumors and traditional beliefs, results in frantic citizens intensely scrutinizing their genitalia. Epidemics within the public have occurred in China as recently as 1987.[37] Similar outbreaks have been reported in Singapore,[38] Thailand,[39] and India.[40]

Biological theories suggesting innate female susceptibility to epidemic hysteria syndrome were popular until the past three decades. Previously, it was commonly believed that females possessed weaker mental constitutions and were prone to emotional liability, making them prime candidates for episodes. This view has been discredited as sexist, with critics arguing that proponents of a biological basis for cases have not taken into account the influence of gender socialization, as females are typically enculturated to possess emotionally expressive, submissive character traits.[41] Further, there is a transcultural tendency for females to be low in the power hierarchy, increasing their susceptibility to long-term emotional frustration.

While social factors are undeniable in precipitating school outbreaks, the historical and cross-cultural overrepresentation of females of school age suggests the possibility that biological factors may exacerbate existing social and cultural forces. For instance, classroom social conditions are fairly uniform for both male and female students in many Western countries, but epidemic hysteria syndrome continues to be reported almost exclusively among females. A plausible physiological mechanism for this occurrence is the innate susceptibility of menstruating females to panic disorder and hyperventilation syndrome.[42] Also, the reporting of individual somatic complaints has been associated with the appearance of puberty and menstruation.[43] Hysterical disorders may have a biological basis because some — such as somatization disorder, globus hystericus, and psychogenic pain disorder[44]— are more frequently diagnosed in females. Also, the incidence of individual conversion disorders appears to be more common in females than males, with reported ratios varying from 2-to-1 to as high as 10-to-1. This parallels the range in prevalence ratios of epidemic hysteria episodes in schools.[45]

Anthropological perspectives focus on the context, social status, and local worldview of pupils, utilizing research by British anthropologist Ioan M. Lewis.[46] This theory is applied to episodes of epidemic hysteria syndrome in non–Western schools by Lee and Ackerman.[47] In observing a preponderance of females in spirit-possession cults and charismatic religious movements within cross-cultural settings, Lewis attributed the situation to their low social status and oppression in male-dominated societies, where they are low on the power hierarchy. Women in many of these societies often experience, sometimes collectively, trance and possession states, psychomotor agitation, and anxiety-related transient somatic complaints. Repressive, intolerable social situations are features of school life in Malaysia and Central Africa, where epidemic hysteria syndrome is endemic. While female redress is culturally unacceptable in these societies, males typically believe that those affected are possessed by spirits. Outbreaks of dissociation, histrionics, and psychomotor dysfunction among predominantly female pupils in these countries often include insulting authorities and frank criticism of administration policies. But these outbursts are accepted with impunity because their temporary possession status deflects the attribution of blame. As a result, they develop into idioms of distress and negotiation whereby outbreaks signal to the wider community that something is amiss. The anthropological perspective assumes that females are not susceptible per se, but rendered vulnerable through gender socialization.

Patterns

Based on the descriptive features of episodes, two distinct presentation patterns are identifiable. These patterns correspond closely with what Simon Wessely terms "mass anxiety hysteria" and "mass motor hysteria."[48] The former is of shorter duration — typically one day — and involves sudden, extreme anxiety following the perception of a false threat. The second type is confined to intolerable social settings and is characterized by dissociative states, histrionics, and alterations in psychomotor activity, usually persisting for weeks or months. Also discussed is an apparently rare third type, "mass pseudohysteria," involving the relabeling of mundane symptoms by hypervigilant authority figures.

TYPE ONE: MASS ANXIETY HYSTERIA

Mass anxiety hysteria is prevalent in Western or developed countries amid a social context that is conspicuously devoid of preexisting stress. Outbreaks are characterized by the appearance of illness signs and symptoms in a single student, which spread rapidly to schoolmates and occasionally teachers. Victims experience a variety of ambiguous, anxiety-related somatic complaints. Occasionally, the index case is a sick teacher or a nearby parent. The behavior of the index subject is often dramatic, engendering consternation among classmates. Often the first affected student exhibits a medical condition such as an epileptic fit, schizophrenia, tonsillitis or heatstroke. The specific cause is typically unknown to the remaining students and is learned retrospectively. Soon after the appearance of the index case, pupils begin to attribute the cause to an unusual odor that is assumed to represent a toxic gas or an agent such as a communicable illness, all of which are believed to pose an immediate personal threat. Commonly, food poisoning from the school cafeteria is indicted. Such determinations are made either nonverbally or through discussion about the incident among classmates. Sometimes rumors play the same role as a precipitating event. The news media, recent events, local traditions, and superstitious beliefs exacerbate the situation.

In non–Western countries, odors or food poisoning are rarely suspected. Instead, suspicion is placed on an array of diminutive supernatural entities. In such settings, the index case typically exhibits screaming, crying, and hyperventilation after seeing what is believed to be such spirits. Fellow pupils typically assume that the index subject is hexed or charmed or that a ghost is roaming the school. This triggers sudden, extreme anxiety because students assume they may be the next victims. The search for potential explanations among pupils is limited only by plausibility. The lack of educational and life experiences can foster hypotheses that are potentially fantastic to adults or individuals living outside of the culture or subculture. Students who are in the closest spatial, visual, or social contact with the index case and subsequent fallen cohorts are most susceptible to developing symptoms. In the majority of cases, investigators identify a downward spread of symptoms along the age scale, with the oldest student(s) affected first, followed by younger classmates. Typical are reports by Schuler and Parenton,[49] Benaim,[50] and Teoh and colleagues[51] that the index case was a prominent group member.

Most episodes last a single day and rarely more than a week. Lengthier cases or episodes involving relapses appear related to the inability of medical, school, and community leaders to convince the affected students and their parents of the psychogenic nature of the symptoms. In rare instances where the imaginary agent is believed to persist, or authorities are not perceived to have thoroughly examined the premises, cases can endure sporadically for several weeks or months. Episodes of mass anxiety hysteria cease rapidly once the students are convincingly reassured that the phantom threat, most typically a harmless odor, has been eliminated or never existed.

A classic episode of mass anxiety hysteria occurred at a girls' secondary school in Blackburn, England, in 1965. It was thoroughly investigated by Moss and McEvedy[52] and reported in the *British Medical Journal*.

On October 6, most of the schoolgirls attended a church ceremony under royal patronage. The service was delayed, and the group had to wait for three hours, during which twenty people fainted. The next day, the fainting incident was the major topic of discussion. At the morning assembly, one girl fainted, which was not uncommon because the assembly averaged two to three faints per week. After the assembly, four girls felt faint and were placed on chairs in a corridor near the center of the building. During the first two periods, six more girls were added. Teachers were concerned that the girls might injure themselves if they were to faint and fall from the chairs, so they were asked to lie on the floor along the corridor. Positioning the first group of symptomatic girls in the highly visible corridors made the situation appear more dramatic. The epidemic spread by line of sight soon after the mid-morning break. By midday, 141 pupils were complaining of a variety of symptoms: dizziness, fainting, headache, shivering, back and stomach pain, nausea, shortness of breath, facial numbness, and tetanic spasms. Ambulances rushed to the scene and transported eighty-five of the most severely affected students to hospital. The mass media speculated as to the source of the mysterious illness, adding further anxiety. Medical tests were unremarkable. Over the next fifteen days, several clusters of cases occurred at the school in a declining fashion. In all, about one-third of the 550 girls were affected:

> What became epidemic was a piece of behaviour consequent on an emotional state: excitement or, in the latter stages, frank fear led to over-breathing, with its characteristic sequelae — faintness, dizziness, paraesthesiae, and tetany. Once learned, this self-reinforcing piece of behaviour restarted spontaneously when the school was assembled. By day 12, however, the hysterical nature of the epidemic was generally accepted, and a firm line prevented the behaviour propagating as extensively as it had on the previous occasions.[53]

Type Two: Mass Motor Hysteria

The second discernible type is typified by an atmosphere of long-term, preexisting tension. Twentieth-century cases are primarily confined to schools in non–Western, technologically underdeveloped, traditional societies. Within such settings, both male and adult-dominated power structures often foster strict disciplinary routines among pupils, especially females. Students have little means of redress as negotiation, and protest channels with authorities are inhibited or nonexistent. They are unable to exit the situation because school is mandatory. By staying at home and feigning illness, homework is still required. Besides, such avoidance strategies will remove them from social contact with many schoolmates. The inescapable, intolerable situation engenders intense frustration that is internalized during the ensuing weeks or months.

This pattern was most prominent in Europe during the latter nineteenth and early twentieth centuries in response to rigid, rationalist educational discipline in many schools in such countries as France, Switzerland, and especially Germany. While the severity of rules varied among districts, the school systems in which episodes occurred were typified by performance pressures, monotonous tasks, rote memorization, repetitive writing, arithmetic drills, and a lack of imagination or individuality.

During this period, curriculums in the French primary-elementary schools were characterized as "too intense" and "far too much composed of memory work."[54] Article 1384 of the French educational code discouraged physical activities and games because teachers were held responsible for accidents occurring under their supervision.[55] Competition was extreme, with excessive pressure to perform coming from teachers, parents, and a list of pupils waiting to take their place: "With such dismissal constantly hanging over their head, pupils appear to be always at high pressure."[56] As early as age eleven, students could enter the secondary schools (*lycées*), which were "a veritable prison-house for all pupils from the youngest equally to the oldest, with a system of continual espionage known as *surveillance* (every minute of the day being duly apportioned, even recreation policed), relieved ... by scarcely a human feature." Dumville described the French teaching method as little more than "monotonous and reiterated preaching" whereby at the close of each lesson, "a tireless *resume*" had to be committed to memory.[57]

In some German districts, discipline was so rigid that, according to Spiller,[58] even "corporal punishment in the elementary schools is harsh and severe." Montgomery observed that the German military-training habits of obedience, order, and self-control were also incorporated into the education of women and children.[59] The Swiss education system during this period was virtually identical to the German system.[60] Montgomery noted that discipline was high, games rare, and free thought and imagination suppressed.[61]

At a girls school in Basel, Switzerland, in 1893, contagious trembling and convulsions affected twenty students, who were prevented from completing written assignments. Symptoms virtually disappeared after school hours, relapsing only upon reentering school grounds.[62] In 1904, the same girls school was swept by a similar outbreak affecting fourteen classes of pupils aged eleven to fifteen. The main symptom was a vibrating tremor

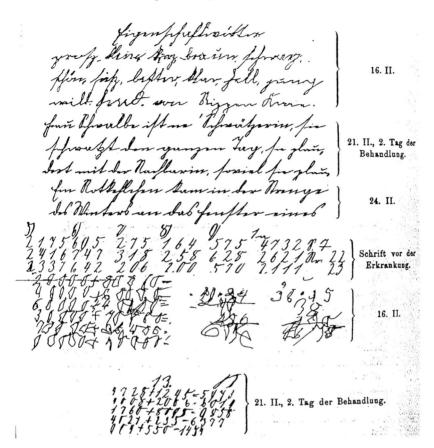

Figure 2.1: In February 1906, Dr. Johannes Schoedel of The People's School in Chemnitz, Germany, observed an outbreak of arm and hand tremors in 21 female students. Remarkably, the tremors only occurred during their writing exercise hour. All other activities were performed normally, including gymnastics. Above are some of the handwriting samples. (Schoedel, J. [1906]. "Uber Induzierte Krankheiten" [On Induced Illness]. *Jahrbuch fur Kinderheilkunde* 14:521–528. The figure appears on p. 522.)

in the right hand and forearm, which began in two students on June 11. Over the ensuing weeks, the symptoms gradually spread until twenty-seven pupils were affected. Rumors started that the school would be closed for six weeks if the tremors continued to spread. The administrators instead announced that the school session would continue, and the affected pupils were instructed in a special classroom with the same teacher for a month. The students were well fed, given a reduced workload, and no blame or punishment was imposed for their inability to complete written work because of their tremors. Despite some disruptions in their arithmetic and handwriting performances, the symptoms gradually diminished. There were six cases of relapse, but the outbreak soon ended.[63] A similar episode took place at Gross-tinz, Germany, between June 28 and mid–October 1892. However, the initial hand tremors soon affected the victims' entire body, and eight of the twenty victims exhibited altered states of consciousness and amnesia.[64] At a school in Chemnitz, Germany, in February 1906, physician Johannes Schoedel observed arm and hand tremors in female elementary students during their writing-exercise hour. The symptoms began in two pupils, but they gradually spread to twenty-one females over four weeks. The pupils performed all other manual tasks normally, including gymnastics class. Schoedel's treatment was to administer electric shocks to those affected and to demand drills in arithmetic. The symptoms ceased soon after.[65] The pupils performed all other manual tasks normally, and they were affected only during written schoolwork. Symptoms ceased soon after it was announced, "Since you are not able to write, you must unfortunately have mental arithmetic again."[66]

Some school episodes during this period appear to have been relatively minor, short-lived, and unrelated to academic discipline or exposure to sudden anxiety,[67] such as the left-arm paralysis in four girls at a London school in February 1907. A girl with infantile palsy of the left arm fractured her right arm. She returned to class several weeks later and "within a few days three children had lost the use of their left arms, and a fourth … had such severe pains in her left arm that she held it to the side and could not be persuaded to use it."[68]

During the present century, mass motor hysteria is most evident in schools within Malaysia or Central and Eastern Africa. The African outbreaks usually affect missionary schools.[69] A typical African case was investigated by Dhadphale and Shaikh. Twitching, mental confusion, uncontrollable laughing, running, and anxiety affected 126 students at a secondary school in Zambia in May, 1976.[70] The researchers noted that "the recent strict disciplinary measures taken by the new administration, such as rigid separation of boys and girls, may have prepared the emotionally charged background."[71] Ebrahim noted that African children are dominated by their "all-powerful elders." Conflict arises from exposure to foreign ideas that challenge traditional beliefs, and escape is sought through conversion reactions. According to Ebrahim, the outbreaks were fueled by "emotional conflict aroused in children who are being brought up at home amidst traditional tribal conservatism, while being exposed in school to thoughts and ideas which challenge accepted beliefs".[72]

In Malaysia, the widespread appearance of mass motor hysteria in schools coincides with rapid social and cultural changes,[73] especially

Islamic revivalism, which has rapidly gained influence since the early 1960s. Islamic by birth, Malays constitute just over half of the population. Yet mass motor hysteria is almost exclusively confined to female Malays attending religious boarding schools. Episodes have become endemic in Malaysian schools since 1962.[74] Malaysian Islamic religious schools are notorious for their strict discipline and lack of privacy, where even basic choices such as which school to attend, courses to take, careers to pursue, and friendships to develop are decided by others.[75] In coeducational Islamic schools, boys and girls are strictly segregated, even within the same classroom. Students must account for their whereabouts at all times. Interaction with the opposite sex is strictly prohibited, courting is forbidden, and even visits by relatives are closely monitored in special public rooms. Hence, mass motor hysteria in Malay boarding schools typically occur amid "a general feeling of unhappiness about some new condition of study or rule among the girls."[76] In conjunction with such oppressive practices, social, cultural, and religious protocols prohibit female Malays from direct confrontation with their superiors.[77]

With the continued presence of strict religious discipline, eventually a small number of students begin exhibiting conversion symptoms. Such events foster widespread anxiety about the existence of demonic agents within the school that posses an immediate personal threat. Teoh and colleagues reported a "monotonously similar" pattern in Malaysian schools:

> [G]irls would scream, shout, and run aimlessly all over in terror, with severe hyperventilation followed by muscular twitchings and tetanic spasms of the limbs. ... Some would fall on the floor in a trancelike state, as though in a stupor. Occasionally one or two of the subjects would speak up on behalf of the group, voicing their misdemeanors and frustrations. Very often they became abusive. They characteristically took hints and cues from one another. Most of the subjects…would swear amnesia. On questioning, the girls would complain of seeing fearsome objects… Some would see dark flying objects or an ugly woman eight feet tall. The occupants of one hostel complained that a hungry spirit was always stealing their food and raiding the refrigerator. Others complained of ghosts stealing their underwear and jamming their doors.[78]

It is vital to realize that while the pupils' interpretations of these events may seem bizarre by Western standards, they are entirely consistent with popular Malay folk beliefs.[79] Animistic customs and superstitions are prevalent in Malay society. There is a widespread belief in the efficacy of magic potions, spells, amulets, charms, and curses, which are easily obtained by consulting a witch doctor (*bomoh*), whose services remain popular. There is also a prevalent belief in the existence of supernatural beings (*Jinn*) that are described in the Koran, diminutive fairylike *toyl* creatures, and ghosts (*hantus*) from Malay culture.

Extreme anxiety, hysterical conversion, and hyperventilation syndrome spread rapidly among pupils who are in closest proximity, in visual contact, or have the strongest social ties with the initial cohort exhibiting dissociative states. These trancelike states sometimes take the form of spirit possession, which can be dramatic and convincing to observers. In virtually every non–Western episode of this type, the services of one or more native healers are solicited to exorcise the evil spirit(s). Repression-induced conversion symptoms typically persist from one month to several years, depending on the changes implemented by authorities in response to the outbreak. If discipline is eased and anxiety levels decline, episodes usually subside. However, if the intolerable situation persists, outbreaks can endure indefinitely.

Contemporary Western episodes are uncommon but occasionally occur. One outbreak of mass motor hysteria took the form of epidemic fainting, dissociation and histrionics among several pupils at a girls school near London amid serious interpersonal and sexual conflicts following the death of a former schoolmate and lesbian advances by a schoolmistress.[80] In this instance, instead of the "drop attacks" instigated by academic discipline, the school premises served as a stage where the girls' personal problems appeared in the form of hysterical conversion dramas over a seven-month period.

Another Western example of mass motor hysteria occurred at an African-American school in Louisiana over a six-month period in 1962. All but one of the twenty-three pupils were female. The students exhibited dizziness, headaches, and epileptic-type seizures. Most of the "blackout spells" lasted for a few minutes, occasionally lasting up to an hour. A considerable number of the students, ranging in age from ten to seventeen, were sexually active. The outbreak coincided with rumors that all of the girls were going to be administered pregnancy tests and, if determined to be pregnant, would be sent away to a correctional school. Treatment with tranquilizers and sedatives was ineffective, and visits by outside authorities exacerbated the situation. Only with the gradual reduction of stress did the outbreak subside seven months later.

The presentation of mass motor episodes is remarkably similar to scores of hysterical fits, dissociation, and psychomotor agitation among nuns secluded in European Christian convents between the fifteenth and nineteenth centuries.[81] Histrionics and role playing were also a significant part of the syndrome. Like their Malaysian counterparts, young females were typically coerced by elders into joining socially isolating religious

165 Girls Faint at Football Game; Mass Hysteria Grips 'Pep Squad'

By The United Press.

NATCHEZ, Miss., Sept. 13—One hundred and sixty-five teen-aged girls on a cheering squad who became hysterical and fainted at a high school football game were reported "all right" today.

Football players dodged ambulances and autos that raced across the gridiron to take the girls to a hospital last night when the mass faintings occurred.

The girls were members of the Tigerettes Pep Squad from Monroe, La.

Paul Neal, principal of Monroe's Neville High School, said that after thirty-five or forty girls had fainted every available ambulance and scores of cars were pressed into service to rush the entire squad to General Hospital.

Dr. James Barnes, who examined and released all the girls, blamed "overheating and mass hysteria." The squad returned to Monroe in its chartered buses. Natchez won the game, 21 to 8.

"They fainted like flies," said Thornton Smith, a spectator. "Men swarmed right around the girls, picking them up and taking them to the foot of the stands."

Mr. Smith said the loudspeakers called for doctors, but the game went on, with players dodging the ambulances. At one time, he said, five ambulances were crossing the field at once.

"It looked like the race track at Indianapolis," Mr. Smith said.

The girls, ranging from 14 to 18 years old, and wearing snappy, gold-trimmed black jackets and white skirts, had paraded on Main Street before the game.

By the end of the first period, Mr. Smith said, they were so excited they mistook the moment for their half-time parade period and started marching toward the south goal line. The loudspeaker called them back. By half-time all were at the hospital.

Figure 2.2: On September 12, 1952, 165 teenage girls from a football pep squad suddenly fainted at a Mississippi football game. The case is unusual in that no perceived threatening agent was present. But at the end of the first quarter, the squad mistakenly marched onto the field for their halftime performance and were embarrassingly called back over the public loudspeaker, generating considerable anxiety. (*New York Times*, September 14, 1952.)

orders practicing rigid discipline in confined, all-female living quarters. Male associations were forbidden. Mass motor hysteria conspicuously appeared under the strictest administrations. Instead of witch doctors, priests were summoned to exorcise the "demonic spirits," and disliked individuals were often accused of casting spells. In both instances, the inmates released frustrations by uttering disrespectful, often blasphemous remarks and engaging in aggressive sexual and threatening behavior, their possession status providing them with impunity.

While Malay schoolgirls often call for the dismissal or transfer of their restrictive headmaster, a despised colleague or restrictive convent priest was typically accused by the possessed nuns of causing their condition through witchcraft. Malaysian episodes usually subside when school figures relax rules or the offending official is removed. In convents, symptoms disappeared soon after the accused was transferred, banished, imprisoned, or more commonly, burned at the stake. While Malaysian episodes typically persist for a few months and occasionally years, convent outbreaks usually endured for several years because lengthy church inquisitions were required and exorcisms were performed to remove the offending person and to administer punishment. During this waiting period, the nuns remained in their repressive situation which continued to incubate symptoms.

Type Three: Mass Pseudo-Hysteria

One surveyed case involved the relabeling of mundane symptoms in closed, cohesive social units, which were instigated and maintained by the erroneous beliefs of hypervigilant authority figures. During a routine social gathering at an elementary school near Atlanta, Georgia, in early September of 1988, the mother of a student attending the school remarked how, since the beginning of the term, her child had appeared pale and experienced minor health problems. Other mothers began scrutinizing their children, noting similar signs and symptoms: pallor, dark circles under the eyes, headaches, fatigue, nausea, and occasional vomiting. They were soon convinced that the school building was responsible. This conviction crystallized further when, on October 11, a small quantity of natural gas leaked during routine maintenance, prompting the school's evacuation. Over the next month, a series of minor gas leaks occurred at the school. Despite health assurances from authorities, many parents became distraught, organized pickets, and highlighted the situation to the mass media. Environmental and epidemiological studies reaffirmed the view of the administration that there was no health threat. Philen et al. remarked that the children exhibited few public illness displays and did not seek attention. Concern was "expressed almost exclusively by the mothers."[82] Attendance levels remained high throughout the term, and the complaints were attributable to ever-present, mundane childhood illnesses.

Conclusions

The characteristic features of epidemic hysteria syndrome in school settings are consistent across diverse geographical areas and historical periods. The classic school outbreak involves a socially cohesive group of female pupils near puberty and early adolescence who are exposed to a stressful stimulus. Transient symptoms spread, subside rapidly, and occasionally reoccur. School episodes manifest themselves as variants of a unitary syndrome that is typified by collective anxiety states and hysterical conversion symptoms. The medical and cultural zeitgeist accounts for the variance in descriptions and nomenclature. Symptoms within each type are interpreted within the prevailing sociocultural milieu. Demonic possession predominates in non–Western, traditional societies experiencing mass motor hysteria. Chemical and food-contamination scares typically involve mass anxiety hysteria, reflecting contemporary Western preoccupations with environmental concerns. While major theories vary in explaining symptom presentation, each theory acknowledges the pivotal role of extreme psychosocial stress.

By its very nature, oubreaks of epidemic hysteria syndrome have the potential to generate public controversy because most investigators view them as a diagnosis of exclusion that can never be confirmed with positive medical test results. A notable exception to this view is Simon Wessely, who does not consider it to be a diagnosis of exclusion because the syndrome is characterized by several distinct features, the collective appearance of which almost certainly indicates the presence of epidemic hysteria syndrome.[83] However, prior to the results of medical and environmental tests and detailed interviews with affected students, physicians can only note the transient, ambiguous, benign symptomatology, the preponderance of female victims, and the lack of a plausible pathogenic agent.

A diagnosis of epidemic hysteria syndrome can only be reasonably determined retrospectively, after eliminating the presence of organic or toxicological pathogens. During the early stages of any outbreak, investigators should be cautious in attributing a psychogenic origin to unidentified illness symptoms prior to receiving laboratory findings. An outbreak of abdominal pain, nausea, and vomiting at a London elementary school in 1990 included such classic epidemic hysteria features as rapid onset and recovery, overbreathing, line-of-sight transmission, and a high female attack rate. Yet subsequent investigation revealed cucumber-pesticide contamination.[84] It may, therefore, be advisable to close a school until such negative results are returned. Closure should also reduce the stress levels among the students and temporarily break up the group.

This will allow time for investigators to determine in detail, if most or all of the characteristics of epidemic hysteria syndrome are present. These are the following: symptoms with no plausible organic basis

symptoms that are transient and benign
symptoms with rapid onset and recovery
occurrence in a segregated group
presence of extraordinary anxiety
symptoms spread through sight, sound, or oral communication
spread occurs down the age scale, beginning in older or high-status students
a preponderance of female participants near puberty and early adolescence

While reports of mass anxiety hysteria dominate the twentieth-century scientific literature, and mass motor hysteria was more prevalent during the nineteenth century, it does not necessarily follow that mass anxiety hysteria was less common in the past century. It may be that during the nineteenth century, psychoanalytic-oriented observers took more notice of prolonged outbreaks affecting small numbers of students while ignoring short-lived, large-scale episodes by passing them off as the behavior of immature schoolgirls.

In managing episodes, school administrators must identify the underlying stressor(s) and take appropriate measures to reduce or eliminate their anxiety-generating effects. This is much easier said than done, as epidemic hysteria diagnoses often engender hostility from defensive parents who challenge claims that the outbreak was "psychological." For instance, physician Joel Nitzkin received a series of threatening telephone calls from belligerent parents.[85] Wong et al. noted considerable public resentment to the epidemic hysteria label,[86] and Cartter et al. observed that "some parents insisted that we had accused their children of faking symptoms."[87]

In controlling short-lived mass anxiety hysteria, administrators should seek the cooperation of teachers, medical authorities, and high-status community members to reassure students and parents that the agent believed to pose a threat was either imaginary or no longer exists. In non–Western countries, the services of native healers are often rendered and provide reassurance.

For more enduring mass motor hysteria, the emphasis should be on identifying and resolving the precipitating conflict. Public confrontation, exhortation, and other coercive measures typically aggravate the situation. In controlling outbreaks or their recurrence, it would be useful to utilize counseling and open communication to counteract misinformation and rumor. In locations such as Malaysia or East and Central Africa, the presence of native healers typically exacerbates episodes because motor symptoms usually take longer to subside than anxiety hysteria. Hence, while the native healer's assistance is viewed as confirming the presence of malevolent spirits, the persistence of cases reaffirms that the school grounds have not been completely exorcised. This supports Wessely's conclusion that to control mass motor hysteria, measures must be implemented "to remove the advantages of the sick-role by the withdrawal of social validation."[88] This could take the form of advising teachers to handle any new cases by appearing confident while publicly labeling the incident as psychological in nature. Removing the victims from the sight and sound of other pupils, sending them home if necessary until their condition completely subsides is an option. This is consistent with the most historically successful means of controlling epidemic hysteria syndrome in schools: disbanding and isolating the group affected, such as granting them leave from school until their symptoms subside.

Table 2.1
Chronological List, Mass Anxiety Hysteria
in School Settings[89]

Source/ Circa	Location	Primary Symptoms	Duration	Sex	Number/ Age Span	Index Noted
Bokai 1892	Hungary	Hyperventilation	-	F	12 (9–15)	-
Legendre 1908	Szechwan, China	Genital sensations	Few days	M	20 (<20)	-
Olson 1928	USA	Fainting	1 month	F	9 (14–17)	+
Pfeiffer 1964	USA	Hyperventilation	1 day	F	8 (16–20)	+
Moss 1966	Blackburn, England	Hyperventilation	2 weeks	F	140 (10–16)	-
McEvedy 1966	England	Vomiting	9 days	F	105 (10–15)	-
(1–2)* 1966	Kajang, Malaysia	Crying, screaming, fainting	1 week	-	18 (<20)	+
Mausner 1967	USA	Gonorrhea-like symptoms	15 days	F (80%)	50–100 (6–12)	+

*Numbers in source column indicate press reports, listed in order in the notes for this table (see Notes section).

Source/ Circa	Location	Primary Symptoms	Duration	Sex	Number/ Age Span	Index Noted
Lyons 1970	Northern Ireland	Fainting	1 day	F	28 (11–14)	+
(3–4) 1971	Pahang, Malaysia	Howling, screaming	~2 days	F	5 (13–17)	–
(5) 1971	Ipoh, Malaysia	Screaming, crying	1 day	–	16 (<20)	–
(6–7) 1972	Junjong, Malaysia	Crying, screaming	1 day	22 F 2 M	24 (6–17)	+
Goldberg 1973	Maryland, USA	Screaming	1 day	47 F 6 M	53 (12–18)	+
Smith 1973	Newcastle upon Tyne, England	Abdominal pain	1 day	76 F 4 M	130 (8–15)	+
Levine/ Polk	Alabama, USA	Pruritus, rash	2 weeks	Ratio: 2 F to 1 M	98 (7–12)	+
Sirois 1974	Quebec, Canada	Fainting	1 day	F	11 (9–11)	–
Sirois 1975	Quebec, Canada	Fainting	6 weeks	–	100 (12–14)	+
Nitzkin 1975	Florida, USA	Headache	1 day	Ratio: 2 F to 1 M	1M 34 (11–12)	+
Levine 1977	Alabama, USA	Fainting	1 day	F and M	57 (14–17)	+
Figueroa 1977	Kingston, Jamaica	Abdominal pain	1 week	Ratio: 3 F to 1 M	196 (10–11)	–
(8) 1978	Kuah, Malaysia	Fainting, screaming, seeing ghosts	1 day	F	7 (~13–17)	+
Forrester 1979	England	Fainting	1 day	F	40 (20<)	–
Bebbington 1980	Nottinghamshire, England	Fainting	1 day	F	414 (7–17)	+
O'Donnell 1980	Ireland	Abdominal pain	1 day	F–M	47 (9–12)	+
Lee 1980	West Malaysia	Screaming	2 days	16 F 1 M	17 (~16–17)	+
Moffat 1980	Montreal, Canada	Dizziness	1 day	23 F 7 M	30 (12–14)	+
Small 1982	Maine, USA	Dizziness	1 day	M–F	34 (9–13)	+
Wong/Tam 1982	Hong Kong	Abdominal pain	3 days	Ratio: 2 F to 1 M	355 (6–14)	–

Source/ Circa	Location	Primary Symptoms	Duration	Sex	Number/ Age Span	Index Noted
(9) 1982	Kuching, Sarawak, Malaysia	Screaming, strange figures seen	3 days	F	30 (~6–17)	+
(10–12) 1982	Kuala Terengganu, Malaysia	Swearing, screaming, crying	3 days	F	~30 (13, 15–16)	-
(13) 1982	Labis, Malaysia	Crying, moaning	8 days	F	20 (12–16)	-
Modan 1983	Jordan, West Bank, Israel	Headache, fainting	14 days	Ratio: 3 F to 1 M	949 (6–18)	-
Small 1983	Massachusetts, USA	Dizziness	1 day	Ratio: 3 F to 1 M	41 (9–13)	+
Wason 1983	Ohio, USA	Headache	1 day	Ratio: 3 F to 1 M	41 (9–14)	+
Roback 1983	Tennessee, USA	Screaming	1 day	F	8 (8–9)	+
(14) 1983	Malacca, Malaysia	Screaming, crying	1 day	F	~30 (12–16)	+
(15) 1983	Seremban, Malaysia	Jumping, screaming, fleeing	6.5 hours	F	15 (20<)	-
(16–18) 1983	Keningau, Malaysia	Fainting, crying, swearing	1 week	F	13 (14–16)	-
Robinson 1984	West Virginia, USA	Pruritus	2 days	Ratio: 3 F to 1 M	57 (9–12)	-
Araki 1984	Tokyo, Japan	Headache	1 day	Ratio: 3 F to 1 M	16 (12–15)	+
(19) 1984	Kuala Terengganu, Malaysia	Itching	½ hour	F	15 (8)	-
(20) 1984	Taiping, Malaysia	Fainting, headache	1 day	M	2 (~6–17)	-
Goh 1986	Singapore	Dizziness	1 day	Ratio: 5 F to 1 M	65 (12–13)	-
(21–23) 1986	Klang, Malaysia	Screaming, fainting, foaming at the mouth	~1 day	F	9 (~13–17)	-
Elkins 1987	Texas, USA	Abdominal pain	1 day	F	30 (14–16)	+
(24) 1987	Johore Baru, Malaysia	Crying	-	F	7 (13–16)	-

Source/ Circa	Location	Primary Symptoms	Duration	Sex	Number/ Age Span	Index Noted
(25) 1987	Seremban, Malaysia	Screaming	—	F	11 (20<)	-
(26) 1987	Pasir Mas, Malaysia	Screaming	1 week	mostly F	43 (13–17)	-
Ruiz 1988	Spain	Fainting	10 days	F	8 (11–15)	-
Cartter 1988	Connecticut, USA	Abdominal pain	1 day	-	39 (12)	-
(27) 1988	Seremban, Malaysia	Screaming	1 day	F	10	+
Gamino 1989	Texas, USA	Hyperventilation, abdominal pain	1 day	-	119 (11–14)	+
Goldsmith 1989	Soviet Georgia	Abdominal pain	1 day	mostly F	40 (<20)	-
Philen 1989	Georgia, USA	Headache	2 months	Ratio 4 F to 1 Male	339 (5–14)	-
Selden 1989	Alabama, USA (?)	Nausea	1 day	Mosly F	15	-
Cole 1989	North Carolina, USA	Headache	Few days	F	103 (10–14)	+
Small 1990	California, USA	Headache	1 day	Ratio: 2.5 F to 1 M	247 (12–18)	-
Baker 1991	Arizona, USA	Headache	1 day	Ratio: 2 F to 1 M	296 (17<)	-
Desenclos 1992	Florida, USA	Abdominal pain	1 day	Ratio: 3 F to 1 M	3 (4–14)	-
Krug 1992	Ohio, USA	Nausea	-	-	116 (10–13)	+
Rockney 1992	Rhode Island, USA	Dizziness, headache, nausea	1 day	18 F 3 M	21 (12–14)	-
Taylor 1992	Canada	Nausea	1 day	2 F 7 Male	19 (9–12)	+
Spitlers et al. 1996	Washington State, USA	Nausea, headache	2 days	63% F	80	-

Table 2.2
Chronological List, Mass Motor Hysteria
in School Settings

Source/ Circa	Location	Primary Symptoms	Duration	Sex	Number/ Age Span	Index Noted
Hirsch 1808	Hanover, Germany	Convulsions	-	F	- (9–14)	-
Regnard 1876	France	Contractures, paresthesia	2 weeks	F	28 (8–13)	+
Armainguad 1879	France	Convulsions, laughing, globus	18 days	F	6 (11–14)	+
Laquer 1888	Germany	Shaking	3 months	F	10 (8–12)	-
Wichmann 1890	Germany	Shaking	7 months	70% F	26 (12–14)	+
Schatalow 1892	Germany	Laughing	14 days	F	13 (10–13)	-
Palmer 1892	Gross-tinz, Germany	Convulsions, tremor	3 weeks	F	20 (10–13)	+
Rembold 1893	Germany	Fainting, laughing	1 day	F	25 (9–10)	-
Hagenbach 1893	Basel, Switzerland	Convulsions	Few days	F	62 (10–20)	+
Sirois 1893	Austria	Abnormal movements	1 month	F	7 (10–20)	+
Leuch 1896	Germany	Coughing, headache, abnormal movements	Few months	96% F	25 (9–11)	+
Von Holwede 1898	Germany	Abnormal movements	10 days	F	42 (8–14)	-
Zollinger 1904	Basel, Switzerland	tremor	Several weeks	F	27 (11–15)	+
Schutte 1906	Meissen, Germany	Abnormal movements	1 month	F	20 (9–13)	-
Schoedel 1906	Chemnitz, Germany	Abnormal movements	4 weeks	F	21 (9–10)	+
Sterling 1936	Poland	Abnormal movements, paresthesia	5 days	F	5 (10–12)	+
Schuler 1939	Louisiana, USA	Abnormal movements	~1 month	F	7 (16–18)	+
Michaux 1952	France	Convulsions	15 days	F	4 (14–16)	+

Source/ Circa	Location	Primary Symptoms	Duration	Sex	Number/ Age Span	Index Noted
Theopold 1955	Germany	Neuralgia	Few days	F	30 (10–20)	-
(26) Rankin 1962	Tanganyika (Tanzania)	Laughing	18 months	Male and F	1000 (12–18)	+
Tan 1962	Johore Baru, Malaya (Malaysia)	Screaming, crying fainting, trance	<1 month	F	29 (~6–17)	+
Kagwa 1964	Uganda	Running, agitation	1 month	M and F	300 (11–40)	
Knight 1965	Louisiana, USA	Fainting, epileptic-like fits, tremor, catatonic posturing	6 months	21 F 1 M	22 (10–17)	+
Helvie 1968	USA	Laughing, crying	1 day	F	16 (14–18)	-
Olczak 1971	USA	Convulsions tremor, stomach cramps	1 week	66% F	55 (15–19)	+
(28–29) 1971	Malaysia	Crying, screaming, fainting, violence	2 days	F	78 (~13–17)	+
Muhangi 1971	Kajara County, Uganda	Grimacing, laughing, foul language, disobedience	-	-	50 (12–20)	+
Teoh 1972	Near Kuala Lumpur, Malaysia	Trance, screaming, hyperventilation	1 month	F	5 (<20)	+
(30–31) 1973	Ipoh, Malaysia	Running, screaming, disobedience	6 days	M	8 (<18)	-
Adomakoh 1973	Africa	Laughing	10 days	F	62 (11–16)	-
Benaim 1973	London, England	Fainting	7 months	F	8 (16–17)	+
Teoh 1975	Kelang, Malaysia	Tetanic spasms, trance, hyper-ventilation, screaming	10 weeks	F	8 (12–15)	+
Ackerman 1978	West Malaysia	Trance, screaming	6 days	8 F 4 M	12 (?)	+
(32) 1981	West Malaysia	Hysterical fits, "dreamy"	1 month	F	several (20)	-

Source/ Circa	Location	Primary Symptoms	Duration	Sex	Number/ Age Span	Index Noted
Mohr 1982	England	Loss of consciousness	21 months	60 F 3 M	63 (12–15)	+
Dhadphale 1982	Mwinilunga, Zambia	Twitching, laughing	3 days	120 F 5 M	126 (16–17)	+
(33–34) 1982	Taiping, Malaysia	Fainting, violent fits	2 months	F	6 (9–11)	-
(35–37) 1986	Bahu, Malaysia	Hysterical fits	1 month	-	29 (~6–17)	-
(38) 1986	Johore Baru, Malaysia	Hysterical fits	2 months	-	several (~6–17)	-
(39) 1986	Johore Baru, Malaysia	Hysterical fits	2 months	-	several (6–17)	-
(40–41) 1986	Bahu, Malaysia	Hysterical fits	1.5 month	-	29 (6–17)	-
(42) 1986	Setiu, Malaysia	Screaming, running	4 weeks	F	10 (~13–17)	-
(43) 1987	Bahu, Malaysia	Screaming, running away	-	-	16 (13–17)	-
(44–47) 1987	Kuala Terengganu, Malaysia	Screaming running, trance	3 weeks	F	100 (12–16)	+
(48–59) 1987	Alor Star Malaysia	Shouting, trance, violence	5 years	F	36 (13–17)	+
(60) 1989	Gurun, Malaysia	seeing ghosts, screaming, fainting	~9 months	F	several (12–16)	-
(61) 1989	West Malaysia	Screaming, seeing ghosts fainting	-	F	18 (13–17)	+
(62) 1989	Klang, Malaysia	Hysteria, seeing ghosts, screaming, fainting	38 days	4 F 1 M	5 (16)	-
Wittstock 1991	South Africa	Fainting, trance	18 months	M and F	60 (6–13)	-
(63) 1991	Johore Baru, Malaysia	Hysterical fits	9 days	F	30	-
(64) 1991	Kluang, Malaysia	Hysterical fits	1.5 months	-	46 (?)	-
(65–67) 1991	Johore Baru, Malaysia	Hysterical fits, violence, tearing clothes, screaming, trance	2 months	most F	120	-

Source/ Circa	Location	Primary Symptoms	Duration	Sex	Number/ Age Span	Index Noted
(68) 1993	Klang, Malaysia	Screaming running	–	–	10 (15–16)	–
(69–70) 1994	Sentul, Malaysia	Screaming, trembling, glossolalia, possession, fainting, verbal abuse	8 days	F	10 (?)	–

Chapter 3

Epidemic Hysteria at Work

We have created an industrial order geared to automatism, where feeble-mindedness, native or acquired, is necessary for docile productivity in the factory; and where a pervasive neurosis is the final gift of the meaningless life that issues forth at the other end. — Lewis Mumford[1]

In this chapter, we identify three presentation patterns in the appearance of epidemic hysteria in work settings. It is important to view these three categories in our taxonomy as a working model and to be mindful that classificatory schemes do not exist as objective elements in nature awaiting description. Thomas Morgan writes that "the arrangement ... into species, genera, families, etc. is only a scheme invented by man (sic) for purposes of classification. Thus there is no such thing in nature as a species, except as a concept of a group of forms more or less alike."[2] In discussing the tendency for mental health practitioners to construct and accept nosologies that conspicuously reflect both the popular and professional zeitgeist, medical anthropologist Arthur Kleinman urges caution in accepting these schemes, given the historical tendency to reify them as part of everyday reality:

> [V]erification of the meaning of the observations in a given social system ... [is crucial as] observation is inseparable from interpretation. Psychiatric diagnoses are not things, though they give name and scope to processes ... [they] ... derive from categories ... [that] are outcomes of historical development, cultural influence, and political negotiation.[3]

It is with this understanding that this chapter should be read.

The author is grateful to François Sirois for his co-authorship of this chapter.

This review examines reported episodes of epidemic hysteria in job settings in the scientific literature for which basic details are available (N = 68). We acknowledge that the term "occupational mass psychogenic illness" (OMPI) is not perceived as neutral in the eyes of those suffering from it or in the eyes of their advocates. However, it is certainly preferable to labels that use the word "hysteria." OMPI is defined as illness symptoms and related beliefs that are collectively reported at a worksite that have no identifiable pathogenic explanation. Our intent is to describe underlying presentation patterns within the reports and account for their irregular appearance. By doing so, we wish to provide historical continuity and perspective to a phenomenon that continues to mystify and frustrate scientists by its sporadic, unpredictable, protean epidemiology. Reports were collected based on a search of MEDLINE, sociological abstracts, psychological abstracts, and cross references for episodes listed under mass or epidemic hysteria, mass psychogenic or sociogenic illness, factory hysteria, assembly-line hysteria, or hysterical contagion.[4] Excluded from this review are various chemical-sensitivity syndromes that appear under different labels: sick-building syndrome, multiple-chemical sensitivity syndrome, total-allergy syndrome, and environmental hypersensitivity. This was done due to their controversial psychogenic status and to keep the survey manageable. For instance, a systematic review by the authors found 346 relevant references for environmental hypersensitivity, 240 for total-allergy syndrome, 218 for sick building syndrome, 416 for Gulf War syndrome, and 4,578 for post traumatic stress disorder.

It is assumed that OMPI is a variant of individual "conversion hysteria," a term that Sigmund Freud devised to explain the converting of psychological conflict and anxiety into involuntary physical symptoms for which there is no corresponding organic etiology. OMPI will therefore refer to the spread of conversion symptoms and anxiety states within a particular cluster of workers following exposure to a common stressor that is either real or imagined.

A fundamental problem with the concept of hysterical conversion is that, like so many psychiatric disorders, the diagnostic criteria are ambiguous and subject to interpretation and misdiagnosis—perhaps hysteria more than any other.[5] Thomas Szasz does not view hysteria as an illness or disorder but as a form of communication precipitated by problems in living.[6] In this sense, it can be interpreted as an idiom of distress. Others have also questioned its existence as a clinical entity, most notably the former editor of the *British Journal of Psychiatry*, Eliot Slater.[7] Certainly the term has been misused to stigmatize a variety of undesirable behaviors and can be analyzed on multiple levels. Indeed, what has been described as hysteria has been interpreted and conceptualized within various academic traditions.[8]

Since the mid–1970s, feminist critiques of hysteria have become fashionable. These critiques deconstruct the term and generally interpret this predominantly female malady as an iatrogenic rubric created and maintained by the male-dominated medical profession.[9] These feminist writers document the clear misuse of the term by male-biased researchers who were/are able to consciously assert social, political, and legal dominance over females and their bodies. This has been achieved by medicalizing femininity and characterizing women's psychological constitution as innately unstable and prone to disturbance, relegating females to the status of the "Other." The ambiguous diagnostic criteria for determining the presence of hysteria was ideal for this purpose because it is said to mimic any organic disease.[10]

The study of conversion symptoms has a history of abuse and misuse, due in large part to ambiguous diagnostic criteria and uncertainty surrounding psychophysiological mechanisms. However, while Kleinman considers conversion symptoms to be "a great mystery at the heart of psychosomatic medicine," he believes that "enough is known about conversion symptoms to describe them as the literal embodiment of conflicted meanings, somatic symbols that have psychological and social uses."[11] In defending the concept, Miller noted that all explanatory models of hysteria have significant weaknesses, but there is a consistent pattern noted by health-care professionals involving subjects with symptoms for which there is no discernible pathology.[12] "If 'hysteria' refers to this and nothing more then the term does carry useful meaning."[13]

OMPI was accorded scant attention by the scientific community until the latter 1970s, when the number of reports increased suddenly. Consequently, interest in the topic quickly shifted from obscure, exotic footnotes in the history of epidemic hysteria to a prominent public-health concern. Workplace episodes have been referred to by various descriptive labels, most commonly "mass psychogenic illness," "mass hysteria" or "epidemic hysteria," "sick-building syndrome" or "tight-building syndrome," and "hysterical contagion." "Mass psychogenic illness" is the most popular contemporary label because it is more neutral than terms containing derivatives of the word "hysteria," which is considered to be pejorative to females.[14] Other phrases such as "group mental disorder" or "mental epidemics" also possess undesirable, potentially stigmatizing connotations. Such labels may also be inaccurate because attempts to identify abnormal personality correlates in participants versus nonparticipants within affected groups are inconclusive.[15]

During the latter 1970s, a cluster of OMPI was reported in several countries, primarily the United States. Colligan and Murphy analyzed these episodes, reviewed the literature, and were surprised to locate just two previous cases in scientific journals during this century.[16] This contrasts sharply with the plethora of prominent reports in schools[17] and communities[18] throughout this century. The two earlier occupational reports both occurred in the United States: the "June Bug" outbreak at a Spartanburg, South Carolina, textile factory in 1962[19] and a 1974 episode in a data center at a major Midwestern university.[20] However, the enigmatic waxing and waning of OMPI reports in the scientific literature may be a function of the prevailing medical zeitgeist and social science ideology in defining and recognizing the problem. For instance, the present definition as to what constitutes OMPI is typically narrow and confined to traditional work settings such as factories and offices.

Presentation Patterns

Three distinct presentation patterns are discernible based on an examination of descriptive features of cases. The first two patterns correspond closely to Simon Wessely's classification scheme of mass hysteria, dividing episodes into two categories: mass anxiety hysteria and mass motor hysteria.[21] The former is characterized by the unexpected presence of what is perceived to be an immediate personal threat, engendering the sudden appearance of a variety of ambiguous, benign, transient somatic complaints. Mass motor hysteria is precipitated within an atmosphere of pre-existing psychosocial stress among dissatisfied employees, fostering dissociation, histrionics, and occasional psychomotor dysfunction such as muscular twitching, falling, and tetanic spasms. A third presentation pattern involves the relabeling of endemic symptoms.

Mass Anxiety Hysteria

While mass anxiety hysteria is not confined to Western settings, in our survey of anxiety hysteria in occupational settings, it is almost exclusive to Western or developed countries. In over half of the reports, the episodes are associated with the perception of an unfamiliar odor that is assumed to be harmful. Occasionally, it involves a potentially infectious agent, such as a visible skin rash that is observed in a colleague. In such cases, the outbreak is less sudden and typically more prolonged. Often there is an identifiable index case in which one of the workers is the first to exhibit conspicuous, often dramatic symptoms. This sometimes results from a preexisting medical condition such as epilepsy, mental disorder, or skin problem.

Upon observing the index subject, colleagues within close visual or social contact rapidly redefine the situation, attributing the symptoms to a plausible toxic agent in their work environment that typically takes the form of a real or imagined odor. As a consequence, work colleagues exhibit sudden, extreme anxiety for their personal welfare. Social and cultural protocols inhibit employees from exiting the workplace. To do so may prompt management sanction, peer ridicule, or even job dismissal, which could result in financial pressures. This situation precipitates internal conflict, which engenders collective anxiety and conversion symptoms, unconsciously allowing workers who are the most concerned for their health or safety to be excused from duty on permissible grounds.

Employees may display an array of psychogenic symptoms, most typically hyperventilation and anxiety. The specific symptoms exhibited usually reflect the perceived threat. For example, skin rashes develop in ceramics factories, while headache, dizziness, and nausea are prominent where a foreign odor is detected. Symptoms may subside rapidly once the threatening agent is convincingly discredited by medical authorities or work management. However, the reverse is often the case, particularly once unions and the mass media become involved. Some episodes continue intermittently for several weeks, particularly in situations where it is perceived that management is taking insufficient measures to investigate the episode and ensure worker health. Attempts to label incidents as OMPI and epidemic hysteria typically engender hostility among employees and residents of the surrounding community, who resent the "hysterical" label or suggestions that the symptoms are psychologically generated. This situation often fosters folk theories.

It is widely assumed that OMPI involves cathartic reactions to pent-up emotions that are incubated in an atmosphere of job dissatisfaction or labor-management conflicts.[22] However, in the case of mass anxiety hysteria, such associations appear unfounded given the distinctive pattern whereby the presence of psychogenic symptoms occur almost exclusively following the sudden, unexpected perception of a foreign odor or agent. There is a conspicuous failure by investigators to mention employee-management conflict. Also, strained management-labor relations and employee dissatisfaction are common in many occupational settings without reports of hysteria outbreaks, the level of which is problematic to quantify and always anecdotal because all episodes are investigated retrospectively.

However, the role of accumulating anxiety in precipitating hysterical reactions is unambiguously evident in repressive work environments that engender mass motor hysteria.

Mass Motor Hysteria

The second type of discernible pattern is mass motor hysteria, which occurs in repressive occupational settings and is incubated amid an atmosphere of preexisting employee dissatisfaction and poor labor-management relations. Social or cultural influences primarily shaped these episodes.

SOCIAL FORCES

The first grouping involves clusters of psychomotor dysfunction and dissociation in Western and Asian settings prior to 1948, with most cases conspicuously coinciding with the Industrial Revolution, which was notorious for repressive, often brutal management practices. Typical policies included child labor, low wages, poor working conditions, long hours, and few rights. In fact, the first recorded outbreak of OMPI occurred at a cotton factory in Lancashire, England, in 1787. The incident involved violent convulsions:

> [A] girl, on the fifteenth of February, 1787, put a mouse into the bosom of another girl, who had a great dread of mice. The girl was immediately thrown into a fit, and continued in it with the most violent convulsions, for twenty-four hours. On the following day, three more girls were seized in the same manner; and on the 17th, six more. By this time the alarm was so great, that the whole work, in which 200 or 300 were employed, was totally stopped, and an idea prevailed that a particular disease had been introduced by a bag of cotton opened in the house. On Sunday the 18th, Dr. St. Clare was sent for from Preston; before he arrived three more were seized, and during that night and the morning of the 19th, eleven more, making in all twenty-four. Of these, twenty-one were young women, two were girls of about ten years of age, and one man, who had been much fatigued with holding the girls... The symptoms were anxiety, strangulation, and very strong convulsions; and these were so violent as to last without any intermission from a quarter of an hour to twenty-four hours, and to require four or five persons to prevent the patients from tearing their hair and dashing their heads against the floor or walls. Dr. St. Clare had taken with him a portable electrical machine, and by electric shocks the patients were universally relieved without exception. As soon as the patients and the country were assured that the complaint was merely nervous, easily cured, and not introduced by the cotton, no fresh person was affected.[23]

THEY ALL FAINTED.

Figure 3.1: In Brooklyn, New York, a girl working in a cigarette factory has a fit of hysterics that spreads to the workforce, forcing temporary closure. (Source: *The National Police Gazette*, October 16, 1886, p. 1, courtesy of the Mary Evans Picture Library.)

It may be significant that one year prior to this episode, Cartwright invented the power loom, which helped to revolutionize the textile industry and supersede the secular order. During this period, women and children were considered best suited for such cotton jobs, often resulting in men being unemployed. Sociologist Neil Smelser specifically examined the Lancashire cotton industry during the period of the outbreak, illustrating how the cotton industry displaced the traditional economic and educational function of the family, resulting in great psychosocial stress on female cotton-mill employees.[24] The absence of contemporary episodes of this type in Western countries may reflect an increasing emphasis on worker rights, improved worksite conditions, occupational legislation, and greater union influence. The disappearance of reports in the former countries of Yugoslavia and the Soviet Union may be related to the rise of anticapitalist political systems.

CULTURAL INFLUENCES

A second subcategory of mass motor hysteria is exclusively reported among indigenous peoples of Malay descent working at factories in Malaysia or adjacent Singapore, a former Malaysian state. Outbreaks are almost always confined to Islamic Malay females amid an atmosphere of employee dissatisfaction or conflict with management. Channels of protest or negotiation are restricted or nonexistent, and there is an absence of unions or liaison officers to redress grievances. Social, cultural, and religious mores inhibit employees from direct confrontation with their almost exclusively male superiors. Female Malays are enculturated to agree with authorities and elders.[25] Workers feel trapped in an intolerable situation where there are considerable financial and peer pressures to remain at their posts, and frustration is internalized over the ensuing weeks or months. A tiny fraction of workers begin exhibiting dissociation, histrionics, and occasional psychomotor agitation such as tremor or twitching. Because of their supernatural worldview and lack of formal education, the observation of "possessed" colleagues fosters extreme anxiety and an array of folk theories pertaining to the presence of a demonic agent. For instance, among many workers of Malayan descent, a pervasive belief exists in the unquestioned reality of *Jinn* and *toyl* spirits, or in the cogency of magic potions, spells, hexes and charms.

In conjunction with this supernatural worldview, the physiological consequences of anxiety and hyperventilation spread rapidly among the workers in nearest proximity or with the closest social ties to the initial cohort exhibiting dissociation or histrionics. These altered states of consciousness are typically regarded as spirit possessions, which can be dramatic and convincing to observers and are interpreted in accordance with an array of Malay folk beliefs. Malays believe in animistic entities known as *toyls*, roaming ghostlike spirits called *hantus*,[26] and *Jinn* creatures, which are referred to in the Koran. In Malaysian and Singaporean factory settings, episodes typically persist from a few days to one month, declining gradually. Often the services of a Malay witch doctor (*bomoh*), usually a male, are sought. Ceremonies are conducted to identify and appease evil or mischievous spirits that are attributed as the cause. Sacrificing a goat or performing incantations intended to ward off the "evil spirits" is common. Often the affected employees convey to the *bomoh* their dissatisfaction with intolerable working conditions, which are believed to have attracted the evil or mischievous spirits. Because of the *bomoh's* status and typical male gender, he serves as a mediator between the employees and management in an attempt to improve working conditions. Episodes may persist if dissatisfaction remains, and the entire cycle is repeated. No known reports of mass motor hysteria in occupational settings have been reported after 1948 among people living in mainstream Western society, presumably as their acculturation into more egalitarian systems provides immunity by offering outlets into which they can channel frustrations.

Relabeling of Endemic Symptoms

This category is by far the most contentious. It involves subjects who are engaged in the redefinition of mundane endemic complaints that are fostered, maintained, and reinforced by a hypervigilant medical community and exacerbating factors. There are two readily identifiable examples.

The first example is characterized by epidemic malaise, emotional liability, depression, gastrointestinal upset, muscle aches, mild fever, and headache. Incidents have been documented since 1934. Episodes primarily occur in closed, socially cohesive populations of hospital staff, physicians, interns, and female nurses, the latter being most heavily affected. Symptoms are protean, often exhibiting considerable variation between outbreaks. Reports have appeared under a variety of descriptive labels: benign myalgic encephalomyelitis,[27] epidemic neuromyasthenia,[28] Iceland disease,[29] and poliomyelitis-resembling.[30] While several researchers argue that the symptoms were elicited by an unidentified virus,[31] no causative agent has been conclusively identified. Many episodes appeared concurrently with epidemics of poliomyelitis in fatigued hospital staff who were in unavoidable close contact with potential vectors.

The origin of these outbreaks has been the subject of medical debate since the publication of three *British Medical Journal* articles suggesting a psychosocial origin,[32] enforced by the relabeling of a variety of mundane complaints that are endemic within the general population by a hyper-vigilant medical community. These articles elicited considerable consternation among many in the medical community who seemed defensive and determined to implicate an organic etiology to vindicate themselves from the stigmatic label of epidemic hysteria, convinced that their educated colleagues were somehow immune from such episodes. Even experienced scientists supporting the presence of an unknown viral agent have concluded that a significant number of participants in the benign myalgic encephalomyelitis and epidemic neuromyasthenia episodes were almost certainly exhibiting conversion symptoms[33] or, at the least, some of the patients were exhibiting psychogenic reactions.[34] In the most famous of these outbreaks, at the Royal Free Hospital in London, McEvedy and Beard used a case-control approach and suggested that "a minority population of hysterics ... attached itself to the true epidemic" of an encephalitic-like illness.[35]

A second example within this category involves variations of writer's cramp and has appeared under the contemporary label of repetition strain injury (RSI) since 1982. Clusters of RSI among Australian keyboard operators qualify under our definition of OMPI, and they have been classified as a form of epidemic hysteria.[36] There is considerable evidence that victims were experiencing a combination of mundane symptoms that became redefined by the Australian medical community, and subsequently in patients, to a new cause. Exacerbating the situation was the prominence of numerous RSI cases that became the focus of false compensation claims by malingerers.[37] Episodes of writer's cramp in the latter half of the nineteenth century[38] and telegraphist's cramp during the first three decades of the twentieth century[39] occurred under similar circumstances. While telegraphist's cramp became covered in 1908 under the British Workman's Compensation Act, it was initially attributed to a variety of organic causes such as muscle failure. The Postal Clerk's Association eventually concluded that it resulted from "nervous instability" in conjunction with fatigued muscles.[40] In fact, by 1912, up to 60 percent of British postal workers reported symptoms. Remarkably, simultaneous surveys conducted in continental Europe identified only sporadic incidents among telegraphists, and the incidence in the United States of cramp symptoms was between 4 percent and 10 percent.[41]

While the majority of the RSI epidemics dating back to the nineteenth century are explainable as the relabeling of endemic symptoms that were supported by the medical community, simple relabeling cannot entirely explain the epidemiology. However, occupational stress was likely a major exacerbating factor. There is a relationship between OMPI reports and the gradual accumulation of somatic symptoms that can be linked to psychosocial factors in the workplace. This association is especially strong in regards to musculoskeletal complaints. For instance, a ten-year study by Leino and Hanninen found that psychosocial factors in work settings "were associated with, and predicted the change in the occurrence of musculoskeletal disorders when age, gender, social class, and physical work load were controlled for."[42] In summarizing the literature in this area, Wessely remarks that "[i]t would be tedious to list all the studies that have considered the influence of psychosocial factors at work and the development of upper limb disorders." He notes a similar pattern in these studies:

> A recent systematic review found 76 relevant references, and concluded that monotonous work and feeling under pressure were closely associated with musculoskeletal symptoms. Certain themes reappear time and again. These are job content (unstimulating); control (low participation in decision making); interpersonal relationships (conflict with supervisors) and general career development (uncertainty, insecurity, poor pay).
>
> There is now a consensus that the psychological environment does affect the production of somatic musculoskeletal symptoms, with a general relative risk of two.[43]

Episode Presentation Patterns: Why Females?

Females are overrepresented in epidemic hysteria episodes, but the reason for this situation is contentious. Some researchers consider biological factors as the primary determinant. Sirois observed that in Western school outbreaks, where the vast majority of participants are also female, social conditions are fairly uniform for both boys and girls. He also noted that these episodes do not appear political or related to any obvious female repression that so conspicuously typify occupational outbreaks.[44] Sirois analyzed forty-five recent school outbreaks, noting that girls near puberty and menarche are the most frequently affected, that a large majority occur at the end of the school year, and that many are associated with galas, graduation and similar gatherings.[45] Sirois believes that unspecified mechanisms associated with sexual arousal may trigger conversion reactions of a benign and age-specific nature.[46]

Klein suggests that the susceptibility of menstruating females to panic disorder and hyperventilation syndrome renders them vulnerable to epidemic hysteria.[47] This is consistent with the presentation of symptoms in mass anxiety hysteria and mass motor hysteria, where the vast majority of participants exhibit anxiety-related symptoms and overbreathing. Hysterical disturbances such as psychogenic pain disorder and somatization disorder are more frequently diagnosed in females, with the latter occurring at a rate about tenfold of that in men.[48] Individual conversion disorders also appear to be more common in females than in males, with reported ratios varying from between two-to-one to ten-to-one.[49]

Any explanation of occupational mass psychogenic illness must also explain its occurrence in males. The only majority male episode of OMPI in our survey appeared as mass anxiety hysteria among a population of all-male military recruits at their California army barracks amid brush fires, an elevated pollution index, and pungent odors. The situation was exacerbated when some recruits unnecessarily received resuscitation because medics had prematurely assessed their conditions as warranting such measures. This unusual set of circumstances generated extreme anxiety among the remaining soldiers. Those observing the resuscitation or witnessing others exhibit symptoms were three times more likely to report symptoms.[50] [51]

Every scientific investigation rests on basic assumptions. With due respect for the biological determinist position of co-author François Sirois, the fundamental working assumption of this book holds that sociocultural factors can fully account for the overrepresentation of female participants in episodes. Females in school settings who are near puberty and menarche are exposed to psychosocial stresses that reflect these new life stages, including common perceptions of themselves as weak and biologically inferior.[52] Further, OMPI reports are virtually never characterized by a preponderance of females near puberty and menarche — they are older females. In other words, the cause of the episodes appears related not to biology, but to social factors for women.

Western females are typically socialized to cope with stress differently than males, often acquiring emotionally expressive, sympathetic, submissive character traits.[53] Such female character traits are also evident in most non–Western countries. Males are typified transculturally by such characteristics as courage, self-reliance, and independence.[54] This socialization pattern may render females more vulnerable to mass psychogenic illness and more likely to seek treatment during an episode, as it is well known that women are more likely to seek medical advice than men.

While there is a general psychiatric consensus that women somatize more than men, the actual role of gender is unclear. Social factors, including observer bias and methodological flaws, can account for some of the discrepancies.[55] Social roles have also been shown to be the main determinant of gender differences in the incidence of depression.[56] While there is an aggregate overrepresentation of females who are diagnosed with psychiatric disturbances, Busfield concluded that "once the data are disaggregated what emerges is a gendered landscape … in which gender also intersects with other social characteristics such as age, marital status, social class and ethnicity. Moreover … the aggregate female predominance in admissions is relatively new."[57]

Females are also overrepresented in the types of jobs that tend to produce dissatisfaction. Kerckhoff observed that an entrenched part of industrial folklore holds that females perform better than males at tedious, boring, repetitive tasks. Hence, women are usually employed in such positions:

> When we review the work situations in which the best-documented cases of mass psychogenic illness have occurred, we find them to be strikingly similar. A room filled with rows of sewing machines operated by women, a series of long benches at which women assemble TV sets, a large room in which many women punch and verify computer data cards, and so on. These are highly regimented work situations in which the workers are all carrying out very boring, repetitive tasks. Hour after hour, they do the same thing over and over again. In most of the cases reported, the degree of regimentation seems to be very high and the workers are permitted only infrequent breaks between which they are restricted in both physical space and their ability to vary their activities. It would be difficult to find situations that would be more conducive to a sense of tension and frustration.[58]

Because females are more likely to externalize emotive responses, if one views epidemic hysteria as the outward "manifestation of psychological stress or anxiety, one might expect those individuals who have been taught to subscribe to the traditional emotionally expressive female role to be most susceptible."[59]

If one were to ask cultural anthropologists specializing in the study of trance and possession states why there is a preponderance of females in epidemic hysteria reports, their responses would likely be affected by a curious observation that ethnographers in various transcultural settings have noted. In many cultures, people exhibit group trance and possession states that are occasionally accompanied by psychomotor dysfunction and/or transient somatic complaints. In most documented instances, the cases involve females experiencing repressive or oppressive conditions or perceptions of themselves as weak and vulnerable.[60] Such cases show remarkable parallels with epidemic hysteria episodes. At least three anthropological perspectives use social and cultural factors to account for the preponderance of females in these group episodes of trance and possession or transient somatic complaints. Yet in rare instances, it occurs almost exclusively among males in situations of perceived weakness and/or extreme psychosocial stress, such as being socially manipulated and forced to live among strangers in a society based on matrilocal residence.[61] Any theory that explains mass conversion symptoms in terms of innate female susceptibility must account for their manifestation in males.

Influential British anthropologist Ioan Myrddin Lewis has observed that there is a global preponderance of females in spirit-possession cults and charismatic religious movements within various cross-cultural settings. Lewis attributed this situation to the women's low social status and oppression in male-dominated societies where they are low on the power hierarchy.[62] Women in many of these societies often experience — sometimes collectively — trance and possession states, psychomotor agitation, and anxiety-related transient somatic complaints. Concordantly, epidemic hysteria is common among Malay females in conspicuously repressive, intolerable occupational settings in Malaysia.[63]

Bartholomew examined the appearance of epidemic hysteria in Malaysia, where episodes are numerous and almost exclusively affect Malay females in school and factory settings. He set out to find out why not a single case of epidemic hysteria was recorded until about 1960.[64] He began with the work of Lewis, who views "spirit attacks" as functional and cathartic, allowing the oppressed to temporarily circumvent their position by inverting the normal social order. Concordantly, beginning in about 1960, the conservative Islamic *dakwah* movement spread across Malaysia, resulting in the implementation of strict Muslim rules and regulations, particularly in the educational system. Ethnic Indian and Chinese Malaysian students, of whom only a tiny portion are Islamic, were not required to adhere to these restrictions. In contemporary Malaysia, intolerable social situations are characteristic features of female Malay school and factory settings. Female redress is culturally unacceptable. Malaysian episodes of mass hysteria are typified by frank criticisms of authorities and administration policies, with the hysteria label deflecting the attribution of blame. Female Malay educational settings are typified by male headmasters who enforce strict academic and religious discipline.

Australian anthropologist Bruce Kapferer has an alternative anthropological explanation. He assumes that social factors can explain the preponderance of females in possession cults in cross-cultural settings, but he believes it is related to the global symbolic identity of females. Kapferer stated that any explanation must consider "the shared constructions and typifications which men and women have of themselves and of each other."[65] A cornerstone of this position is the widespread transcultural reality among both men and women that women are subordinate to men and are thus more susceptible to spirit possession.[66] If this approach is applicable, we should be able to identify cultural constructs that render female Malays vulnerable to collective spirit-possession and conversion symptoms in schools and factories.

Ackerman reported that submissiveness to males is a female Malay cultural trait. Malays also hold a folk belief that they are inherently suggestible, especially females. This position was even espoused by a former Malaysian prime minister.[67] Also, Malay females are believed to possess a weaker life force (*semangat*) making them susceptible to possession. Female Malays are the precise group that is affected by occasional episodes of mass spirit possession in educational and factory settings. So in addition to repression and submissiveness, which typify OMPI in Malaysia, cultural constructs of Malay female vulnerability to supernatural entities is another contributing factor to epidemic hysteria outbreaks. For example, in explaining an outbreak of mass spirit possession at a college hostel for female Malays, Raymond Lee and Susan Ackerman observed that events surrounding the episode were generally interpreted as spirit possession: "The ideas by which they made this interpretation were based on a worldview which places heavy emphasis on the supernatural and female vulnerability."[68]

Kapferer's perspective may also account for the overrepresentation of females in global reports of mass conversion reactions in schools and factories outside of Malaysia. While factors like status ambiguity and male dominance in repressive settings can engender episodes, a major overlooked element may involve female perceptions of innate vulnerability in countries where epidemic hysteria cases occur.

Any discussion of social factors that are correlated with the preponderance of women in spirit-possession religions and behaviors must include the meticulous research of anthropologist Erika Bourguignon, who like Kapferer, is critical of Lewis. Bourguignon believes that Lewis's thesis is only a partial explanation for the culturally patterned model of altered states of consciousness that results from a combination of economic and social structural factors. Using ethnographic data collected from 488 societies, she found that trance states are predominantly a male phenomena associated with less complex, low-accumulation subsistence economies (i.e., hunting, gathering, fishing), which typically socialize for traits such as self-reliance, assertion, and independence. However, possession-trance typically involves women in complex, high-accumulation societies (i.e., pastoralism and/or agriculture), who socialize for obedience, compliance, and dependence in their ecological adaptations.[69] In this latter instance, females entering possession-trance deal with the "spirits" through impersonations and by dramatizing the importance of compliance made by these powerful spirits. However, because "humans play the roles of these impersonated entities, the ASC (Altered States of Consciousness) allow those in possession-trance to act out their own needs for assertion, and they present them with an opportunity to manipulate others and their own real-life situations as well."[70] This finding is entirely consistent with Malay society, where females are socialized to be obedient and dependent. It is precisely in such societies that females "will not seek spirit help to augment their own powers to be able to deal with a hostile group. Instead, the [women] call on powerful, authoritative spirits to *act in their place*."[71] To summarize, Bourguignon's findings indicate that trance states are typically male and involve interaction with another person to increase individual power in subsistence societies, while possession-trance is common among females and entails becoming another person, which allows subservient women to act out their needs.

Familiarity with the transcultural, transhistorical pattern of human behavior can be fruitful in understanding the common, unsubstantiated, Western biomedical folk theory of innate female susceptibility to epidemic hysteria by providing an ethnographically informed global and contextual perspective.

The Pattern of Report Incidence

The array of headings under which OMPI appears is often devoid of any reference to such terms as "mass psychogenic illness," "mass hysteria" or "epidemic hysteria." For instance, Ackerman and Lee's ethnographic description of an episode at a Malaysian shoe factory was labeled as "a spirit-possession event."[72] An Australian outbreak among textile workers in 1956 appeared under the title "Fumigation with Dichlorethyl ether and Chlordane: Hysterical Sequelae."[73] Other potentially misleading or ambiguous episode descriptions include "epidemic faintness,"[74] "acute illness,"[75] and "epidemic of 'shocks.'"[76] Donnell and colleagues used the nondescript title, "Report of an Illness Outbreak at the Harry S Truman State Office Building,"[77] while Sparks and colleagues investigated "An Outbreak of Illness Among Aerospace Workers."[78] Even a literature search by Colligan and Murphy of OMPI from the beginning of the nineteenth century to the mid–1970s failed to locate details of a 1967 case at an Olivette, Missouri, assembly plant,[79] which was summarized by Robert Markush under the title of: "Mental Epidemics: A Review of the Old to Prepare for the New."[80]

This book would have been further complicated if we had attempted the daunting task of including illness reports appearing under the heading of "sick-building syndrome," "multiple chemical sensitivity syndrome," "total-allergy syndrome," and "environmental hypersensitivity." Reports of sick-building syndrome (SBS), for instance, exemplify the problem of these categories. The prevalence of SBS in office-building employees since the early 1980s has been labeled as OMPI. Some episodes may be related to air pollution and poor ventilation and/or the mixture of low-level toxicants,[81] while others are characterized by the inability to identify any pathogenic agent in sufficient amounts to pose a plausible threat. Given instances of the latter, and in conjunction with symptomatology closely following social networks, some investigators suggest a psychogenic etiology.[82] Disparate assessments of SBS among scientists occur because OMPI is a "diagnosis of exclusion," and its presence is subject only to circumstantial verification.

Because OMPI is referred to by a variety of descriptive labels, reviews are prone to information bias, as the literature is more diffuse than researchers may realize. Those reviewing the OMPI literature face a formidable task in locating cases distributed across a variety of interdisciplinary journals in such domains as psychology, sociology, anthropology, psychiatry, and occupational or epidemiological medicine. OMPI is subsumed within the epidemic hysteria literature, which is fraught with similar labeling problems. The diversity of names used to label "epidemic hysteria" is a source of further confusion, often implying the presence of mental disorder (e.g., shared psychopathology, mass psychosis), sometimes denoting normalcy (e.g., group conformity, social contagion), and occasionally described in neutral terms (e.g., mass phenomena, collective behavior). Bartholomew (1990) identified eighty-two separate synonyms for the term.[83]

A further exacerbation is the interdisciplinary nature of the topic, prompting the use of diverse methods and assumptions in interpreting social delusions. Physicians typically write on singular cases of mass psychogenic illness that they have encountered, but sociologists often discuss communitywide episodes involving unsubstantiated beliefs or perceptions. Psychologists tend to focus on the psychometric characteristics of those affected, social psychologists explore the influence of rumor and gossip, and psychoanalytical approaches seek to identify deep-seated, subconscious psychological conflicts. Historians usually limit discussion to medieval dancing "manias." Anthropologists emphasize the cultural context of outbreaks and the position of subordinate females within repressive social structures. Some folklorists study the influence of urban legends in precipitating collective delusions in addition to similarities between recurring folkloric genres. Journalists examine the mass media's impact in perpetuating such mass phenomena. Finally, political scientists are known to employ the vernacular meaning to describe what they may view as overzealous or unsubstantiated adherence to a particular opinion that is unfounded.

The enigmatic temporal clustering of scientific reports on OMPI may reflect the prevailing medical zeitgeist and psychiatric ideology in terms of the recognition, prevalence, and seriousness of episodes.[84] A major factor affecting the seemingly sporadic report pattern is scientific awareness of cases. This was illustrated by psychologist Michael Colligan, who attended an American Footwear Manufacturers Association Conference where nearly half of the audience acknowledged familiarity with OMPI cases.[85] One of the authors, Bartholomew, has recently served as a consultant to several multinational corporations operating in Malaysia and the Malaysian Ministry of Human Resources. The author is aware of four OMPI episodes since 1992, one involving over three hundred workers. The managers in these factories are reluctant to disclose incidents because of adverse publicity. This view is reinforced by the media-sensitive government, which is concerned over any portrayals of the country as backward, primitive, or underdeveloped. In fact, during a spate of at least seventeen school episodes in 1971, the Malaysian government prohibited the press from reporting on mass hysteria cases.[86]

Another factor affecting the clustering of reports may be the heightened public and scientific awareness of occupational and environmental issues that can foster hypersensitivity and preoccupation with workplace health. For example, as SBS has risen in prevalence during the past two decades, environmental legislation has grown concurrently voluminous. As a result, various mundane symptoms that are prevalent in any general population may have become relabeled and attributed to a new cause. This may account for the almost exclusive confinement of SBS to Western countries.

Concluding Remarks

In this chapter, we have discussed the attribution of agency to social and cultural influences. Western reports of OMPI appear to line up almost exclusively under the social-factor category, and non–Western ones are largely cultural. It appears that people experiencing OMPI in the West are responding to external factors arising from powerlessness (i.e., low participation in decision-making, performing unstimulating tasks, job insecurity, low pay, conflict with supervisors). In non–Western settings, a critical factor in OMPI episodes is the endemic belief structure harbored in the minds of suffers. When discussing non–Western beliefs that appear to engender outbreaks, we have been careful to use the term "folk beliefs" and avoid words such as "superstition" because most dictionaries define "superstition" as a lack of logic and reasoning. Another culture's assumptions and, therefore, its steps in reasoning may differ from one's own. This suggests that to refer to another culture's beliefs as "superstition" is ethnocentric. While many OMPI reports tend to describe the illness associations made by the affected people and groups as false or erroneous, such descriptions are pejorative because there is no demonstrable alternative or agreed-upon agent. Therefore, we have substituted such words as "unsubstantiated" and "perceived illness."

It may be less confusing and more accurate to refer to the three discernible OMPI presentation types as "occupational mass psychogenic illness syndrome" (OMPIS), as symptomatology is distinct and consistent over time. Investigators of outbreaks with psychogenic features have a responsibility to thoroughly examine the occupational environment for the presence of infectious or toxicological agents.

Incomplete environmental investigations following outbreaks of illness symptoms among the predominantly female workforce at a garment industry in Mayaguez, Puerto Rico, resulted in management labeling the complaints as OMPI. A more thorough examination revealed the presence of toxic fumes that had precipitated degenerative diseases, respiratory-tract damage, and even death.[87]

Most episodes of OMPI are readily identifiable — even before environmental testing is completed — by the presence of certain characteristic features, the presence of which should heighten suspicions of a psychogenic origin. These include extraordinary anxiety among a segregated group of workers; ambiguous, benign, transient symptomatology featuring a rapid onset and recovery; transmission by sight, sound, and along social networks; and a disparity between affected workers and cohorts of equal or greater exposure who remained asymptomatic. Conspicuously absent from this list is female susceptibility. As stated earlier, the working assumption of this book is that sociocultural factors can account for the disproportionate number of female participants in episodes. Hence, the overrepresentation of females will not be considered as a risk factor.

Since the eighteenth century, authors have documented a fascinating array of OMPI forms, from writer's cramp and repetition strain injury to fainting factory workers and epidemic malaise. It remains to be seen what new forms future episodes will take and the corresponding medical labels they will receive. A key factor in the prevalence of future episodes will hinge on how workers are treated. It is clear that underlying factors in many outbreaks are the dehumanizing aspects of certain types of jobs and the way that management treats employees. For decades, those studying OMPI episodes have sought the causes by scrutinizing the affected workers. It is now evident that many episodes can be prevented by building trust and open communication between workers and management. For instance, in episodes of mass anxiety hysteria involving the perception of strange odors (the most common type), a positive climate can prevent outbreaks or reduce their extent, open communication channels and trust serve to dissolve suspicions, rumors, and conspiracy theories that typify outbreaks. In episodes of mass motor hysteria, listening and responding to worker concerns can reduce the long-term buildup of anxiety that eventually triggers outbreaks. The incidence of OMPI can be further reduced by resolving supervisory conflicts, by providing stimulating positions that offer appropriate pay, future security, and career development, and above all, by treating workers with respect, equality, and sensitivity.

This chapter's senior author can recall serving as a management consultant to several Malaysian factories in Shah Alam during the mid–1990s, where outbreaks of mass motor hysteria were a monthly occurrence (and probably still are). Many of these factory workers wore shirts that simply read: "Human being is not machine." In an age of technology, assembly lines, deadlines and quotas, where profit margins are often placed ahead of people and workers can feel like numbers, we could do well to listen to these voices.[88]

Table 3.1
Occupational Mass Psychogenic Illness
Involving Mass Anxiety Hysteria[89]

Source/ Circa	Location/ Circa	Work Setting	Primary Symptoms	Duration	Sex	No.
Parigi/ Giagiotti 1956	Italy 1956	Gold work	Hyper- ventilation	2 weeks	F	30
Bell/Jones 1958	Australia 1956	Textile	Dizziness	12 days	F	55
Champion et al. 1963	USA 1962	Textile	Fainting	1 week	F	62

Source/ Circa	Location/ Circa	Work Setting	Primary Symptoms	Duration	Sex	No.
McEvedy et al. 1966	UK 1966	Textile	Dizziness, blurred vision	-	F	22
Markush 1973	USA 1967	Ordnance	Hyper-ventilation	11 days	mostly F	50
Stahl 1982	USA 1972	Data center	Dizziness, nausea	2 days	F	30
Phillips 1974	USA 1974	Manufacturing	Headache, respiratory	-	F	54
Folland 1982	USA 1975	Manufacturing	Dizziness, nausea	-	mostly F	144
NIOSH a 1976	USA	Electronic	Headache, light-headed	-	F	51
NIOSH b 1977	USA	Furniture	Headache, foul taste	-	48 F 3 M	51
NIOSH c 1977	USA	Fish packing	Headache, respiratory	-	33 F 2 M	35
NIOSH d 1978	USA	Shoe	Headache, weakness	-	35 F 1 M	36
NIOSH e 1978	USA	Smoke detector	Headache, light-headed	-	F	66
NIOSH f 1978	USA	Garment storehouse	Headache, light-headed	-	53 F 19 M	72
NIOSH g 1978	USA	Shoe	headache, sleepiness	-	92 F 29 M	121
NIOSH h 1978	USA	Engine assembly	Headache, dry mouth	-	F	49
Maguire 1978	UK 1976	Ceramics	Dermatitis	Few Weeks	F	10
Maguire 1978	UK 1976	Ceramics	Dermatitis	Few Weeks	F	17
Cunliffe 1978	UK 1978	Textile	Dermatitis	2–3 days	F	8
Cohen et al. 1978	USA 1978	Electronic	Headache	2 weeks	F	50
Murphy/ Colligan 1979	USA 1979	Shoe	Headache	1 week	F	*60
Boulougouris et al. 1981	Greece 1981	Telephone exchange	Fainting	2 weeks	F	250
Phoon 1982	Singapore 1978	Ball-bearing	Fainting, screaming	2 days	F	4
Phoon 1982	Singapore 1978	Ball-bearing	Fainting, screaming	1 day	F	8

Source/ Circa	Location/ Circa	Work Setting	Primary Symptoms	Duration	Sex	No.
Boxer 1985	USA 1984	Electronic	Headache	5 weeks	F	*29
Ilchyshyn/ Smith 1985	UK 1985	Ceramics	Dermatitis	Few weeks	-	8
Alexander Fedoruk 1986	USA 1986	Telephone exchange	Headache	4 weeks	F	81
Donnell et al. 1989	USA 1989	Civil service	Headache	4 days	mostly F	305
Hall and Johnson 1989	USA 1989	Garment	Headache	-	-	*100
Sinks et al. 1989	USA 1989	Machine shop	Headache	1 day	mostly F	21
Yassi et al. 1989	Canada 1989	Telephone exchange	"Shocks"	2 weeks	-	55
Sparks et al. 1990	USA 1990	Aircraft industry	Dizziness	weeks	mostly F	53
Struewing/ Gray 1990	USA 1990	Military camp	Coughing	1 day	M	164

Table 3.2
Occupational Mass Psychogenic Illness
Involving Mass Motor Hysteria[90]

Source/ Circa	Location/ Circa	Work Setting	Primary Symptoms	Duration	Sex	No.
St. Clare 1787	UK 1787	Cotton	Convulsions	6 days	23 F 1 M	24
Seeligmuller 1876	Germany 1875	Farming	Convulsions, globus	10 days	F	9
Bouzol 1884	France 1882	Silk	Abnormal movements	3 weeks	F	12
Schatalow 1891	Russia 1891	Lace	Neurological	5 days	F	20
Bechtereff 1914	Russia 1914	Rubber	Neurological	1 week	F	90
Franchini 1947	Italy 1941	Soap	Convulsions	1 day	F	16
Parin 1948	Yugoslavia 1948	Army	Convulsions	15 months	mostly F	-
Chew 1978	Malaysia 1972	Plastic Toy	Crying, trance	4 days	F	5

Source/ Circa	Location/ Circa	Work Setting	Primary Symptoms	Duration	Sex	No.
Ackerman/ Lee 1981	Malaysia 1981	Shoe	Fainting, trance	2 weeks	F	30
Phoon 1982	Singapore 1973	Television	Screaming, fainting, trance	*2 week	F	84
Phoon 1982	Singapore 1973	Electrolic Capacitors	Screaming, crying trance	*10 days	F	12
Phoon 1982	Singapore 1973	Cuttlefish	Screaming, crying, violence, trance	18 days	26 F 2 M	28
Phoon 1982	Singapore 1976	Battery	Screaming, fainting	8 days	F	18
Phoon 1982	Singapore 1976	Camera	Headache, screaming	7 days	22 F 1 M	23
Phoon 1982	Singapore 1977	Telephone Exchange	Screaming, fainting	13 months	F	22
Chan/Kee 1983	Singapore 1983	Electronic	Screaming, trance	-	F	108
Ong^ 1987	Malaysia 1975	Electronic	Trance	-	F	40
Ong^ 1987	Malaysia 1978	Electronic	Trance	*3 days	F	120
Ong 1987	Malaysia 1978	Electronic	Trance	*3 days	F	15
Ong 1987	Malaysia 1980	Electronic	Trance	-	F	21

Table 3.3
Occupational Mass Psychogenic Illness
Involving Relabeling of Existing Symptoms[91]

Source/ Circa	Location/ Circa	Work Setting	Primary Symptoms	Duration	Sex	No.
Beard 1879	UK 19th century	Writer	Muscle and joint pain	Years	-	100s
Smith et al. 1927	UK 1908–1930	Telegrapher	Muscle and joint pain	Years	-	1000s
Gilliam 1938	USA 1934	Hospital staff	Malaise, liability	7 months	168 F 30 M	198
Acheson 1954, 1959	UK 1952	Nursing staff	Malaise, stiff neck	10 weeks	F	14

Source/ Circa	Location/ Circa	Work Setting	Primary Symptoms	Duration	Sex	No.
Acheson 1955	UK 1953	Hospital staffs	Sore throat, light fever	*2 months	F	13
Macrae 1954	-	-	Difficulty concentrating	-	-	-
Shelokov et al. 1957	USA 1953	Hospital staff	Malaise, headache, liability	3 months	49 F 1 M	50
Anonymous 1955; Hill 1955; Hill et al. 1955	South Africa 1955	Hospital staff	Muscle ache, liability	Months+	92 F 8 M	-
McEvedy/ Beard 1970	UK 1955	Hospital staff	Malaise	4 months	265 F 27 M	292
Poskanzer et al. 1957	USA 1956	Hospital staff	Malaise	Months+	-	-
Geffen/ Tracy 1957	UK 1956	Hospital staff	Malaise	Months+	-	-
Daikos et al. 1959	Greece 1958	Hospital staff	Malaise, liability	42 days	F	27
Ikeda 1966	Japan 1960	Hospital staff	Liability	-	F	-
Albrecht 1964	USA 1961	Convent	Malaise	Months+	F	26
Dillon et al. 1974	UK 1974	Hospital staff	Malaise	Months+	141 F 4 M	145
Lucire 1986	Australia 1980s	Civil service	Muscle and joint pain	Years	mostly F	1000s

SECTION THREE

*Mass Hysteria
in Communities*

Chapter 4

The Mad Gasser of Virginia

All our separate fictions add up to joint reality. — Stanislaw Lec[1]

From December 1933 to February 1934, residents in a rural Virginia county were terror stricken by reports that someone was sneaking up to homes at night and spraying the occupants with a sickly sweet, noxious gas. Over the next few weeks, the local press published numerous reports of attacks by the elusive fiend. Frustrated police were baffled and unable to identify a single solid clue. It was as if the gasser would appear and vanish into thin air. By mid–January, families in remote parts of the county were sleeping with neighbors, and vigilante farmers were patrolling roads at night with their guns at ready.

The psychological nature of the scare was soon evident. After several incidents of shooting at shadowy figures in the dark, one police officer warned that residents were so on edge that he feared innocent people would be shot. In late January, a physician told county legislators that not all cases appeared genuine, and it was disclosed that at the site of one of the "attacks," the offending fumes were traced to a coal stove.

In early February, the "gassings" shifted to another county. Most calls consisted of jittery citizens smelling odors that were traced to mundane sources, and few people reported becoming sick. In most cases, a common cause was readily detected: coal fumes, burning rubber, exhaust from a passing car. Given the edgy state of many residents, it is not beyond the realm of possibility that a few calls may have even been triggered by passing flatulence. "Attacks" ceased in both counties after the police concluded that the "gas man" was a figment of imagination.

The author is grateful to Robert Willis for his co-authorship of this chapter.

Setting the Stage

Cradled in the picturesque Valley of Virginia, Botetourt County[2] is surrounded by the Blue Ridge Mountains to the east and the Alleghenies to the west. The county has always been rural. It is a neighborly place where even today, on its back roads, on foot or by car, people wave to one another as they pass—whether they recognize each other or not.

Botetourt is also rich in history. King George III's administrators carved it out of Augusta County and part of Rockbridge County to the east in 1769, naming it for Norbourne Berkley, Baron Botetourt, a governor of the colony from 1760 to 1770. The new jurisdiction, the first of His Majesty's to be formed beyond the Blue Ridge, came into being as the American colonies' population began moving westward toward open lands. Botetourt settlers had their share of trouble with the Indians. In 1756, a twenty-four-year-old officer, Colonel George Washington, came to inspect the forts where the pioneers took refuge from attacks.[3]

In its infancy, the county stretched to the Mississippi River and, fanning northwestward, took in all or part of what would become seven states. To this day, people come from all over America to delve into the circuit court's records for information on ancestors who lived somewhere in the once-vast county.

Fincastle, the county seat, was founded in 1772. Thomas Jefferson designed the courthouse. The little town served as a sort of staging area for the Lewis and Clark expedition of 1804–1806.

Like most of the United States during the Great Depression, Botetourt was poor. By 1933, its fifteen thousand inhabitants subsisted on an economy that was primarily agricultural, with a few small factories and some timbering and quarrying. Support businesses such as retail stores made up the rest. The county had lost population, probably to nearby cities such as Roanoke. Spendable income per capita had fallen from $231 in 1925 to $167. The average annual gross farm income was less than $1,000, while the average wage for manufacturing workers was under $500 a year. A third of the farm products were consumed by the farming families and 40 percent of the 529 farm owners cleared $600 or less for a year's labors.[4]

Less than one of every three Botetourt homes had telephones, and about the same number had electricity. The 1930 Census turned up 907 illiterates, 7.8 percent of the population, compared with a 8.7 percent rate in Virginia and 4.3 percent nationwide. Outside the towns, there still were many one-room schools. This was Botetourt County, Virginia, on the eve of a bewildering spate of reported gas attacks in late 1933. In the ensuing weeks, news of the bizarre events in the sleepy Virginia Valley would rise to international prominence, only to fade rapidly into obscurity.

The Gasser Strikes

The strange story of "the mad gasser of Botetourt"[5] began shortly before Christmas of 1933 in Haymakertown, a community of fewer than thirty people. A mysterious figure reportedly struck three times at the Cal Huffman farmhouse between the evening of December 22 and the early morning of December 23. At about 10 P.M., Mrs. Huffman detected a gassy odor and became nauseated. Despite the incident, she retired to bed while her husband remained awake in hopes of catching the perpetrator if there was a repeat attack.[6] About thirty minutes later, the smell of gas again permeated the house so Mr. Huffman telephoned police, who did not arrive until about midnight because of the remote location.[7] Botetourt County Special Officer O.D. Lemon responded to the Huffmans' residence, a 165-year-old stone house known as the McDonald property, which was on the farm of K. W. Henderson.[8] A search of the area revealed nothing. As a veteran deputy, Lemon — who also farmed — was paid only about $30 a month. However, he was a diligent and formidable lawman, as would be proved a few months later during the long investigation of the celebrated Major Kent murder case, when Lemon figured prominently in bringing the culprit to justice.[9]

Lemon left at about 1 A.M. Soon after, there was a third gas attack. This time, all of the seven or eight family members experienced choking fumes that made them temporarily ill. The Huffmans' twenty-year-old daughter, Alice, was most seriously affected and fainted. The *Roanoke Times* reported that when nearby Troutville physician S.F. Driver arrived on the scene, he dramatically administered artificial respiration to "resuscitate" Alice. In just a few hours, she appeared to have completely recovered. She later relapsed and was described as "seriously ill," but doctors attributed her symptoms to "nerves."[10] After this third attack, Mr. Huffman and a neighbor who was staying with them, Ashby Henderson, thought they may have seen a man running away from the house.[11]

Dr. W.N. Breckinridge, the county coroner, thought that the spray was not ether, chloroform, or tear gas. He said the effects were "suggestive of 'chicken gas,' said to be sometimes used by chicken thieves to 'knock out' chickens temporarily" while they snatched the groggy birds.[12]

The next press reports appeared on December 27. An article in the *Roanoke Times* was typical, treating the gas attacks as factual ("Gas Attacks on Homes Continue") and adding a new case involving Mr. and Mrs. Clarence Hall of Cloverdale. The couple returned home with their three children Sunday night at about 9 P.M. after a church service. Within five minutes, they detected sickening fumes that left a sweet taste in their mouths. Symptoms included extreme nausea, smarting eyes, and weakness. Mr. Hall had preceded his family into the house. He was quickly overcome by noxious fumes that seemed to come from the stove. The couple's daughter Catherine said, "When he didn't come back out, mother went in and pushed him out of the house."[13] Dr. Breckinridge answered the call from the Hall home, this time accompanied by Dr. R.B. Easley of Richmond. Dr. Breckinridge thought that the gas was a cocktail of chemicals, including formaldehyde.[14]

Shaken by the ordeal, the entire Hall family spent the night nearby with their grandmother, Mrs. William Guy. The women and children tried to sleep in the cramped quarters while the men stayed out in the woods all night, armed. "It was a very frightening time," Catherine said. "How could anybody do this, two days before Christmas? It was just a terrible time, a lot of lives were torn up."[15] The next evening at 6:20 P.M., Mrs. Hall's sister and brother-in-law, Mr. and Mrs. Claude Arthur, drove by the Hall residence, glimpsing what appeared to be a figure with a flashlight near a side window. No more was ascertained because the couple did not leave the safety of their car to investigate.[16]

Neither the Huffmans nor the Halls could mention anyone who might wish to harm them. At this point in time, Botetourt officers thought the gassings "were either intended as a prank by some boy or that it was the work of a crank."[17]

The gasser struck again on December 27 at Troutville, when acetylene welder A.L. Kelley reported that he was attacked about 10 P.M. in his upstairs room. Curiously, no one else in the house was affected.[18] This was followed by a temporary respite in press coverage and reported incidents. Most residents breathed a sigh of relief, confident that the gassings were over.[19]

Meanwhile, police were still hoping to bring the culprit to justice, despite having virtually nothing to go on. A *modus operandi* was emerging by the time of the third attack. A *Roanoke Times* reporter noted that the gasser's technique was always the same; the cunning fiend found an opening into the house, chose the victims, and released the spray. "The operation last night was typical. The front door of the Kelley dwelling was opened. This leads into a hall from which a stairway leads upstairs. At the head of the stairway is Kelley's room. Leaving the door open the rush of cold air sent the gas true to its mark and the victim was made deathly sick for a time."[20] From his welding experience, Kelley said the gas left a taste "similar to that of copper and that arising from the welding of bronze."[21]

After this attack, Officer Lemon divulged the meager evidence that police had accumulated so far. The sum of the evidence was a clue he had found after the first incident: the print of a woman's high-heel shoe found under the window where the gas was apparently sprayed into the Huffman's porch. Lemon believed the perpetrator had hidden under the porch before attacking the home a second time.[22] But a day later, he and Deputy T.D. Zimmerman were looking for a man and woman said to have been passing the Kelley place "several times" near the time of the attack. They were in a 1932 Chevrolet with license plates 248-11. The fourth digit was obscured. A police check of similar plate numbers and vehicle types proved a dead end. Although police now concluded for the first time that the separate attacks were related and probably not the work of pranksters,[23] their sense of urgency in solving the case gradually eased. After all, it appeared the gassings had ceased.

The Gasser Returns, January 1934

Two and a half weeks passed after the report of the Henderson home's being gassed, and people were beginning to relax. Then on January 11 at about 10 P.M., the gasser struck the Homer Hylton home at Howell's Mill near the Pleasantdale Church a few miles west of Fincastle. The Hyltons slept upstairs, and Mrs. Moore — the wife of a traveling salesman — slept with her baby in a downstairs room. Moore reported hearing muffled voices in the yard, followed by a rustling shade near a window that had been broken for some time. According to the *Roanoke* Times, Mrs. Moore immediately noticed the smell of gas, then "grabbed her baby and ran out to give the alarm, but not until experiencing a marked feeling of numbness." The couple who owned the house were unaffected by the gas. They were even unaware of the incident until hearing Mrs. Moore's cries.[24] Once again the press reported the gasser's existence as a certainty, beginning their account of the attack as follows: "Nocturnal dispensers of a nauseating and benumbing gas were abroad in Botetourt county again last night."[25] Homer Hylton stood guard over his residence with a shotgun the remainder of the night, fearing another attack.

Hylton also warned his neighbors, Tom and Sally Harris, who lived on an adjoining farm. One of the Harrises' seven children, Ruth, said her mother became alarmed and went around plugging any holes in windows with rags to keep gas from being sprayed in. "Back then," she said, "you couldn't replace a broken window pane right off."[26] Another neighbor, G.E. Poague, said he thought the fiend had contemplated an assault on his residence, as family members had heard muffled tones outside at about the same time of the attack on the Hylton household.[27] By this time, lawmen and amateur criminologists were grasping at any straw, and people and events were scrutinized on the most flimsy evidence. One reporter noted that Mr. Poague's daughter had just attended a neighborhood meeting of young people "and reports having met several boys on the road near her home as she returned, and an automobile was heard to pass along the highway at the Hylton place a short time before the attack."[28]

Another of the Harris children, Roy, relayed the warning to the family of Emmett and Lura Lee, who also lived near the Hyltons.[29] Thelma Lee Kyle of Troutville, a cousin to the Harris children, said all ten of the Lee offspring were moved upstairs for safety at night, and her father got out his shotgun. Meantime the Lee family hastily patched up holes in window panes with what they had, including a piece of tin. A few nights later, Mrs. Kyle said they'd gone to bed but were still awake when they heard what sounded like someone messing with the tin. "Daddy went to the top of the stairs and said, 'What are you trying to do down there?' Then he took his shotgun, raised an upstairs window and fired it up in the air. They never bothered us no more."[30]

At about the same time, the home of G.D. Kinzie in Troutville, a town of about five hundred people, was gassed by what Dr. S.F. Driver concluded was potentially lethal chlorine gas.[31] This statement only served to heighten tensions. A few nights later on January 16, Mr. F.B. Duval told police that upon arriving at his home between Cloverdale and Bonsack about 11:30 P.M., he learned that his family had been gassed. On his way to meet with police, he "encountered a man standing beside the road. The man ran to a nearby car, the motor of which was running, and escaped."[32] Duval was too far away to give chase. Duval and Lemon patrolled roads of the area for several hours afterward but found nothing — except that where the auto had stopped, Lemon spotted footprints from a woman's shoe, just as he had near the Cal Huffman home the night of the very first gas attack.

Another pattern had emerged. In most cases the attacks were at homes where the perpetrators could see there was no telephone line leading in, thus no chance of police being summoned at once. Less than a third of Botetourt homes had telephones then, and less than two-thirds had cars. By this time, about a dozen attacks had occurred, yet there was still no clear motive. Without any real clues, authorities were baffled, and residents were growing increasingly frightened. Some investigators believed that the attacks were the work of a demented soul, while others subscribed to the prankster theory. Either way, as one journalist remarked, "all who have been victims of the gas agree to the fiendish efficiency of the perpetrator's efforts."[33] Officers were also at a loss to explain how the gas was being dispensed. Some thought that a gas gun or gas-filled capsules were being used.

On January 19 at 7:30 P.M., a Mrs. Campbell was sitting near a window at her Carvin's Cove home near the Roanoke County line when she noticed the curtains flutter. Immediately following this was a strange odor that made her ill.[34] This time authorities thought they had cornered the culprit. Officers from Botetourt and Roanoke counties quickly converged on the house from different directions, thinking they would trap the gasser on the road. The phantom eluded them without a trace.[35] Other traps also failed, including officers hiding in the night at various spots in anticipation of where the gasser would strike next.[36]

On January 21, Mr. and Mrs. Howard Crawford returned home in Colon at about 9 P.M. after visiting friends. Mrs. Crawford, while trying to light a lamp, was staggered by fumes.[37] One reporter described the mood of Botetourt County citizens at this time as tense:

> Doors and windows are securely locked at night and men with shotguns ready keep nocturnal watch over their homes to guard against the stealthy marauder who hurls gas into rooms where sleeping families are overcome or made violently ill.
>
> Rural sections have been terrorized for a month and as yet authorities who have been called out repeatedly in the dead of night after the attack have obtained no more than shadowy clues as to the perpetrator. Once or twice victims have caught glimpses of a man fleeing in the night and twice an automobile has been seen speeding away from the scene of attacks, but no one has been able to see either closely enough to obtain a good description.[38]

By January 23, the fear of being the gasser's next victim had reached new heights. Families in remote sections of the county were sleeping at neighbors' houses, and vigilante farmers were "patrolling roads at late hours of the night or sitting on their doorsteps with guns in their hands."[39] One police officer expressed concern "that some innocent person passing a house or calling upon a neighbor may be wounded or killed through nervousness" by those fearing they were next on the gasser's list.[40] On the morning of January 24, Mrs. R.H. Hartsell of Pleasantdale returned home at about 4:30 A.M. after sleeping with a neighbor (because she feared the gasser!), only to find that the house had been gassed.[41] On that day, the Botetourt police inadvertently heightened tensions after a misunderstanding

Virginians Are Terrorized by Gas Thrower, Who Flees in Night After Making Victims Ill

By The Associated Press.

FINCASTLE, Va., Jan. 21. — Farmers' families of Botetourt County, terrified by a stealthy marauder who hurls gas into rooms, overcoming his victims or making them violently ill, are locking doors and windows securely these nights. Men keep their shotguns ready to guard their homes.

Rural sections have been terrorized for a month, but authorities, called out repeatedly in the dead of night after attacks, have obtained no more than shadowy clues as to the perpetrator.

Once or twice victims have caught glimpses of a man fleeing in the night and twice an automobile has been seen speeding away from the scene, but no one has been able to obtain a good description.

Several times a woman's footprints have been found, leading to belief that the gas thrower may have a confederate.

What motive is behind the attack none can say. Circumstances suggest to some investigators that the attacks are the work of a prankster and to others of a demented person.

One doctor, who has treated sev-eral of the victims, is convinced that on one occasion, at least, deadly chlorine gas was used.

Beginning on the night of Dec. 22, the attacks have continued at the rate of two or three a week, the most recent being in Carvin's Cove, near Hollins College, over the week-end.

Officers think that the marauder uses either a gas "gun" or capsules.

The last attack resulted in making a woman, Mrs. Campbell, wife of a former magistrate, ill. She was sitting beside a window and saw the curtains flutter. A second later she detected the odor of gas. Officers, quickly summoned, found no trace of the culprit.

F. B. Duval, whose home near Bonsack was gassed Thursday night, caught only a fleeting glimpse of a man running to a near-by automobile, the motor of which was running. A woman's footprints were found where the car had been parked.

All of the gassing has been confined to the southeastern corner of the county in the vicinities of the towns of Troutville, Cloverdale, Daleville and Haymakertown.

Figure 4.1: The *New York Times* published this singular account of Virginia's phantom "gas thrower" on the front page of its January 22, 1934, edition. (Reprinted with permission of the Associated Press.)

with Roanoke County Police resulted in their erroneously announcing three separate attacks on homes in the vicinity of Carvin's Cove two nights earlier.[42] In actuality, there had been one report, at the residence of a man named Reedy. Immediately upon detecting the odor, one of Reedy's sons grabbed a shotgun, ran outside, and fired at — but apparently missed — what appeared to be a man running across a field.[43]

On January 28, five people at the Ed Stanley residence near Colon Siding were overcome by noxious fumes while sitting in a room. Symptoms included a severe choking sensation and nausea. While none of the victims lost consciousness, Mrs. Henry Weddle suffered extreme nausea and had to be carried from the house. She was then taken home to recover. When one of the victims, Frank Guy, a hired hand for the Stanleys, managed to reach fresh air, he saw what appeared to be four men running near the woods. Guy fired a shotgun at them.[44] Mrs. Stanley and a guest, Dorothy Garrett, were reportedly still groggy the following day, although one doctor thought their prolonged "stupor" may have been from sedatives and "nerves."[45]

The situation was reaching crisis proportions, and something more needed to be done. As news of the latest attack circulated, the Botetourt County Board of Supervisors held a hearing on the matter the next day. Drs. Driver and Breckinridge also appeared, expressing doubt that all the alleged gassings were genuine. While believing the gasser was real, Dr. Driver said that not all cases appeared to be genuine gassings. It was also disclosed that at one of the "attacked" homes, the offending fumes were traced to a coal stove.[46] Dr. Driver said that he had been unable to detect a gas odor at the homes of any victims he had attended to, but the symptoms in all of these cases were similar: nausea, headaches, and swelling. He did acknowledge that in each case, by the time he arrived, the house's doors had been opened for ventilation. Before the meeting ended, the board authorized a $500 reward for apprehension and conviction of the gasser.[47]

The next day, members of the Virginia State Assembly took action. Not to be outdone by their county colleagues, a bill was proposed calling for a prison term of up to ten years or a fine of $500 or one year in jail for anyone convicted of releasing noxious gasses in public or private places.[48] In the event the incident caused injury to a person or animal, the gasser "would be deemed guilty of malicious wounding and punished with from between one and twenty years in the penitentiary in the discretion of the court."[49] Delegates M.R. Morgan of Botetourt and W.H. Scott and Blair Fishburn of Roanoke introduced the bill, which was passed after a vote of the House of Delegates at the Capitol on January 30.[50]

Growing Skepticism

With the lack of concrete evidence, an inkling of skepticism appeared in press reports for the first time on January 24. Perhaps they were triggered by the first obvious false alarm. In Fincastle on the night of January 24, a

Reward Offered By County Board To Catch Gasser

Another Home In Botetourt Attacked With Nauseating Fumes At Usual Hour

Fincastle, Jan 29. (AP),—A reward of five hundred dollars was offered today for the apprehension and conviction of Botetourt county's mysterious "gas man" whose latest attack with a nauseating gas on a dwelling last night was brought to the attention of the county board of supervisors.

The attack last night was described by authorities as probably the most far-reaching in results of any of the series of attacks made by the stealthy marauder since he started operations in this section more than a month ago.

Victims of this latest attack at the home of Ed Stanley, near Cloverdale, were Stanley, his wife, a visitor named Dorothy Garrett, and Mrs. Henry Weddle, and Frank Guy, who works at the Stanley place.

Others were present, but none suffered materially, although all told officers they smelled the fumes.

Officers reported in Fincastle today that Mrs. Stanley and Miss Garrett were in a stupor as late as 11 o'clock today, although they were not made unconscious at the time of the gassing. Mrs. Weddle was so overcome that she had to be carried from the room for air, in extreme nausea, and later was removed to her home.

Figure 4.2: In late January 1934, the Botetourt County Board of Supervisors was so alarmed by the gasser crisis that they passed a resolution offering $500 for information leading to his capture and conviction. This was a huge sum for Depression-era Virginia and was more than most County factory workers made in a year. (Source: *Lynchburg News,* January 30, 1934, p. 1.)

woman living near the jail, Mamie Brown, dashed from her residence screaming that her home had just been gassed. A crowd quickly formed, and she described to the excited audience that "she heard the gasser run across her porch as a projectile containing the noxious fumes plopped against the kitchen wall."[51] The enthralled crowd was then led to her house by jailer C.E. Williamson and watched in suspense. He picked up the container, sniffed, and deflated the gathering as he proclaimed that someone "had tossed a common fly-killing fluid into the kitchen — apparently as a joke."[52]

Just after 9 P.M. on January 25, a watch dog at the Chester Snyder farm near Cloverdale began barking. Prepared for the gasser, Snyder leaped from bed, grabbed a shotgun, and raced across the yard. Spotting what appeared to be a man creeping along a ditch, he launched a hail of buckshot from his single-barrel, 12-gauge shotgun. However, he said the figure was nowhere in sight.[53] The incident may have been unrelated to the gasser, although it was reported as a potential attack. On January 28, a journalist jokingly interviewed Mr. Snyder's five-month-old pup: "He [the dog] was friendly and apparently willing to help 'make copy,' but when he was asked whether a man he detected prowling...was the 'gas' man, the pup merely pointed his ears ... and barked a single bark."[54] By January 30, some citizens expressed the view that "the whole gassing case is a mere hoax, or figment of imagination of reported victims."[55] The statement of Sheriff L.T. Mundy typified the mood at this time. He declared himself a doubting Thomas unless he was gassed himself. Meanwhile, his wife was busy stuffing keyholes on their farm in an effort to thwart the gasser.[56]

A New Target: Roanoke County

Early on the evening of February 3, the gasser's activities shifted for the first time to adjacent Roanoke County. Three people were sickened by fumes at the Hamilton residence just outside Vinton, when a family was entering their home after an absence of several hours.[57] Local Deputy Sheriff J.T. Wood said when he arrived, there was a distinct smell of tear gas lingering in the air.[58]

Later that evening, the Troutville home of Mr. A.P. Scaggs was reportedly gassed, sickening five persons and their dog.[59] As usual, the attack occurred between 8 and 9 P.M. A doctor was summoned to treat the victims, all of whom quickly recovered, including the pet.[60] As was often the case, later that night the Scaggs house was visited by curiosity seekers. Suddenly, someone shouted, "Gas!" The house emptied as if someone had yelled, "Fire!" One man dashed through the wrong door and was "trapped" in an interior room. A short time later, the man complained of a bad headache. No one else experienced symptoms, and several people made light of the incident.[61]

While there were claims of subsequent gassings in Botetourt County, none involved actual symptoms or the detection of gas by residents. For instance, the next evening when John Shanks noticed a suspicious car not far from his Troutville home, he fired three shots into the air as the vehicle disappeared into the darkness. At about the same time, another Troutville man became fearful of a gas attack after hearing a strange noise on his porch. Police, however, noted that the incidents were vague and may have been unrelated to the gasser.[62]

The gasser next struck a residential section of Roanoke at about 8 P.M.

on February 7. Mrs. A.H. Milan was alone in her living room with her twelve-year-old daughter, Josephine, who noticed a "funny" smell coming from the door. The girl paid little attention to the odor until several minutes later when Mrs. Milan, who had been feeling unwell for two days, felt more sick. It was then that Josephine felt dizzy.[63] Mrs. Milan spent the night in the hospital as a precaution, although her daughter suffered no aftereffects.[64]

The next night, Roanoke police received five more gasser calls within two hours, only to be frustrated by a lack of clues. The first call was at about 8:55 P.M., when J.F. Clay of the city health department reported an attack on his family at their home. Mr. Clay was with his wife and two children in the front room when they noticed a strange odor. He and one of his children then felt dizzy for the next few minutes. By the time police detectives arrived, they could detect no trace of the gas.[65] Most of the calls consisted of residents smelling fumes but not becoming sick. One of the reports was a clear false alarm when a woman overreacted upon hearing a car stop near her residence.[66]

The following night, February 9, seemed to usher in a major turning point because the Roanoke County gassings peaked with seven separate reports investigated by police, who curiously noted that "[i]n no instance did the officers detect any nauseating fumes, and no occupants of any of the homes were affected."[67] In most instances, police readily detected a mundane source of the odors. In one case, three detectives rushed to a home, only to implicate coal fumes from a stove. At another residence, gas fumes were believed to have belched from a passing car:

> Residents at 316 Howbert Avenue, Wasena, detected strange fumes near a furnace register about 8:25 but no one suffered any ill effects and police said they believed the fumes had come from the furnace. No one was seen or heard about the house before the odor was detected....
>
> Three reports were received between 10 and 11 o'clock ... at 551 Washington Avenue, S.W.—both occupants and police detected fumes, but they came from a thawing automobile radiator which contained alcohol. Several persons were playing bridge when the fumes were noticed. Police found that an automobile had been driven into a garage at the rear of the house and the smell of alcohol was decidedly noticeable.
>
> A resident at 311 Broadway, South Roanoke, entered a bedroom and detected a peculiar odor. Police said they failed to find any trace of a noxious gas.
>
> Residents at 811 and 813 Shenandoah Avenue, N.W., noted a peculiar odor about 11 o'clock. Police said they believed that the occupants had smelled sulfur in coal smoke from passing trains.[68]

On the morning of February 10, armed with the knowledge of the seven pseudoattacks of the previous night, a further revelation eroded confidence in the gasser's existence. It was disclosed that Mrs. E.L. Langford, who suddenly took ill after hearing a "gas canister" strike her door on the evening of February 8, was being released from the hospital after rapidly recovering. Police concluded the noise was actually rice thrown at her door. Three other residents of the dwelling had been unaffected.[69]

On February 11, there was one final flurry of gassings. At about 7 P.M., employees of the Roanoke Gas Light Company were called to repair what was believed to be a leaking gas main at the J.M. Duncan home. The lines appeared to be in working order. Meanwhile, jittery occupants told workers that the gasser must have paid a visit and that they had stuffed their doors and windows with towels. The workers carefully searched the premises for any clues and found several tiny particles of a mysterious gray substance, which they carefully wrapped and gave to police. It was later identified as pieces of an eraser.[70]

At 7:15 P.M. a baby was suddenly seized with a coughing fit. Thinking the infant had been gassed, the parents frantically summoned police to the Robert L. Caywood residence. No trace of noxious fumes was detected by the officers, and by this time the baby was fine.[71] No sooner had police dispensed with this call when at about 7:50 P.M., a loud thud was heard at the front door of 823 Tazewell Avenue, S.E. Police rushed to the scene in hopes of catching the gasser in the act. They found only bits of a lump of coal scattered at the base of the door.[72] In another false alarm, Mrs. Saide Johnson became suspicious of a man standing near a parked car. Within moments she felt a "tingling" in both arms and hands, and shortly thereafter she detected a strange odor like burned powder near the front door. Another woman in the house said it resembled sulfur. When police arrived at 8:45 P.M., they too could detect a peculiar odor, but it seemed harmless and was attributed to a mundane source.[73] By 11:15 P.M., weary officers were called to the residence of Mrs. H.R. Bishop after she noticed a strange smell. The officers' noses could detect nothing unusual.[74]

Also on February 11, police had a potential break in the case, announcing that they had scooped up a sweet-smelling, oily liquid found in the snow near the scene of a suspected attack at a home in Botetourt County, the first incident reported in that county in over a week.[75] On February 12, local chemist Leroy H. Smith told police that the mystery liquid was nothing but a mixture of substances that were harmless to humans and most likely an insecticide "similar to that of fly exterminators used in practically every household."[76] Reported gassings ceased entirely in both counties after the night of February 11. In all, Roanoke police tallied nineteen calls, the last of which occurred when several officers responded to a gassing that was traced to burning rubber, prompting them to suggest that the gas man was "a product of overwrought imaginations."[77] This conclusion was supported by an editorial in the *Roanoke Times* that proclaimed, "Roanoke Has No Gasser."[78] In the article, it was stated that "[t]his newspaper has so believed from the first [in the gasser's nonexistence], but it seemed best to permit the police to go ahead and investigate without whatever handicap they might be under were cold water to be thrown on their search in advance." Despite this claim, in an earlier editorial in the same newspaper it was clearly stated that the gasser was real, concluding that "the series of gas attacks is being engineered by irresponsible practical jokers, with more zest for adventure than brains."[79]

In 1998, Lomax Breckinridge of Fincastle related his recollections of the case to journalist Robert Willis. His father, Dr. W.N. Breckinridge, had been the county coroner and was involved in the investigation. He was also the mayor of Fincastle at the time. Later, after gas attacks had become international news, someone in England wrote to "The Lord Mayor of Fincastle" seeking additional information and enclosing a ten-shilling note to cover expenses. The doctor turned the request over to his son, who put some material together and retained the old currency until his death in 1998.[80]

The reported attacks ended as suddenly and mysteriously as they had begun in the late winter of 1934. Days and weeks passed without a further report. Gradually people began to relax, and life returned to normal. There was no more sitting up at night with shotguns or stuffing rags in the cracks of closed-up houses to keep out an invasion of gas. But the case was far from closed. Some residents treated it as an unsolved crime; others accepted the hysteria hypothesis. What was clear was that the gassings had stopped, much to everyone's relief. Ten years, six months, and twenty days later, another extraordinary and remarkably similar series of events would terrorize the small city of Mattoon, Illinois, about five hundred miles to the northwest in America's heartland.

Chapter 5

The Mad Gasser
of Mattoon

*Or in the night, imagining some fear, How easy is a bush sup-
pos'd a bear!*— William Shakespeare, "A Midsummer Night's
Dream"

The best-known case of mass hysteria of the twentieth century was
the "mad gasser" of Mattoon,[1] Illinois, which occurred in September 1944.
It is easily the most widely cited case by scientists over the past one hundred years. The episode captured the imagination of the country for a few
days in the late summer of 1944, but it was quickly forgotten and faded
into obscurity amid the tumultuous events that made headlines in the final
year of World War II. Interest was rekindled when an undergraduate student in education at the University of Illinois, Donald Max Johnson, wrote
about it in a 1945 issue of the *Journal of Abnormal and Social Psychology*.[2]
The case was soon recognized as a classic. The "mad gasser of Mattoon"
has been cited ever since in numerous introductory psychology and sociology textbooks and within the subfields of social psychology and collective behavior, two branches of the social sciences devoted to studying mass
behavior.[3] Discussion of the event also appears occasionally in publications on mysteries and the paranormal, where it is often suggested it may
be an unsolved crime or the work of an extraterrestrial or supernatural
creature.[4] While the 1938 Martian panic triggered by the Orson Welles
radio dramatization of the H.G. Wells novel *War of the Worlds* has likely
gained more publicity, technically it was not a case of mass hysteria involving the spread of illness symptoms. The "invasion" was a mass panic and
exaggerated at that, as will be discussed in greater detail in Chapter 14.
    The city of Mattoon is located in east-central Illinois, in Coles County,
about forty miles from Indiana to the east. Surrounded by farmlands and
reliant upon the railroad, it was a typical, small, Midwestern city whose

residents were preoccupied with the outcome of World War II. The 1940 census listed its population as 15,827. By late 1944, this figure was closer to 17,250.[5] Its economy was enjoying a mild boom, and it was home to several small industries, including furniture and shoe factories, a foundry, and a Diesel engine manufacturer.[6] But the events of September 1944 would etch the name of this previously obscure city prominently into the annals of mass psychology.

It was a clear, cool night when the saga began, shortly after 11 P.M. on September 1, 1944. In a small, tree-shaded home in the city's north end, a young housewife named Aline Kearney had just retired to her bedroom with her three-year-old daughter, Dorothy Ellen. Her sister Martha Reedy, a permanent guest in the house while her husband was away in the U.S. Navy, was lying awake on a bed in the front room while Mrs. Kearney's other daughter and her sister's son were asleep in a back room. Mrs. Kearney closed the door and began reading the newspaper in bed. She noticed a "sickening, sweet odor" that she first attributed to a flower bed situated near her open window, which was just inches from the bed. She called Martha to the room to see if she could smell it, but she couldn't smell a thing. As the scent grew stronger, she felt a paralyzing sensation in her legs and lower body. Her throat was unusually dry, and her lips were burning. Panicking, she screamed for Martha in the living room. Upon opening the bedroom door, Martha too noticed the smell. After being told of the paralysis by her sister lying in the bed, she raised the alarm to a next-door neighbor, Mrs. Earl P. Robertson, who phoned police. Mr. Robertson then searched the area without success. When police arrived, they also found no trace of an intruder.[7]

Seventieth Year. No. 192   MATTOON, ILLINOIS, SATURDAY EVENING, SEPTEMBER 2, 1944   All Phones 2*·

Yanks in Germany by Night
"Anesthetic Prowler" on Loose

MRS. KEARNEY AND DAUGHTER FIRST VICTIMS

Both Recover; Robber Fails to Get Into Home

A prowler who used some kind of anesthetic or gas to knock out his intended victims was on the loose in Mattoon Friday night.

Mrs. Bert Kearney and her three-year-old daughter, Dorothy Ellen, were victims of the anesthetic prowler as they slept in bed at their home, 1408 Marshall Avenue. Both had recovered today, although Mrs. Kearney said that her mouth and throat remained parched and her lips burned from effects of whatever was used by the prowler who was unsuccessful in getting into the house.

Figure 5.1: Is this the story that triggered an outbreak of hysteria? Mattoon police did not take the first several gassings seriously, attributing them to imagination. It would be difficult to tell this from reading the local paper. The top headline is significant. As the episode began, Allied forces were driving toward Germany, and there were widespread fears that German commanders might defend their homeland by drenching Allied cities with poison gas. (Source: *Daily Journal-Gazette*, September 2, 1944, p. 1.)

Meanwhile, Bert Kearney, a taxi driver, headed home after hearing of the attack on his family. Pulling in front of his house, he caught a glimpse of what appeared to be a man near the bedroom window. Kearney gave chase, but the figure disappeared into the night. Police again searched the area even more thoroughly than before, but to no avail. Mr. Kearney said the man was tall and wore dark clothes and a tight-fitting cap over his head.[8]

Authorities surmised that someone may have sprayed the bedroom with ether, chloroform, or a mixture of both. Mrs. Kearney said that the paralyzing sensation in her legs completely abated within thirty minutes of the initial incident. Her daughter also felt ill, but she recovered by the next morning. Martha Reedy and two other children in the house at the time of the event were unaffected. Shaken, Mrs. Kearney, her sister, and the three children spent the rest of the night with a relative in another section of the city.[9]

The next evening, September 2, the editors of the Mattoon *Daily Journal-Gazette*[10] published the first report on the incident, sensationally proclaiming, "Anesthetic Prowler on Loose." The existence of a gasser was treated as a certainty. The subheadline read, "Mrs. Kearney and Daughter First Victims ... Robber Fails to Get into Home." The *Journal-Gazette* was Mattoon's only large circulation newspaper and was read by 97 percent of families.[11]

After reading the *Journal-Gazette* story, several other local families reported similar attacks on their homes—some dating to before the attack on the Kearney house. At about the same time as the attack on the Kearney residence, Mrs. George Rider said that the gasser had struck her home. Waiting for her husband to return from work, she was alone with her two children, Ann Marie, 5, and Joe, 2, who were sleeping in a middle bedroom. She had an upset stomach and began drinking excessive amounts of coffee. She told a doctor that she had drunk "several pots" and then took stomach medication before, as she put it, she "popped her cookies" and began to vomit.[12] Until this point, there was no sign of the gasser. She then went in and lay in bed near her children. The window was shut because the baby had a cold. She then heard a peculiar noise—like a "plop"—followed by a odd smell that gave her a strange sensation of floating.[13] Numbness in her fingers and legs accompanied this lightheadedness. Just then, her baby began coughing. A psychiatrist who later interviewed Mrs. Rider called her account one of "retrospective rationalization." Dr. Harold Hulbert said, "Yes, she believes it NOW and as a consequence is still in terror. But she didn't believe it THEN. It was only later, after she had heard of the supposed attack on Mrs. Kearney, that such a possibility entered her head."[14] He said the sensations of numbness and feeling dizzy were not unusual after a bout of vomiting.[15]

Also, apparently about the same time, just a few blocks from the Rider house, a woman said she awoke to a "sickly sweet odor" and noticed her children were vomiting. It was assumed that the gasser had forced the fumes through a bedroom window.[16]

Mr. and Mrs. Orban Raef said the gasser struck the night before making Mrs. Kearney and her daughter sick. He and his wife were asleep at 3 A.M. when, he said, fumes came through the bedroom window. Both experienced "the same feeling of paralysis" and felt unwell for about ninety minutes. Friends sleeping in another room were unaffected.[17]

Mrs. Olive Brown told authorities that several months earlier, she had been gassed but did not report the incident due to its fantastic nature. She said that around midnight, when "she and her daughter had retired to separate rooms, she had an experience similar to that related by persons during the past few days."[18]

The gasser claimed his next victim at about 10:15 P.M. September 5, when Mrs. Beulah Cordes, 45, was overcome by fumes after finding a strange, neatly folded, white cloth lying on her front porch. She picked up the cloth, which was about six by nine inches and with a wet spot in the middle, sniffed it, staggered, and yelled, "That went right to my toes!"[19] She said it felt as if an electric current was passing through her legs. She said, "It was a feeling of paralysis." Her husband Carl then helped her inside. She felt sick for the next two hours: "Her throat and mouth were so badly burned by the fumes she inhaled that blood came from cracks in her parched and swollen lips and her scarred throat and the roof of her mouth." She also had trouble swallowing and speaking.[20] Mrs. Cordes speculated that the gasser may have been trying to knock out their dog when he was frightened off, although she didn't see or hear anything. She also found a skeleton key and a used lipstick tube on the sidewalk nearby. The cloth was later sent for analysis to the State Police Crime Laboratory in Springfield, where chemical expert John Sutter could detect no trace of the gas used. Sutter said that it must have evaporated.[21]

At about this time, Mattoon Mayor E.E. Richardson, himself a physician, expressed doubt that chloroform or ether was being used. He said that oil of mustard could account for the numbing sensation widely reported by victims. Meanwhile, a reporter for The International News Service contacted experts at the U.S. Army's Chicago-based Chemical Warfare Service. They suggested that the mystery gas may have been chloropicrin, a widely available poison gas that has a sweet odor and was used commercially to exterminate vermin.[22]

The major Chicago newspapers entered the fray on September 6. Most sent reporters to Mattoon and afforded the story considerable space. These papers had a significant readership in Mattoon and undoubtedly affected public perceptions of the episode. The *Chicago Daily Tribune* was read by 24 percent of residents; the *Chicago Daily News* reached 20 percent.[23] While the *Chicago Herald-American* covered only about 5 percent of Mattoon,[24] its audience during the gassings was likely higher. During times of crisis it's only natural that people seek out alternative news sources. Johnson said the *Herald-American*'s detailed, alarming headlines and photographs were often cited to him in the course of his investigation.[25] The editors of the *Herald-American* played the story for all it was worth. Consider the account that appeared on September 10: "Groggy as Londoners under protracted aerial blitzing, this town's bewildered citizens reeled today under repeated attacks of a mad anesthetist who has sprayed deadly nerve gas into 13 homes and has knocked out 27 known victims."[26]

By September 6, Mattoon's modest police force of two officers and eight patrolmen was being overwhelmed by the nightly barrage of gassing reports, and the situation was escalating out of control.[27] The city was in a state of fright. The Mattoon Commissioner of Public Health and Safety, Thomas Wright, sent an urgent message to the Illinois Department of Public Safety, seeking help in solving the "anesthetic prowler" case. That night, the mood in the city was tense as volunteers patrolled with an already fed-up police force. Despite these extraordinary measures and scores of other citizens closely watching their neighborhoods for any sign of the gasser, four more victims were added right beneath their very noses. There were also several additional reports of prowlers across the city, although none directly linked to the "mad anesthetist."[28] The first gassing report occurred at about 9 P.M. when Mrs. Glenda Henfershott reported a prowler lurching near her residence. When her eleven-year-old daughter Glenda became ill two hours later, Henfershott believed she had been drugged by the gasser.[29]

At 10 P.M. Mrs. Ardell Spangler was overcome by "sickly sweet fumes." She was attacked in her bedroom. Like most other victims, she felt nauseated and had a parched throat and lips. Despite this, she was able to work the next day.[30]

A third attack was reported just moments after midnight as restaurant owner and operator Mrs. Laura Junken was entering her apartment. She told police that the smell had made her legs "weak as if paralyzed." She compared the odor to "cheap perfume." Her bedroom window had only been open about four inches, and she surmised that someone must have forced gas through the window space just as she was about to enter the apartment.[31]

The fourth report occurred about an hour past midnight when sixty-year-old Fred Goble, a foundry worker, told police that he awoke feeling very ill, "apparently from the effects of something sprayed through a bedroom screen window."[32] His symptoms included nausea and vomiting, and they persisted for two hours. His wife, who was sleeping next to him, experienced no symptoms, perhaps because the open window was farther away. His next-door neighbor, Robert Daniels, was awake at the time to spot a "tall thin man" running from Mr. Goble's yard.[33]

The hunt for the gasser was reaching a fever pitch in the city by September 7, with authorities expressing concern that innocent people might accidentally be shot.[34] At least one minor injury occurred during the day: Hiram Weaver fell and broke his hip while checking his daughter's home to ensure that it was free of the phantom anesthetist.[35] That same day, police accused a youth of the gassings, but after questioning and passing a lie-detector test, he was released.[36] The boy had gone to the residence of a female acquaintance and, as a prank, rapped on the side of the house. He then knocked on the front door and, when she answered, whispered, "May I leave my skull cap and spray gun here for a while?" He continued to tap on the house at intervals until police were called and nabbed him.[37] The story of the boy and the skull cap implies that he was Jewish, possibly reflecting rural Midwestern anti–Semitism of the time, where Judaism was often associated with the "evils" of secularism and big-city life. Ironically, during this same period, millions of Jews were being systematically gassed to death in Europe.[38]

By September 7, state investigator Richard Piper and his assistant, Francis Berry, arrived. Piper began questioning victims that same day. He remarked, "This is the strangest case I've ever encountered in many years of police work."[39] As Piper and Berry arrived, details of another gassing were coming to light. Mrs. Leonard Burrell said that on September 5 at about 11:15 P.M., she awoke "coughing and strangling from fumes in the room."[40] Grabbing her eighteen-month-old son, Dennis Lee, she fled and spent the night with neighbors, where she called her husband at work. He telephoned police. Mrs. Burrell was still experiencing chest soreness the next day, but she said the baby was not affected.[41]

On September 8, a lengthy editorial in the *Journal-Gazette* was critical of anyone who considered the reports to be a product of fantasy. It was a veiled reference to a statement made earlier in the week by Police Chief C. Eugene Cole who said that many gassing reports were probably triggered by nerves:[42]

> One of the principal difficulties throughout has been that the whole matter was taken too lightly. It was easy to say, "Oh, it's just imagination!" and shrug the whole thing off with a disdainful air.
>
> But Mrs. Carol Cordes, who suffered burns, couldn't laugh about it. Neither could Mrs. Bert Kearney, who suffered complications which could have cost her very life! Neither could Mrs. George Rider, whose two youngsters were found vomiting and who was nauseated herself! Neither could any of the other citizens who had the same terrifying experience![43]

The editorial also noted that after initial skepticism, the police department was viewing the reports with extreme seriousness and "doing everything in its power to solve the case." Meanwhile, on the night of September 8, seventy people poured onto Dewitt Avenue after hearing that the gasser had been spotted nearby. When someone in the crowd detected the smell of gas, some in the group were convinced that the "mad man" had targeted them.[44]

The episode peaked on the weekend of September 9 and 10, as the gasser was seemingly everywhere. The mood was electric and terrifying as police crisscrossed the city in an effort to answer dozens of calls from frantic citizens, each claiming to have smelled the sickly sweet odor of the "mad chemist." When the weekend came to a close, one reporter described the scene: "As the friendly rays of the morning sun spread across this tortured city today sweeping away the night, Mattoon residents breathed easier and hundreds of persons who bordered on hysteria and fear of attacks from the 'mad anesthetist' returned to calmer states of mind."[45]

On both September 9 and 10, parts of the city resembled scenes from a B-monster movie, as hundreds of citizens gathered near city hall to hear the latest developments. As a patrol car would speed off into the night to answer a call (presumably the gasser), it would be followed by a procession of vehicles whose occupants were intent on seeing the latest victims and, perhaps, the gasser himself being caught. This prompted Police Commissioner Wright to order his officers to arrest "chasers."[46] Meanwhile, vigilante gangs of men and boys roamed the streets on foot and in vehicles touting everything from clubs to rifles and shotguns. A group of armed farmers also patrolled the city,[47] while the aid of fifty more farmers—of the Anti-Theft Association, formerly the Anti-Horse Theft Association[48]—was pledged if needed. The commissioner expressed grave fears that innocent people would be hurt or killed by a jittery resident with his or her finger on the trigger.[49] He exclaimed "I wouldn't walk through anybody's backyard at night now for $10,000."[50] His concerns were justified. One woman whose husband was away in the U.S. Army loaded his shotgun for protection, only to blow a hole in the kitchen wall.[51]

MATTOON GETS JITTERS FROM GAS ATTACKS

MATTOON, Ill., Sept. 9.—Groggy as Londoners under protracted aerial blitzing, this town's bewildered citizens reeled today under the repeated attacks of a mad anesthetist who has sprayed a deadly nerve gas into 13 homes and has knocked out 27 known victims.

Seventy others dashing to the area in response to the alarm, fell under the influence of the gas last night.

All skepticism has vanished and Mattoon grimly concedes it must fight haphazardly against a demented, phantom adversary who has been seen only fleetingly and so far has evaded traps laid by city and state police and posses of townsmen.

With lips still swollen from effects of the bitter-sweet gas which to date has defied analysis, three women of a single family became the latest known victims today when they told a Herald-American reporter about the madman's four visits to their home on two consecutive nights.

Figure 5.2: This front-page article in the *Chicago Herald-American* of September 10, 1944, fueled public anxiety over the Mattoon gasser by describing the episode in dramatic fashion.

By September 9 there wasn't a flashlight available in the city, and terrified families were huddled in their homes with shades drawn, as many men laid in wait, hoping to catch the "mad chemist." September 9 was also the day when the most dramatic and vivid encounter with the gasser came to light. Sisters Frances and Maxine Smith recounted to police a series of attacks on their home. Frances was a well-known, middle-aged community figure and the principal of the Columbian Grade School. On the night of September 6, the pair said they were frightened by "noises outside their bedroom windows" and thought it may have been the gasser. The following night, they reported three attacks.

The first infiltration of gas caught them in their beds. Gasping and choking, they awoke and soon felt partial paralysis grip their legs and arms. Later, while awake, the other attacks came and they saw a thin, blue smoke-like vapor spreading throughout the room.

Just before the gas with its "flower-like" odor came pouring into the room they heard a strange "buzzing" sound outside the house and expressed the belief that the sound probably was made by the "madman's spraying apparatus" in operations.[52]

In the early hours of September 9, four people in the same bedroom were hit by the gasser as they slept in the Baily home. Mrs. Russell Baily and her sister Katherine Tuzzo and two neighbors staying with them were sprayed at about 1:45 A.M. All four became ill in the night with nausea, vomiting, stomach pains, and dry mouth and throat. Their bedroom windows had been left open.[53] Just hours before the attack on the Baily residence, police rushed to 2320 DeWitt Avenue, where passing taxi driver Leroy Cook noticed a strong, sweet-smelling odor as he turned the corner near a house. The smell seemed particularly strong near the bedroom window of the C.W. Driskell home, but there was no odor inside the house.[54]

Two separate weekend incidents resulted in women being sent to Memorial Hospital for examination. One was Mrs. Virginia Kaly, who reported feeling unwell after smelling gas while sitting in Mattoon's crowded theater. She was nauseated and her body rigid. Others in the audience were convinced that the bold and cunning gasser had snuck in and sprayed poor Mrs. Kaly.[55] The other hospitalized woman was Mrs. George Hampton, who was diagnosed as suffering from extreme anxiety despite her husband's claims that he too began choking and gasping at the same time. The attack supposedly occurred at their home. Both women were nauseated. The same physician, Dr. C. Raymond Coles, examined both women. Coles noted that besides nausea, he could find no evidence of exposure to poison gas or other toxic agents. He concluded that they were experiencing the effects of "extreme nervous tension."[56] However, as a precaution he ordered tests of their stomachs to determine if there was any gas or chemical residue. There was not.

The first call on the night of September 10 saw authorities rush to the scene of a reported gas attack at the Stewart Scotts house, four miles south of the city. Sheriff Leroy Boggs was surprised to find the house empty. He said the Scotts and a guest, James Tanner, had "run wildly out the front door and down the dark, country roads the minute they felt symptoms... Their nearest neighbor was a quarter of a mile away. I found them there."[57] Meantime, Frances and Maxine Smith, who had reported three attacks on September 7, told police that someone tried to gas them again at their home on the night of September 10.[58]

Later on September 10, two people were hit by gas as they slept in twin beds. Mrs. Lucy Stevens was baby-sitting a nine-year-old boy overnight in his house when the incident occurred. They suffered fits of choking and coughing.[59] At 11 P.M., a strange vapor sickened a couple living in the city's northwestern sector. Kenneth and Mary Fitzpatrick were in their living room playing cards. When Mrs. Fitzpatrick went to the kitchen she was enveloped by strange vapors, felt nauseated, weak, and a burning sensation

STATE HUNTS GAS MADMAN

Terrorized Citizens Ask Aid

Figure 5.3: Another dramatic headline with one and a half inch bold letters in the *Chicago Herald-American* of September 11, 1944.

BY GLDAYS ERICKSON.
(Chicago Herald-American Staff Correspondent.)
MATTOON, Ill., Sept. 18.—Re-sponding to frantic pleas from terrified citizens, state highway police under Chief Harry Yde were preparing to move in emer-gency units to aid in the search for the gas-spraying madman who has terrorized the community for the past 10 days.

on her lips. She screamed for her husband, who managed to get her to safety despite enduring similar symptoms. Their two-year-old daughter Jo, asleep nearby, was unaffected.[60] A short time later, another gassing was reported six blocks away at the John Grafton residence. His daughter, Mrs. Richard Daniels, was baby-sitting her one-year-old son Michael and her two sisters. One of the girls heard a noise at the front door and upon entering the living room screamed, "I smell ether!"[61] There was a frantic scramble to get out. In her haste, Mrs. Daniels grabbed her son and fell hard to the floor. She had to be helped from the house by concerned neighbors. All four grew ill — the most serious being Mrs. Daniels, whom a doctor ordered to bed.[62] Investigators later found a can of model-airplane glue containing ether, which was lying on the couch at the time.[63] Police answered no less than fifteen other alarms during the night.

It seemed as if everyone had a pet theory. There was the "mad scientist" hypothesis, which posited that an evil genius was busy concocting the gas in a secret laboratory. There was talk of a demented high school chemistry student. A variation of this view held that a well-intentioned but misguided "eccentric inventor was trying out the effectiveness of a new wartime gas."[64] There was even conjecture that it was an ex-soldier trained in chemical weaponry.[65] But by far the most outlandish discussion centered on "the Ape Man."

The Ape Man theory began circulating after claims made by Mattoon fortune-teller Mrs. Edna James, owner of a men's hotel, the Lincoln Inn. While she was lying in bed the night of September 7, she said, a strange odor filled the room. She went to the kitchen to investigate. There stood a strange-looking Neanderthal-type man, about twenty-five, with stooped shoulders and facial warts. She said, "He was like an ape standing there, crouched, his long arms reaching out as he held the spray gun in his hands."[66] She said the "phantom" then let out an unintelligible grunt, raised his spray gun, and doused her with three clouds of gas that numbed her arms and legs. She claimed that in a second encounter on September 9, the Ape Man appeared in her hotel lobby in the presence of several guests, but she was the only one who saw him, and he suddenly disappeared.[67] Mrs. James may have fabricated the Ape Man story for financial gain. What was playing in Chicago cinemas at that time? "The Hairy Ape" starring William Bendix and Susan Hayward. Was she drumming up business with her sighting?[68]

In response to the weekend bedlam, by September 11, law enforcement officials were blanketing the city. Illinois State Police Chief Harry Yde ordered five Springfield squad cars with two officers each to mobilize in Mattoon to fight the gasser. Each car had a local volunteer to assist with directions, and each officer carried a shotgun.[69] They arrived later that day. Three police officers from Urbana were also dispatched to patrol the streets that night. It was also disclosed that two FBI agents were in Mattoon. Their chief interest was in finding out what type of gas the "madman" was using "to knock out his victims."[70] That night there were no new reports, but one woman was so frightened of an attack that she was taken to Memorial Hospital suffering from "extreme mental anguish." She was given a sedative and released.[71]

Beginning on September 11, there was a concerted effort by both the *Journal-Gazette* and police to paint many of the events of recent days as episodes of mass hysteria, perhaps to reassure the public. With a small army of police patrolling the streets, Police Commissioner Wright remarked that they were often able to answer a call "before the phone was back on the hook."[72] At 11:30 A.M. that morning, the only daylight gassing was reported by Mrs. Eaton Paradise, who frantically told police, "I've just been gassed." City and state police raced to the house—only to find that she had accidentally spilled a container of nail-polish remover.[73] This case and the many obvious false alarms from the weekend that had been triggered by nerves prompted Police Chief Cole to make a surprise announcement on the afternoon of September 12—it was all mass hysteria. He said the case of the "mad anesthetist" was "a mistake from the beginning to end."[74] Cole blamed the episode on large amounts of carbon tetrachloride emitted by the Atlas Imperial Diesel Engine Company, which produced army shell casings. He said the odor was apparently carried around the city by shifting winds. Cole's announcement was stunning and divisive.[75]

Mattoon was split by a bitter rift between Police Chief Cole and many people who rejected the hysteria theory, resented it, and portrayed Cole and the police as bumbling incompetents. They viewed his finger-pointing at Atlas as an easy scapegoat that conveniently diverted attention away from himself. Siding against Cole was State Attorney William E. Kidwell, who branded the hysteria hypothesis "ridiculous" and said police had let the situation needlessly escalate out of control by failing to act promptly at the start.[76] Other authorities appeared to distance themselves from Cole, including State Police Captain Harry Curtis, who said he believed most reported gassings were false alarms but some of the earlier reports may have been real — but he couldn't prove it.[77]

Meanwhile, Atlas officials immediately and vehemently denied the charge, saying it was not the source of the mystery gas. While admitting that the facility used a quantity of trichlorethylene, they pointed out that it was only common sense that the strange odor could not have come from their plant. Otherwise their workers would have either noticed the fumes or been sickened themselves. The manager of the plant, W.J. Webster, said the charges were ludicrous: "There is some trichlorethylene in the plant but the concentration is so small that the fumes wouldn't travel more than ten feet."[78] Company officials said they had used the chemical for the past four years without a single report of a fume-related illness. Their statement said, "Trichlorethylene is used in practically every war plant in the country, and it seems strange if a mystery gas is put out by factories using trichlorethylene, that other communities throughout the nation have not been similarly affected."[79] They also noted that the plant had just recently been inspected by Dr. Kronenberg from the State Health Department. In an interview, the doctor was emphatic in saying that "there was no possibility of trichlorethylene vapors getting into the outside atmosphere in any amount of concentration that would even closely approximate a toxic condition."[80]

By the night of September 11, gassing claims and theories were growing even more improbable and elaborate. Bertha Bence, a fifty-four-year-old widow living in a cottage told police that she was convinced the gasser was a woman. She said, "Monday night I was asleep in the front bedroom of our home when I heard a peculiar whirring noise through a partly opened window. Suddenly I felt faint and nauseated."[81] Her three sons responded to her cries by running outside to nab the gasser. Only twenty-year-old Orville thought he saw something — "a shadowy form" disappearing into an alley. The next morning high-heel shoe prints were found near Mrs. Bence's bedroom window. She concluded that the gasser was a woman dressed in men's clothing. How he or she was able to elude capture and dash down the alley strapped in high-heel shoes was not discussed!

Despite Coles's claims of hysteria, the investigation behind the scenes was as intense and vigorous as ever. On September 12, Police Commissioner Wright announced that investigators had narrowed their list of suspects to four; two were amateur chemists and the others "crackpots." It was revealed that one of the chemists was under police surveillance. The disclosure was made only after a Chicago newspaper published confidential details of the case.[82] The paper in question, the *Chicago Herald-American*, had a different version of events, saying the information was willingly released without restriction.[83] It also reported that police told them they had secured a warrant for the man's arrest, but it wasn't used for lack of conclusive evidence. He was described as a wealthy eccentric with a cellar laboratory who lived where most of the gassings were reported: "His scholastic record at Mattoon High School and the University of Illinois, they said, was brilliant, but his actions in recent years, his aversion for his neighbors, have led to a belief that he was partially demented."[84] The notion of a mad scientist threatening women was a popular literary image in the two decades leading up to the Mattoon episode. Science-fiction expert Stuart Schiff observed that a common theme of pulp magazines in the 1920s and 1930s was to depict "an obviously mad scientist among an array of test tubes, electrical sparks, and fantastic machines. In the foreground ... one usually found a beautiful but scantily clad young woman ... obviously threatened by the deranged scientist."[85] The scientist was typified as a genius blinded by power, greed, or scientific advancement.

Meanwhile, State Police Captain Harry Curtis announced that every person reporting a gas attack was being asked to sniff small amounts of various chemicals to see which was closest to the agent that the gasser used. These included mustard gas, tear gas, chloropicrin, Lewisite, and methol chloride. Chloropicrin was the gas of choice, but it was not a unanimous choice.[86] Also on September 12, State Attorney Kidwell was busy contacting state mental hospitals to see if any former patients had an obsession or expertise in poison gas.[87]

By September 13, the gasser was now being called the "phantom anesthetist" and "Mattoon Will-o'-the-Wisp."[88] The press reported on two more false reports overnight "as the city began a slow return to normalcy."[89] In one case, a doctor was caught trying to get into his office after locking his keys inside. The other call turned out to be a black cat on a porch.[90] Meanwhile, Police Chief Cole continued his offensive on the mass hysteria front. After the stinging criticism from Atlas officials, he widened his scope to include many Mattoon factories using chemicals such as those involved in dyeing and cleaning processes. He said that the fumes might be carried across the city by shifting winds, but he pointed out that no one had been made seriously ill and all had recovered quickly. In either case, he said, if a gas were being used, it certainly wasn't doing serious harm. Also, warfare-type gasses almost always hover near the ground and linger for long periods, whereas the Mattoon gas rapidly dissipated.[91]

Some speculated that the gasser was engaged in war sabotage. Others thought it was an escaped Nazi. However, why would a Nazi or saboteur be going to such lengths and taking such risks to spray what was clearly a nonfatal gas into homes occupied most often by anxious women and their children?[92] Indeed, the hysteria explanation best fits the reported events. No known gas could have been so potent and stable as to affect some people in a room and not others, to dissipate without a trace so quickly, and to leave no lasting aftereffects. Hysteria explains why the gasser was able to roam neighborhoods and not be caught, despite a massive civilian and police presence. Finally, what was his motive, as no money was taken? Why did not dogs bark to alert residents of the intruder's presence?[93] Vague descriptions also did not tally. One person said he was tall and thin; another witness said a fat man had squirted gas through her bedroom window.[94] Also, while many of the symptoms were similar, all were vague and indicative of anxiety, and no one reported her eyes being affected. As psychiatrist Harold Hulbert observed, "Remember the eyes. They couldn't have escaped a volatile, poisonous gas."[95]

The symptoms were not suggestive of any known poison gas of the period. There are two types of poison gas: persistent and nonpersistent. Persistent gasses linger for hours or days and would have been readily detected by investigators or have made others in the house at the time sick. Nonpersistent gasses are dispensed into the air but quickly disperse and lose potency. Common lung irritants or suffocants of the time included such gasses as phosgene, chlorine, and chloropicrin. Even a small exposure causes definite breathing problems that would require medical attention. Any examining physician would have almost certainly detected it. Other nonpersistent agents in use at the time were tear gasses such as chloracetophenone and sneezing gasses like diphenylchlorarsine. While burning lips were reported by some residents, no burn marks were ever identified by doctors. Such sensations may have been caused by dry and cracking lips or anxiety.[96]

By September 14, gassing reports in Mattoon stopped for good. The only call was of a prowler on Richmond Avenue. Police rushed to the home to find neither evidence of a gassing nor a prowler. At this point, both police and the press were ridiculing claims. The *Mattoon Journal-Gazette* began its account of the previous night's activities by writing, "One call! No paralyzing gas! No madman! No prowler!"[97] September 14 was also notoriously eventful because a major train crash in Terre Haute, Indiana, about fifty miles from Mattoon, helped to further divert waning attention from the gasser.[98] Also on September 14, police in Cedar Rapids, Iowa, reported that a woman called them in a frantic state, claiming that she saw a man holding a spray gun outside a window. She said the man pointed the gun at her and pumped her room with gas. Police said when they arrived, "they found no madman and no gas, but did find a billy goat tied in the yard and an odor that seemed to come from the animal."[99]

No one likes to be made a laughingstock, but the conclusion by Mattoon police that mass hysteria was responsible for the mad gasser proved embarrassing for the city. On September 19, an editorial in the *Decatur Herald* made fun of imaginative Mattoonites, noting that autumn was a season of odors: flowers, picnic fires, industrial wastes, and rotting produce from Victory gardens: "At this season of the year odors are sniffed not merely by individuals but by entire communities. Our neighbors in Mattoon sniffed their town into newspaper headlines from coast to coast."[100]

ALL QUIET ON MATTOON'S "GAS FRONT"

Police Get Only One Call; Find Neither Prowler Nor Gas

With nightly calls for police assistance and investigation reaching an all-time high a week ago when the city was gripped by the case of the "mad anesthetist," Mattoon officials were amazed Wednesday night when only one call—far below the normal number—was received.

The lone call was a report of a prowler in the 3000 block of Richmond avenue. Police, guided by two-way broadcasting equipment loaned by the state, investigated and reported finding no prowler or evi-

Figure 5.4: By the second week of September, and just days after the case had reached a fever pitch, gassing reports suddenly stopped cold. This occurred amid press reports making fun of the case and police who continued to push the hysteria explanation. (Source: "All Quiet on Mattoon's 'Gas Front,'" the *Daily Journal-Gazette*, September 14, 1944, p. 1.)

Meanwhile, editors of the Mattoon *Journal-Gazette* suggested that "Decatur's famous odors, carried Mattoonward by the wind" might have been to blame for the gas mania. The editorial also claimed that the first few reports were caused by a real gasser who was not caught due to police ineptitude, but mass hysteria quickly took over as public fear spiraled out of control.[101] At about this juncture, a reporter for *Time* magazine humorously noted that gasser symptoms in Mattoonites consisted of temporary paralysis, nausea, and "a desire to describe their experiences in minutest detail."[102] Other letters to the *Journal-Gazette* during late September ridiculed the episode, such as one from Corporal Richard Littleton stationed in Camp Haan, California, who noted that Mattoon residents were even more advanced in their poison-gas training than his unit.[103] Another writer referred to the incidents as "hysteria," remarking that events had finally died down.[104] The strange case of the mad gasser of Mattoon had come to an end.[105]

The Mad Gasser in Context

To understand a particular set of human behaviors, it is important to examine the context in which it occurred. For instance, some scientists have concluded that the Nazi movement resulted from a mass mental disturbance. They assume that no one in their right mind could engage in such obviously sick behaviors as exterminating millions of Jews. Similar claims have been made about the European witch-hunts.

Nazis have been viewed as suffering from mass mental disturbance,[106] as have Japanese imperialists during World War II.[107] William Brown claimed that Hitler's "hysterical and paranoid tendencies" were a form of collective insanity that found "their counterparts in the reactions of the entire nation."[108] Medical historians Frederick Cartwright and Michael Biddiss view the allegiance to Hitler as the product of a group mental illness, a basic premise underlying the "culture and personality" critique of Nazism as pathological: "Germany was a sick nation, in that so many of her individual members were mentally sick, defeated and disillusioned [from World War I], translating their sufferings into a fantasy of persecution [by the Jews]."[109]

To characterize mass adherence to Nazism as a psychological disturbance is inappropriate and misleading. While we are not advocates of such destructive social movements, grassroots support for Nazism is more comprehensible when examined within the context of numerous classic studies demonstrating the impact of social and cultural norms on conformity,[110] with later studies specifically applied to Nazism.[111]

A similar case can be made for understanding the sixteenth- and seventeenth-century witch-hunts. Despite interpretations of people labeled as witches as mentally ill or social misfits, a relativistic, contextual view helps to understand the motivations of those involved.[112] For instance, any interpretation of the 1692 Salem, Massachusetts, witch trials must include an understanding of the community's social setting. The trials were not a

Mattoon Terror Like Salem Witch Hunt

BY EFFIE ALLEY.

MATTOON, Ill., Sept. 21.— Mattoon's gas phantom can boast a long and 100 per cent American ancestry, dating back to the witch hunts of colonial days.

According to Dr. Harold S. Hulbert, psychiatrist, who has just completed an investigation of Mattoon's epidemic of mass hysteria, the same forces which created the recent terror here have at one time or another manifested themselves in nearly every American community, sometimes with tragic, sometimes with comic results.

All of which is just the doctor's way of saying that Americans are a suggestible people, quick to take up a fad or a fetish. He wants it made clear that while it lasted Mattoon's terror of the supposed gas-sprayer was a fad.

COULD BE GRAVE.

Though fads of this kind are harmless enough, the same emotional forces which give rise to them may, when centered on a different object, create ugly and even grim situations.

Take, for example, the earliest manifestations of this kind in America—the Salem, Mass., witch hunts.

It all began with two hysterical girls who accused a hunchback woman of having bewitched them and exhibited self-inflicted blisters and swellings to prove it.

A lot of people paid off their secret hatreds on the witches.

The people of Rensselaer, Ind.,
in the year of our Lord, 1939, didn't, of course, believe in witches. But they did believe in lions, after farmers in the vicinity had reported mysterious killings of farm animals.

POSSES ORGANIZED.

Dozens of armed posses were organized, expert big-game hunters called in, lions were seen here, there and everywhere in Jasper County. After a month's excitement, the big lion hunt came to a humiliating end with the killing of two dogs whose prints proved to be identical with tracks supposed to have been made by the maurading lions.

As for police who have such a situation to deal with, Dr. Hulbert believes that they couldn't do better than follow the example of Mattoon's Police Commissioner Thomas V. Wright.

When he gave every individual reporting an attack the choice of an immediate medical examination or a night in jail, the attacks ceased as if by magic.

As the antidote for fear is trust, Dr. Hulbert points out that in any similar situation every effort should be made to build up the faith of the people in constituted authorities.

They should be assured and reassured that if there is a culprit at large, the police, using ordinary police methods, will soon have him under lock and key. And that, according to Dr. Hulbert, who is a criminologist as well as a psychiatrist, isn't just baloney.

Figure 5.5: Illinois psychiatrist Dr. Harold Hulbert likened the episode to that of the Salem witch trials of 1692. (Source: The *Chicago Herald-American*, September 22, 1944, p. 4).

simple cause-and-effect reaction to pent-up stress. Historians Paul Boyer and Stephen Nissenbaum concur:

> When "Salem witchcraft," like some exotic cut flower, is plucked from the soil which nurtured it ... [it] cannot rise above the level of gripping melodrama. It is only as we come to sense how deeply the witchcraft outbreak was rooted in the prosaic, everyday lives and how profoundly those lives were being shaped ... by the times in which they lived. For if they were unlike any other men, so was their world unlike any other world before or since.[113]

While the seventeenth century may be remembered as the Age of Enlightenment, a belief in witches and demons was promoted and institutionalized by prominent period intellectuals known for their scientific prowess. British chemist Robert Boyle (1627-1691) suggested that English miners be interviewed to determine whether they encountered underground demons, while his countryman, philosopher Sir Francis Bacon, held that "malign spirits" might be responsible for witchcraft.[114] On the subject of interpreting witchcraft beliefs, many researchers note "the absolutism and ethnocentricity involved in evaluating historical events such as the witch hunts in terms of modern constructions of reality" and the failure to take a relativistic position that considers "past beliefs and actions in terms of the historical, social, and intellectual contexts in which they were imbedded."[115]

Diagnosing Germany as a sick society is an example of what Wolfgang Jilek calls a "positivistic fallacy" involving the psychopathological labeling of collective beliefs that do not fit into the framework of the logico-experimental explanatory theories of positive science.[116] Jilek sagely noted that the Nazi's racist ersatz-religion preaching of the superiority of a "Nordic-Aryan master race" was proclaimed in the nineteenth century by "Ariosophers" and elitist writers such as Count Gobineau and H.S. Chamberlain. Jilek observed that in the same category fall "doctrinaire Marxist beliefs in mankind's salvation through the inevitable coming of the 'classless society' against all bourgeois-imperialist conspiracies, and also the witchcraft and demon beliefs held by millions of nonpsychotic individuals in societies that make demoniac forces responsible for perceived evil or misfortune."[117]

Mindful of the importance of context in the understanding of human behavior, we should ask ourselves, "What were the circumstances that the first reported 'victim,' Mrs. Kearney, found herself in on the night of September 1, 1944, just before 11 P.M.?" We can make a pretty good guess. We know that there was a great deal of publicity over the possible use of poison gas during World War II. The gassing also broke out during a burglary wave and a hunt for an escaped Nazi. On August 29, police were searching Mattoon for an escaped Nazi from Camp Ellis.[118] The next evening, two city homes were broken into.[119] On August 31, three Mattoon businesses were burglarized, and a fourth was reportedly robbed.[120] We also know that for months before the outbreak, the *Journal-Gazette* had been highly critical of the police department's ability to maintain law and order.

What had Mrs. Kearney been doing just prior to going to bed that fateful night? She had a considerable sum of money for the time — $75 — from her government allotment check that had been cashed earlier in the day. Also, she and her sister were counting it near a window that was visible from the street. Given this setting, her reaction to detecting the odor — that of being gassed by a prowler intent on taking her money — was not such a bizarre assumption for the time period.

After the initial sensational case and subsequent police search for the gasser, which received spectacular press coverage, residents began reinterpreting mundane occurrences such as nocturnal shadows and chemical odors from numerous local factories. Residents also began paying close attention to ever-present body complaints and new symptoms resulting from heightened anxiety states. The result was a wave of gas attacks in both communities. The symptoms in both episodes were similar, as residents focused on body symptoms that mirrored common and well-publicized poison-gas complaints: nausea, vomiting, dry mouth, palpitations, difficulty walking, and a burning sensation in the mouth. However, symptoms were transient and benign. That is, they didn't last long and were not serious.

The Mattoon *Journal-Gazette* practically created the whole gasser scare. We know the police had not taken seriously the first several gassing reports. A later editorial criticizing police in the *Journal-Gazette* points this out.[121] Police had not taken Aline Kearney seriously. Neither did they place much credence in the three reports that quickly followed, where residents had claimed gassings only after learning of the Kearney case. According to the *Journal-Gazette*, police concluded that these cases were "just imagination."[122] But this police skepticism is not reflected in the press reports in the early going. On September 2, the *Journal-Gazette* carried the first report on the incident: "Anesthetic Prowler on Loose." Not only was the gasser's existence treated as fact, but the subheadline implied that more gassings may follow: "Mrs. Kearney and Daughter First Victims ... Robber Fails to Get into Home."

After reading of the initial gasser story in the *Journal-Gazette*, several Mattoon residents reported similar home attacks either near the time of the reported incidents at the Kearney residence or days—even months before. These additional reports are dubious. Why? At the time of the supposed gassings, no one reported the incidents to police, friends, or relatives, or even fled their house or bothered consulting a doctor. Just imagine—you suspect someone has sprayed poison gas into your home, making you and your family ill with dizziness, burning lips, vomiting, partial limb paralysis. It was well-known that poison gas could cause permanent disabilities or prove lethal. And what do these early gas victims do? They remained in the house and, soon after the supposed attack, went back to sleep without telling a soul! This behavior makes no sense unless, after learning of the mad gasser, those involved in the three earlier attacks began redefining ambiguous events and reconstructing what had actually happened.

This is reminiscent of the case of Father William Gill, an Anglican priest who made spectacular claims about communicating with aliens. The case is often repeated in UFO books as proof of alien contact. Early on the evening of June 27, 1959, Gill and a small group watched an illuminated object in the sky near Boianai, Papua New Guinea. They became excited after thinking they could see humanlike figures waving back at them. The exchange of waves continued and a flashlight was turned on and off toward the "craft," which seemed to respond by moving in a pendulum fashion. It is unlikely that Father Gill and part of his congregation made this story up. Yet as UFO investigator Philip Klass sagely points out by using Father Gill's own log, once the claims are examined in greater detail, they simply do not make sense. After claiming to have just communicated with the "craft's" occupants and having watched the object for only thirty minutes, the group must have been very excited. Would it land? Might they try to communicate again? At this point, and with the object still in view, what did Father Gill and his companions do at this potentially historic juncture in history? They went to dinner—and resumed viewing half an hour later![123]

This makes for an exciting story, but human memory does not recall events as they happened, but as we think they happened. Even when we do remember relatively accurately, details can change after the fact.[124] It brings to mind the saying, "The older I get, the better I was." If I had been convinced an alien craft was hovering over my house, I would have certainly called the police and every friend and relative I had, and told them to get there—fast. Such stories sound exciting after the event, but logic and common sense dictate otherwise.

Perhaps the best explanation for the "Mad Man of Mattoon" was offered by five Chicago chemists, who dismissed the case as a hoax after weighing the evidence. They concluded that the recipe for "a nonexistent prowler" was rumor, a whiff of sour milk, clover, ragweed, or smoke, and a lot of imagination.[125]

How do we explain that most victims were women? It seems to reflect the plight of the many Mattoon wives, whose husbands were in the service or working at night.[126] A writer observed that one serviceman's wife who was frightened to stay in her own home with her tiny son moved in with her parents, but those with nowhere else to go "live in fear each night, waiting for daylight to come."[127] The preponderance of females gassed is also an artifact of research. Journalists from four Chicago newspapers who went to Mattoon to cover the story reported suffering lingering effects of the gas after visiting attack scenes. Symptoms included headache and swollen tongues.[128] They were not counted as victims in Donald Johnson's famous study because he assumed that women were more prone to hysteria.[129] Several attacks involved husbands accompanying their wives, and while both described suffering from the effects of the gas, only wives were counted by Johnson as victims.[130] Suspicion that the culprit was female, which also occurred in the Botetourt drama, is conspicuous because we don't typically think of women committing such macabre crimes. This may reflect a deeper societal dread during the 1930s and 1940s that women were emerging as a social force that would soon challenge male supremacy. Indeed, there was an omnipresence of sinister *femme fatales* in numerous films of this period.[131]

Could the case of Mattoon's mad gasser have been initially triggered by a real gasser? It is improbable given the facts. Such theories are highly speculative and typically made in ignorance both of basic theories of social psychology and the scientific literature on epidemic hysteria and collective delusions. If there were a real gasser, he would have had to possess superhuman strength and guile, run the one hundred-yard dash like Jesse Owens, and had the luck of a lottery millionaire. Then there is the motive. Nothing was ever reported taken, no clear facial description was given, and no gas was ever detected. Some cases occurred in different parts of the city at almost identical times. The only substance in the case was that there was no substance, only vague clues, shadowy figures, and vague symptoms reported by jittery residents. Suggestions of the existence of a paranormal ghostlike entity gassing residents are even more implausible. Among the many drawbacks was the absence of credible, replicable evidence for the existence of a single paranormal event.[132]

The mad gasser may seem unique in the annals of mass behavior, but in reality it is just one in a long series of epidemic hysterias and mass delusions occurring during the twentieth century that coincided with

Figure 5.6: Did the motion picture industry contribute to the scare? The two main movies playing at the Mattoon Theater in early September were *The Phantom Shadow* and *Invisible Man's Revenge*. (Source: The *Daily Journal-Gazette*, September 7, 1944, p. 2.)

heightened awareness of pollution and chemical-warfare concerns triggered by imaginary or exaggerated contamination threats. These are an especially common theme in epidemic hysteria cases. This is the context in which the strange case of the Mattoon gasser should be understood. The form seems bizarre only to those who are unfamiliar with the basic underlying elements, which are all too familiar.

It is inevitable that comparisons will be made between the events in Virginia and Illinois. In both episodes, local newspapers played an instrumental role in spreading the story and presenting the gasser's existence as certain. Later, near the end of each outbreak, press accounts turned overwhelmingly skeptical, contributing to the rapid decline and cessation of cases. Both gassing episodes occurred almost exclusively at night to populations who were preoccupied with the threat of poison gas. It was noted in Virginia that a woman's high-heel shoe print was found near a window where the gas was believed to have been sprayed. In Mattoon, high-heel shoe prints were also found and were scrutinized as perhaps gasser-related items (as were a dropped lipstick tube, a discarded cloth, fluttering curtains, mundane noises, and a black cat). Such observations are purely coincidental and not surprising, any more than there were trees and grass near the bedroom windows of victims in both Mattoon and Botetourt. To fully appreciate the two episodes, superficial comparisons can be misleading. It is important to look at the bigger picture and the larger context to see where the two episodes fit.

The remarkable parallels between the phantom anesthetist of Mattoon and the mad gasser of Botetourt are not coincidental. They are fascinating examples of epidemic hysteria within community settings. During the entire interwar period, Americans were preoccupied with the issue of chemical weapons during wartime.

With horrific images of gas warfare still vivid, early in the postwar period there was considerable public interest as the U.S. government embarked on a national policy for the use of poison gas in wartime. In 1919, General John Pershing captured the mood, proclaiming, "Whether or not gas will be employed in future wars is a matter of conjecture, but the effect is so deadly to the unprepared that we can never afford to neglect the question."[133] For instance, according to a U.S. government survey published in the *New York Times* of January 8, 1922, Americans overwhelmingly favored a total abolition of gas warfare. That same year, the Washington Arms Conference resulted in the United States agreeing to a prohibition of gas as an offensive weapon. Significantly, defense measures involving poison gas were allowed. Fear of gas warfare was still very much on the public mind in 1922, with Frederick Brown describing the year as one in which "gas had become the *cause celebre* of World War I memories."[134]

Throughout the rest of the 1920s, gas warfare remained a major issue in American politics. Public debates ebbed and flowed around various forums. The high-profile venues were the 1925 Geneva Gas Conference and ongoing discussions held at the League of Nations. While a U.S. delegation signed the Geneva Gas Protocol in 1925, the Senate refused to ratify it, and the debate over whether or not to ratify continued throughout the decade. For instance, the influential American Legion denounced the protocol at its annual conventions in 1925, 1926, and 1927. One of its prominent members, Colonel John Taylor, even wrote and distributed twenty-five thousand copies of a Legion booklet titled *The Truth About the Geneva Gas Protocol — America Should Reject It — Its Preparedness Essential to Our National Security*. Many other veterans groups opposed the gas treaty, such as the Veterans of Foreign Wars, Military Order of the World War, Spanish-American War Veterans, and the Reserve Officers Association, among others, but there was opposition.[135] For instance, a founder of the American Legion, Congressman Hamilton Fish, stood before the House of Representatives in 1927 and accused Taylor of "misrepresenting the views of the rank and file" and using chemical-industry money to defeat the Geneva Gas Protocol.[136]

Between 1926 and 1934, the U.S. government engaged in a series of ongoing preparatory discussions for the World Disarmament Conference. The result was to keep the issue of gas warfare in the public eye and within political circles. Scores of articles appeared discussing the various positions on gas warfare. During the latter 1920s, even more books and periodicals fueled the debate.[137]

During the early 1930s, a number of books discussing gas warfare also appeared, such as J.M. Kenworthy's *New Wars: New Weapons* and Liddell Hart's *The British Way of Warfare*.[138] In *The Air Menace and the Answer*, Elvira K. Fradkin described America during the early 1930s as living through the "poison gas scare."[139] He noted that "development of poison gas and the exploits of the airplane are becoming daily more of public concern."[140] The League of Nations also published many documents addressing the issue, and proceedings of the many conferences held on the topic appeared.[141]

While certainly not a common event, placing the Botetourt gasser within this historical gas-scare context renders it more plausible. In 1933, the year of the Botetourt gassings, the *New York Times* published twenty-one stories on the subject of chemical weapons.[142] Separate accounts described the preparations for poison-gas defense in Holland, Denmark, England, Australia, and Germany,[143] as there was a growing view that the use of poison gas in warfare was inevitable.[144] Scores of widely read periodicals published stories on the perils of gas warfare around this time.[145] Far from a bizarre episode of epidemic hysteria affecting an enclave of Virginia hillbillies, the imaginary gassings could have happened anywhere in America.

By the late 1930s, fear over the use of poison gas had become indelibly imprinted upon the American psyche. In his study of *The War of the Worlds* panic in October 1938, Princeton University psychologist Hadley Cantril concluded that a major contributing factor to the panic was the plausibility of the broadcast, as a substantial portion of listeners had assumed that the Martian gas raids were actually a German gas attack on the United States. One typical respondent told Cantril: "The announcer said a meteor had fallen from Mars and I was sure that he thought that, but in back of my head I had the idea that the meteor was just a camouflage … and the Germans were attacking us with gas bombs."[146]

Throughout World War II, Allied and Axis powers alike lived day by day under the specter of poison gas. In *A Higher Form of Killing*, Robert Harris and Jeremy Paxman note that "years later it is difficult to appreciate just how great the fear of gas was" for both the military and civilians.[147] Many unfounded rumors of Japanese gas atrocities circulated in America during the war, prompting calls in the U.S. press for retaliation. A typical 1944 headline proclaimed, "You Can Cook 'Em Better with Gas."[148]

By 1944, the year of the Mattoon gassings, there were no less than 112 articles in the *New York Times* on the subject of chemical warfare.[149] Popular and scientific periodicals around this time also discussed the poison-gas peril and its possible use.[150] Until this point, gas had not been used in the war for fear of retribution. By the fall of 1944, the war had clearly turned in favor of the Allies. With a victory seen as inevitable, there was grave concern that an increasingly desperate Germany might resort to the use of gas warfare. The Allies were so worried of the possible use of poison gas during their June 6, 1944, D-Day invasion of Normandy that they had a plan to retaliate within forty-eight hours with two bombing raids of four hundred planes each, all carrying chemical weapons designed to drench selected targets.[151] Gas-warfare expert Frederic Brown states that D-Day was the "most dangerous period for German [gas] initiation"—a credible threat that was widely discussed in the press during latter 1944. The mad gasser appeared just two and a half months after D-Day. There was also discussion as to whether the United States should be the first to use gas.[152] This view came under a firestorm of criticism by many commentators, who were fearful that the Axis powers would think that the use of gas was imminent and initiate a first strike. Following editorials favoring the idea in the *Chicago Tribune*, the *New York Daily News*, and the *Washington Times-Herald*, Norman Cousins branded their editors as "incredibly irresponsible."[153]

In this century we are no longer oppressed by demons and spirits, at least not in the developed world, but our modern demons take new forms. It is perhaps part of the human condition to harbor fears about the

Figure 5.7: Collage of press reports on the mad gasser of Mattoon. The press was influential in perpetrating the scare.

environment, and to believe in the existence of powerful yet invisible forces with the potential to control our destiny. To the medieval mind, demonic possession was a reality. To the inhabitants of interwar Virginia, such fears would have seemed quaint, but a threat from mysterious gases was viewed as all too real. The future use of poison gas against civilian populations was part of the mental landscape of the interwar period. From early in World War I until the first atomic bomb was dropped on Hiroshima, Japan, on August 6, 1945, Americans lived in fear of the world's most devastating weapon at the time: poison gas.

Descriptions of gas attacks in Europe during World War I are devastating and hellish. At 5 P.M. on April 22, 1915, the Germans released the first chemical weapons of the war — a chlorine gas attack near Ypres, Belgium. Five thousand Allied soldiers died, and ten thousand were injured. It is estimated that through the end of the war, ninety thousand people were killed by various poison gasses that were used on both sides, and over 1 million were hurt.[154] Given the tremendous publicity on the dangers of chemical weapons, especially chlorine and mustard gasses, it was probably not coincidental that during the Botetourt episode, medical authorities initially suspected chlorine gas was being sprayed,[155] but tests eventually ruled this out.[156] In Mattoon, chloropicrin — also in the chemical arsenals of some countries at the time — was wrongly suspected.[157] Clearly, the mad-gasser episodes were not flights of irrationality that occurred out of thin air. They were grounded in plausibility, fueled by the mass media, and engendered by the major preoccupation of the period: the poison-gas dilemma.

Chapter 6

Pokémon TV Show Sickens Thousands in Japan

The new electronic independence recreates the world in the image of a global village. — Marshall McLuhan[1]

The word "Pokémon" is a shortening of the term "pocket monsters," from the original Japanese name *Poketto Monsuta*. It was created as a video game for the handheld Nintendo Game Boy system. Pokémon creator Satoshi Tajiri introduced the game in 1996, and within a few months it became a best-seller. Following this success, Nintendo created a television cartoon version. Animated by Shogakukan Productions and directed by Hidaka Masamitsu, it debuted in Japan on April 1, 1997. To date, 120 episodes have aired in Japan.

Sales of Pokémon products generate over $1 billion annually for Nintendo from such items as video games, tapes, comic and coloring books, Internet sites, magazines, clubs, music CDs, trading cards, and feature films. Pokémon has become a recognizable global icon that is so popular in America that *Time* magazine featured it on the cover of its November 22, 1999, edition. The animated series airs in America on the WB Network and attains consistently high ratings.

The television cartoon centers on young boys and girls who wander the world of Pokémon looking for small creatures (called Pokémon) to capture, befriend, and train for battle against other trainers (and their Pokémon) in the Pokémon League. The ultimate goal is for the kids to collect one of every species and become Pokémon Masters. There are currently at least 151 different Pokémon characters, each with unique powers and

The author is grateful to Benjamin Radford for his co-authorship of this chapter.

individual personalities. The most popular character, Pikachu, resembles a yellow rat and has the ability to shock opponents with electricity.

The Episode

At 6:30 P.M. on December 16, 1997, Pokémon episode number thirty-eight — titled *"Dennou Senshi Porigon"* ("Computer Warrior Polygon") — aired across Japan on TV Tokyo. The program was popular and held the highest ratings for its time slot with an average market share of about 15 percent. In the episode, Pikachu and his human friends Satoshi, Kasumi, and Takeshi have an adventure that leads inside a computer. About twenty minutes into the program, the group encounters a fighter named Polygon. A battle ensues, during which Pikachu uses his electric powers to stop a "virus bomb." The animators depicted Pikachu's electric attack with a quick series of flashing lights.

Millions watched the program. In one city, Toyohashi, over 70 percent of the twenty-four thousand elementary school students and 35 percent of the thirteen thousand junior high school students watched the program, for a total of over twenty-one thousand children in Toyohashi alone.[2] In Tokyo, the Kawasaki education board found that 50,714 students, or 55 percent of the students in public kindergartens, primary, and middle schools in the area, watched the episode.[3]

At 6:51 P.M., the flashing lights of Pikachu's attack appeared on television screens. By 7:30 P.M., according to Japan's Fire-Defense Agency, 618 children had been taken to hospitals complaining of various symptoms. News of the illnesses spread rapidly through Japan and became the subject of media reports later that evening. During the coverage, several stations replayed the flashing sequence, whereupon even more children fell ill and sought medical attention. The number affected by this second wave is unknown. Reported symptoms included convulsions, altered levels of consciousness, headache, breathlessness, nausea, vomiting, blurred vision, and general malaise.[4]

The Aftermath

On December 17, 1997, TV Tokyo issued an apology, suspended the program, and said it would investigate the cause of the seizures. Officers from the Atago Police Station, acting on orders from the National Police Agency, questioned the program's producers about the cartoon's contents and production process. The Japanese Health and Welfare Ministry held an emergency meeting, discussed the case with experts, and gathered information from hospitals. Meanwhile, video retailers across Japan withdrew the series from their rental shelves.

Outraged mothers accused TV Tokyo of ignoring their children's health in the quest for ratings. Other parents called for the implementation of an electronic screening device to block intense animation. Japanese Prime Minister Ryutaro Hashimoto expressed concern, stating that rays and lasers might be dangerous—after all, they had been considered for use as weapons—and that their effects are not fully understood. While a Nintendo representative quickly explained that the only link between its game and the cartoon was the characters, the company's shares immediately dropped nearly 5 percent on the Tokyo stock market.[5] TV Tokyo placed warning labels on all future and past Pokémon episodes. Despite the scare, and buoyed by the show's enormous popularity and revenue-generating capacity before the illness reports, the Pokémon TV program returned to the air in Japan in April 1998. To date, no reports of collective illness coinciding with the program's broadcast have occurred.

Bright, flashing lights are known to trigger seizures in epileptics. In 1994, British commercial television ads and programs were limited to a rate of three flashes per second. The limit followed a 1993 incident in which a noodle ad featuring fast-moving graphics and bright flashes triggered three seizures. After several teens experienced seizures while playing Nintendo video games, the company began including warning labels on much of its software. The warning stated that the games' graphics and animation could cause a *shigeki*, a strong stimulation resulting in unconsciousness or seizures.

The Pokémon case was alarming and enigmatic due to the large number of (almost exclusively) children reportedly affected and the array of symptoms. While bright flashes seemed to be the likely culprit, the flashes had been used hundreds of times before without incident. The technique, called *paka-paka*, uses different-colored lights flashing alternately to create tension. It is common in *anime*, the distinctive Japanese animation technique used in Pokémon and many other cartoons, such as *Voltron*, *Sailor Moon*, and *Speed Racer*. There was no apparent difference between episode thirty-eight and the other Pokémon episodes. Producer Takemoto Mori had used virtually identical *paka-paka* in most of the previous episodes, with slight variations in color and background combinations. All Pokémon episodes were prescreened before airing, and no problems were reported.

A clear genesis of the Pokémon panic remains elusive. After four months, Nintendo announced that it could find no obvious cause for the outbreak, and Pokémon returned to the airwaves. Further research was left to the scientific community. Hayashi et al. surveyed patients in the Yamaguchi prefecture (population 1,550,000) and found twelve affected children with no history of epilepsy.[6] During the program, two had fainted and ten had tonic-clonic convulsions. Eleven of the twelve had photosensitivity or epileptic EEG abnormalities. The researchers concluded that the children had latent photosensitive conditions predisposing them to exhibit seizures when exposed to the flashing lights.[7] Hayashi et al. estimated the incidence of seizures triggered by Pokémon at 1.5 per 10,000, ten times the incidence found by British researchers.[8]

Yamashita et al. investigated every child in eighty elementary schools in the central Fukuoka prefecture on Kyushu Island (population 470,807). On December 22, 1997, six days after the outbreak, teachers asked whether any pupils had experienced symptoms after seeing the episode. Questionnaires were also sent to medical facilities in the prefecture. Of the 32,083 enrolled students, only one child experienced a convulsion, while 1,002 reported minor symptoms. As half of all boys and girls saw the program, Yamashita et al. estimated that 6.25 percent of the children were affected.[9] A survey of twelve hospitals in the prefecture revealed that seventeen children ages two to fifteen were treated for convulsions. Tobimatsu et al. studied four children who had been affected by Pokémon and diagnosed all with photosensitive epilepsy.[10] The researchers believe that the children's sensitivity to color, in particular rapid changes between red and blue, may have played an important role in triggering the seizures.

Furusho et al. surveyed patients who visited pediatric clinics from January 8 to February 28, 1998. Of the 662 children surveyed, 603 (91 percent) watched the Pokémon episode. Of those, two reported seizures, nine had headaches, eight had nausea, four had blurred vision, one vomited, two had vertigo, and two had dysthymia (depression). A slight majority of the children (sixteen) did not develop symptoms during or immediately after viewing the program but much later.[11]

Epidemic Hysteria: A Broad Overview

Hysteria is characterized by the impairment or loss of sensory or motor function for which there exists no organic basis.[12] The modern name for hysteria is conversion disorder, the converting of emotional conflicts and anxiety into physical symptoms. Epidemic hysteria refers to the rapid diffusion of conversion symptoms and anxiety states. While epidemic hysteria is often referred to as a diagnosis of exclusion even before tests are complete, it is possible to render an accurate diagnosis based on the criteria listed in Chapter 1.

Epidemic hysteria is most commonly reported in small, cohesive social units within enclosed settings such as schools and factories. Simon Wessely identifies two types of hysterical reactions in groups: anxiety and motor hysteria.[13] Anxiety hysteria has a rapid onset and recovery period, usually twenty-four hours, and is precipitated by the sudden perception of a threatening agent, typically a strange odor or rumor of contaminated food. Stomach pain, nausea, vomiting, and diarrhea typify suspected food-poisoning cases.[14] Suspected toxic-gas leaks commonly provoke headache and dizziness.[15]

Most reports involve an identifiable index case who is the first to exhibit illness symptoms that are usually highly visible and dramatic.[16] Often, unbeknown to the group, the index case is suffering from a physical illness such as an epileptic seizure, influenza, or schizophrenia. Symptoms are often spread through line of sight.

Mass motor hysteria incubates more slowly than anxiety hysteria, and develops in an atmosphere of accumulating long-term group stress. It is prevalent in intolerable social settings, most commonly in schools enforcing extreme disciplinary measures.

There have been numerous reports of mass motor hysteria in Western countries prior to the mid-twentieth century. These cases were correlated with strict educational policies or dehumanizing factory conditions prior to the rise of unions. Modern-day reports are rare except for non–Western schools and factories, where episodes remain prevalent amid strict capitalist discipline or academic regulation coupled with limited or nonexistent grievance channels. Mass motor hysteria was common in European convents between the fifteenth and nineteenth centuries.[17]

In theory, both motor and anxiety hysteria are controlled by removing the stressful agent. This may be easier said than done due to the emotionally charged nature of many outbreaks and the difficulty that is often encountered in convincing skeptical group members. In anxiety hysteria, the key is to persuade those affected that the toxic agent has either been eliminated or never existed. Episodes of motor hysteria are often interpreted by the affected group to confirm the presence of demonic forces, making it vital to convince group members that the offending "spirits" have been eliminated or appeased.

Epidemic Hysteria in Japan

Periodic outbreaks of collective frenetic emotional displays that have been labeled as mass hysterical outbreaks have been recorded in Japan in 1705, 1771, 1830, and 1867. These episodes conspicuously coincide with oppressive feudal regimes and accompanying social crises. They may have functioned as cathartic responses to long-standing repression by releasing pent-up anxiety. Historian E. Herbert Norman labeled these events as a combination of hysteria and ritual through which a collective catharsis is achieved under the guise of *okage-mairi*, a custom involving a pilgrimage to give thanks to the Sun Goddess by visiting the Ise shrine.[18] Outbreaks were characterized by collective frenetic dancing, crying, singing, obscene and bizarre behavior, amnesia, trance states, and other transient ailments. For instance, in 1771, Shinto philosopher Motoori Norinaga described an outbreak firsthand. As people flooded roads to make the pilgrimage, many carried pictures that depicted obscene or absurd figures or events:

> There is much roistering and noisy talk going on and some of it of a nature similar to the pictures. The people go along clapping their hands, shouting, singing *"okage de sa! nuketa to sa!"* and becoming more and more excited. Both young men and old women forget their natural modesty and indulge in this frenzy so that it is quite a disturbing sight to see. They seem to have abandoned themselves to utter madness, as well as ribaldry and horseplay.[19]

These episodes resemble the famous medieval dancing manias[20] involving masses of Europeans who, it has been widely argued, were engaging in a ritualistic mass catharsis by partaking in pilgrimages to St. Vitus shrines and chapels during periods of famine, pestilence, and disease to obtain divine favor. Medical historians George Mora[21] and George Rosen[22] take this view. Mora stated that dance manias were a socially acceptable means of "expression, through ritual, of deeply rooted emotional conflicts," with participants engaging in psychotherapeutic coping strategies to individual or societal problems.[23]

In modern times, epidemic hysteria outbreaks in Japan have taken a different form to reflect changing fears that characterize the industrial age, namely environmental contaminants. Twentieth-century outbreaks are typified by the sudden manifestation of mass anxiety symptoms of a transient, benign nature. These have occurred in response to the perception of an imaginary or exaggerated harmful agent in the immediate environment.[24] The one known exception to this trend occurred in 1960, when a Japanese hospital staff of mostly females was swept by an epidemic of

digestive disorders and mood liability that has been interpreted as an outbreak of epidemic hysteria.[25] The modern trend of epidemic hysteria in
Japan manifesting itself in response to environmental concerns continued
into the mid–1990s, when several incidents of sudden anxiety hysteria—
typified by fainting and breathing problems—took place in the Japanese
subway system. A few well-publicized real attacks involving sarin nerve
gas by the Aum Shinrikyo sect triggered the outbreaks.[26]

Discussion

Massey et al. discussed "the jerks," a hysterical epidemic in which
many attendants of emotionally charged, nocturnal, religious revival meetings in the seventeenth- and eighteenth-century southern United States
exhibited psychomotor agitation of the arms or limbs and often ended in
collapse. After examining firsthand accounts, they suggested that "the
jerks" may have been triggered by epilepsy, which was then imitated by
hypersuggestible group members. The researchers stated that among the
throngs of participants "there were perhaps some who had epilepsy. Some
meetings were held during the evening with only light from torches flick-
ering in the night. Did this trigger any seizures? Did those few with epilepsy
set the stage by example to trigger mass hysterical response from others?"[27]

The outbreak of illness symptoms coinciding with the broadcast of
the Pokémon television program fit the profile of mass anxiety hysteria
triggered by either observing someone exhibit a genuine seizure or upon
learning of the illness reports through the media or by word-of-mouth.
While epidemics of mass anxiety hysteria are often triggered by the sudden stress and uncertainty surrounding a single index case experiencing
a real illness, a few mass anxiety hysterias have a viral, bacterial, or toxicological component that triggers or contributes to the psychogenic illness outbreak.

One example is the outbreak of collapse in three British secondary
schools that coincided with a viral infection.[28] Radovanovic noted that an
influx in respiratory infections accompanied an epidemic hysteria episode
in the former Yugoslavia during 1990.[29] Another case involved three fourth
graders at a California school who on September 23, 1998, inadvertently
ingested LSD and were hospitalized. Eleven other students who had sam-
pled a white powder from a vial believed that they too had ingested LSD
and were hospitalized. Despite exhibiting symptoms ranging from violence to hallucinations, tests were negative, and the pupils were released
within a few hours.[30] In other instances, actual events, such as a chemical

leak, serve as a trigger. For example, on February 19, 1986, nineteen workers at a U.S. compressor-manufacturing factory were suddenly stricken with headaches, nausea, and light-headedness after detecting a harmless odor. Following extensive tests with negative results, investigators determined that a recent real hazardous chemical exposure at the same facility, and media conjecture over plant safety, fostered epidemic hysteria.[31]

The Pokémon episode meets many of the criteria for epidemic hysteria. Many of the children's symptoms had no identifiable organic basis, other than the verified cases of seizures. The symptoms reported were minor and short-lived. The victims were nearly exclusively schoolchildren in early adolescence. Anxiety from dramatic media reports of the first wave of illnesses was evident. Most of the Pokémon-induced symptoms, such as headaches, dizziness, and vomiting, are less typical of seizures than of mass hysteria. Conversely, symptoms that are typically associated with seizures (e.g., drooling, stiffness, tongue-biting) were not found in Pokémon victims. Three other symptoms, convulsions, fainting, and nausea, that were found in Pokémon victims are also associated with both seizures and mass hysteria.

It is important to distinguish seizures from epilepsy. A seizure is a symptom of epilepsy, which in turn is a general term for an underlying tendency of the brain to produce electrical energy that disrupts brain functions. Seizures can be brought about through various ways (e.g., a lack of oxygen, brain injury, high fever), and one seizure does not in itself establish epilepsy. There are several types of seizures. Research by Tobimatsu et al. found that the Pokémon victims had generalized tonic-clonic seizures.

While the mass media is rarely implicated in triggering epidemic hysteria outbreaks, the reporting of existing outbreaks typically exacerbates the situation. Media reports and publicity fuel the hysteria as news of the affliction spreads, planting the idea or concern in the community while reinforcing and validating the veracity of the illness for the initial victims.[32] This may result in emotionally charged public meetings and the reporting of misinformation[33] or in social-protest movements that thrive on media publicity surrounding a hysteria outbreak.[34] In the Pokémon episode, the jump in reported cases is strong evidence for the role the media played in the episode. According to news accounts of the time, the number of children said to be affected was around seven hundred the evening of the Pokémon episode. The next morning, the episode dominated the Japanese news. Japanese children who had not heard about their peers from the news or from their parents learned of it that morning, when the seizures "were the talk of the schoolyards."[35] Once the children had a chance to hear panicky accounts of what had happened through the media, their friends, and their schools, the number of children reported the next day to have been affected increased to twelve thousand.

One common component of mass hysteria is an exaggerated overestimation of risk to a perceived threat. For hysteria to spread, those affected must not only perceive the risk as real and present, but they must also believe they are vulnerable to it. Researchers surveying epileptics have found that "[m]ore than a quarter of those surveyed indicated that they thought that a substantially greater proportion of people with epilepsy were at risk from [video games] than the estimated real risk suggests. One in thirteen perceived that every individual with epilepsy is at risk of a seizure as a result from playing video games.... [T]he proportion of individuals with epilepsy surveyed who saw themselves to be at risk from video games is two to three times the estimated real risk."[36] The risk overestimation may have been associated with the cartoon version of Pokémon.

Hysteria, Epilepsy or Both?

The late Canadian cultural theorist Marshall McLuhan observed that the technological revolution has recreated the world in the form of a "global village."[37] The continuing reliance on mass communications, especially television and the Internet, gives the novel nature of the Pokémon illness outbreak added significance. Technological innovations are occurring at unprecedented rates and have the potential to influence significant masses of people beyond the typical number in traditional mass hysteria episodes. Rapid and perpetual technological innovations are changing the face of how and where we work, how we interact with others, how we play, and many other facets of everyday life. Whereas epidemic hysterias in earlier periods were limited by geography, they now have free and wide access to the globe in seconds. The 1938 Martian-panic radio broadcast exemplified the potential impact of the mass media in spreading social delusions, as it is estimated to have frightened about 1.2 million Americans.[38] The incident is not considered a case of epidemic hysteria however, as illness symptoms were not associated with the episode.[39]

While a small number of people affected by the Pokémon animation were confirmed as suffering from photoepilepsy, most of those examined or retrospectively surveyed by physicians clearly were not. Indeed, the incidence of photosensitive epilepsy is estimated at one in five thousand.[40] Such an incidence (.025 percent of the population) cannot explain the number of children affected (in some cases nearly 7 percent of the viewers).

The question remains, what were the vast majority of children experiencing? Inexplicably, no outbreaks of mass illness symptoms associated with viewing television were ever reported before and have not been reported since the episode. The large numbers of children affected and the transient, benign nature of their symptoms—typical of anxiety—is consistent with a diagnosis of mass anxiety hysteria.

Given the chameleonlike nature of hysteria, it should not be surprising that as we enter the new millennium, it would manifest in a television-related setting. Epidemic hysteria has been known to take many forms, depending on the historical and cultural context. These include shaking, crying and glossolalia accompanying Melanesian cargo cults and Holy Spirit movements,[41] running and laughing fits in central and southern Africa,[42] "demon possession" in Malaysia,[43] fainting in response to imaginary bug bites in the southern United States,[44] clay-eating among Australian Aborigines,[45] and strange odors in modern Western schools and factories.

In 1959, Marshall McLuhan first proclaimed that in the case of mass communication, especially television, "The medium is the message."[46] In other words, it is not the content per se, but the mode of communication that is paramount. More of our senses are engaged during the act of communicating to the masses.

In one sense, the cause of the Pokémon illness is irrelevant. If the Pokémon illness symptoms resulted in mass photosensitive epilepsy, the case is unprecedented. If it is epidemic hysteria, it is also without precedence given the large numbers affected. The most likely explanation is a combination of both. Mass photosensitive epilepsy engendered a media-nurtured overlay of mass hysteria, which accounted for the vast majority of cases. The Pokémon episode may be a harbinger of future technological hysterias that have the capacity to affect unprecedented numbers of people at a phenomenal speed.

Chapter 7

Rethinking the Medieval Dancing Mania

One morning, without warning, the streets were filled.... They danced together, ceaselessly, for hours or days, and in wild delirium, the dancers collapsed and fell to the ground exhausted, groaning and sighing as if in the agonies of death. When recuperated, they swathed themselves tightly with cloth around their waists and resumed their convulsive movements. They contorted their bodies, writhing, screaming and jumping in a mad frenzy. One by one they fell from exhaustion.... Many later claimed that they had seen the walls of heaven split open and that Jesus and the Virgin Mary had appeared before them. — Benjamin Gordon[1]

No book on epidemic hysteria and mass delusions would be complete without some discussion of dancing mania. Pick up a textbook on abnormal psychology, and in the first chapter you are likely to find a description of the medieval dance "plagues." Popularly known as St. Vitus's dance, between the eleventh and seventeenth centuries this seemingly bizarre behavior swept across Europe. Tens of thousands of people joined in frenzied public orgies and wild dances lasting for days and sometimes weeks. It is little wonder that psychiatrists and medical historians typify these episodes as epidemic hysteria affecting people who were overwhelmed by unprecedented stresses of the period. The behavior is totally bizarre and chaotic by any modern standard. Groups of people seemed to go temporarily insane.

During outbreaks, many people ripped off their clothes and paraded around naked. Others screamed and pleaded to be tossed into the air. Some danced furiously in what observers described as strange, colorful attire. Some placed wreathes on their heads and held wooden sticks. A few reportedly laughed or wept to the point of death. People screamed and made

St. Vitus's Dance victims go on pilgrimage to Echtemach, Luxembourg. (Courtesy of the Mary Evans Picture Library.)

obscene gestures. Others squealed or howled like animals. Some rolled themselves in the dirt like pigs or took great delight in being struck on the soles of their feet. After a while, some dancers would fall into trances or begin twitching uncontrollably. As if this was not strange enough, in several reports it was said that dancers could not stand pointed shoes or the color red, often becoming violent upon seeing either.

An Italian variant was known as tarantism. Victims were believed to have been poisoned by the bite of the tarantula spider, or less commonly a scorpion, for which the only cure was thought to be frenetic dancing to certain music, which supposedly dissipated the venom from their blood.[2] Converse to their European neighbors to the north, *tarantati*— as victims were known, could not stand seeing the color black. They sometimes tied vines around their necks and struck each other with whips, or they made believe they were fencing with swords. Many revelers drank heavy amounts of wine. All of this bedlam occurred to the accompaniment of music and singing. Many of the dancers said they longed for the sea, perhaps because of the summer heat and their physical exertion. Some accounts tell of dancers jumping into the sea and perishing.[3]

The term "dancing mania" is derived from the Greek word "*choros*," a dance, and "*mania*," madness. The literal translation of "*choros mania*" is "dancing madness." The name was adopted after about two hundred people danced so spiritedly on a bridge above the Maas River in Germany in 1278 that it collapsed, killing many participants. Survivors were treated in a nearby chapel dedicated to St. Vitus, and many were reportedly restored to full health. Prior to the twentieth century, it was commonly referred to as epidemic chorea or choreomania. The word "chorea" was erroneously evoked to describe these behaviors. Participants were often thought to be exhibiting symptoms of chorea, a central nervous system disorder that causes irregular jerking movements that can resemble dancing.

"Tarantism" and "dancing mania" are often used synonymously because they share overlapping features. Tarantism was mainly confined to Southern Italy. Gloyne described it as the "mass hysterical reaction" to perceived bites of the tarantula spider.[4] The first recorded episodes appeared in the thirteenth century and persisted on a widespread scale in Southern Europe for four hundred years, reaching its height in the seventeenth century, after which it virtually disappeared. Small annual episodes persisted in Southern Italy well into the twentieth century. Hans Schadewaldt investigated an outbreak in Wardo in 1957.[5] Italian religious-history professor Ernesto de Martino identified thirty-five tarantism cases near Galatina in 1959. De Martino conducted his survey between June 28 and 30, as June 29 is the festival day of St. Peter and St. Paul. On that day, "victims" travel from regional villages to the chapel of St. Paul to obtain a cure for various ailments.[6] More recently, it has been observed near Sardinia, Italy.[7]

Medieval tarantism was almost always reported at the height of the hot, dry summer months of July and August:

> People, asleep or awake, would suddenly jump up, feeling an acute pain like the sting of a bee. Some saw the spider, others did not, but they knew that it must be the tarantula. They ran out of the house into the street, to the market place dancing in great excitement. Soon they were joined by others who like them had just been bitten, or by people who had been stung in previous years, for the disease was never quite cured. The poison remained in the body and was reactivated every year by the heat of summer.... Music and dancing were the only effective remedies, and people were known to have died within an hour or in a few days because music was not available.[8]

Symptoms included headache, giddiness, breathlessness, fainting, trembling, twitching, appetite loss, soreness, and visions. Sometimes it was claimed that a sore or swelling was caused by a tarantula bite, but such assertions were difficult to verify because the bite resembled those of other insects. The dance-frenzy symptoms resemble typical modern episodes of epidemic hysteria, in addition to expected reactions from exhaustive physical activity or excessive alcohol use.

Many psychiatrists label tarantism as a form of epidemic hysteria due to its psychological character and the claims that mostly females were affected.[9] Early physicians theorized that a venomous species of tarantula found only near the Italian state of Apulia was producing sporadic tarantism symptoms each summer, but tests on spiders of the region have not substantiated this.[10] *Latrodectus tarantula* is a nonaggressive, slow-moving spider common in Apulia that can produce psychoactive effects in people it bites. In severe cases, its bite may temporarily mimic many tarantism symptoms, including twitching and shaking of limbs, vomiting, weakness, nausea, muscle pains, and hallucinations.[11] Ironically, *Lycosa tarantula* was commonly blamed for tarantism symptoms because it is larger, more aggressive, ferocious-looking, and has a painful bite. When de Martino conducted his study in 1959, he surveyed doctors in the region and found that authentic cases of residents being poisoned by either spider were virtually unheard of. This is not surprising because the same people would report relapses annually about the same time of year. *Latrodectus tarantula* is also found in other countries where tarantism does not occur,[12] including the United States.[13] Could a tarantula with a hallucinogenic bite have once existed near Apulia but since died out? It is unlikely. During the Middle Ages, some people devised a clever test to determine if Apulian tarantulas were any more poisonous than others. They tried shipping tarantulas from Apulia to different parts of Italy, but people didn't "catch" tarantism from them or experience hallucinations.[14] It is doubtful that some other insect or agent caused the attacks, as most victims did not even claim to have been bitten and would only participate in tarantism episodes at designated times.

Clearly, most cases were unrelated to spider bites. Another psychological aspect was the only reliable cure: dancing to certain music. Victims would typically perform one of numerous versions of the tarantella, rapid-tempo music with brief, repetitive phrases that mount in intensity. These performances also allowed victims to exhibit social behavior that was prohibited during any other time. Dancing persisted intermittently for hours and days— even weeks. Participants would eventually proclaim themselves cured for the remainder of the summer, only to relapse in subsequent summers. Many never claimed to have been bitten, but were believed to have been infected by those who had been bitten, or by brushing against a spider. All that was needed to reactivate the venom was to hear the strains of certain music being played to cure those who had already been bitten.

Dancing Manias

A variation of tarantism spread throughout much of Europe between the thirteenth and seventeenth centuries, where it was known as the dancing mania or St. Vitus's dance, because participants often ended their processions in the vicinity of chapels and shrines dedicated to this saint. Like tarantism, outbreaks seized groups of people who engaged in frenzied dancing that lasted intermittently for days or weeks. These activities were typically accompanied by symptoms similar to tarantism: screaming, hallucinations, convulsive movements, chest pains, hyperventilation, crude sexual gestures, and outright sexual intercourse. Instead of spider bites, participants usually claimed that they were possessed by demons who had induced an uncontrollable urge to dance. Like tarantism, music was typically played during episodes and was considered to be an effective remedy. Social scientists typified victims as females who were maladjusted, deviant, irrational, or mentally disturbed. Detailed accounts of many episodes appear in a classic book by German physician Justus Hecker, *Epidemics of the Middle Ages* (1844). He considered the origin of these epidemics as "morbid sympathy" because they often coincided with periods of severe disease, such as widespread pessimism and despair after the Black Death.[15] This epic plague, which by some estimates killed half of the world's population at that time, subsided about twenty years prior to 1374, the year that most scholars identify with the onset of the dance mania.

As with tarantism, dance manias occurred spontaneously. Participants, mostly mentally disturbed females, were unable to control their actions. Influential New York University psychiatrists Harold Kaplan and Benjamin Sadock stated that the manias represented "collective mental disorder."[16] Carson and his colleagues viewed St. Vitus's dance and tarantism as collective hysterical disorders.[17] A researcher in abnormal psychology, Ronald Comer of Princeton University, used the term "mass madness."[18]

The dance manias occurred so long ago that it is hard to be certain what actually happened. The most popular explanation today is that many participants were psychologically disturbed. Without a doubt, some were. Prominent medical historians such as Henry Sigerist, George Mora, and George Rosen each noted aspects of Greek or Roman rituals in tarantism, but each assumed that the participants used these rites to work themselves into frenzied states of physical and mental disturbance to experience cathartic reactions to intolerable social conditions. They also assume that most participants were hysterics. In other words, the victims used these ancient festivals or carnivals to whip themselves into a frenzied state of physical and emotional exhaustion that allowed them to relieve pent-up stress while fostering a group sense of togetherness.

Mora wrote that tarantism and dance manias used rituals as psychotherapeutic attempts to cope with individual or societal maladjustments that fostered mental disturbances.[19] Sigerist held a similar view. An abnormal psychology text by Robert Carson of Duke University cited Sigerist to support the view that St. Vitus's dance and tarantism were similar to ancient Greek orgiastic rites that Christian authorities had outlawed but that were secretly practiced anyway. Carson jumped to the wild conclusion that these "secret gatherings … probably led to considerable guilt and conflict" that triggered collective hysterical disorders.[20] Dance frenzies appeared most often during periods of crop failures, famine, floods, epidemics, and social upheaval, leading Rosen to conclude that stress triggered widespread hysteria.[21] Yet these very tragedies prompted attempts at divine intervention through ritualized dancing and often produced trance and possession states. Indeed, many symptoms associated with tarantism and dancing mania are consistent with sleep deprivation, excessive alcohol consumption, emotional excitement, and vigorous, prolonged physical activity. A German chronicle reported that during a dance frenzy at Strasbourg in 1418, many people fasted for several days and nights.[22] Could it be that many victims were simply suffering from exhaustion in their attempts to receive divine favor and were not hysterical?

The European dancing manias and their Italian variant, tarantism, are portrayed within the psychiatric literature as spontaneous, stress-induced outbursts of psychological disturbance that mainly affected females. This depiction is based on the selective use of period quotations by medical historians such as George Rosen and Henry Sigerist, who were reflecting popular stereotypes of female susceptibility to mental disorders. But based on Backman's translations of medieval European chronicles describing these events, many firsthand, it is evident that present-day depictions of dancing manias are wrong. Contrary to popular psychiatric portrayals, females were not overrepresented, and episodes were not spontaneous but structured, involving unfamiliar religious sects engaging in strange or unfamiliar customs that were redefined as a behavioral abnormality.[23] Let us examine the evidence.

First, as to the claim that most dancers were mentally disturbed, period chronicles reveal that most participants did not reside in the municipalities where the manias occurred but hailed from other regions, traveling through communities as they sought out shrines and churchyards to perform in. As a result, they would naturally have had unfamiliar customs. The largest and best-documented dance plague, that of 1374 involving throngs of dancers in Germany and Holland, involved pilgrims from Bohemia, Hungary, Poland, Carinthia, Austria, and Germany who were joined by locals along the route.[24]

Although they exhibited actions that were part of the Christian tradition and paid homage to Jesus, Mary, and saints at chapels and shrines, the dancers were described as strange because other behaviors were foreign. Radulphus de Rivo's chronicle *Decani Tongrensis* stated that "in their songs they uttered the names of devils never before heard of ... this strange sect." The *Chronicon Belgicum Magnum* described them as "a sect of dancers." The actions of dancers were often depicted as immoral because there was much uninhibited sexual intercourse. The chronicle of C. Browerus, *Abtiquitatum et Annalium Trevirensium*, stated, "They indulged in disgraceful immodesty, for many women, during this shameless dance and mock-bridal singing, bared their bosoms, while others of their own accord offered their virtue." In *A Chronicle of Early Roman Kings and Emperors*, it states that many engaged in "loose living with the women and young girls who shamelessly wandered about in remote places under the cover of night." Backman asserted that most of the dancers were pilgrims of Bohemian and Czech origin. During this period, Czechs and Bohemians were noted for their "immorality," including prostitution and annual festivals where there was the free partaking of sex.[25]

What about the claim that there was a spontaneous, uncontrollable urge to dance? Period chronicles reveal that dance manias were mainly composed of pilgrims engaging in emotional, highly structured displays of worship that occasionally attracted locals. This social patterning is evident in the firsthand account of September 11, 1374, by Jean d'Outremeuse in his chronicle *La Geste de Liege*. He wrote that "there came from the north to Liege ... a company of persons who all danced continually. They were linked with clothes, and they jumped and leaped.... They called loudly on St. John the Baptist and fiercely clapped their hands." Slichtenhorst, in describing the dance frenzy of 1375 and 1376 in France, Germany, and Gelderland (now southwestern Holland), noted that participants "went in couples, and with every couple was another single person ... they danced, leaped and sang, and embraced each other in friendly fashion."[26]

A similar pattern was evident in tarantism. While *taranti*, as victims were also known, were typically described as participating in uncontrollable behaviors in chaotic, frenzied throngs like modern-day ecstatic religious sects, adherents worshipped in a set pattern. Australian medical historian and tarantism expert Jean Russell stated that victims would typically commence dancing at sunrise, stop during midday to sleep and sweat, then bathe before the resumption of dancing until evening, when they would again sleep and sweat, consume a light meal, then sleep until sunrise. This ritual was usually repeated over four or five days and sometimes for weeks.[27]

Clearly, tarantism episodes were not spontaneous, and the same is true of dance manias. German magistrates even contracted musicians to play for participants and serve as dancing companions. The latter was intended to reduce injuries and mischief during the procession to the St. Vitus chapel.[28] In the case of tarantism, during the Apulian summer, musicians holding everything from pipes and harps to cithers and drums traveled the countryside and made a living by playing curative tunes.

Hecker stated that the dancing mania was a "half-heathen, half-christian festival" that incorporated "the kindling of the 'Nodfyr,' which was forbidden them by St. Boniface"[29] into the festival of St. John's day as early as the fourth century. This ritual involved leaping through smoke or flames, which was believed to protect participants from various diseases over the ensuing year. A central feature of the dance frenzy was leaping or jumping continuously for up to several hours through what were claimed to be invisible fires, until dancers collapsed in exhaustion.

Not only were episodes scripted, but dance processions were swollen by spectators,[30] including children searching for parents who were among the dancers and vice versa.[31] Some onlookers were threatened with harm for refusing to dance.[32] Many took part out of loneliness and carnal pleasures; others were curious or sought exhilaration.[33] Hecker remarked that "numerous beggars, stimulated by vice and misery, availed themselves of this new complaint to gain a temporary livelihood," while gangs of vagabonds imitated the dance, roving "from place to place seeking maintenance and adventures."[34] Similar observations have been noted of tarantism episodes.

And what of claims that most dancers were hysterical females? A revisiting of the descriptions of dancing manias based on early chronicles of these events shows that both men and women were equally affected. Petrus de Herenthal's chronicle *Vita Gregorii XI* stated: "Persons of both sexes ... danced." Radulpho de Rivo's *Decani Tongrensis* said: "persons of both sexes, possessed by devils and half naked, set wreathes on their heads, and began their dances." Johannes de Beka's chronicle stated that in 1385, "there spread along the Rhine ... a strange plague ... whereby persons of both sexes, in great crowds ... danced and sang, both inside and outside of churches, till they were so weary that they fell to the ground." According to *Koelhoff's Chronicle* published in 1499, "Many people, men and women, old and young, had the disease [of dancing mania]." This gender mixture is evident in more recent tarantism reports near Sardinia, Italy, where Gallini found that the vast majority of "victims" were male,[35] while de Martino reported that most participants that he investigated near Apulia were female.[36]

What Caused the Dance Manias?

Ergot poisoning has been blamed for hallucinations and convulsions accompanying the dance mania. Nicknamed St. Anthony's Fire, ergotism coincided with floods and wet growing seasons that foster the growth of the fungus *claviceps purpura*, which thrives in damp conditions and forms on cultivated grains, especially rye. While this could account for some symptoms, many outbreaks did not coincide with floods, wet growing seasons, or harvest periods. Convulsive ergotism could cause bizarre behavior and hallucinations, but chronic ergotism was more common and typically resulted in the loss of fingers and toes from gangrene, a feature that is distinctly not associated with dance manias.[37] As for tarantism, most episodes occurred only during July and August and were triggered by real or imaginary spider bites, by hearing music, or by seeing others dance. Tarantism involved structured annual rituals. Also, while rye was a key crop in central and northern Europe, it was uncommon in Italy. Surely a few participants were hysterics, epileptics, mentally disturbed, or even delusional from ergot, but the large percentage of the populations affected and the circumstances and timing of outbreaks suggest otherwise. Episodes were pandemic, meaning that they occurred across a wide area and affected a very high proportion of the population.[38]

So, what is the most likely explanation for dance manias? I think the most likely explanation is ancient ritual. There were religious sects who gained followers as they made pilgrimages through Europe to receive divine favor during years of turmoil. Their symptoms such as visions, fainting, and tremor can be expected for any large population engaging in prolonged dancing, zealous worship, and fasting. Eventually, this ritual grew out of fashion as they found other means to fulfill their needs. Tarantism was a regional variant of the dancing mania that developed into a local tradition and was mainly confined to southern Italy. Apulia had once been part of Greek culture, but once Christianity took control, church leaders outlawed the classical Greek practices involving the catharsis of built-up stress or Dionysian festivals that were characterized by drunken orgies and violence where pretty much any behavior was acceptable.[39] As a way to circumvent the church and legitimize dancing, "the idea emerged that a person poisoned by spider bite had to dance to be 'cured.'"[40]

This discussion of the dancing mania shows the importance of consulting original sources and the realization that we are all products of our social, cultural, and historical milieu. When assessing normality, it is vital to look at the context of the participants and those making the evaluations.

Could phenomena similar to the dance manias return? Yes. The medieval dancing manias have a modern-day counterpart: all-night dance raves.[41] Participants in both activities engage in prolonged dancing to music and behavior deemed as nonconformist or bizarre (but not necessarily pathological) by those outside of the subculture. Dance-mania participants typically ingested wine, while their contemporaries prefer mood-altering or hallucinogenic substances.

Raves began in the mid–1980s in the United States and Great Britain as clandestine gatherings at secret venues, with the location revealed just hours before the event to deter law-enforcement surveillance. Sigerist contended that St. Vitus's dance was similar to ancient Greek orgiastic rites that had been outlawed by Christian authorities but were secretly practiced. Eventually, they grew more open when authorities realized the could not suppress them.[42] In a bid to reduce harm to participants, volunteer groups attend raves to offer safety advice. Some government agencies, such as in Canada, sanction supervised raves. Six hundred and fifty years ago, German magistrates paid musicians to perform for participants and provided dancing companions as a form of social control.[43]

Ravers represent a mixture of male and female participants who espouse counterculture values. A prominent harm-reduction strategy at supervised raves includes taking dancing breaks and drinking plenty of fluids. Medieval dance mania and tarantism participants also adhered to a discernible pattern that involved taking breaks for eating, bathing and sleeping.[44] Modern-day raves may be similar to the dance manias within a different historical and cultural context, fulfilling similar social and psychological needs.

SECTION FOUR

Collective Delusions

Chapter 8

Penis Panics:
Collective Delusions
Outside the West

I woke up at midnight and felt sore and numb in my genitals. I felt ... [my penis] was shrinking, disappearing. I yelled for help, my family and neighbours came and held my penis. They covered me with a fishnet and beat me with branches of a peach tree.... The peach tree branches are the best to drive out ghosts or devils. They said they'd catch the ghost in the net. They were also beating drums and setting off firecrackers....They had to repeat the procedure until I was well again, until the ghost was killed by the beating. — Report by an 18-year-old agriculture student with no family history of mental illness at Leizhou Peninsula, China, near the end of a major penis-shrinking scare in 1985.[1]

When mass delusions occur in non–Western countries, it may be tempting to think of the people in the cultures affected as backward, primitive, or uneducated. It cannot be overemphasized that collective delusions and epidemics of hysteria are limited only by plausibility. If an idea is believable to members of a particular group, then it can become real in its consequences.

In parts of Asia, entire regions are occasionally overwhelmed by terror-stricken men who believe that their penises are shriveling up or retracting into their bodies, whereupon they will die. Those affected often place clamps or strings onto the precious organ or have family members hold the penis in relays until an appropriate treatment is obtained, often from traditional healers. Occasionally women are affected, believing their breasts

The author is grateful to Wolfgang G. Jilek and Louise Jilek-Aall for their co-authoring of this chapter.

or labia are being sucked into their bodies. Episodes can endure for weeks or months and affect thousands. Psychiatrists are divided as to the cause of these imaginary scares. Some believe that it is a form of group psychosis triggered by stress, while others view it as mass hysteria. How can any sane group of people become so out of touch with reality as to believe that their sex organs are shrinking and disappearing? We will try to unravel this mystery by briefly describing several genital-shrinking scares, their similarities, and the factors involved in triggering them. While these episodes may appear humorous to Westerners, they offer a valuable lesson because they show how vulnerable we all are to mass delusion.

While genitalia-shrinking is known by a variety of names in different cultures, psychiatrists refer to it by the generic term "*koro.*" A Malay word of uncertain derivation, *koro* may have arisen from the Malay word "*keruk,*" meaning "to shrink,"[2] although it is more likely a reflection of the Malaysian-Indonesian words for "tortoise" (*kura, kura-kura,* and *kuro*). In these countries, the penis, especially the glans or tip, is commonly referred to as a tortoise head. This led Dutch scientist P. M. Van Wulfften-Palthe to conclude that this is how the modern term "*koro*" most likely got its name: "The fact that a tortoise can withdraw its head with its wrinkled neck under its shell literally into its body, suggested ... the mechanism ... in '*koro*' ('*kura*') and gave it its name."[3]

According to Van Wulfften-Palthe, the term "*lasa koro,*" ("shrinking penis") was first published in 1874 in Matthes's *Dictionary of the Buginese Language* of Celebes, now Sulawesi.[4] In traditional Chinese medicine, the equivalent term is "*suo-yang,*" denoting reduction of the "warm" male principle *yang*, which results in an excess of the "cold" female principle *yin* and thereby disturbs the *yin-yang* equilibrium essential for the preservation of health. This doctrine is formulated in the *Canon of Internal Medicine* of Yellow Emperor Huang Di, compiled 600–400 B.C., in which *suo-yang* is already referred to as a serious disorder. In traditional Chinese medicine, ancient revitalizing remedies are indicated for the treatment of *suo-yang*.[5] In his *New Collection of Remedies of Value*, published in 1834, Bao Sian Ow wrote that *suo-yang* was a life-threatening condition if the retraction of the genitalia into the abdomen could not be prevented.

At the turn of the nineteenth to the twentieth century, the *koro* syndrome became known to Western medicine through the clinical reports of Dutch and British physicians working in Southeast Asia. Psychoanalytically oriented psychiatry assumed it to represent a concrete manifestation of oedipal castration anxiety, while the later school of ethnopsychiatry viewed the *koro* syndrome as culturally determined. Psychiatrist Pow Meng Yap elevated *koro/suo-yang* to a classical paradigm of what he termed "culture-bound syndromes," assuming it to be the product of popular conceptions of traditional Chinese medical theory imported into other parts of Asia by Chinese immigrants.[6] However, it has since become evident that the *koro* syndrome has for ages been endemic in populations not exposed to Chinese cultural influence (e.g., among aboriginal tribes on the island of Flores[7] or among Muslim inhabitants of interior Mindanao, Philippines).[8] Not a single Chinese person was affected during *koro* epidemics in Thailand, India, or Nigeria. Apart from ethnographic data showing that the Freudian oedipal complex is far from universal, the notion of *koro* manifesting oedipal castration anxiety is dispelled by the fact that females have also been affected by it. What the manifestations of *koro* in quite diverse populations of Asia and Africa have in common is that they are triggered by imaginary threats to procreative ability in cultures that place a very strong emphasis on this ability. This also explains why some young male victims of *koro* or *suo-yang* suffer at the same time from anxiety over "semen loss," which in several traditional Asian medical systems is listed under specific terms denoting a serious malady, considered the cause of declining energy and virility, and is the basis for multiple, vague somatic complaints.

The first European medical report of a *koro/suo-yang* epidemic in Asia was published by the French physician J. Legendre, who in 1907 observed a sudden but short-lasting mass panic of penis-shrinking among young students in Szechuan, western China. He considered the condition an "Asiatic psychosis" associated with the fear of being unable to procreate, "terrifying to the Chinese."[9]

The first well-documented outbreak in recent times occurred in October and November 1967, when hospitals in Singapore were inundated by frantic citizens who were convinced that their penises were shrinking and would eventually disappear, at which time, many believed, death would result. Victims used everything from rubber bands to clothes pins in desperate efforts to prevent further perceived retraction. These methods occasionally resulted in severe organ damage and some pretty sore penises. At the height of the scare, the Singapore Hospital treated about seventy-five cases in a single day. As the symptoms were patterned according to the *suo-yang* descriptions in classical texts of Chinese medicine, the conclusion of the investigating *Koro* Study Team was that indoctrination with traditional Chinese medical theory was a causative factor.[10] However, only 25 percent of the *koro* victims had any prior knowledge of such a theory. In fact, the mass panic started with rumors that pork had been poisoned by the swine-fever vaccination of pigs before slaughter, which was supposed to cause genital shrinkage. One erroneous report even claimed that a pig dropped dead immediately after inoculation when its penis retracted! This *koro* epidemic in Singapore happened at a time of political uncertainty. British withdrawal from the Malayan peninsula occurred amid high ethnic tension between the Muslim Malays, who never eat pork, and the pork-eating Chinese, many of whom suspected the Malays of engineering the alleged swine poisoning.[11]

The panic abruptly ended when the Singapore Medical Association and Health Ministry held public news conferences to dispel fears. Writing in the prestigious *British Journal of Psychiatry*, Singaporian doctor C.T. Mun described two typical cases. In one, a pale sixteen-year-old boy rushed into the clinic accompanied by his parents. The boy was clutching his penis. After reassurance and a sedative were provided, there was no recurrence. The frightened boy said that he had heard the rumors of contaminated pork at school but had eaten pork that morning. Upon urinating, his penis appeared to have shrunk. At that point, he hung on for all he was worth and shouted for help. In a second case, a mother dashed into the clinic clutching the penis of her four-month-old baby and frantically asking for help. Dr. Mun wrote that "the child had not been well for two days with cold and a little diarrhoea. The mother was changing his napkin ... when the child had colic and screamed. The mother saw the penis getting smaller and the child screamed, and [she] thought he had *koro*. She had previously heard the rumours. The mother was first reassured, and the baby's cold and diarrhoea treated. The child was all right after that."[12]

Epidemics of *koro/suo-yang* (in Cantonese, *suk-yang*) are well known in South China. In the southern part of Guangdong province, outbreaks of genital-shrinking panics were officially recorded in 1865, 1948, 1955, 1966, 1974, 1984-1985, and 1987. Most of these years were times of political and socioeconomic unrest in China. A major *koro* epidemic struck the area of Leizhou Peninsula and Hainan Island between the summer of 1984 and the summer of 1985.[13] Several thousand people were affected, most of them males in younger age groups but also young females and even some small children — as diagnosed by the parents. Toward the end of this epidemic, Wolfgang Jilek and Louise Jilek-Aall went to the area to interview adult victims of diverse educational background, among them a college student and an accountant. All admitted to a terrifying fear of death when they felt their genitals were shrinking and retracting. They described concomitant symptoms of intense psychomotor agitation and autonomous nervous system excitation. Ubiquitous among the area population was the belief in female fox spirits possessing young men and causing the disappearance of their genitalia. Decades of indoctrination of the atheist Marxist ideology of communist China have not changed the traditional belief

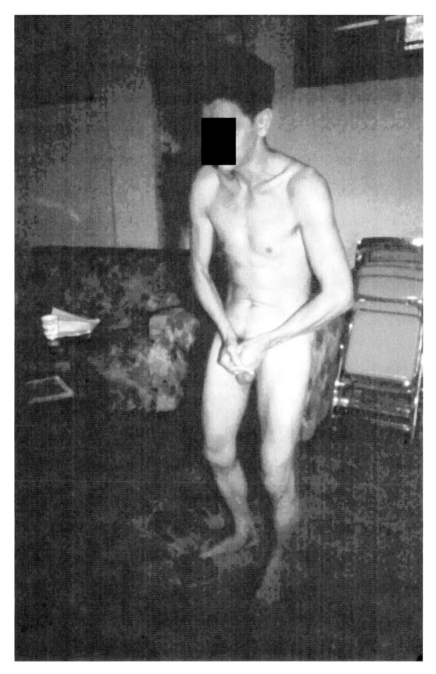

Figure 8.1: Acute *koro* attack during the 1985 epidemic in Guangdong, China. (Photograph by Dr. Wolfgang Jilek.)

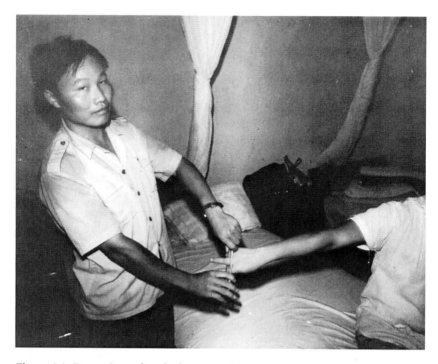

Figure 8.2: Extracting a female fox spirit from a *koro* sufferer by squeezing and pulling the middle finger with chopsticks during a *koro* epidemic in southern Guangdong province, China, in 1985. (Photograph by Dr. Wolfgang Jilek.)

in supernatural fox maidens with magic powers, who roam the countryside in search of male victims. The female fox ghost transforming herself into a *femme fatale* is a classical theme of Chinese literature.[14] During the 1984-1985 epidemic, such a beautiful, bewitching, and castrating fox maiden called Hu Li Jing was supposedly seen in the area trying to rob young men of their precious organs and thereby threatening their lives. In line with the popular belief in possession by evil fox spirits, therapeutic efforts were focused on exorcising the dangerous intruders from the patients and, at the same time, preventing the supposedly lethal total retraction of the genitalia by holding on to them by all means available. Exorcism was performed by beating the evil spirit out of the possessed victim with sandals, shoes, or more traditionally, with branches of the peach tree, which in China has the reputation of warding off demons. The possessed person received the blows and was covered with a fishnet to catch the exiting fox spirit. Often, the possessed person's left middle finger was squeezed between chopsticks and pulled to remove the supernatural intruder. To chase the evil spirits from the neighborhood, people produced

Figure 8.3: Dr. Wolfgang Jilek and Chinese colleagues examining *koro* sufferers during the 1985 epidemic in the southern Guangdong province. (Photograph by Dr. Louise Jilek-Aall.)

loud noises by yelling, by beating drums, gongs, or metal barrels, or by setting off fire crackers—all of which had the effect of exacerbating collective anxiety in the community. Supernatural protection against the evil spirits causing *suo-yang* was sought by displaying images of the divine physician Zhong Kui or Mao-Tse-tung, who in some rural areas of China is today identified with a demon-slaying god. Each of the 232 victims surveyed by University of Hawaii psychiatrist Wen-Shing Tseng and his colleagues was convinced that an evil, female fox spirit was the culprit, while 76 percent of those affected had witnessed others being "rescued." Most of these cases occurred at night following a chilly sensation, which would appear before a feeling of penile shrinkage. Tseng and his researchers reported, "Thinking this [chill] to be a fatal sign and believing that they were affected by an evil ghost, they [*koro* victims] became panic stricken and tried to pull at their penises, while, at the same time, shouting for help."[15] Interestingly, several children reported shrinkage of their tongue, nose, and ears, reflecting the prevalent ancient Chinese belief that any male (yang) organs can shrink or retract. Tseng investigated another episode in 1987 that affected at least three hundred residents on the Leizhou Peninsula of Guangdong province.

Tseng has sought to determine why episodes repeatedly occur in the area of Leizhou Peninsula and Hainan Island but never spread to the principal section of Guangdong province or other parts of China. Another question is why only certain residents in a region report *koro*, while others do not. It was found that those affected held the more intense *koro*-related folk beliefs relative to a control group from the adjacent nonaffected area, helping to explain "why each time the *koro* epidemic spread from the Peninsula, it would cease when it reached the urban area of Guangzhou (Canton), where the people are more educated and hold less belief in *koro*."[16]

A *koro* outbreak occurred in Thailand in November and December 1976. Originating in the area bordering Vietnam, the epidemic moved inland. It eventually affected at least two thousand people in the northeastern provinces of the country, primarily rural Thai residents and not one member of the sizable Chinese minority. Jilek and Jilek-Aall traveled in the area at the time and were the first to report their observations in scientific journals in the West.[17] Later, a detailed analysis was presented by Sangun Suwanlert and D. Coats.[18] Panic anxiety in male victims was typically triggered by the perception of shrinkage and numbness of the penis, followed by impotence. Females complained of shrinking, itching, and numbing of breasts and vulva with sexual frigidity. Associated with this basic complaint were diverse other symptoms such as dizziness, nausea, headache, abdominal pain, diarrhea, and discomfort at urination. Most of the afflicted were afraid of dying, and some of them fainted. Suwanlert and Coats studied 350 subjects in detail, irrespective of whether they sought treatment from native healers or physicians, and found that most patients recovered within one day and all recovered within one week. Jilek and Jilek-Aall were told of the folk treatment applied to *koro* victims which consisted of pulling and fastening the genitalia, then feeding the victim food locally considered to have sexually roborant properties, such as crab meat mixed with raw eggs. The outbreak started among students of a technical college in the Udon Thani province with rumors that Vietnamese immigrants had deliberately contaminated food, milk, and tobacco with a *koro*-inducing powder. Strong anti–Vietnamese sentiment in the region and the "domino theory" that the victory of the communists in Vietnam would cause neighboring countries to fall into their hands enhanced the collective anxiety, which fed on the general suspicion, reflected by the mass media, that communist Vietnam was attempting to sabotage the procreative capability of the Thai nation through specific poisonous substances. Anti-Vietnamese sentiments in the region were especially strong in the month before the episode,[19] with allegations by Thailand's interior minister that there was "solid evidence" of a plot whereby "Vietnamese refugees would incite rioting in northeast Thailand, providing Vietnam with an excuse to invade" on February 15.[20] As the episode continued, the poisoning rumors became self-fulfilling. Numerous Thai citizens recalled that previously consumed food and cigarettes recently purchased from Vietnamese establishments had an unusual smell and taste. However, an analysis of suspected sources by the Government Medical Science Department "detected no foreign substance that could possibly cause sexual impotence or contraction of the male sex organ."[21]

Koro rumors, combined with preexisting awareness of the "disease," served to foster and legitimate its plausible existence. Suwanlert and Coats (1979) found that 94 percent of victims studied "were convinced that they had been poisoned."[22] Contradictory statements issued by authority figures undermined negative government analysis of alleged tainted substances. Security officials attributed the substances in food responsible for causing *koro* to a mixture of vegetable sources undetectable by medical devices.

Northeastern India was hit by a mass outbreak of *koro* from July 2 to September 1982. It spread through the states of Assam, West Bengal, and Meghalaya. It became popularly known by the name "prickle disease," as those affected reported a sensation of prickling or tingling all over the body preceding the symptoms of classic *koro*. Several Indian psychiatrists reported the epidemic.[23] Thousands of people of different social class and caste, from diverse ethnic and religious backgrounds were afflicted. Psychiatric investigators could not elicit any underlying major psychological disorder in the examined victims. The majority of the *koro* victims were younger men, but at least one-quarter were women and children. Men felt their penises and testicles retracting, while most women felt their breasts shrinking or "going in." Chakraborty et al. reported that victims developed the *koro* syndrome only a few hours after hearing about it. Hundreds of people succumbed within a day or two at the locality where the condition appeared.[24] The panic reached such levels that medical personnel toured the region, reassuring people by loudspeaker. In the Darjeeling district, doctors measured penises at intervals to allay fears by demonstrating there was no shrinkage. Some parents tied strong thread to their young sons' penises, securing them to threads around the waist, a practice that occasionally resulted in penile ulcers. Besides grasping the affected body part tightly, a folk remedy was pouring buckets of cold water over the sufferer's head. During another *koro* episode in 1985 in North Bengal, Hindus, Muslims, and mountain tribespeople of both sexes were affected.[25] Female victims, complaining mainly of breast flattening and nipple retraction, were investigated in a special study that failed to find a woman with an underlying psychotic illness among the probands.[26] Ajita Chakraborty, well-known Indian social psychiatrist, concludes that the *koro* epidemics in northeastern India developed amid the collective fear of the rural population that they would be inundated by land-hungry immigrants.[27]

Magical Genitalia Loss in Nigeria

If *koro* panics now top your list of the most bizarre human delusions, you may have to rejuggle that list. For in parts of Africa, there is an even stranger behavior: vanishing genitalia! The influence of social and cultural context is evident in collective episodes of magical genitalia loss in Nigeria, which have been reported for at least twenty years. While working at a teaching hospital in Kaduna, northern Nigeria, in 1975, psychiatrist Sunny Ilechukwu[28] wrote in the *Transcultural Psychiatric Research Review* that he was approached by a police officer who was accompanied by two men. One of the men made the startling claim that the other had caused his penis to vanish. The officer, acting on orders from his superior, was to obtain a medical report to settle the dispute. The patient explained that he was walking along a street and "felt his penis go" after the robes worn by the other man had touched him. Incredulous, Ilechukwu initially refused to handle the case, but he later agreed to conduct a physical exam, which transpired in full view of the concerned parties. The patient stood and stared straight ahead until it was announced that his genitals were normal. Reacting in disbelief, the patient glanced down at his genitals and suggested that they had just reappeared! The policeman then indicated that charges would be filed against the man for falsely reporting a crime.

This case may appear to some readers to be a clear case of isolated, individual mental disturbance, as it is beyond Western credulity that people could believe that entire body parts were missing when clearly they were not. Yet Ilechukwu reported on epidemics of magical penis loss in Nigeria during the mid–1970s and again in 1990. A major Nigerian episode of "vanishing" genitalia in 1990 mainly affected men while walking in public places. Accusations were typically triggered by incidental body contact with a stranger that was interpreted as intentionally contrived, followed by unusual sensations within the scrotum. The affected person would then grab his genitals to confirm that all or parts were missing, after which he would shout a phrase such as "Thief! my genitals are gone!"[29] The victim would then completely disrobe to convince quickly gathering crowds of bystanders that his penis was actually missing. The accused was threatened and usually beaten (sometimes fatally) until the genitals were "returned." While some victims soon realized that their genitalia were intact, "many then claimed that they were 'returned' at the time they raised the alarm or that, although the penis had been 'returned,' it was shrunken and so probably a 'wrong' one or just the ghost of a penis."[30] In such instances, the assault of the accused would usually continue until the "real" penis reappeared.

Ilechukwu reported that incidents quickly spread like wildfire across the country: "Men could be seen in the streets of Lagos holding on to their genitalia either openly or discretely with their hands in their pockets. Women were also seen holding on to their breasts directly or discreetly by crossing the hands across the chest. It was thought that inattention and a weak will facilitated the 'taking' of the penis or breasts. Vigilance and anticipatory aggression were thought to be good prophylaxis."

The role of sociocultural traditions in triggering episodes is evident. Many Nigerian ethnic groups "ascribe high potency to the external genitalia as ritual and magical objects to promote fecundity or material prosperity to the unscrupulous. Ritually murdered persons are often said to have these parts missing."[31] The reality of vanishing genitalia is institutionalized to such an extent that during the 1990 episode, several influential Nigerians, including a court judge, protested vehemently when police released suspected genital thieves. Many knowledgeable citizens "claimed that there was a real — even if magical — basis for the incidents."[32] One Christian priest supported cultural beliefs of genital theft by citing a biblical passage in which Christ asked, "Who touched me?" because the "power had gone out of him," claiming that it was a reference to genital stealing.[33] Ilechukwu concluded that sociocultural beliefs related to magical genitalia loss in Nigeria render sexually maladjusted individuals susceptible to attacks.

Unraveling the Mystery

Since Emil Kraepelin, the famous German psychiatrist and initiator of comparative cultural psychiatry, mentioned the *koro* syndrome in his widely used textbook under "Ethnic Peculiarities-Specific Forms,"[34] sporadic cases of European and Euro-Americans with *koro* symptoms have been reported in medical journals, increasingly so with the growing interest in transcultural psychiatry. However, *koro* symptoms in the West are, in general, part of a chronic neurotic, psychotic, or neurologic disorder. While the temporary victims of the *koro* epidemics in Asia and Africa share a cultural belief or social delusion with many or most of their peers—and are not suffering from a chronic mental disorder—the individual Western patient's conviction of suffering from genital shrinking is an autistic delusion not shared by the patient's human environment. Common themes include preoccupations with masturbation and nocturnal emissions, perceived sexual inadequacies or excesses, and ignorance, inexperience, or insufficient confidence in sexual relationships. Social and cultural beliefs about sexuality may reinforce these factors. Unlike epidemics, individual cases can persist for months or years in people with obvious psychosexual problems and psychiatric disturbance. For instance, psychiatrist R.A. Emsley described the case of a man who became mentally traumatized and developed a great fear of impotence after being unwillingly circumcised in a tribal ritual. He then failed to get an erection while trying to have sex— at which point he could feel his penis shrinking.[35] Many disturbed men who believe their penis is shrinking suffer from schizophrenia, a condition where overvalued notions or delusions regarding damaged or impaired sexual organs can occur.[36] In one case recorded by psychiatrists Edward Kendall and Peter Jenkins while working in a hospital in Columbia, South Carolina, a thirty-five-year-old schizophrenic man was hospitalized after experiencing delusions of having "the largest penis in the world." A few days later, he tied cloth around his penis to prevent retraction, believing he was changing into a woman.[37]

Large-scale genitalia-shrinking episodes are typified by the symptoms of anxiety persisting for a few minutes to several days. Those affected always experience a complete recovery upon being convinced they are no longer in danger. Isolated singular cases experience more severe symptoms and may never recover. For instance, British psychiatrist Anne Cremona[38] treated a man who, at age eighteen, was unable to get an erection while attempting intercourse on three different occasions. He came to believe that his penis was abnormal. He experienced great anxiety and violence, abused drugs, began hearing voices, and became a hypochondriac. At age twenty-one, while walking down the street, he suddenly felt his penis shrink half an inch. After two years of such delusions, his *koro* symptoms were "as frequent and distressing as ever" and were unresponsive to drug treatment. In another case, an Englishman with *koro* was afraid to urinate in public, fearing that friends might spot him being "unable to find his penis when using a urinal" and tease him. His symptoms persisted for twenty years, but they disappeared after he received psychotherapy and drugs.[39] With cases like these on record, it's no wonder that some psychiatrists have assumed that similar psychological disturbances trigger epidemic *koro*. Yet a closer look at mass outbreaks reveals that they result from an entirely different process.[40]

The few isolated, individual cases often take years to recover, and they do so only after the underlying sexual problems are addressed. Victims of genitalia-shrinking panics recover within hours or days after being convinced that the "illness" is over or never existed, and most clearly lack any psychosexual problems. Episodes also share similar symptoms: anxiety, sweating, nausea, headache, transient pain, pale skin, palpitations, blurred vision, faintness, insomnia, and the belief that body parts are shrinking. These symptoms are normal body responses to extreme fear. The penis, scrotum, breasts, and nipples are the most physiologically plastic external body parts, regularly changing size and shape in response to stimuli ranging from sexual arousal to temperature changes. Studies also reveal that stress, depression, illness, and urination can cause small but discernible penis shrinkage.[41] Another key factor is the nature of human perception, which is highly unreliable.[42] A person's mental outlook and social and cultural reference system also preconditions perception. In each of the countries reporting epidemic *koro*, there were preexisting beliefs that genitalia could shrivel up under certain circumstances.

Far from exemplifying group psychosis, mental disorder, or irrationality, penis-shrinking panics are a timely reminder that no one is immune from mass delusions and that the influence of culture and society on individual behavior is far greater than most of us would like to admit. This is a valuable lesson to remember at the dawn of a new millennium. It is easy to think of past or non-Western delusions with a wry smile as if we are somehow now immune or that those involved were naive and gullible. Yet the main reason for the absence of penis-shrinking epidemics in Western societies is their incredible nature. It is simply too fantastic for modern Westerners to believe. But it was not that long ago that some Westerners believed in disappearing genitals. In parts of Europe during the witch-hunts until the late seventeenth century, one popular folk belief held that witches could cause a man's penis to vanish. Even the infamous *Malleus Maleficarum*, which led to countless witchcraft executions, gave examples of temporary penis loss.[43] These claims resemble genitalia-vanishing epidemics in modern-day Nigeria.

The key point is that any delusion is possible if the false belief underlying it is plausible. So while we may laugh at the poor, "misguided" Asian or African for believing in penis- and breast-shrinking, we are haunted by our own unique delusions: crashed saucers, alien abductors, and CIA cover-ups of just about everything.

Chapter 9

Imaginary Air Raids on Canada: Xenophobia During World War I

When the truth cannot be clearly made out, what is false is increased through fear.[1] — Quintus C. Rufus

In late August 1914, Canada entered World War I following the unanimous vote of a special session of Parliament. This event occurred amid great exuberance and unanimity, and it was marked by "parades, decorations, cheering crowds and patriotic speeches."[2] Canada was situated far from the European frontlines, and its distant, vast land mass and cold climate also contributed to a feeling of insulation from attack or invasion. However, despite an initial enthusiasm to enter the war and a general feeling of distance from its unfolding events, there was a rapidly growing realization that German sympathizers and enemy agents might pose a more immediate threat.

During World War I, a series of espionage dramas unfolded among the protagonist countries. Canada and the United States had their share of confirmed spy scandals, acts of subversion, and sabotage. There was considerable concern among Canadians that German Americans and sympathizers acting on orders from Berlin or independently might cross the border intent on crippling Canada's war efforts. In reality, the acts of espionage, sabotage, and subversion that took place had relatively little impact on everyday life in the United States or Canada or on the war's outcome. The few successful incidents that did occur only heightened fears and suspicions surrounding the intentions of German sympathizers in Canada and, especially, the United States. It is difficult to give an exact figure to the number of enemy acts in Canada during the war because "there was hardly a major fire, explosion, or industrial accident which was not attributed to enemy sabotage." By the time an incident had been thoroughly investigated, it "invariably led elsewhere."[3] Beginning in 1914, an anti–German hysteria steadily rose in North America, and it would not subside until well after the Armistice agreement ended the war on November 11, 1918.

During World War I, vivid imaginations and wild rumors were the order of the day, and politicians did little to ease fears. For instance, in the United States, President Woodrow Wilson told Congress that Germans "filled our unsuspecting communities with spies and conspirators."[4] In America, the German scare reached such proportions that foods, streets, schools, businesses, and cities with Germanic names were renamed. Communities prohibited German music or theater performances. Suspected traitors were occasionally assaulted, tarred and feathered, or hanged by vigilantes.[5]

A similar social paranoia swept across Canada. Schools and universities stopped teaching German as a language. The city of Berlin was renamed the town of Kitchener. The Anti-German League was formed to rid Canada of all German influence, including products and immigrants.[6] In August 1915, miners in Fernie, British Columbia, refused to work until alien employees at the Crow's Nest Pass Coal Company were dismissed, after which they were promptly placed in a makeshift internment camp.[7] As in the United States, Canadian politicians further stoked the fires of public hysteria. For instance, the former Saskatchewan lieutenant governor made the sensational claim that 30 percent of Canada's newer provinces were composed of "alien enemies, who made little secret of their desire to see the flag of Germany waving over the Canadian West."[8] Between 1914 and 1918, 8,579 German and Austro-Hungarian Canadian men were placed in internment camps.[9] But clearly, Canadians viewed the greater threat as coming from the United States, where in 1910 there were nearly 10 million German Americans.[10] Initially, the German scare was more intense in Canada because it entered the war in 1914, while the United States remained neutral in the conflict and did not officially join the war effort until April 1917.

Of the many rumors to circulate across Canada during the war, one was particularly persistent and widespread. From the very onset of hostilities, it was widely rumored that German Americans sympathetic to the kaiser had been secretly preparing large-scale military raids or an invasion of Canada.[11] During January 1915 alone, the British consul in Los Angeles warned Canadian authorities that German sympathizers were planning attacks on Port Arthur, Fort William, and Winnipeg.[12] Meanwhile,

> The consul general in New York, growing increasingly agitated, claimed
> that a raid on Canada was imminent and that the Germans had mustered
> five thousand men in Chicago and up to four thousand in Buffalo. The
> foreign office in London [claimed]...that a 'reliable source' had reported
> that a group of eight thousand men had been formed in Boston and that
> bombing raids on Halifax and St. John's could be expected.[13]

As "imaginations ran wild, and on the flimsiest of what passed as evidence," there were scores of false accusations about scheming Germans on both sides of the border.[14] The British consul-general, Sir Courtney Bennett, stationed in New York, held top honors for being the worst offender.[15] During the early months of 1915, Bennett made several sensational claims about a plan in which as many as eighty thousand well-armed, highly trained Germans who had been drilling in Niagara Falls and Buffalo were planning to invade Canada from northwestern New York state. Despite the incredulity of his assertions, it was a testament to the deep anxiety and suspicion of the period that Prime Minister Sir Robert Borden requested a report on the invasion stories, which Canadian Police Commissioner Sherwood assessed to be without any foundation.[16]

In conjunction with the German scare, rapid advances in aeronautics contributed to a growing insecurity among Canadians that they could be vulnerable to an aerial attack. Amid these concerns, rumors circulated that German sympathizers from within Canada or the adjacent United States—and almost exclusively the latter—were planning to launch surprise bombing raids or espionage missions using airplanes flown from secret, remote airstrips.[17]

It was within this context that a series of phantom airplane scares swept across Ontario and Quebec between 1914 and 1916. Airplanes of the period were crude affairs, very limited in maneuverability. Night flying held its own risks, and the first nocturnal flight did not occur until 1910 and lasted just twenty kilometers.[18] Sightings over Canada during the war were almost exclusively confined to observations of nocturnal lights.

The first reports were confined to southeastern Ontario. They began in the village of Sweaburg, six miles south of Woodstock, on August 13, 1914, when High County Constable Hobson and numerous residents reported seeing "two large aeroplanes" pass from east to west at about 7:30 P.M.[19] Sporadic sightings of mysterious airplanes continued over the next two weeks. They were reported by many farmers in the region, and in such places as Aylmer, Tillsonburg, and Port Stanley.[20] As a result, a special guard was placed at the wireless station in Port Burwell on Lake Erie.[21] The next major incident occurred at about 9 P.M. on September 3, when three airplanes were observed in the oil town of Petrolea[22] as powerful search-

Figure 9.1: While the German air bomber pictured never flew over Canada during World War I, a moral panic causing fear of all things German led to misperceptions of mundane objects as German aircraft. (National Archives of Canada PA 164607, courtesy of Michael Bechthold.)

lights swept the countryside. Scores of residents watched the spectacle for hours as "every field glass in Petrolea was brought into requisition."[23] The "aeroplanes" were widely thought "to have some connection with Great Britain's war against Germany."[24] One plane was observed to fly in the direction of Oil Springs, while a second hovered near Kingscourt, and a third appeared to travel eastward toward London along the Grand Trunk, "evidently scanning the line carefully."[25] Petrolea Police Chief Fletcher was in communication with nearby communities, and he immediately began conducting witness interviews.[26] Meanwhile, military authorities attempted to allay fears and suggested that the planes were privately owned aircraft.[27] There were also reports that the planes may have been owned by an American pilot crossing the border at night.[28]

Several observations of "a mysterious aeroplane" were reported near Hamilton during early September, prompting military personnel to investigate.[29] After a spate of sightings between September 8 and 10 at Springbank, residents were described as "greatly stirred."[30] One witness was Fred Bridge, who urged Canadian authorities to take the reports seriously:

> With my neighbor, I have seen the flashlights which swept the countryside and have heard the roar of the motors. Last night three of them came down over Springbank...
>
> The people of London [Ontario] are not taking this matter seriously enough. Some of those fellows will drop something in the reservoir and cause no end of trouble. I am a time-expired man of the British army ...

> [and if] the call is urgent I am prepared to respond. ...every farmer in
> the community should be given a rifle and service ammunition by the
> department of militia, that these spy aviators might be brought down.[31]

By mid–September, the military had issued orders to fire on airplanes
seen within fourteen miles of any wireless station,[32] and one American
plane was even shot at near the border.[33] As the war tension continued, a
short-lived panic occurred in Toronto on the morning of October 10, when
a large, fluttering kite flown in the city's center caused a traffic jam as anxious crowds gathered to try to identify the object. Some residents even dove
for cover. The incident exemplified the "nervous state into which even
Toronto is thrown by the talk of war and of raiding aeroplanes."[34] During mid–October, several residents on the outskirts of Sault Ste. Marie
claimed to have observed an illuminated airplane rise into the sky from
the American side of the border near Soo Locks and sail over the river
above the Canadian locks, which were under close guard by militiamen.[35]

Considerable alarm was caused in the city of London on the morning of October 21, when several soldiers reported that an airplane carrying a powerful spotlight flew directly over the Welseley Barracks and nearby
ordnance stores at about 5:50 A.M. Sergeant Joseph, who was on guard
duty, stated that

> It was an aeroplane all right.... I and three members of the guard were
> sitting around the campfire when we heard the purr of engines and look-
> ing up saw the aeroplane coming from the northeast of the barracks. It
> had a bright light and was traveling rapidly. It came practically over us
> and the ordnance stores and then turned to the east and south. There
> was no use firing at it for it flew too high and at too rapid a rate. It was
> an aeroplane, of that we are sure.[36]

This incident followed a series of airplane sightings and reports of aerial
motor sounds in the vicinity of London over the previous several weeks,
which investigations had traced to causes such as toy balloons or boat
engines.[37] Meanwhile, shortly after the barracks sighting at London, Canadian military authorities once again reiterated the unlikelihood of a spy
or war plane flying overhead because, it was argued, spies could travel the
city unmolested in broad daylight and achieve similar results. The authorities also wondered why planes on a secret mission would use brilliant
searchlights that would surely attract attention.[38]

Scattered sightings continued during November. On the Canadian
portion of Niagara Falls, guards watching over the Toronto power plant
reported seeing what appeared to be signal lights being flashed from the

American side of the border across Lake Ontario. The lights would appear during the early morning hours and consisted of red, yellow, and green colors. The militiamen believed the lights were used "to form different combinations. A close watch is being kept for spies."[39] During this period, there were also rumors of sightings in numerous Canadian villages, including Forestville, Quebec.[40]

In the early morning hours of December 3, a major scare occurred in Toronto, when a series of ambiguous rumbling noises were widely thought to be an airplane raid. It was later suggested that the city's cyclone dredge, in conjunction with war jitters, was responsible for the scare. A cyclone dredge is a machine for removing river sediment. Its droning motor could easily have been mistaken for distant airplanes.

In the light of day, when it was realized what had happened, the *Toronto Daily Star* somewhat sarcastically described the episode as follows:

Aeroplane Raid Robs Citizens of Slumber
Ominous Rumbling, Apparently Coming from Sky, Caused Widespread Uneasiness

> Half of Toronto sat up in bed last night and held its breath, listening to the Germans in aeroplanes flying about over the roof. Towards five o'clock ... the Star office was deluged with reports that included window and picture rattling, purring noises and everything but bombs. From their reports it was learned that the Germans had investigated Bleecker street at 12 p.m., Indian road and Clinton street at 4 a.m., and had stood directly over 45 St. George street at 4.30 a.m.[41]

The sightings were sporadic until mid–February, with reports of airplanes near Niagara Falls on December 10[42] and Montreal during the early morning hours of January 11.[43]

The biggest scare began on February 14, 1915, at 9:15 P.M. in Brockville, a community on the U.S. border nestled along the St. Lawrence River. Constables Storey, Thompson, Glacier, and several residents became convinced that three or four airplanes had passed by the city to the northeast, heading in the direction of Ottawa, about sixty miles due north. The actual observations were vague with the exception of "light balls" falling from the sky.[44]

"The first machine was flying very rapidly and very high. Very little could be seen, but the unmistakable sounds of the whirring motor made the presence of the aircraft known."[45] Five minutes later, a second machine was heard, then suddenly three balls of light descended from the sky, plunging several hundred feet and extinguishing as they hit the river. A few

Figure 9.2: On February 14, 1915, the biggest air-raid scare of the war occurred when German planes were "detected" crossing the New York state border in the direction of Ottawa. As word of the sightings spread, Parliament Hill was blacked out, and marksmen were deployed to counter the expected attack. (National Archives of Canada RD 254, courtesy of Michael Bechthold.)

minutes thereafter, vague observations of two more airplanes passing over the city were reported.[46]

As word of the sightings spread throughout Brockville, its inhabitants became "wildly excited."[47] At 10:30 P.M., the Brockville police chief sent an urgent telegram to Prime Minister Sir Robert Bordon, who summoned Colonel Percy Sherwood, chief of Dominion Police. After consultation with military authorities, all lights in the Parliament buildings were extinguished, and every blind was drawn.[48] Marksmen were posted at several vantage points on Parliament Hill, while the prime minister and cabinet ministers kept in close communication in the event of an attack during the night. News of the possible attack spread rapidly, and several members of Parliament rushed to the roof of the main building to see if they could spot any aircraft.

The scare in Canada was intensified the following morning, when the *Toronto Globe* implied that an attack had actually happened. Its banner, front-page headlines stated: "Ottawa in Darkness Awaits Aeroplane Raid. Several Aeroplanes Make a Raid into the Dominion of Canada. Entire City of Ottawa in Darkness, Fearing Bomb-Droppers. Machines Crossed St. Lawrence River ... Seen by Many Citizens Heading for the Capital — One Was Equipped with Powerful Searchlights — Fire Balls Dropped." On the

American side, the *New York Times* description of the incident the next morning was much more cautious, with its headlines stating in part, "Scare in Ottawa Over Air Raid ... but Police Chief's Report Is Vague." The *Times* also noted that the police chief in Ogdensburg, New York, just twelve miles down the St. Lawrence River from Brockville, stated that no one had reported seeing or hearing anything at the time the airplanes were said to have passed near Brockville. In addition, flying machines were also sighted at Gananoque, Ontario.[49] Other observations of unusual aerial objects were redefined. For instance, once the news of the sightings spread, an Ogdensburg farmer told police that he had seen an airplane on February 12 flying toward Canada.[50]

It is important to note that within the context of the outbreak of World War I and Canada's involvement, the airplane raid appeared plausible. One press account stated, "the fact that the country is at war and the Germans and pro-Germans abound across the border renders it quite within the bounds of possibility, if not probability, that such a raid might occur."[51]

On the night of February 15 and the early morning hours of February 16, the Parliament buildings again remained dark, and marksmen were posted at strategic locations.[52] This appears to have been both a precautionary and a face-saving measure. Information was rapidly coming to hand indicating that a series of toy balloons mistaken for enemy airplanes, had been sent aloft the previous night on the American side. Prime Minister Borden was defensive. When asked for information about the "invasion," he replied that when informed of the reports, he had left the matter to the judgment of the chief of staff and chief of Dominion Police.[53] The Canadian press, such as the *Toronto Globe*, was also embarrassed, as it had reported the aerial incursion as a certainty in its previous edition. However, in the paper's next edition, it blamed the affair on "hysterical" residents in Brockville.[54] Meanwhile, the charred remains of two large toy balloons[55] had been found in the vicinity of Brockville. Local residents blamed the balloons on boys from nearby Morristown.[56] A number of toy balloons in other locations had also been sent aloft by Americans on February 14 and 15, in commemoration of the centenary of peace.[57] An adviser for the Canadian Aviation Corps, J.D. McCurdy, stated that a mission by German sympathizers from northern New York was highly improbable, especially given the difficulty of night flying.[58]

The last major sighting wave during World War I occurred in July. In the first week of the month, an airplane reportedly landed in a field near Nolan Junction, Quebec. It was claimed that two men carrying plans and papers disembarked, then shortly after flew off toward Montreal.[59] On

July 16, an illuminated airplane was seen by blacksmith Silvanus Edworthy in London.[60] On the morning of July 17, a craft was seen near Massena, Ontario.[61] During mid–July, airplanes were widely reported flying in the vicinity of Quebec City[62] and Montreal.[63] When aircraft were seen near a factory in Rigaud, the lights were extinguished and precautions "taken to protect the place from possible attack."[64] On the night July 18, a military guard at the Point Edward wireless station fired five shots at what he took to be airplanes, and two large paper balloons plummeted to earth.[65]

At 11 P.M. on July 20, when a mysterious aircraft was sighted by several citizens of Chateauguay near Montreal, speculation was rife that a German resident of that town for the past five years had secretly flown across the border to the United States. The man had been closely watched since the outbreak of hostilities, and he disappeared the night the plane was sighted.[66]

Widely scattered nocturnal airplane sightings continued, including sightings at Tillsongburg on July 22[67] and London on August 8, 1915.[68] On February 5, 1916, a railway worker spotted two airplanes near Montreal. There was thought to be a connection between this sighting and a suspicious man who was seen at about the same time under the Victoria Bridge. Fearing an attempt to blow up the bridge, guards on the structure opened fire on the figure, who fled.[69] On February 13, a rare configuration of Venus and Jupiter resulted in a brilliant light in the western sky that was mistaken by hundreds of residents of London as an airplane about to attack.[70] Finally, the last known scare during the war occurred at Windsor, when a biplane was sighted by hundreds of anxious residents for about thirty minutes on July 6, 1916. Several people using binoculars actually claimed "to distinguish the figure of the aviator.[71]

Social Psychological Aspects of the War Scare

The phantom airplane raids and spy missions across Ontario and Quebec during World War I are classic examples of a collective delusion. The literature on such episodes indicates the pivotal role of several key factors. These included the presence of ambiguity and anxiety, the spread of rumors and false but plausible beliefs, and a redefinition of a potential threat from general and distant to specific and imminent. Exacerbating factors included the fallibility of human perception, mass media influence in spreading the fears, recent geopolitical events, and actions or reassurances from authority figures and institutions of social control, such as the police and military.[72]

Figure 9.3: A sentry standing guard in Toronto in early 1916. The ability of Germany to launch an air attack on Canada during World War I was nonexistent. Supposed sightings, fueled by eyewitness claims published in newspapers, led many to believe that attacks were possible if not imminent. (National Archives of Canada PA 2598, courtesy of Michael Bechthold.)

The outbreak of World War I generated extraordinary anxiety in Canada, as did concerns about the allegiance of German Canadians and German Americans, which was unclear. It was not known whether they possessed the motivation, means, and resources to launch aerial missions. Recent advances in aviation technology lent plausibility to the rumors.

The ambiguous nighttime sky was ideal for fostering misperceptions of stars, planets, and other natural phenomena. When an observer scrutinizes an object such as a star, it can appear to change color, flicker, and move.[73] Of particular interest is what social psychologists call the autokinetic effect. This illusion was first identified by Muzafer Sherif in 1936,[74] who found that when people stare at a single point of light in a dark environment, the light appears to move — often dramatically — even though it is stationary. The difficulties in judging distance and movement under such conditions occur because objects such as buildings, cars, and people usually provide a familiar frame of reference with which to base judgments.

However, in dark settings these cues are either greatly diminished or not available.[75] This situation is similar to Canadians staring at the sky in search of German airplanes at night. Human perception is highly unreliable,[76] and people are prone to interpreting objects in their environment that reflect their mental outlook or worldview at the time.[77]

It is difficult to imagine Canadian military authorities handling the sporadic sightings more successfully than they did, short of censoring press accounts. While realizing a responsibility to investigate reports, they simultaneously issued confident, reassuring press statements that helped to contain the spread of each episode and avoid public panic. Ironically, the very act of conducting an investigation may have lent credence to public perceptions that there was something to the sightings. The Canadian press was more influential in triggering episodes. On several occasions, the language of their accounts treated the existence of a hostile airplane as a certainty, and the publication of eyewitness reports intermittently rekindled public attention on the issue, providing a semblance of legitimization to the rumors of the planes' existence.

I suspect that the series of group delusions in Ontario and Quebec coinciding with World War I are relatively common occurrences during periods of war or war threats.[78] At the time of occurrence, such episodes may appear to be of paramount importance, but once their psychological origin becomes evident, they are soon forgotten. Unfortunately, little has been written on the subject, which is a fascinating part of our war heritage.[79]

Chapter 10

The Phantom Sniper of Esher, England: How a Community Created an Imaginary Assailant

Man is not the creature of circumstances,
Circumstances are the creatures of man.
— Benjamin Disraeli[1]

Collective delusions are often regarded in social science literature as rare events and freak occurrences. Yet until the relatively recent information age, most social delusions were simply forgotten because there was no one to preserve them. Numerous delusions of the past few centuries may have been recorded but were quickly forgotten. One fascinating aspect of the social-delusion literature is that the most seemingly bizarre episodes that one might think would never occur again — recur. As we read in Chapters 4 and 5, the "mad gasser" of Mattoon occurred almost a decade after a remarkably similar event in Virginia, known locally as "the phantom gas tosser." Chapter 1 included the case of the phantom slasher of Taipei, Taiwan, who in 1956 supposedly went around slashing residents with a razor-like instrument. In the late 1930s, a similar razor-welding maniac appeared in England and was dubbed the Halifax Slasher — until police realized there was no such person.

One particularly fascinating parallel involves a famous case familiar to most sociologists and social psychologists as "the Seattle windshield-pitting epidemic." In March 1954, police in the city of Bellingham in northwest Washington state were baffled by reports that a ghostly sniper was shooting at car windshields. The situation soon reached crisis proportions.

The author is grateful to Paul Chambers for his co-authorship of this chapter.

Over a one-week period in early April, over fifteen hundred windshields were reported damaged. Despite the massive number of "attacks," Police Chief William Breuer had no suspects and no tangible evidence. Authorities surmised that the most likely weapon "was a BB-gun barrel attached to a compressor in a spark-plug socket, fired from a moving car."[2]

At the height of the episode people across the city of thirty-four thousand placed various items over their windshields for protection — from newspapers to door mats and even plywood. Meanwhile, downtown parking garages were under heavy security. The phantom pellet-shooter seemed to be everywhere — even police cars reported being struck. In lieu of a lack of evidence, by mid–April local and national media began emphasizing the mysterious nature of the damage. On April 12, a reporter for *Life* magazine came to Bellingham and referred to the episode as "ghostly" and the perpetrators as "phantom"-like. The next evening, the *Seattle Times* talked about "elusive BB-snipers."[3] In time, reports of the mysterious windshield attacks moved closer to Seattle, eighty miles to the south. Reports of strange pit marks on windshields first reached Seattle on the evening of April 14. By the end of the next day, weary police had answered 242 phone calls from concerned residents reporting tiny pit marks on over three thousand vehicles.[4] In some cases, whole parking lots were reportedly affected. The reports quickly declined and ceased. On April 16, police logged forty-six pitting claims. They logged ten on April 17, after which no more reports were received.

Nahum Medalia of the Georgia Institute of Technology and Otto Larsen of the University of Washington studied the episode. They stated that the most common damage report involved claims that tiny pit marks grew into dime-sized bubbles embedded within the glass, leading to a folk theory that sand-flea eggs had somehow been deposited in the glass and hatched. The sudden presence of the pits created widespread anxiety because they were typically attributed to atomic fallout from hydrogen-bomb tests, which had been recently conducted in the Pacific and had received media publicity. At the height of the incident, the night of April 15, the Seattle mayor even sought emergency assistance from President Dwight Eisenhower.

In the wake of rumors (such as the existence of radioactive fallout) and through a few initial cases amplified in the media, residents began looking at — instead of through — their windshields. An analysis of the mysterious, black, sooty grains that dotted many Seattle windshields was carried out at the Environmental Research Laboratory at the University of Washington. The material was identified as cenospheres — tiny particles produced by the incomplete combustion of bituminous coal. The particles were a common feature of everyday life in Seattle, and they could not pit or penetrate windshields.

Medalia and Larsen noted that as the pitting reports coincided with the hydrogen bomb tests, media publicity on the windshield damage seems to have reduced tension about the possible consequences of the bomb tests: "[S]omething was bound to happen to us as a result of the H-bomb tests—windshields became pitted — it's happened — now that threat is over."[5] Second, the very act of phoning police and appeals by the mayor to the governor and even president of the United States "served to give people the sense that they were 'doing something' about the danger that threatened."[6]

In a remarkable parallel, another social delusion involving marks on windshields began several years earlier in England. Between early December 1950 and December 7, 1953, police received over fifty reports of projectiles thought to have been bullets or BBs striking automobile windscreens (referred to in America as windshields) along a small stretch of a busy road southwest of the London outskirts. Police later concluded that the sniper was imaginary. Most of the reports occurred along a mostly isolated 3.4 kilometer section of road linking Esher and Cobham, which is a village located to the south-southwest of Esher. A smaller cluster of nine incidents was reported along a more populated area about two kilometers northeast of Esher, where the road diverges into the communities of East Molesey, Thames Ditton, and Hinchley Wood. Despite its notoriety at the time, these events were quickly forgotten and would have likely escaped attention altogether if one the authors (Chambers) had not spotted a reference to it in the book *Stranger Than Science*, written by Frank Edwards in 1959.[7]

The episode began on December 2, 1950, when British media celebrity Richard Dimbleby told police that his car windscreen was struck by what appeared to be a .22 caliber bullet. The incident received minor national media attention in England.[8] Dimbleby was a political journalist who worked for the British Broadcasting Corporation on both radio and television. One week later, on January 9, two more "shootings" were claimed. Mr. H. Tickner of Esher said that while driving south toward Cobham, there was a flash followed by a loud noise before his screen was starred to the extent that he was forced to stop.[9] He scrutinized the car but found no trace of a projectile.[10] His description would typify those of many people in the months to come. A second incident was reported on the same morning by Reginald Kingshott of Belham whose screen "was badly cracked by a missile."[11]

At least three competing folk theories were discussed at this time.

The most popular views were that someone was deliberately shooting bullets at windscreens or that stones were flying up from the road after being propelled by car tires.[12] A more esoteric view held that an experimental road surface may have created a "peculiar vibration" capable of shattering glass.[13] After a three-week break, on February 9, 1951, a seventh incident was reported by Robert Southern, who said his windscreen was "smashed" by an unknown projectile while driving near Fairmile Lane.[14] The reports stopped for about ten months. In all, six cars and a truck had been hit by what some residents were dubbing "the sniper."[15]

The attacks resumed during the Christmas period of 1951. On December 15, a master of Milbourne Lodge Senior School was driving south near Blackhills when he "heard a crack like a pistol shot and saw his complete windscreen frost over."[16] Mr. S. Jay managed to maintain control of the vehicle and pull over. Cobham police investigated the possibility that the projectiles were either from a .22 caliber rifle, an air gun, or a catapult.[17] The incident marked the start of a prolonged period of local, and eventually national, interest in the "strange happenings" on Portsmouth Road. By January 11, 1952, the *Esher News and Advertiser* (hereafter referred to as the *Esher News*) had recorded twelve sniper incidents from the same stretch of Portsmouth Road. By mid–March this total had risen to fourteen, and reports in the *Esher News* had taken on a more serious tone. One article asked authorities, "When will action be taken to end this menace at Esher?"[18] By now the *Esher News* was firmly backing the idea of a sniper with an air gun being responsible, a position that would seem justified by an incident that occurred on March 20, 1952. On that date, Frank C. Smith from Thames Ditton was driving north along Portsmouth Road when he "felt the car rock and pulled up to find out what happened."[19] Examining his car, he found a nine-millimeter hole in the driver's door, about eight centimeters below the handle. It appeared as though someone had taken a shot at him. The *Esher News* ran a picture of a worried-looking Mr. Smith sitting in his damaged car and commented on the case: "A ballistic expert has since said that it was probably a .317 bullet, an unusual calibre for a British gun, but one quite common in Italy. If it was fired from a high bank along the side of the road, it might have ricochetted [sic] off the road surface before hitting the panel. If the gun had been aimed at the door, the bullet would have killed the driver."[20]

Mr. Smith's incident was a turning point in the history of the phantom sniper. From this moment on, local police and the Esher council took the concerns of the *Esher News* and the local community seriously. After the next series of smashed windscreens, which were reported within two weeks of Mr. Smith's shooting, the police began to patrol Portsmouth Road and even instigated a detailed search of the surrounding common land.[21] However, this did nothing to lessen the activities of the phantom sniper. By May 16, there were a total of twenty incidents,[22] and interest in the happenings at "Hell-Fire Pass" began to attract attention from outside the region. The shattered windscreen of Eric Sykes, which occurred on May 9[23] is the first of the phantom sniper incidents to make it into the back pages of the *London Evening Standard*, where the newspaper glibly stated that the police were "looking for someone with a gun."[24]

By mid–June, 1952, it was hypothesized that supersonic aircraft were responsible for the shattered windscreens because sonic booms were known to break house windows. A local editorial dismissed the theory, noting that sound waves would not be as selective as to affect "one road only and nowhere else," asking, "why are windscreens only shattered, not the side windows of cars? Why are private cars always the victims, never lorries or buses?" The editorial went on to suggest that air guns were responsible.[25]

During June 1952, more reports of damaged cars poured in. For the first time, a car windscreen was shattered not on Portsmouth Road, but a couple of kilometers to the east on Copsem Lane, which leads into the town of Oxshott. The phantom was spreading further afield and becoming more adventurous, not only targeting windscreens but the headlights of an ambulance and a private motorist.[26] In light of these revelations, the local council swept the Portsmouth Road between Esher and West-End Lane in the hope that loose stones and not a gunman might be the cause.[27]

The first national coverage came at this time, advancing the sonic-boom theory from low-flying aircraft.[28] In an editorial on the matter, the *Esher News* rejected the idea in favor of a lone gunman. It also summarized its involvement in the development of the phantom sniper mystery:

> Months ago, when we started to report it, we were alone. Then, via the county and evening Press, the affair reached the nationals. Last month, over months after the first incident, Esher Council took official notice of the matter. We are now waiting with bated breath for a question to be asked in Parliament. That, our readers will be interested to learn, is how the machinery of democracy creaks to an ultimate solution. But what an awful time it takes![29]

Reports of broken windscreens kept being reported, but the sniper was also held responsible for other crimes, including the smashing of a shop and a pub window in Esher itself.[30] Intense police activity accompanied some of these incidents such as the broken windscreen of Mr. V. J. Wood, which prompted ten constables to search surrounding woodland and undergrowth.[31]

Complaints from residents spurred the local council to demand a statement from the Metropolitan Police on their plans to catch the sniper. "The ratepayers are entitled to know what actions are being taken," wrote councillor N. Jones.[32] The request produced a reply from the police commissioner, who said that a "special observation had been kept on the road by selected officers, and would be continued for a further period, but that at present there was no evidence to support the theory that the damage was being caused maliciously."[33] It was also mentioned that the Ministry of Transport had plans to investigate the matter. It is clear from these statements that the Metropolitan Police did not favor the sniper theory and thought loose stones were responsible. Council members disagreed. During a debate on the matter, several council members expressed concern at the police attitude toward the problem. Councillor E. Royston said, "There is a solid basis of concern, and it would be wrong for us to shrug our shoulders or laugh at it, and wrong to say that we know what the cause is."[34] By September 1952, the number of incidents numbered at least thirty-three, but there was yet to be found a single bullet, pellet, or other missile in connection with the broken windows. To explain this, readers of the *Esher News* proposed their own theories, including catapults,[35] falling pine cones,[36] and pellets made from frozen carbon dioxide (dry ice) that would melt on contact.[37] Following attention from the national press, the police, and the council, local interest peaked between May and September 1952. It was noticeable that from August to October, the reports of shattered windscreens came not only from Portsmouth Road but from surrounding areas: East Molesey, Thames Ditton, and Hinchley Wood. Between October 16 and December 1, 1952, there were no reports of shattered windscreens at all, the longest period of quiet in nearly a year.

The Final Phase

The six weeks of quiet from the phantom was only a lull before one final burst of sniping. In December 1952, five reports of broken windscreens were recorded in the *Esher News*.[38] More incidents in January led journalists at the paper to ask if a new phase of shootings was beginning,[39] but despite this blip in activity the reports were only a trickle in comparison to the previous year. The most serious incident was four windscreens shattered in the same week in April.[40] Other theories continued to be espoused. In February, the Metropolitan Police informed the council that "in spite of intensive observation over a prolonged period, the police have no evidence that the damage is being caused maliciously."[41] Some theories were not so cautious. Gordon Slyfield suggested that the explanation might necessitate calling in the Institute of Psychical Research:

> The metaphysical theory must not therefore be ruled out. I am familiar with the physical results attached to psychical phenomena of the séance room. If there is a powerful spiritualist medium dwelling on this road, he or she may be ignorant and need not go into a trance.... A rod of ectoplasm proceeding from the medium is strong enough so that an entity can lift physical objects. This is what happens with poltergeist phenomena in the presence of adolescents.
>
> If such the entity were the spirit of a dastardly highwayman, might not he still operate against lawful users of the highway?[42]

Mr. G. Bird responded by asking sarcastically, "Why stop at earthbound highwaymen firing ectoplasmic bullets; why not the vibrations of harps twanged by little men landing from flying saucers?"[43] Bird went on to tout the gunman theory and suggest that local patrols were the answer to catching the culprit.

These debates in May of 1953 largely mark the end of the incidents on Portsmouth Road. Afterward, there were only another five reports of broken windscreens, three of which did not occur locally. As the number of weeks increased between articles, the *Esher News* was reduced to making the odd report near the back of the paper. The last report is from their December 11, 1953, issue when Mrs. L. Perry reported having her windscreen shattered while driving in Ealing, many kilometers northwest of Esher.[44]

What Was Happening on Portsmouth Road?

We will test the four main theories put forward as the cause of the broken windows at the time. The first explanation was that sonic booms from low-flying military aircraft were shattering windscreens on Portsmouth Road. Both the *Esher News*[45] and some its readers picked up this idea.[46] The first acknowledged breaking of the sound barrier occurred in October 1947, only a few years before the Esher incidents. In the years following this achievement, the term "supersonic" entered popular culture as a euphemism for anything that was fantastic or great. There was, however, also concern over the effect of supersonic booms on local property, especially windows, which could potentially shatter as a consequence. Although few, if any, people in Esher could ever have heard a supersonic boom at this time, there was already talk about the possibility of these noises being heard in the region.[47] Also, the town itself is on the flight path to nearby Heathrow. It is probably for this reason that this theory gained local popularity. Yet the pattern of windscreen shattering does not suggest a supersonic origin. Surely, cars from a wider area would be affected, as would the windows of houses, let alone the side windows of cars. It is also questionable how many supersonic aircraft would have been operating in the area at that time. With the aid of hindsight, we now also know that supersonic aircraft may rattle a few windows, but they rarely break them and then certainly not the toughened glass of car windscreens.[48]

Another reason for rejecting the sonic-boom theory is that in a large majority of cases, motorists reported hearing an object strike their windscreen. Also, in a number of cases, there was clear evidence in the form of circular pock marks in the glass (e.g., Robert Bruce had a circular crack in his windscreen after driving along Portsmouth Road on June 4, 1952).[49] In the majority of cases, it seems as though a missile of some kind is the most likely explanation. It is the origin of these missiles that forms the mystery. Throughout its coverage of the windscreen incidents, the *Esher News* favored the idea of a genuine sniper hiding at the roadside and taking shots at passing cars. In favor of this idea are the tight distribution of incidents, most of which occurred along the same short section of Portsmouth Road, and the sound of a gunshot that accompanied many of the broken windscreens. With reports like that of Mr. Tickner, who said he saw a flash and then heard an explosion just prior to his windscreen shattering,[50] it is no wonder that a gunman was suspected. The one consistent problem with this theory was the lack of a single recovered bullet either from inside the car or from the roadside. At other incidents where windows or cars have been shot at, the bullet is normally quite easy to find.[51] The *Esher News* and members of the local council overcame the problem of a lack of bullets by consistently advocating that an air gun must have been used. An air gun is a light rifle that uses compressed air to fire light bullets, pellets, or even stones over relatively short distances. They are low-powered, and their ammunition is fragile. So while it is possible for an air-gun shot to break or damage a windscreen, the bullet itself might not survive the impact and certainly wouldn't penetrate the glass to land inside the car. This would adequately explain the lack of a bullet at the scene of the crime. In addition, air guns are light, cheap, and do not require the owner to hold a license. So a local youth or other mischief maker could easily have operated an air gun. Although air guns vary in power and accuracy, a pellet or rock fired from one could shatter a windscreen. Several experiments were performed with air guns and windscreens, the results of which all show that air-gun pellets can indeed shatter all types of windscreen glass.[52]

While an airgun-wielding sniper could have been hiding in the bushes surrounding Portsmouth Road, there are problems with this idea. One problem is accuracy. The effective range of most air guns is only a few hundred meters. Like all guns, their accuracy decreases with increased distance from the target and with increased wind and rain. Despite these factors, the sniper seems to have been an uncannily good shot under all types of light and weather conditions. The sniper managed to accurately shoot the windscreens of dozens of cars without missing and hitting other parts of the car, most notably the body or side windows. On top of this, the sniper was capable of doing this at night and in all weather conditions, including — on one occasion — a blizzard![53] To accomplish this, the sniper would have to be very close to the roadside indeed. Yet he or she was never once spotted by passing motorists, police patrols, or people who pulled over after their windscreens shattered. This seems very strange indeed.

The strongest piece of evidence favoring a sniper was the case of Frank Smith, whose car was apparently hit on the driver's door by a .317 bullet that left a sizable hole. All this would seem to suggest strongly that Smith was shot at, but there are some strange inconsistencies noticeable in the reporting of this incident. First, there is the caliber of the bullet. At .317, it is much larger and more powerful than the air-gun pellets believed to be responsible for the other broken windscreens. Either the sniper changed his means of operating, or he was using a different gun for this one occasion. More puzzling was the lack of any mention of a bullet found embedded in the door even though, according to the *Esher News* article, a "ballistic expert" was involved in the case.[54] The article never stated that the ballistic expert examined the car, merely that he suggested that it could be a .317 bullet. Stranger still was the unnamed ballistic expert's assertion that the bullet could have "ricochetted [sic] off the road surface before hitting the panel." Does this imply that the angle of entry was such that the missile had to come from a downward direction? That would seem to be very odd indeed. We are not given enough information to decide, but this case has enough inconsistencies to suggest that either a bullet was not involved, or that this shooting was not related to the other windscreen incidents. It is also interesting that despite this apparent *prima facie* case of a shooting along Portsmouth Road, for several months afterward, the police still maintained that there was no evidence of malicious damage to any of the cars involved in the sniper incidents.

A suggestion made on many occasions was that schoolboys with catapults were responsible for the damage. A good catapult with a stone or steel ball bearing could easily damage a car windscreen and could even be more powerful than some air guns. The suggestion that schoolboys were involved came early in the second wave of incidents, when a police sergeant told the *Esher News*, "Perhaps it will stop when the children go back to school."[55] However, the catapult theory, which was suggested on more than one occasion, has all the same problems of accuracy in adverse conditions as the air gun does. There is also the prolonged time period over which the incidents occurred and the diffusion of incidents beyond Portsmouth Road — all of which works against nonmobile children with catapults. There was also only one windscreen broken at a time, which suggests a remarkable patience for impudent children.

The British Automobile Association (AA) was quoted as saying that the damage was most likely due to inferior glass. It is unknown how inferior glass could be responsible for the Esher incidents, except possibly in conjunction with movements in the frame of the vehicle causing the glass to flex and crack. This, however, would not explain the starred windscreens or other evidence of impact that most people reported.

Loose Stones, Heavy Traffic, and an Active Press

An obvious explanation for the broken windscreens is that loose stones on the road were being flicked into the air by passing traffic and then striking windscreens of other cars. This possibility was suggested from the outset of the Esher incidents and was repeated many times by many different people.[56] It is also clear that local authorities favored this theory when they sent a sweeper lorry to clear Portsmouth Road.[57] The police and the Ministry of Transport, with their insistence that there was no evidence of malicious damage, also favored an explanation along these lines.[58] There is little doubt that flying stones can cause the damage seen along Portsmouth Road, but given the large number of incidents in such a short space of time, how likely is it? When looking at the likelihood of stones as the cause of the Esher incidents, it is necessary to take a number of factors into account, including traffic volume, the pattern of windscreen breakage, and the type of glass used in cars of the day. We shall address these points individually.

The windscreen shootings occurred during a period of extraordinary concern within Esher, when the townsfolk had become obsessed with its traffic problem. The old A3 (now the A307) ran straight through the town center, taking all of the traffic from London to the cities of Portsmouth, Winchester, and Southampton. Residents were concerned over traffic accidents, road improvements, and noise on the road. Many residents, spurred on by the *Esher News*, campaigned for a bypass road to be built around the town, which came to fruition in the late 1960s.

During the early 1950s, Portsmouth Road (then the A3 road) was the major means of driving between London and south-coast cities such as Portsmouth, Brighton, and Southampton. The *Esher News* had been campaigning for some time on the issue of traffic accidents and pollution through Esher itself—and with good cause. In September 1951, a census by the AA showed that there was an average of 987 cars an hour passing through Esher during the daytime, making that stretch of Portsmouth Road officially Britain's busiest highway.[59] Allowing for slack periods at night, that would mean that between twelve thousand to fifteen thousand vehicles a day passed through Esher's center, a staggering number for an old Roman Road not designed for the purpose. When one realizes that during the three years in which the phantom sniper operated, over 12 million cars traveled the road, then the fifty-one recorded damaged windscreens during this time actually looks statistically quite low (it equates to a 0.004 percent chance of a car along Portsmouth Road being damaged during this time). In other words, the damage occurring to the windscreens is not that statistically unusual.

There are statistics for everything in this world, including stone damage to windscreens. In a survey of nearly four thousand parked cars, 45 percent showed evidence of stone damage on their windscreens. This survey was backed up with another statistic that states that "stones cause 90 percent of windshield replacements."[60] The seriousness of stone damage was also outlined in a report for the Ministry of Transportation and Highways of British Columbia, Canada, where loose stones on roads were causing broken and damaged windscreens. The report recommended using smaller aggregate during their winter road-gritting program.[61] These results appear to suggest that windscreen damage by loose stones is very common indeed, with up to half of all cars showing evidence of stone damage. When these statistics are put together with the huge volume of traffic seen on Portsmouth Road, the number of incidents does not look statistically abnormal.

One reason that the Esher incidents look so abnormal is because of the large number of windscreens that were not just chipped or starred but actually shattered. According to the information given by the *Esher News* and other sources, of the fifty-one damaged vehicles the authors studied, thirty-two had their windscreens fully broken. This may come down to the windscreen types used in the 1950s. Virtually all modern cars have laminated windscreens, which have a thin layer of rubbery plastic sandwiched between two layer of glass. When hit by an object, a laminated windscreen will not shatter or frost over, it will merely produce a spider-web pattern. However, laminated glass was just coming into regular use in the early 1950s, and many cars traveling along Portsmouth Road would have had windscreens that were made of tempered glass that, when hit by an object, shatters into thousands of small pieces. It is this shattering that produces the characteristic frosted-over effect that can still be seen in broken side and rear windows of modern cars. This difference in design leaves tempered glass more open to shattering than laminated glass. In the early 1950s, tempered glass was more common than laminated glass, which would explain why so many windscreens were shattered. The glass type was only mentioned in two of the Esher incidents. Both of these were laminated windscreens and only received minor damage, not shattering.[62] While not conclusive, this follows the above pattern.

Further evidence favoring loose stones as the culprit comes from the pattern of windscreen damage. Most damage was to windscreens, suggesting that the missile was coming toward the vehicle. While a sniper could hit windscreens, it would be more likely that they would end up taking out side windows instead. Only one side shot was reported, and that was the "bullet hole" in Frank Smith's car door.[63] A second piece of evidence comes from the area in which the windscreen was hit. Of the four reports in which the area of impact is listed, all are on the driver's side of the car.[64] This is significant because stones flicked into the air are usually done so by traffic going in the opposite direction, which means that stones are most liable to hit the drivers side. However, stones lifted by a car in front can hit the windscreen anywhere. The noise of a stone hitting a windscreen, from firsthand experience, is a loud, sudden crack. Some people associated this noise with the shot of a gun.[65] However, given that the weapon commonly cited was an air gun and that the noise always came with the damage (a shot would be expected to be heard after the damage if the shot came from some distance away), this is better evidence of a stone rather than a gunman. It is also possible that there was something wrong with the road surface between Esher and Cobham that led to an excessive amount of loose stones on the road. It should be noted that an abnormal road surface is not necessary to produce the level of damage seen.

The majority, if not all, of the incidents along Portsmouth Road can be explained by flying stones, which correspond with the volume of traffic, pattern of damage, and windscreen type. The authors acknowledge that some damage seems unlikely to have been caused by flying stones, such as the hole in the car door and the two incidents of a rear window breaking. Yet a natural explanation is likely, rather than the presence of a lone gunman.

Given that the majority of smashed windscreens on Portsmouth Road are likely to have been caused by loose road chipping, how is it that something so inoffensive could lead to a national mystery? There are two crucial factors in the origin and level of interest of the phantom sniper: the volume of traffic along Portsmouth Road and the campaigning nature of the *Esher News*. When visiting modern-day Esher, one is struck by how dominant Portsmouth Road is within the village. This road is one of the main truck routes from London to the south coast, and it cuts through the middle of the village. Even now, years after the building of the Esher bypass road, it carries a massive volume of traffic along it, creating much noise and congestion. At the time of the sniper incidents, there was great concern in Esher about the level of traffic running through the village and the number of accidents this was generating. Articles about the road dominated practically every issue of the *Esher News*. Each issue would carry several items concerning that week's traffic accidents, and each month there would be a tally of accidents in comparison with the previous month. Throughout the period of the sniping claims, the *Esher News* showed extreme concern at what the traffic was doing to the village, and the paper was actively involved in the local campaign for a bypass road to be built.

Portsmouth Road was then the busiest highway in Britain, and it is no wonder that traffic would be high on the list of local concerns. This local obsession with traffic may have laid the foundations for the phantom sniper. It is probably no coincidence that the first acknowledged shooting was a high-profile incident involving the celebrity journalist Richard Dimbleby, who reported his broken windscreen to the Esher police. This made local people and the *Esher News* aware of the idea that there was a sharpshooter on Portsmouth Road. As further reports of smashed windscreens came in, the *Esher News* assumed that there was a connection between them. The paper promoted the idea of a sniper. Judging by the number of times that the newspaper mentioned the Esher Police Station, it appears that the paper was getting most of its reports from a contact inside the police station. This would explain how the *Esher News* heard of so many broken windscreens and why the incidents were so tightly clustered on the road between Esher and Cobham. Anybody who received a damaged windscreen on this stretch of road and thought that they had been shot at would automatically call the nearest police station, which would be in either Esher (if heading northbound) or Cobham (southbound). Assuming that there was some communication between the Esher and Cobham police stations, the *Esher News* would hear of all such incidents.

It is noticeable that many of the drivers reporting these incidents lived locally, were aware of the sniper rumors, and would be more likely to report their damaged windscreens to the authorities than passing motorists who might attribute an incident to loose stones. After the start of the second wave of damaged windscreens, the *Esher News* took a keen interest in the "shootings" and actively campaigned to get the claims scrutinized by the authorities. This campaigning, which resulted in the paper publishing forty articles on the matter in thirty-six months, fueled a social delusion in which any windscreen damage from anywhere within a twenty-kilometer radius of Esher would get reported. The eventual involvement of the national press, the local council, the Ministry for Transport, and the Metropolitan Police was seen by the *Esher News* as a vindication of its position on the matter. The editorial of June 20, 1952, makes it clear that the *Esher News* saw itself as crucial in the promotion of this affair, and they were probably correct in this.[66]

Like all bouts of social delusion, there comes a point when the number of incidents peaks and interest begins to fall. This seems to have been reached in about late September or early October 1952, when after over six months of solid coverage, the number of reports and news items began to decrease markedly. Although there was the odd burst of interest, the phantom sniper became yesterday's news.

The last piece of the puzzle concerns the large number of smashed windscreens on that one small stretch of Portsmouth Road — at least forty-three over thirty-six months (this excludes windscreens broken outside the Esher area). It was this large number that drew the *Esher News*'s attention in the first place and helped to perpetuate the idea of a local sniper. Is it feasible that loose stones or structural failure could cause so many breakages in such a short period? Unfortunately, we do not have the police incident books from Esher or Cobham, so it is impossible to know how many reports of windscreen damage they received in the periods before and after the sniper incidents. On average, there were one or two broken windscreens a week reported to the *Esher News* during the peak period between March and October 1952. According to the traffic census and stone-damage data quoted earlier, the number of incidents are perfectly within the bounds of normality. The levels of damage are not excessive when compared to the volume of traffic and the susceptibility of car windscreens to damage from loose stones.[67]

Chapter 11

The Ghost Rockets:
Anatomy of a Moral Panic

Imagination frames events unknown,
In wild, fantastic shapes of hideous ruin,
And what it fears creates.
                    — Hannah More[1]

History is replete with instances involving the rapid spread of false accusations and rumors about the existence of a group of deviants who are intent on perpetrating nefarious deeds on innocent community members. This form of social delusion has been identified by various loosely conceptualized labels at different times and places: terror, fear, scare, contagion, panic, rumor-panic, witch-hunt, persecution, craze, delusion, moral crusade, moral outrage, hysteria, or mass hysteria. In 1971, sociologist Jock Young originated the term "moral panic" to describe such episodes.[2] The following year, the term gained widespread circulation and rapid acceptance within the British social science community with the publication of *Folk Devils and Moral Panics: The Creation of Mods and Rockers* by Stanley Cohen.[3] The book examined the exhibition of relatively minor deviance among two British youth factions known as the Mods and the Rockers following a disturbance in Clacton, England, on Easter Sunday in 1964 and the exaggerated public reaction that ensued. In defining what constitutes a moral panic, Cohen used a symbolic interactionist or labeling perspective to analyze deviance, a precursor to what is now known as social constructionism.[4]

The labeling, interactionist, symbolic interactionist, or social interactionist approach is also referred to in general terms as the particularist, humanist, antipositivist, qualitative, or subjectivist position. The kindred

The author is grateful to Glenn Dawes, Anders Liljegren, and Clas Svahn for their co-authorship of this chapter.

theme of a social interactionist perspective is a shift from narrow, individual, etiological causes of deviance to a relativist definition emphasizing its ambiguous and dynamic nature, the role of social controlling agents in creating and maintaining deviant labels,[5] and the consequence of such designations in fostering further deviations.[6]

Cohen states that a moral panic is a societal reaction to a perceived threat to fundamental interests and values by moral deviants, whereby a "condition, episode, person or group" becomes defined as a danger:

> [I]ts nature is presented in a stylised and stereotypical fashion by the mass media; the moral barricades are manned by editors, bishops, politicians and other right-thinking people; socially accredited experts pronounce their diagnosis and solutions; ways of coping are evolved or (more often) resorted to.... Sometimes the panic passes over and is forgotten, except in folklore and collective memory; at other times it has more serious and long-lasting repercussions and might produce such changes as those in legal and social policy or even in the way the society conceives itself.[7]

Since the appearance of Cohen's seminal book in 1972, the term "moral panic" has grown increasingly popular as a useful analytical framework to understand collective actions in the fields of sociology, social and community welfare, social problems, social movements, deviance, and history.

While widely utilized by behavioral scientists in the United Kingdom, more quantitative-oriented sociologists from the United States have failed to embrace the concept of moral panics until recently, citing the ambiguity of Cohen's moral panic indicators. In an effort to remedy this situation, American sociologist Erich Goode and Israeli sociologist Nachman Ben-Yehuda refined Cohen's ambiguous conceptualization of a moral panic, identifying five characteristic features: concern, hostility, consensus, disproportionality, and volatility.[8]

The first core component is the presence of sufficient, measurable *concern* about a perceived threat to the public well-being. This concern typically involves fear and anxiety. It can be measured by opinion polls, media commentaries, or through organized social movements. Second, the public concern must generate heightened *hostility* toward an identifiable agent, group, or category that is perceived as a community threat. The appearance of hostility toward those believed responsible for the threat to core societal values and beliefs produces a dichotomy of good and evil stereotypes. For instance, "good" individuals wish to expunge society of the undesirable threat posed by the "devils," while "sinister" agents are identified. In discussing this good-versus-evil polemic, Barlow noted how police routinely round up crime suspects based on stereotypical features such as age, race, and socioeconomic background.[9] Third, a moral panic cannot exist unless a *consensus* forms within a particular segment of the society that the threat exists and poses a danger. While moral panics may be limited to a geographical region or section of society, a substantial number of societal members must be affected for the episode to develop.[10]

Goode and Ben-Yehuda identified the fourth characteristic feature of moral panics as *disproportionality*. Concern about the threat posed by moral deviants and their numerical abundance is far greater than can be objectively verified, despite unsubstantiated claims to the contrary. Sociologist Jeffery Victor noted that despite significant measurable concern, "the numbers of deviants are minimal or even nonexistent and their harm is very limited or even nonexistent."[11] According to Goode and Ben-Yehuda, during a moral panic, "the generation and dissemination of figures or numbers is extremely important — addicts, deaths, dollars, crimes, victims, injuries, illnesses — and most of the figures cited by moral panic 'claims-makers' are wildly exaggerated."[12] If the degree of disproportionality cannot be determined, it is not possible to conclude that the appearance of significant concern actually represents an episode of moral panic. Media amplification and stereotyping are relevant in contributing to the disproportionate way in which a threat is portrayed, raising the issue of social constructionism. A fifth essential feature of moral panics is *volitility*. The threat may appear or disappear suddenly, or it may gradually wax and wane. It may last for a few weeks or endure for years. It may remain dormant for decades only to suddenly resurface in another location. While episodes may be short-lived, there are often historical antecedents that lay dormant over time and reappear in the same or other locations. While volatile and socially constructed, their appearance is typically related to structural elements in society, as in the case of the early-modern witch-hunts that were fueled by political, gender, and demographic factors.[13]

Three Theoretical Models of Moral Panics

Goode and Ben-Yehuda offer three theoretical frameworks for analyzing the origins of moral panics. The *grassroots model* postulates that episodes are generated spontaneously from a broad cross section of the general public, who express widespread concern over moral deviants who are perceived to be involved in a particular event or issue. These concerns typically spread to other influential sectors of society including the mass media, politicians, and police. Often, concern builds to the extent that it is widely deemed that immediate action is required to resolve the threat, which commonly takes the form of organized social movements. The role of special-interest groups is not essential to generate moral outcry against a particular group of perceived deviants, as agents of social control such as the police, military, or mass media can serve the same purpose.[14] A moral crusade precipitated by a groundswell of grassroots participation occurred in the United States between 1983 and 1993 in reaction to an urban myth about the existence of a network of satanic cultists kidnapping and murdering children in ritual sacrifices. At least sixty rumor-panics were triggered in various sections of the country.[15] These episodes coincided with the disintegration of family structures and the desire to find scapegoats to serve as a metaphor for prevailing concerns over the weakened family and its capacity to protect children.[16]

According to the *elite model*, which utilizes a Marxist orientation, powerful societal members can consciously engineer a moral panic by initiating a campaign to generate and sustain moral outcry toward an invented or exaggerated threat from a specific group of targeted deviants. Their intention is to divert public attention from the actual problems of society which threaten their hold on power. The mass media, politicians, religious institutions, police, and military can be manipulated to mold public sentiment through such means as public policy and fund allocations. An example of the elite model was the European Renaissance witch-hunts in the wake of the rapidly eroding influence of the Catholic Church, which was threatened by new social, economic, religious, scientific, and political institutions. In response, the Catholic Church organized moral panics to reassert their waning power and influence by targeting groups of deviants, especially females, who were accused of colluding with the devil and were imprisoned, tortured, or executed.[17]

The *interest-group model* emphasizes the key role of special-interest groups in the formation of moral crusades. Middle-class and professional groups are more likely to initiate and sustain a moral panic of this type as an unintended consequence of focusing public attention on moral deviants and their supposed threat to the community good. Goode and Ben-Yehuda contend that professional associations such as church leaders may have personal interests in highlighting a certain issue and be responsible for focusing media attention away from a particular position. This may contradict the interests of elite groups, empowering interest groups in terms of the direction or timing of moral panics. While interest-group members may be sincere in advancing a cause, they may also be simultaneously elevating their status and power. A classic example of this type of moral panic was the antiprostitution crusade led by the female suffragette movement and fundamentalist Protestants who formed interest groups that fostered the U.S. "white slavery" scare of 1907–1914. During the episode, false stories that young women were being kidnapped and forced to work as prostitutes by organized crime gangs prompted widespread public outrage. As a result, hundreds of people involved in adulterous relationships or young men living with a lover outside of marriage were branded as participating in white slavery, and some were even imprisoned.[18]

We shall next describe the context and circumstances surrounding the formation of waves of claims and public discourse about the existence of imaginary German V-rockets allegedly test-fired over Scandinavia by the Soviet Union shortly after the end of World War II. We shall utilize Goode and Ben-Yehuda's schema for identifying moral panics in understanding the origin and nature of this significant, but little-known episode in Scandinavian history.

The Ghost Rocket Scare: A Synopsis

Between early May and June 30, 1946, a significant and widespread fear swept across Sweden and, to a lesser extent, Scandinavia in general as tens of thousands of Swedes reported observing mysterious, rocketlike projectiles streaking through the skies. The episode coincided with the Soviet military occupation of Peenemunde, the former center of German rocket development, and engendered a popular folk belief that the Soviets were test-firing German V-rockets as a means to demoralize or intimidate the Swedish population or as a prelude to an invasion. Conspicuously, not a single piece of tangible evidence was ever recovered to confirm the rockets' existence. On October 10, the Swedish Defense Staff released their results of a four-month investigation of about one thousand reports, finding no compelling evidence that even one sighting originated from a foreign government. The report attributed most sightings to astronomical and meteorological causes.

Astronomer Louis Winkler correlated the projectile sightings to a rare confluence of meteorological and astronomical events, namely geomagnetic comets and the periodic disbursement of their orbital streams in combination with an unusual influx of solar activity, producing extraordinary auroras, meteors, and cometary spray streaking through the atmosphere. Winkler stated that

> The uniqueness of the ghost rocket activity is emphasized by additional and accompanying phenomena. Scandinavian newspapers gave accounts

of spectacular auroras occurring over Helsinki on February 26 and Stockholm on July 26. The preliminary aurora correlates well with the spray date of Encke on February 25, whereas the July 26 aurora corresponds to the onset of the main ghost rocket activity.[19]

The historical and political contexts were also key factors in the shifting interpretation of the objects from naturalistic to Soviet-made causes, including rumors to this effect and a long history of Soviet mistrust, which has preoccupied Swedes for centuries. Top Swedish military officials, politicians, scientists, police, and journalists made public statements reinforcing the existence of the rockets. Near the end of World War II, German V-rockets devastated parts of the United Kingdom. Occasionally, they strayed into Scandinavia, raising concerns but causing no damage. One V-2 fell near Backebo in southeastern Sweden, leaving a crater five meters wide and two to three meters deep. Fears over a repeat of the recent, vivid, and highly publicized destruction in England were rekindled in Sweden during 1946, since Russian forces had occupied Peenemunde. Soviet troops controlled much of northern Europe during this period, and it was unclear how much Scandinavian territory they might claim in the political uncertainty following the war.[20] It is within this context of centuries-old Russian invasion fears and postwar political ambiguity involving possible Russian claims on Swedish territory that plausible rumors began circulating about potentially hostile Russian intentions.

There was speculation as early as March 19 that the Soviets would soon begin test-firing rockets. A newswire from the Swedish newspaper agency *Tidningarnas Telegrambyra* appeared in numerous domestic papers on March 19, including *Sydostra Sveriges Dagblad, Umebladet,* and *Norra Vasterbotten,* serving as a prelude of what was to occur in the spring and summer. It quotes the London *Daily Mirror's* Berlin correspondent as stating that "German scientists and technicians who work under Russian supervision will shortly release a number of V-2 bombs from secret research stations on the Baltic." Xenophobia of Russians again resurfaced between April 23 and 26, as a series of earth tremors were reported in the Swedish counties of Blekinge, Skane, and Kalmar, and in the vicinity of the Danish island of Bornholm in the southern Baltic. The *Helsingborgs Dagblad* of April 27 suggested that the tremors were Russian nuclear weapons tests. On April 28, the Swedish foreign affairs minister, Osten Unden, met privately with his Norwegian counterpart, Halvard Lange, who warned that there was great consternation in American political circles that the Soviets would soon possess atomic weapons. Lange stated "that there was an imminent danger of war" and that a group aligned with General Dwight Eisenhower felt that "differences between the U.S. and the

Soviets had taken on such a nature that the U.S. ought to strike with a preventative war. President Truman, however, was opposed to this."[21] These events and circumstances provide a context for the mass sightings of ghost rockets and the ensuing fear that was about to sweep across Sweden.

Moral Panic Indicators

CONCERN

Measurable, extraordinary disquiet throughout Sweden that Russia posed an imminent threat to its sovereignty characterized the episode. This fear was manifest in rocket-sighting reports, media commentaries and editorials, views expressed by authority figures, in letters to the editor, and even period poetry.

Anxiety was often expressed following eyewitness accounts of aerial observations interpreted as rockets. Between January and early May 1946, observations of fireballs streaking above Sweden were reported. This includes meteor sightings at Fransborg, northwest of Stockholm,[22] and over Ljungdalen in Jamtland, both on January 9,[23] and in Dalarna County on January 17.[24] In the wake of rumors that began circulating in mid–March that the Soviets would soon begin test-firing V-rockets over Sweden, rising anxiety quickly turned to fear. On May 21 when a yellow fireball was sighted at Halsingborg, some residents were described as "disturbed."[25] By May 24, the first rocket report was recorded with an early morning sighting over Landskrona. While night watchmen described it as a "fireball with a tail," another witness said it was a "wingless cigar-shaped body" spurting exhaust sparks.[26] Some newspapers described the incident with such terms as "rocket bomb,"[27] "remote-directed bombs,"[28] "projectile"[29] "V-bomb,"[30] and "V-1 bomb."[31] Media speculation that some sightings may have been remote-controlled rockets provided a convenient, familiar, unitary label with which to classify ambiguous stimuli. As the sightings continued, the Swedish and foreign press increasingly described the rockets as factual, and the previous reports of naturalistic aerial phenomena (i.e., meteors, aural phenomena, and fireballs) were overwhelmingly being described as dangerous Soviet weapons.

Many Swedish press reports expressed concern and explicit fear that the Soviet's newly acquired missile technology would soon be equipped with atomic weapons that would be used on Sweden. American political commentator Marquis Childs warned in a major Swedish daily that the rocket intrusions were a portent of how the next war would be waged: "If the arms race ends in a new and more terrible war, Sweden's advanced civilization will be torn asunder along with nearly any other.... It is this which makes the use of Sweden as a suitable military laboratory so serious."[32] The *Svenska Dagbladet*'s New York editor, Per Persson, concurred with this view: "If these projectiles carried explosive charges of atomic bomb character and if they were directed against industrial centers...Sweden would be destroyed and the war would be over."[33] The Swedish magazine *Se* described the rocket scare as "a premonition of 'push-button war.'"[34] One press columnist suggested that the United States should drop "atom bombs on Moscow, before ... the ghost rockets become palpable."[35] Some commentators expressed this atomic fear in poems.[36]

Hostility

During the episode, there was heightened hostility toward the Soviets, given the long history of bitter Swedish-Russian relations. Hence, once the sightings were attributed to the Soviets and were rumored to have been V-rockets over the country, many Swedes were described as angry[37] at the Soviets, and heated political accusations were exchanged as to the rockets' origin. The Soviet journal *Novoie Vremia* (New Times) denounced the test-firing claims as anti–Soviet "slander which is poisoning the international atmosphere."[38] The same publication, characterized the allegations as "Swedish lies" precipitated by mass panic.[39] When the Swedish Defense Staff issued its August 6 communiqué vindicating foreign-power involvement in the rocket sightings, *Ny Dag*, a communist newspaper published in Stockholm, chided the "meddlesome" Swedish press for blaming the Russians, making analogies to Pinocchio in noting that "the nose is lengthened ... among the Swedish newspaper family."[40] One newspaper commented that the Russians were using Sweden "as a shooting range and as a guinea pig at trials with new weapons."[41] In some circles it was speculated that the missiles were being guided over Sweden as a tactic of intimidation to either "scare us somehow"[42] or, as a report in the *Smalands Folkblad* of July 27 suggested, as a Soviet response to the well-publicized atomic detonations on Pacific atolls at this time.

Under the category of hostility are evil stereotypes of the nefarious folk devil — in this case the Soviets. A columnist for a major Swedish daily newspaper noted the unsubstantiated portrayals of the Russian during the scare, remarking that their portrayal "is a villainy, a bare and unromantic villainy."[43]

CONSENSUS

During June and July, a widespread consensus emerged across Sweden that the Soviet rocket threat posed a real and imminent danger among a substantial segment of society. This is evidenced by the volume of rocket sightings, media handling of such claims, and military activities reinforcing a conviction in the rockets' reality. In the wake of recent sightings and increasing concern as to the rockets' widely assumed hostile Russian origin, the Swedish Defense Staff distributed 221 copies of a memo to national and regional army, navy, and air force units, asking anyone who had recently observed mysterious aerial objects to complete a questionnaire about the sighting. The memo also provided guidance for interviewing civilians who reported observations of rocketlike objects, stating, "It cannot be ruled out that these [recent sightings] could be connected to tests, by a foreign power, of types of remotely piloted weapons."[44]

After a series of spectacular rocket observations, July 10, the Swedish Defense Staff issued a public appeal for all citizens to immediately report any unusual aerial sights or sounds to their nearest troop unit,[45] underscoring the potential gravity of the situation. The military's public involvement and high-profile inspections of numerous "crash" sites began at this time, reinforcing the widespread belief that the Soviets were test-firing V-rockets. While the existence of even a single missile was never verified, press descriptions of these "crashes" contributed to the prevailing definition of the situation.[46]

Prominent foreign newspapers circulating in Sweden further reinforced the domestic media reports about the rockets' existence. An editorial in a leading British paper stated that "it does not need much imagination to see Russian engineers, no doubt assisted by obedient German scientists, operating from a research station on the Baltic coast."[47] The *New York Times* of August 12 began a dispatch as follows: "A swarm of rocket bombs passed over Stockholm at 10 o'clock tonight."

DISPROPORTIONALITY

The episode was disproportionate to the Soviet threat to Sweden at the time. Because the United States already possessed atomic weapons and was a strong Swedish ally, one Swedish commentator asked

> But what in heaven's name is the reason for shooting over us? Why make the Swedish newspapers report about how the projectiles go when they own hundreds of well-controlled square miles to test in? Why put pressure on us—when the first rule behind spanking a child is that he should

know the reason for it? We doubt the ghost rockets ... and should they all be true, Russians would have to put the whole German toy industry changing to production of ghost bomb launchers.[48]

These sentiments were echoed by R.V. Jones, then director of intelligence of the British Air Staff, who noted while many of his staff believed that Russian rockets were violating Swedish air space, this assessment was counter to the facts at hand and to the political circumstances. Jones remarked that if the Russians possessed a controllable V-rocket, it would do more harm to their cause to test it because it would "alert the West to the fact that they had such an impressive weapon." Second, Jones questioned the remarkable reliability of the flying bombs:

> The Germans had achieved no better than 90 per cent reliability in their flying bomb trials of 1944, at very much shorter range. Even if the Russians had achieved a reliability as high as 99 per cent over their much longer ranges, this still meant that 1 per cent of all sorties should have resulted in a bomb crashing on Swedish territory. Since there had been allegedly hundreds of sorties, there ought to be at least several crashed bombs already in Sweden, and yet nobody had ever picked up a fragment. [Jones, R.V. (1978) *Most Secret War*. London: Hamilton, p. 641.]

Throughout the scare, numerous exaggerated claims were made that V-rockets were invading Swedish air space and had crashed and inflicted damage. Yet once thorough investigations were conducted, not a single claim was verified. For instance, various ground marks and objects found near the scene of rocket sightings were commonly portrayed in the media as having an association with the projectile reports. In central Sweden, a "pit in the ground" was inspected by air-defense officers as a possible "ghost bomb mark."[49] When a deposit of slag and coal-like material was found in central Sweden, it was assumed that it must have fallen from the sky, and an investigation was demanded.[50] At one typical crash site, a "projectile find" was subsequently identified as a steam-valve spindle.[51] On August 5, a farmer in southern Sweden discovered a "missile" embedded up to thirty centimeters into the ground in a remote area of Blekinge.[52] One reporter concluded that based on the details, "the object fell from a very great height," suggesting that it was part of a rocket.[53] Authorities later identified it as a dislodged airplane antenna.[54] The unexplained death of three cows belonging to Jamtland farmer Andera Edsasen was attributed to a missile carrying poisonous material.[55] On a farm in Somlingbacken, Jamtland, when Maria Vastfeldt heard a loud noise before a henhouse was razed by fire, a V-rocket was blamed.[56] Investigators later traced the cause to a blasting cap and nitrolite cartridge.[57] When a barn in mid–Norrland collapsed for no apparent reason on August 11,[58] it was "connected to the appearance of the ghost rockets," which were seen the same day. Police subsequently determined that a tornado was responsible.[59] While a concurrent fire in the Svartvik sulfite factory's timber store near Sundsvall was also blamed on a "ghost bomb fall," police found no specific evidence to support the theory.[60] Investigators from the Institute of Criminology Research later identified the probable cause as an overheated engine transmission bearing.[61]

A letter dated August 9 from Swedish Defense Staff archives reveals that when a metal fly caterpillar infestation appeared in the southern Swedish provinces of Skane, Blekinge, and Oland during mid–July, Jan Flinta of Stockholm wrote to the military theorizing that the rockets were designed to dispense caterpillar eggs.[62] After a Swedish B-18 bomber crashed at Valdshult on August 12, intense speculation ensued as to whether it has collided with a rocket bomb because observers reported that it had suddenly plummeted almost vertically to the ground.[63] An inquiry commission later dismissed this claim.[64]

The Swedish Defense Staff announced the results of its four-month investigation on October 10, concluding that about eight hundred reports resulted from "celestial phenomena." While the remaining two hundred cases were classified as unexplained, there was no credible evidence to conclude that any sightings were missiles or other objects of either domestic or foreign origin.[65] The report stated that

> The majority of sightings with certainty result from celestial phenomena… [which] often occur but usually do not attract any special attention. Since the interest of the general public was awoken…[they] started to take a closer note of them…therefore the large number of reports.
>
> Some sightings cannot, however, be explained but this should not be attributed to some sort of object of a different kind. Not enough information is in hand…to be able to draw firm conclusions with any certainty concerning their nature, origin and appearance. Through a collaboration with astronomers it was clear that the two "peaks" in July and August probably were caused by meteors or meteorites. … [Of the alleged crashes] remains mainly consist of coke or slag-like formations.… In no case has anything come forth that can be considered as if the material came from any kind of space projectile. In certain lakes very thorough investigations have been made because of supposed crashes. So far, however, no find has turned up which can be presumed to originate from a V-type weapon.

In all, military officials received about one hundred reports of alleged crashes.[66] On at least twenty-eight occasions, personnel conducted on-site inspections.[67] Thirty "bomb fragments" were collected from both civilians and Swedish Defense Staff representatives, but all were eventually traced to mundane sources.

VOLATILITY

Volatility was a feature of the episode which began slowly on May 21 when the inhabitants of Halsingborg reported a yellow fireball passing overhead. Observation reports and press discourse continued in a sporadic but increasing fashion until a dramatic influx of sightings and concern over the existence of V-rockets occurred on June 9. Reports continued intermittently through July 9, when a second peak occurred after an object subsequently identified as a bolide crossed eastern Sweden. The sightings ebbed and flowed throughout the remainder of the episode, declining rapidly by early September. In September, while sightings decreased dramatically, press coverage remained high, but much discourse was of a more skeptical nature.

Conclusion

In tracing the cause of the phantom-rocket moral panic, there is neither evidence of a conspiracy among elites using institutions of social control to fabricate the scare nor indications that interest groups formed to oppose the perceived threat during the episode. The Swedish missile scare of 1946 conforms to the grassroots model of moral panics because it originated from popular public concern over Russian access to destructive German V-rockets in nearby eastern Europe. Heightened anxiety first took the form of rumors to this effect that appeared in March, which were based on stereotypes dating back centuries depicting the Soviets as an evil, hostile, militarily aggressive empire with aspirations of acquiring Swedish territory. It was members of the public who first began reinterpreting ambiguous aerial stimuli as rocket-related incidents, and these views were quickly amplified in the subsequent mass media descriptions of these rockets as indisputable missiles of Russian origin. The views of Swedish and foreign authority figures (e.g., police, military officers, politicians, journalists) further crystalized this popular consensus. While no specific social movements or special-interest groups arose during the ghost rocket scare to focus moral outcry against the perceived Russian folk devil, reporting by the mass media widely described ambiguous observations of mysterious aerial stimuli as possible or certain V-rockets. Visual observations and verbal opinions by scientists and politicians further congealed public consensus about the reality of the missile flyovers and the threat that they supposedly posed.

Sweden's ghost rocket panic of 1946 was one in a series of moral panics involving security concerns about the Soviet Union, dating back to at least the nineteenth century. Northern Europe has a two-hundred-year history of antagonisms with the former Soviet Union, including ideological disputes, espionage claims, border conflicts, warfare, and invasion fears.[68] Between 1899 and 1914, itinerant Russian workers popularly dubbed "saw-filers" traversed rural Sweden. Known for their expertise in sharpening tools, the name soon became synonymous among Swedes for Russian spies. These accusations were never confirmed, despite police monitoring of their movements and their occasionally masquerading as saw-filers.[69] Historian Franklin Scott remarked that "[a]lmost certainly they were saw-filers and nothing more."[70] Between fifty and three hundred saw-filers, most hailing from the Novgorod region, traveled to Sweden from autumn to winter and earned high pay.[71] Speculation about their possible clandestine activities was especially intense between 1899 and 1902 and 1910 and 1914.[72] Newspaper editors were mainly responsible for depicting saw-filers as potential spies.[73]

During the 1930s, intermittent waves of sighting claims and public discourse over the existence of mysterious "ghost planes," occurred in northern Sweden. Also referred to as the "ghost flier" or "flier x," thousands of Swedes reported seeing the craft, predominantly at night. They were typically described as grey monoplanes devoid of identifying insignias or markings, sporting landing skis and a powerful searchlight. There were thousands of eyewitness sightings, and on occasion observers even claimed that they could discern the outline of a pilot.

There are many conspicuous aspects to the flier x episode, including its supernatural and folkloric qualities. For instance, the ghost flier was frequently observed or heard in impossible flying conditions for the period, even alighting and departing during fierce blizzards in remote areas where other planes and pilots would not dare venture. Period aircraft were incapable of operating under treacherous blizzard conditions for several consecutive hours, performing the bold maneuvers described by observers, and eluding the massive military search that ensued during the heaviest concentration of sightings, which was between December 1933 and February 1934. No confirmation of the plane or its secret airfield was ever given. The prevailing folk theory held that the sightings were Russian reconnaissance missions.[74] However, there were occasional speculations that the mysterious ghost planes originated from Germany[75] or Japan,[76] or were smugglers of liquor[77] or weapons.[78]

Since the early 1980s, thousands of alleged submarine intrusions, widely believed to be Soviet spy vessels, have been recorded in Swedish territorial waters. Between 1981 and 1994, a Swedish government commission assessed over six thousand reports of suspected underwater incursions.[79] Despite concluding that a few major incidents involving Soviet submarines were real, most claims were attributable to naturalistic explanations and involved unverified ambiguous perceptions such as wave movements, marine sounds and lights, and divers. The commission also noted a relationship between the influx of reports in relation to media publicity. There is considerable literature on the submarine debate in the Swedish media.[80] Intermittent claims of Soviet submarines violating Swedish waters have occasionally appeared throughout the twentieth century, but they have intensified dramatically since 1981, when a Soviet Whiskey Class U137 ran aground during a spy mission. While it was widely reported but never conclusively proven that the vessel carried nuclear weapons, analysts from the Research Institute of National Defense found traces suggestive of nuclear activity, and the incident precipitated a frenzy of domestic and international media interest and Swedish political protests.

Since the nineteenth century, Sweden has experienced several recurrences of a singular moral panic involving exaggerated domestic-security concerns in relation to the Soviet Union, from the saw-filers and flier x to ghost rockets and phantom submarines. Goode and Ben-Yehuda's moral panic model is useful in identifying and understanding the origin and nature of the ghost rocket panic of 1946, placing it in context with similar Swedish episodes. Given the continuation of Swedish-Russian antagonisms and social and political uncertainties following the breakup of the Soviet Union—and perhaps instigated by a relatively small number of genuine espionage attempts—there is every reason to expect future episodes of this moral panic to surface. Only the form these episodes take will change, reflecting the dynamic political and technological circumstances.

Chapter 12

The Wish Mania as a Moral Panic in Reverse

What ardently we wish, we soon believe.[1] — Young

Taxonomies of human behavior are often based on social outcomes of an insidious, value-laden process that may reflect the milieu and Zeitgeist of the evaluator. A classic example of subjectivity in constructing classification schemes was the creation of hierarchies of human social evolution in the nineteenth century. During this period, popular racist stereotypes of native people, minorities, and various deviants, were used to support so-called culture- and value-free scientific theories of degeneration, European intellectual superiority, and the genetic basis of behavior.[2] A more recent illustration of this point is the publication of the *Diagnostic and Statistical Manual of Mental Disorders*, which has been widely criticized for placing medical labels on deviant social roles in Western society and creating such dubious categories as alcoholism as a disease,[3] compulsive gambling,[4] and homosexuality as a mental disorder.[5] Far from reflecting universal elements in nature awaiting cross-cultural, transhistorical discovery and identification, these categories were human creations involving ambiguous, arbitrary criteria. Mindful of this caveat about the subjective, socially constructed nature of classification systems, and using a cognitive psychology-social interactionist approach, I propose the existence of a category of collective behavior termed "wish manias."

Moral Panics: A Brief Overview

British sociologist Stanley Cohen originated the term "moral panic" in 1972 in his seminal study of exaggerated negative public reaction to a relatively minor disturbance in Clacton, England, by two British youth

197

factions (the Mods and the Rockers) in 1964. His subsequent use of the term "moral panic" has since entered the mainstream sociological vocabulary and has become an integral part of the literature on collective behavior, social movements, and social problems. As noted in the previous chapter, Cohen defined a moral panic as a societal reaction to a perceived danger from moral deviants.[6]

This definition uses a labeling or societal-reaction paradigm to understand crime and deviance, which was an easy precursor to contemporary models of social constructionism.[7] The presence of a perceived long-term threat within a diffuse geographical setting typifies moral panics. It can be confined to a community, region, country or group of countries. Primarily symbolic and rumor-driven, the panic consists of general anxiety over exaggerated perceptions of eroding traditional values.

Self-fulfilling stereotypes of xenophobic scapegoats and deviants who are unjustly accused of evil acts characterize moral panics. Panics typically include subversion myths in which a particular alien group is perceived as threatening fundamental social values.[8] Ethnic and minority groups, heretics, and the poor have been common scapegoats throughout history. Subversion myths flourish during periods of social tension and economic hardship and are typified by dramatic, plausible rumors containing meaningful, topical morals or messages reflecting popular fears. During oral transmission, local details are substituted, and a credible source is identified.[9] For instance, the recent American satanic-cult scare coincided with eroding family structures and a search for scapegoats[10] in an effort to protect a way of life.[11] Rumors and urban legends of satanic cults are metaphors about the inability of the weakened family to protect children.[12] American sociologist Erich Goode and Israeli sociologist Nachman Ben-Yehuda identified five moral panic indicators: concern, hostility, consensus, disproportionality, and volatility.[13] In this chapter, the context and circumstances surrounding the formation of a wish mania, involving mass sightings of imaginary airships in the United States during a seven-month period between 1896 and 1897, is described.

From November 17, 1896, to mid–May 1897, waves of claims and public discourse about the existence of airships spread rapidly across the United States amid rumors that an American inventor had perfected the world's first heavier-than-air flying machine. Tens of thousands of citizens reported seeing airships. The ship was typically described as cigar-shaped with wings or propellers, an attached undercarriage, and a powerful headlight. The widespread reports of phantom-airship observations coincided with an American national obsession with science, invention, and rationalism. Voluminous, plausible newspaper speculation, in conjunction with publicized attempts at powered flight, resulted in tens of thousands of citizens misperceiving mundane astronomical and meteorological phenomena as airships far exceeding the period technology.[14] Hoaxes and press fabrications or exaggerations added further fuel to the airship mania, although these report types were in the minority.[15] The sightings served as a projected Rorschach test of the collective psyche, underscoring the promise of rapid technological advancement during a period of spiritual decline.[16]

While moral panics are well-documented incidents, little has been written on wish manias. The collective-delusion literature is almost exclusively filled with descriptions of episodes involving the perceived existence of imaginary negative agents that engender mass anxiety and fear within a community or region. These include descriptions of phantom monsters,[17] gassers,[18] slashers,[19] genital-stealing ghosts,[20] atomic fallout,[21] cattle mutilators,[22] rockets,[23] and satanic cults.[24] Conversely, the literature is virtually devoid of descriptions of social delusions involving the rapid spread of positive agents that produce exaggerated feelings of hope and transformation. It should be noted that we have not included behaviors involving millenarianism because they are not typically classified within the collective-delusion literature but under such headings as social movements and religious cults and sects. Why? Because they are not considered spontaneous.

Setting Parameters

A wish mania is defined as the rapid, spontaneous spread of false, exaggerated, or unsubstantiated beliefs within a diffuse collective such as a community, region. or country. The belief is deemed plausible within a specific sociocultural context, whereby many members of the affected population become preoccupied with the perceived existence of a benevolent rumor-related object, agent, condition, or circumstance. As people attempt to substantiate the existence of a positive or benevolent agent, they overscrutinize and redefine ambiguous, ordinarily mundane objects, events, situations, and circumstances, generating a self-fulfilling prophesy that reflects the emerging definition of the situation.

The origin and nature of moral panics revolve around the appearance of what Cohen described as "folk devils," the nefarious agent or agents believed responsible for the deterioration of traditional morals and values.[25] Correspondingly, wish manias center on the appearance of what I shall term "folk angels," an exaggerated public reaction to a positive agent that is highly desirable and widely viewed as having the potential for significant public good. Exacerbating factors contributing to a redefinition of the situation and the development of a wish mania include exaggerated media reporting, human perceptual fallibility and memory reconstruction, charismatic leaders, conformity dynamics, cultural folk beliefs and stereotypes, and major social or economic crises. Wish manias typically persist from a few weeks to several months, occasionally lasting for years, and recur periodically. They usually decline rapidly once the expected positive agent fails to materialize. Near the end of the episode, a barrage of negative mass media accounts questioning the folk angel's existence further adds to its demise.

Excluded from my definition of wish manias are spontaneous ecstasies arising within organized, ritualized, or institutionalized social environments, although once an episode starts, it may become the subject of such activities. Goode defines ecstatic collectives as "Highly emotional states and trances, in which the dominant mood is positive, joyous, rapturous, even frenzied."[26] This includes such behaviors at certain sporting events (e.g., the emotional zeal associated with Brazilian soccer matches),[27] charismatic[28] and "primitive"[29] religious groups, collective glossolalia,[30] political rallies,[31] South American carnivals,[32] and rock concerts.[33]

Millenarian movements embody each wish mania element, but they are a different genre. While wish manias may engender or stem from millenarian movements, in other respects they are distinctly separate entities. Wish manias may include any of the three central elements of cargo cult movements as outlined by Goode:

> Three basic ingredients that make millennial (or millenarian) religious cults possible are one, some sort of cultural disaster or crisis; two, a prior set of millennial ideas from the original culture, and three, the emergence of a charismatic leader to put together, articulate, and propagate these ideas.[34]

Millenarian movements appear to be a special category of social delusion that is related to, but separate from, my definition of wish manias.

The use of the word "wish" is not intended to be interpreted in any psychoanalytic or psychodynamic sense such as unconscious fantasies. Instead, I emphasize the socially constructed nature of reality.[35] The use of the word "delusion" is not employed in the psychiatric sense but in the sociological context of adherence to false but plausible folk beliefs.

Wish Mania Indicators

CONCERN VERSUS ENTHUSIASM

The first key ingredient in a moral panic is the existence of sufficient concern or even fear about the perceived threat to the community well-being. The concern should be measurable (e.g., opinion polls, organized social movements, public commentary in the media). In a wish mania, there is a measurable presence of collective enthusiasm about the existence of an agent or object that is believed to embody features that can positively affect community well-being in a significant way.

HOSTILITY VERSUS HOPEFULNESS

Public concern must engender increased hostility toward the identifiable agent that is perceived as threatening to the community. The advent of hostility toward those responsible for the threat produces a dichotomy of stereotypes consisting of "good" or respectable individuals who want to rid themselves of the undesirable threat posed by the "folk devils." Wish manias involve a preoccupation with a positive agent or object that can potentially benefit the community and revolutionize lifestyles either physically (through some new invention or miracle cure) or spiritually (believe in "x" and you'll live forever).

NEGATIVE CONSENSUS VERSUS POSITIVE CONSENSUS

The existence of moral panics is dependent upon a consensus that a problem or threat exists among at least some section of the society. Conversely, the wish mania must involve a substantial number of community members in agreement that the positive agent or object can solve long-standing problems, the solution to which will benefit the community. While moral panics may be limited to a region or section of society, if the number of people affected is insubstantial, there is little chance that a moral panic will exist.[36] The same is true of wish manias.

DISPROPORTIONALITY

There is an assumption that the degree of public concern or number of affected persons is disproportionate to the real threat: "In moral panics, the generation and dissemination of figures or numbers is extremely important — addicts, deaths, dollars, crimes, victims, injuries, illnesses — and most of the figures cited by moral panic 'claims-makers' are wildly exaggerated."[37] The same is true of wish manias.

VOLATILITY

They may suddenly appear or disappear, or surface or subside in a waxing and waning fashion. They may persist for weeks or decades, suddenly lie dormant, then just as suddenly resurface. Many short-lived moral panics have historical antecedents that lay dormant over time and reoccur in the same or other locations. Again, the same is true of wish manias.

Examples of wish manias appear in chapter one. Prominent recurrent episodes include Virgin Mary "appearances,"[38] reports of British fairy encounters,[39] and UFO sightings.[40–41] For instance, accounts of UFO occupants and fairies depict Otherworldly beings that are functional equivalents of religion. They are substitutes for god in a secular age that are camouflaged for modern-day reception.[42] Episodes even focus on the existence of imaginary or extinct creatures such as Bigfoot or the Tasmanian "Tiger," linking these animals with UFOs or the supernatural. Bigfoot's reported capabilities now rival those of aliens and fairies in terms of their power and function, including the ability to vanish or materialize, become transparent, communicate telepathically, change shape, withstand motor vehicle impacts and bullets.[43] Recent Australian folk theories consider the Tasmanian "Tiger" as a possible extraterrestrial or paranormal creature.[44]

The Airship Episode and Wish Mania Indicators

ENTHUSIASM

There was a measurable presence of excitement across the country during the 1896-1897 airship episode. This was reflected in media commentaries, letters to the editor, airship-sighting reports, and the opinions of authority figures. In many instances, enthusiasm was engendered after eyewitness accounts of ambiguous aerial objects interpreted as the airship.

In describing the first sighting, involving hundreds of witnesses in Sacramento, California, on November 17, one typical press report began as follows: "A vast amount of excitement was created among residents in the outskirts of the city tonight by the appearance of what they claim to have been an airship" (*The* San Francisco *Call*, November 18, 1896, p. 3). Ten days later, as the sightings continued, the same newspaper reported, "The subject of the airship and lights seen by the people of half a dozen counties has not lost any of the interest in the public mind" (*The Call*, November 27, 1896, p. 14).

As the sightings spread across the rest of the country between January

Figure 12.1: Sketch of an airship with birdlike wings reported by California residents in November 1896. (*San Francisco Call*, November 23, 1896, p. 1.)

and May 1897, considerable excitement was also in evidence. In Nebraska, it was reported that "Kearney is the latest town that is involved in the throes of excitement over the mysterious light" (*York Daily Times*, February 23, 1897, p. 3). When a strange light was spotted near Mansfield, Texas, the *Dallas Morning News* of April 18 published a report by a telegraph operator who wrote, "Great excitement prevails here." On the evening of April 12, the residents of Jewell, Iowa, "were greatly excited ... by the appearance of the so-called airship" (*Iowa State Register*, April 14, 1897, p. 5), while in Cedar Rapids, another airship report caused "considerable excitement" (*Waterloo Daily Courier*, April 14, 1897, p. 14). After the craft was rumored to have floated over Cripple Creek, Colorado, the community was described as "wildly excited over the affair, and it is the general talk" (*Denver Times*, April 19, 1897, p. 1). When the vessel was sighted in West Virginia, it was reported that "the mysterious air ship seems to be the all-absorbing topic at present" (*Parkersburg Sentinel*, April 21, 1897, p. 1).

Many authority figures such as police officers, politicians, and prominent business people were cited as airship believers. Groups of witnesses in communities across the country commonly signed or offered to sign affidavits to this effect. In Cincinnati, Ohio, police officer John Ringer saw a mysterious aerial light and stated emphatically, "I believe it was the

Figure 12.2: An eyewitness sketched this drawing of an airship with huge fanlike propellers flying over Oakland, California, on November 20, 1896. Hundreds of other residents claimed to have seen it that evening. (*San Francisco Call*, November 22, 1896, p. 1.)

airship" (*Toledo Evening Blade*, April 30, 1897, p. 2). In Farmersville, Texas, the city marshal spotted the mysterious vessel and claimed to discern the figures of two men inside (*Austin Daily Statesman*, April 19, 1897, p. 7). One witness was the mayor of Hermann, Missouri (Herman *Advertiser-Courier*, April 21, 1897, p. 3). Among a large number of citizens who report-

Figure 12.3: On April 10, 1897, Chicago newsstand dealer Walter McCann used a box camera to take a spectacular photograph of an airship over north Chicago. The object in the original photograph was vague and enhanced by the artist. (*Chicago Times-Herald*, April 12, 1897, p. 1.)

edly observed the vessel in Albert Lea, Minnesota, was "ex-mayor Gillrup" (*St. Paul Pioneer Press*, April 12, 1897, p. 4.). When Russellville, Kentucky, residents observed the airship "plainly and distinctly," witnesses included Mayor Andrews and prominent merchant James McCutchens (*Louisville Evening Post*, April 16, 1897, p. 5). Among several prominent citizens who observed the airship at Storm Lake, Iowa, was Justice Lot Thomas and his wife (*Evening Times-Republican*, April 9, 1897, p. 9). Some people even organized themselves to watch for the vessel. For instance, in Belton, Texas, a crowd of respected citizens "assembled for the purpose of watching for that much-talked-of airship" (*Houston Post*, April 22, 1897, p. 9).

Press sensationalism was another factor in perpetuating the episode and contributing to the enthusiasm, first in California and later across the United States. Amid intense public interest in airship development, newspaper editors published a barrage of articles speculating as to whether someone had invented the world's first practical airship. Yellow journalism was rife during the episode, as certain newspaper editors would sensationalize, exaggerate, and on rare occasion, falsify stories to boost circulation. This was a common strategy for a few American newspapers between 1880 and 1900.[45]

HOPEFULNESS

The long-anticipated perfection of the airship was overwhelmingly viewed as a positive occurrence that would benefit humanity. In commenting on the significance of the initial sighting of the airship, a letter published in the *Sacramento Bee* on November 19, 1896, stated, "I believe that aerial navigation has been successfully accomplished and that those who were fortunate enough to be gazing into the sky [the] night before last saw that which will revolutionize the world." An editorial in the *Daily Humboldt Times* (December 2, 1896, p. 2) proclaimed, "Wonderful, indeed, are the discoveries of science. With these facts before us who dare say that the successful navigation of the air will never be accomplished? Who can say that it has not already been successfully accomplished?" A commentary in one Texas newspaper concluded that the airship was real, would revolutionize transportation and communication, and would "contribute towards the onward progress of the world" (Brownsville, Texas, *Daily Herald*, April 29, 1897, p. 2). When the airship was seen near Elyria, Ohio, prominent Judge E. H. Hinman was a witness and remarked, "It is truly a wonder" (*Toledo Blade*, April 23, 1897, p. 2). After the initial spate of sightings in California in November 1896, the *San Francisco Call* carried the headline, "Exclusive Account of the Greatest Invention of the Age Is Now Corroborated by Thousands."

During the 1890s, Americans were enchanted with literature on inventions, which had become a national obsession because people were "in love with the great wonders of science."[46] This buoyant mood fostered a widespread feeling that almost any invention was possible. The second half of the nineteenth century was marked by revolutionary inventions: telephone, gramophone, filament lamp, motor car, steam turbine, diesel engine, X-ray devices, and radio. The imminent perfection of the first practical airship was widely hailed as a landmark for America and civilization as a whole. The airship was to be the pinnacle in a series of technological advancements during the latter nineteenth century. The age-old dream of heavier-than-air flight was of particular interest, as during this period "magazines devoted to science and engineering vied with Jules Verne's *Robur the Conquerer* and other fictional publications to describe the flier which would soon succeed."[47] The reams of aviation literature "fed the public a steady diet of aeronautical speculation and news to prime people for the day when the riddle of aerial navigation finally would receive a solution."[48] This social climate fostered an exaggerated feeling that the perfection of the world's first heavier-than-air flying machine was imminent. In 1893, aviation pioneer Octave Chanute characterized this collective optimism in the last decade of the nineteenth century:

> [L]et us hope that the advent of a successful flying machine…will bring nothing but good into the world; that it shall abridge distance, make all parts of the globe accessible, bring men into closer relation with each other, advance civilisation, and hasten the promised era in which there shall be nothing but peace and good-will among all men.[49]

During the 1880s and 1890s, backyard tinkerers in America and Europe claimed to be perfecting the first practical airship. They were often afforded hero status, with their exploits glorified in the press and by science-fiction writers. Competition was intense to be the first to patent such a vessel, resulting in a flurry of submissions to the Washington, D.C., patent office. A shroud of secrecy prevailed because many inventors withheld vital data on their patents and experimental craft.[50] This ambiguity surrounding the state of aerial development further heightened public perceptions of the airship's existence.

The moral panic counterpart to hopefulness is hostility toward a particular group or category perceived as a community threat. The appearance of hostility produces stereotypes of "good" community members who desire to eliminate the threat posed by folk devils. Barlow drew a parallel to how police routinely round up stereotyped suspects based on such characteristics as race, age, and socioeconomic background. During wish manias, a converse process occurs.[51]

This point is illustrated by the many people who reinforced the airship's existence by speculating about its inventor's identity, with local residents and reporters scrutinizing every activity. Amateur inventors of the period were typified as independent, wealthy eccentrics. Hence, in one Nebraska city, intense press speculation focused on John Preast, an educated recluse residing on the outskirts of Omaha (*Omaha Globe-Democrat*, April 10, 1897). As partial confirming evidence, the paper reported that "The two times in the past week that the (airship) light has been seen at Omaha it disappeared near Preast's home." In Michigan, suspicion fell on "an ingenious Battle Creek mechanic" (*Evening News* [Detroit], April 16, 1897, p. 4). In western Missouri, it was G.D. Schultz "a retired capitalist of decidedly sedentary habits" (*Kansas City Times*, April 3, 1897,

p. 1). In California, the activities of dentist Elmer H. Benjamin were scrutinized and redefined as airship-related by such state newspapers as the *Weekly Visalia Delta, Tulare County Times, Woodland California Daily Democrat, Sacramento Evening Bee* and *San Francisco Chronicle*:

> This gentleman is six feet in height, about 40 years of age, and as far as his mysterious habits are concerned [Mr.] Keiser said last night: "We have had him in the house for two years and don't know any more about him than on the day he came in. He goes away every little while on trips to Oroville, Sacramento and Stockton, sometimes staying a few days, sometimes a month. He has plenty of means and fills his time when at his room experimenting with various metals, principally aluminum and sheet copper.
>
> "He is a dentist by profession, I think. I know he has friends and one relative in Oroville who are experimenting on some invention or other, but what it is I don't know. He has told me once or twice that attorney Collins does his law business for him, and I have often wondered what law business a dentist in a small way would be likely to have."
>
> "Dr." Benjamin's name is not in the directory, nor in the list of dentists in the city. Nobody could be found last night who had ever heard of him practicing his profession. His room contains very little to show what his real business is. There are a few drawings and charts scattered around bearing trigonometrical figures, two very ancient teeth on the mantle shelf and a litter of aluminum and copper shavings all over the carpet (*San Francisco Chronicle*, November 23, 1896, p. 12).

In Nevada, speculation turned to George Cummings, an unsuccessful candidate for governor who was rumored to have hidden a 150-pound, gas-powered, cigar-shaped vessel in a house and secretly test-flown it at night on two or three occasions (*Virginia* [Nevada] *Evening Chronicle*, November 25, 1896, p. 3). In Goldendale, Oregon, it was a local inventor, Mr. Parrott (*The Dalles Times-Mountaineer*, December 12, 1896, p. 4). In Montana, it was said to be Albert Zoske (*Darby Sentinel*, May 11, 1896, p. 1). In Savannah, Ohio, a letter to the editor of the newspaper identified a wealthy genius with "a large barn on his property which he keeps carefully guarded, allowing no one to enter except two strangers who came with him from the West" (*Salem Daily Herald* [OH], May 8, 1897, p. 2). Reporters and local townsfolk often followed these suspects day and night and interviewed their friends in an effort to verify their suspicions. Often these gentlemen appeared to relish in the publicity and acted in a manner that only heightened rumor and speculation.

POSITIVE CONSENSUS

There was a consensus of the folk angel's existence among certain segments of American society, as evidenced in thousands of airship-related press reports representing tens of thousands of sightings, claims, and speculative stories.[52] Often, the entire population of cities and towns reported sightings.

According to the *Quincy* [Illinois] *Morning Whig* of April 13, 1897, "It is the general belief that an airship ... [exists]. This belief is entertained by men of scientific attainments as well as those not so well versed in the field of natural philosophy." On November 30, 1896, it was reported that "Los Angeles is excited and people are gazing upward from every corner at what all who have seen them declare are the lights of an airship" (San Francisco *Call*, December 1, 1896, p. 7). In Eureka, California, one newspaper editor expressed personal skepticism regarding the airship, but he noted that "there is as little doubt in the minds of many people that the question of aerial navigation has been solved and that some inventive genius has constructed a real flying machine" (*Daily Humboldt Standard*, November 28, 1896, p. 2). According to an Illinois paper, "A vast amount of speculation concerning the mysterious airship ... has been indulged in by all classes of citizens" (*Decatur Evening Republican*, April 15, 1897, p. 8). Following a spate of sightings near St. Louis, Missouri, during mid–April, excitement peaked on the evening of April 13, when it was estimated that half the city's population was scanning the skies (*St. Louis-Post Dispatch*, April 14, 1897, p. 7). In Ashland, Nebraska, the *Ashland Gazette* of April 16, 1897, remarked that "newspapers are full of accounts of mysterious lights that have appeared in the heavens in different localities and the general theory in regard to them is that they are lights from an airship." On April 20, the *Columbus* [Ohio] *Evening Press* stated that while the airship may be imaginary, "you cannot convince all the inhabitants of this great and glorious country ... and it is a useless task to attempt it."

Excerpts from a series of reports appearing in the *Dallas Morning News* of April 18, 1897, highlighted the voluminous press space devoted to the sightings, the prevailing excitement, and the large number of residents from various walks of life who either reported seeing it or were on the lookout:

> **Waxahachie, Ellis Co., Tex., April 17.**—Many people sat up the major part of last night looking for the airship.
>
> **Hillsboro, Hill Co., Tex., April 17.**—[T]he airship that has been seen in different portions of the state has been the sole topic of conversation on the streets and elsewhere in the city to-day.

Since the reliability of the witnesses that have seen it is unimpeachable, many persons now come forward and admit having seen it.

Texarkana, Bowie Co., Tex., April 17.—The mysterious bright light that has been visible in the heavens for the past fortnight has been seen from this point.

Garland, Tex., April 17.—The airship which created so much excitement Thursday night, was seen in Garland by several.

Denton, Denton Co., Tex., April 17.—The airship reports of which have appeared in the news from this and so many other places, is causing a great deal of talk here.

Bohham, Fannin Co., Tex., April 17.—The mysterious airship passed over the northern part of this city last night at 8:15.

Celeburne, Johnson Co., Tex., April 17.—The much advertised airship seen by so many was seen here last night by two gentleman of undoubted integrity.

Davis, I.T., April 16.—The stories about the famous and much-heard-of airship were satisfactorily proven to the people of this vicinity.

Tioga, Grayson Co., Tex., April 17.—James Daugherty, a young farmer living near town, saw the airship at 11:30 last night.

Greenville, Hunt Co., Tex., April 17.—Several persons here say they saw the mysterious aerial visitor the night of April 15.

Mansfield, Tex., April 17.—Great excitement prevails here. An airship or something of the kind made its appearance above the city about 9:45 o'clock last night. When first seen it was about 500 feet high.... It appeared about as large as a box car, main part of the vessel cigar-shaped with wings or sails extended on either side.

Ladonia, Tex., April 17.—There seems to be no more doubt in the minds of some regarding the airship.

Ennis, Ellis Co., Tex., April 17.—People here are deeply interested in the published accounts of the airship as seen and reported from various points.

Forney, Kaufman Co., Tex., April 17.—Mrs. G.W. Voiers, wife of Cashier Voiers, states that she is of the opinion she viewed the airship last night.

DISPROPORTIONALITY

Certainly the rumors of the airship's existence were disproportionate to its speculated existence because the vessel was entirely imaginary. The airship was often seen simultaneously at many locations hundreds and even thousands of miles apart. Three illustrations from Indiana during mid–April 1897 are representative of the national press. The Marion, Indiana, *Morning News* calculated that the vessel had been reported in "a dozen places at once." The *Fort Wayne Daily News* noted its "omnipresence," while the *Newton County Enterprise* announced, "Too many airships spoil the lie." If someone had developed such a craft and demonstrated it in public, they would have almost certainly received instant wealth and worldwide acclaim if they had made their invention public. No remains of such a vessel have ever been found, and it is difficult to fathom how and why it could have been kept secret.

Nineteenth-century science lacked the technological sophistication to navigate heavier-than-air machines.[53] This event was many years away, and when it happened, it was a modest achievement by any modern standard. The first recorded self-powered flights of Orville and Wilbur Wright at Kitty Hawk, North Carolina, occurred on December 17, 1903, consisting of four brief hops totaling just one minute and thirty-seven seconds. Crude prototypes were constructed during this period, but they held little practical value. Aerial navigation over the next decade was dangerous because a sudden wind gust could easily down the fragile, clumsy vessels of the era, and night flying held special perils. Despite heavy press coverage of the numerous flight trials during this period, most were woeful failures, and aerial navigation was primitive. Historian David Jacobs stated that "all evidence indicates that scientific knowledge about powered flight in 1896 and 1897 could not have led to the invention of airships with the characteristics witnesses described."[54] Charles Harvard Gibbs-Smith, a specialist in aeronautical flight before 1910, was emphatic on this point: "I can say with certainty that the only airborne vehicles, carrying passengers, which could possibly have been seen anywhere in North America ... were free-flying spherical balloons, and it is highly unlikely for these to be mistaken for anything else." Gibbs-Smith concluded that "No form of dirigible ... or heavier-than-air flying machine was flying — or indeed could fly — at this time."[55]

VOLATILITY

The airship episode was highly volatile. It began suddenly on the evening of November 17, 1896, with a spectacular sighting over Sacramento. It quickly snowballed in the wake of massive California press publicity and subsequent sighting reports. Folklorist Thomas Bullard stated that the 1896 airship wave in California "burst onto the scene unheralded and unrivalled" in an "explosive" manner, but by mid–December only "a few last reports straggled in."[56] The wave rekindled in February in Kansas and Nebraska, peaked during April 1897 with dozens of major sightings in most states, only to rapidly decline in early May. By the end of the month, the sightings had ceased abruptly.

Concluding Remarks

Since the early 1970s, the concept of moral panics has gained increased prominence and usefulness among social scientists. In this chapter, the notion of wish manias has been conceptualized as a subcategory of social delusion that has been neglected in the scientific literature. Waves of claims and public discourse regarding imaginary sightings of airships in the United States in the 1890s has been used as a case study to illustrate the characteristic features of a wish mania. While there have been a few scattered discussions in the scientific literature of social delusions involving exaggerated hopes such as Virgin Mary appearances and sighting waves of extinct or mythical creatures like the Tasmanian Tiger or Bigfoot, such episodes have heretofore been conceptualized as a generic form of collective delusion. In this chapter, wish manias are identified as a specific form of social delusion that is related, but in opposition to, moral panics. For the first three categories of moral panics (concern, hostility, consensus), wish manias contain the corresponding oppositional elements of enthusiasm, hopefulness, and positive consensus. The remaining two moral panic categories of disproportionality and volatility are overlapping features of wish manias. Examining the origin and nature of wish panics can contribute to understanding why, and under what conditions, they occur.

Just as moral panics are symbolic reflections of prevailing anxieties and stereotypes, wish manias are collective functional attempts to confirm the existence of unsubstantiated social realities that provide hope, certainty, and psychological comfort in an uncertain world. A similar degree of psychological satisfaction and fulfillment can be obtained by adhering to a philosophical outlook that includes basic principles of logic, reason, and science that have contributed to so much recent progress for humanity. These principles are preferable to the seductive, idealized social world of religion, wish manias, and pseudoscience.

Chapter 13

Before Roswell:
The Meaning Behind
the Crashed-UFO Myth

*Doth any man doubt that if there were taken out of men's
minds vain opinions, flattering hopes, false valuations, imaginations as one would ... it would leave the minds of a number
of men poor shrunken things, and full of melancholy and indis-
position.* — Francis Bacon[1]

An alien spaceship crashes to Earth, killing its occupants. Roswell,
New Mexico, 1947? No, a remote Indian Ocean island, 1862. Another ship
plunges from the sky above a small town in the southwestern United States,
extinguishing the life of its extraterrestrial pilot. Roswell? No, Aurora,
Texas, 1897. In July 1947, a flying saucer supposedly crashed in the desert
near Roswell, New Mexico, killing or critically injuring its crew. U.S. military personnel are said to have sealed off the area, carted away the evidence, and engaged in a cover-up. Yet stories of crashed UFOs are not
new. While dozens of crashed UFOs have been reported at sites around
the world since 1947, reports of crashed alien craft date back to at least the
middle part of the nineteenth century.[2]

History is a valuable tool in the scientist's arsenal because it distances
observers from events, allowing for a less emotional, more contextual perspective in evaluating incredible claims. For instance, between 1900 and
1950, humanlike aliens typically landed in saucers with protruding exhaust
pipes and clumsy disembarking ladders, wore Buck Rogers–style space
suits, carried pistol ray guns, and usually hailed from Mars. This cari-
cature is laughable in comparison to present-day aliens, who have large
heads and bulbous eyes, float from their ship, and can communicate telepathically. The same comparative historical approach can be applied fruit-

fully to crashed-saucer claims to show that they are part of a broader myth.

In a letter to the *Houston Post* of May 2, 1897, John Leander wrote that an elderly sailor from El Campo, Texas—identified only as "Mr. Oleson"—claimed to have been shipwrecked on a tiny, uncharted Indian Ocean island in 1862. He said that during his ordeal, an immense airship sporting gigantic wings crashed into a rock cliff. Inside were the bodies of twelve-foot-tall creatures with dark, bronze skin: "Their hair and beard were also long and as soft and silky as the hair of an infant." The surviving sailors lived inside the wrecked airship and eventually "summoned courage to drag the gigantic bodies to the cliff and tumble them over." After building a raft and being rescued by a passing Russian vessel, Oleson retained a ring from the thumb of one of the creatures as the only proof of the events. Two and one-quarter inches in diameter, it was "made of a compound of metals unknown to any jeweler ... and [was] set with two reddish stones." As luck would have it, by the time the vessel reached port, the remaining airship sailors died, leaving Oleson as the sole survivor.

This story bears an uncanny resemblance to Roswell. The account is a secondhand narrative of alien creatures in a space vessel crashing in a remote location. The craft was destroyed, and foreign writing was found inside. The alien bodies were disposed of and the debris lost. A piece of confirming evidence was retained (in the form of an immense ring with unknown properties), but the witness failed to allow public scrutiny. It is important to remember that our interest in such accounts is in their narrative content and not in their truth or falsity *per se*.

During a wave of phantom-airship sightings in the United States between 1896 and 1897, there were several crashed–UFO claims. On the night of December 3, 1896, a wrecked airship was found in the gully of a cow pasture in a San Francisco suburb after dairy farmers heard a loud bang followed by cries for help. Rushing to the scene, they found two dazed occupants staggering near a forty-foot-long, cone-shaped tube of galvanized iron with broken wings and propellers. After causing a local sensation, and under questioning by those inspecting the "wreckage," the alleged pilot, J.D. deGear, confessed that the "ship" had been pulled to the hilltop on a wagon and pushed over.[3] The spot was chosen for its proximity to a nearby saloon, which enjoyed a brisk business during the spectacle.[4]

On the night of April 4, 1897, an airship supposedly crashed on the J.D. Sims farm near Bethany, Missouri, killing its pilot.[5] Within a week, a flying machine reportedly plunged into a reservoir near Rhodes, Iowa.[6] No debris was ever found. On April 16, another vessel allegedly crash-landed outside Waterloo, Iowa.[7] In Tennessee, it was rumored that a craft had plunged to Earth in the middle of the night, sinking without a trace into the Sycamore Creek.[8]

Finally, there was the Aurora, Texas, hoax. A craft carrying what appeared to be a Martian allegedly crashed there, and its pilot was supposedly buried nearby.[9] In *UFOs — Explained*, the former senior editor of the respected publication *Aviation Week and Space Technology*, Philip J. Klass, demonstrated that this was undoubtedly a hoax. Yet scores of UFO researchers have traveled and continue to travel to the community of Aurora, armed with cameras, Geiger counters, metal detectors, pickaxes, and shovels in hopes of locating the purported grave of the unfortunate alien.

It is also notable that there were theories of government cover-ups during the airship wave. The *Galveston Daily News* of April 29, 1897, argued that airship reports were secret U.S. government experiments, noting that "A profound secrecy has been maintained as to what has been accomplished, even army officers themselves only getting vague inklings of what is going on."[10] There were also claims of airships being constructed and hidden in U.S. military installations, including Fort Sheridan near Chicago and Fort Logan in Colorado.[11]

Pre-Roswell crashed–UFO claims have also occurred outside the United States. In 1909, a wave of phantom-zeppelin sightings spread across New Zealand amid rumors that Germany was planning an aerial attack. Within this context, a zeppelin reportedly crashed at Waikaka, killing those on board.[12] In Scandinavia during the 1930s, mysterious "ghost aeroplanes" were frequently spotted. On February 5, 1933, several Norwegians became convinced that the "ghost flier" had crashed into Mount Fagar. A police search party revealed nothing.[13] During World War II, the British government was reported to have captured a crashed saucer and tiny aliens.[14] In 1946, dozens of UFOs reportedly crashed in Scandinavia after rumors that the Soviets were test-firing V-rockets. No confirming evidence was ever found despite intense military investigations.[15]

If there is any mystery surrounding accounts of crashed UFOs, its solution lies not in examining some secret military hangar but in examining the human mind. We need to ask ourselves, what makes this myth so appealing? Folklorist Jan Brunvand contends that for legends to persist in modern society "as living narrative folklore," they must contain three key elements: "a strong basic story appeal, a foundation in actual belief, and a meaningful message or 'moral.'"[16] Accounts of crashed saucers and government cover-ups easily meet each of these criteria. They make for fascinating reading and discussion. They are rendered plausible in the many dubious books, pseudoscientific "docudramas," and speculative movies that suggest their existence. These narratives contain a poignant message about a secular age that has used science and reason to expel gods, ghosts, and demons from our minds. These haunting images have been replaced with more plausible contemporary themes: a world of government mistrust, nefarious conspiracies, and alien abductors. Ironically, as scientists delve deeper into the mysteries of our universe, they generate more questions. New scientific discoveries continue to reveal a world that is every bit as fascinating as that any pseudoscientist could imagine.[17]

Chapter 14

The Martian Invasion Panic

Human beings have a demonstrated talent for self-deception when their emotions are stirred.[1] — Carl Sagan

Shortly after 8 P.M. on October 30, 1938, many Americans became anxious or panic-stricken after listening to a live, one-hour radio play depicting a fictitious Martian landing at the Wilmuth farm in the tiny hamlet of Grovers Mill, New Jersey. Those living in the immediate vicinity of the bogus invasion appeared to have been the most frightened, but the broadcast could be heard in all regions of the continental United States, and no location was immune. The play included references to real places, buildings, highways, and streets. The broadcast also contained prestigious speakers, convincing sound effects, and realistic special bulletins. The drama was produced by a 23-year-old theatrical prodigy named Orson Welles (1915–1985), who was accompanied by a small group of actors and musicians in the New York City studio of the Columbia Broadcasting System's Mercury Theater. The broadcast script was written by Howard Koch, who loosely based it on the 1898 book *The War of the Worlds* by acclaimed science-fiction writer H.G. Wells. The incident remains arguably the most widely known delusion in U.S. history, and perhaps even in world history. Many radio stations around the world continue to broadcast the original play each Halloween.

Over six decades after the Martian panic, it is timely to reflect on the lessons we can glean from the incident by using the wisdom that hindsight can provide.

Human Perception and Memory Reconstruction Are Remarkably Flawed

Today, many people seem to forget that the "Martian invasion" illustrates far more than a short-term panic. It is a testament to the remarkable power of expectation on perception. A person's frame of reference has a strong influence on how external stimuli are interpreted and internalized as reality.[2] Perception is highly unreliable and subject to error.[3] This effect has long been known to be pronounced under situations of stress, ambiguity, and uncertainty.[4] This message cannot be overemphasized but continues to go widely unheeded. Visual misperceptions are a common thread in many reports of such diverse phenomena as religious signs and wonders, UFOs, and Bigfoot.

In his famous study of the Martian panic, Princeton University psychologist Hadley Cantril discussed the extreme variability of eyewitness descriptions of the invasion. These examples have been usually overlooked in subsequent popular and scholarly discussions of the panic. One person became convinced that they could smell the poison gas and feel the heat rays as described on the radio, while another became emotionally distraught and felt a choking sensation from the imaginary gas.[5] During the broadcast, several residents reported observations to police "of Martians on their giant machines poised on the Jersey Palisades."[6] After checking descriptions of the panic, Bulgatz reported that a Boston woman said she could actually see the fire as described on the radio. Other people told of hearing machine-gun fire or the "swish" sound of the Martians. A man even climbed atop a Manhattan building and described seeing "the flames of battle."[7]

The event also reminds us that the human mind does not function like a video camera, capturing each piece of data that comes into its field of vision. People interpret information as it is processed. These memories are not statically locked away in the brain forever. Our memories of events are reconstructed over time.[8] Cantril cited the case of Jane Dean, a devoutly religious woman who, when recalling the broadcast, said the most realistic portion was "the sheet of flame that swept over the entire country. That is just the way I pictured the end."[9] In reality, there was no mention of a sheet of flame anywhere in the broadcast.

The Mass Media Are a Powerful Force in Society

Not only does the Martian panic demonstrate the enormous influence of the mass media in contemporary society, but in recent years an ironic twist has developed. There is a growing consensus among sociologists that the extent of the panic, as described by Cantril, was greatly exaggerated.[10] The irony here is that for the better part of the past sixty years, the media may have misled many people to believe that the panic was far more extensive and intense than it apparently was. However, regardless of the extent of the panic, there is little doubt that many Americans were genuinely frightened, and some did try to flee the Martian gas raids and heat rays, especially in New Jersey and New York.

Based on opinion polls and estimates, Cantril calculated that of about 1.7 million people who heard the drama, nearly 1.2 million "were excited" to varying degrees.[11] Yet there is only scant anecdotal evidence to suggest that many listeners actually took some action — such as packing belongings, grabbing guns, or fleeing in cars after hearing the broadcast. In fact, much of Cantril's study was based on interviews with just 135 people.[12] Bainbridge criticized Cantril for citing just a few colorful stories from a small number of people who claimed to panic. According to Bainbridge, on any given night, out of a pool of over 1 million people, at least a thousand would have been driving excessively fast or engaging in rambunctious behavior. From this perspective, the event was primarily a media creation. Miller supported this view, noting that the day after the panic, some newspapers carried accounts of suicides and heart attacks by frightened citizens, which proved to have been unfounded but have passed into American folklore.[13] Miller also took Cantril to task for failing to show substantial evidence of mass flight from the perceived Martian attack. Cantril cited just a few examples that did not warrant an estimate of over 1 million panic-stricken Americans.[14] While Cantril cited American Telephone Company figures indicating that local media and law-enforcement agencies were inundated with up to 40 percent more telephone calls than normal in parts of New Jersey during the broadcast, he did not determine the specific nature of these calls:

> Some callers requested information, such as which units of national guard were being called up or whether casualty lists were available. Some people called to find out where they could go to donate blood. Some callers were simply angry that such a realistic show was allowed on the air, while others called CBS to congratulate Mercury Theater for the exciting Halloween program. ... We cannot know how many of these telephone calls were between households. It seems ... (likely) many callers just wanted to chat with their families and friends about the exciting show they had just listened to on the radio.[15]

Goode agreed with Miller's assessment, but he also noted that to have convinced a substantial number of listeners "that a radio drama about an invasion from Mars was an actual news broadcast has to be regarded as a remarkable achievement."[16] Whether tens of thousands of people or over 1 million listeners became panic-stricken, there is no denying that the mass media have significantly influenced public perception of the event. There is also no disputing that similar broadcasts have resulted in full-fledged panics.

It Can't Happen Again

Only someone with an ignorance of history would assume that similar panics could not recur. More recent mass panics and delusions have involved the pivotal role of the mass media, especially newspaper and television. For instance, the media were instrumental in triggering a widespread delusion about the existence of imaginary pit marks on windshields in the state of Washington during 1954. The marks were erroneously attributed to atomic fallout.[17] The relative ease with which a spate of media hoaxes were perpetrated across the country in the early 1990s prompted the Federal Communications Commission to fine TV stations up to $250,000 for knowingly broadcasting false information. But could a repeat of the 1938 Martian panic occur? The answer is, "Yes."

A widespread panic was triggered following a broadcast of the Welles play by a Santiago, Chile, radio station on November 12, 1944. Upon hearing the broadcast, many fled into the streets or barricaded themselves in their homes. In one province, troops and artillery were briefly mobilized by the governor in a bid to repel the invading Martians. The broadcast was highly realistic. It included references to such organizations as the Red Cross and used an actor to impersonate the interior minister.[18]

On the night of February 12, 1949, another radio play based on *The War of the Worlds* resulted in a pandemonium in Quito, Ecuador. Tens of thousands of panic-stricken residents ran into the streets to escape Martian gas raids. The event made headlines around the world, including the front page of the February 14, 1949, edition of the *New York Times*.[19] The drama described strange Martian creatures heading toward the city after landing and destroying the neighboring community of Latacunga, twenty miles south of Quito. Broadcast in Spanish on Radio Quito, the realistic program included impersonations of well-known local politicians, journalists, vivid eyewitness descriptions, and the name of the local town of Cotocallo. In Quito, a riot broke out and an enraged mob burned down the building housing the radio station that broadcast the drama, killing fifteen people.

The tragic sequence of events began when a regular music program was suddenly interrupted with a news bulletin, followed by reports of the invading Martians wreaking havoc and destruction while closing in on the

'Mars Raiders' Cause Quito Panic; Mob Burns Radio Plant, Kills 15

By The Associated Press.

QUITO, Ecuador, Feb. 13—An enraged mob that hurled gasoline and flaming balls of paper took fatal vengeance here last night for a panic caused by an Orson Welles-type radio dramatization of an "invasion from Mars." The mob attacked and burned the building of the newspaper, Comercio, which housed the radio station, and killed fifteen persons and injured fifteen others.

Army troops were called out and used tanks and tear gas to restore order.

The mob wrecked the newspaper building, its equipment and the radio station. Damage was estimated at more than $350,000.

Indictments were drawn against Leonardo Paez, director of art at the station, known as Radio Quito, and Eduardo Alcaras, a Chilean who is the station's dramatic director. Heads of the station said the two men prepared and directed the dramatization without their knowledge.

Police detained ten suspects and more arrests were ordered. The Government appointed Diaz Granados, Minister of Defense, to investigate the rioting.

As in the Orson Welles broadcast that caused panic in the United States in 1938, the populace had been terrified by a radio dramatization of H. G. Wells' fantastic novel, "The War of the Worlds," localized to describe strange creatures from Mars landing near by and heading for Quito.

Hysteria drove most of the population of Quito into the streets before the program directors learned how much consternation they had caused. Frantically they appealed to the people to be calm, and assured them it was all fictional.

When the people finally were convinced, they swept upon the Comercio Building, which housed Ecuador's principal newspaper, showering it with stones and driv-

Continued on Page 7, Column 4

Figure 14.1: A Martian panic in Ecuador on February 12, 1949, took fifteen lives and caused widespread havoc. (*New York Times*, February 14, 1949, p. 1. Reprinted with permission of the Associated Press.)

city. A voice resembling that of a government minister appealed for calm so the city's defenses could be organized and citizens evacuated in time. Next, the "mayor" arrived and made a dramatic announcement: "People of Quito, let us defend our city. Our women and children must go out into the surrounding heights to leave the men free for action and combat." An announcer said he was positioned atop the tallest building in the city, the La Previsora tower, and that he could discern a monster engulfed in plumes of fire and smoke advancing on Quito from the north. It was at that point, according to a *New York Times* reporter, that citizens "began fleeing from their homes and running through the streets. Many were clad only in night clothing."

Other radio adaptations of *The War of the Worlds* have had less dramatic consequences but have resulted in some frightened listeners in the vicinity of Providence, Rhode Island, on the night of October 31, 1974, and in northern Portugal in 1988.[20]

What of the Future?

Since 1938, the world's rapidly expanding population has grown increasingly reliant on the mass media. People generally expect the news to contain immediate, accurate information on nearly every facet of their lives. By most projections, the twenty-first century will bring an even greater dependence on information and mass media. While it may be true that you cannot fool all of the people all of the time, as the *War of the Worlds* panics and other mass scares attest to, you need only fool a relatively small portion of people for a short period to create large-scale disruptions to society. That is the lesson we can glean from the reaction to the 1938 broadcast. It can and will happen again. Only the mediums and forms will change as new technologies are developed and old delusional themes fade away while new ones come into vogue.

Each era has a set of taken-for-granted social realities that define it and manifest themselves in unique delusions. During the Middle Ages, scores of popular delusions, panics, and scares surrounded the belief that humans could transform into various animals, especially wolves.[21] In the seventeenth and eighteenth centuries, most recorded delusions were precipitated by a widespread fear of witches and manifested themselves in episodes of mass demon possession and moral panics involving a hunt for imaginary witches.[22] These episodes often resulted in torture, imprisonment, or death for various minority ethnic groups such as Jews, heretics, deviants, the aged, women and the poor.[23] Twentieth-century mass delusions overwhelmingly involved two themes. The first was a fear of environmental contaminants, mirroring growing concern about global pollution and heightened awareness of public health. This situation triggered scores of mass psychogenic illness in schools, factories, and occasionally communities. There were also numerous social delusions without psychogenic illness. A second series of delusions spread widely in Western countries that have become dependent on child-care facilities. Their prominence since the mid–1980s coincided with a series of moral panics involving exaggerated claims about the existence of organized cultists kidnapping or molesting children. These myths function as cautionary tales about the inability of the weakened family to protect children.[24]

At the dawn of the twenty-first century and a new millennium, we can only ponder what new mass panics await us. It is beyond the realm of science to accurately predict what these will entail. However, it will be vital for scientists to respond to the challenge of this new era of ideas and technologies that will engender an unforeseen set of circumstances that characterize and define each age. For mass panics and scares can tell us much about ourselves and the times in which we live. Part of this challenge entails remembering the lessons of the past.

SECTION FIVE

Major Issues and Future Directions

Chapter 15

From Demon Possession to Environmental Fears: The Changing Face of Mass Delusions and Hysterias

I believe the future is only the past again, entered through another gate.— Sir Arthur W. Pinero[1]

The spread of mass delusions and hysterias mirrors popular social and cultural preoccupations that define each era and reflect unique social beliefs about the nature of the world. Prior to the twentieth century, most epidemic hysteria reports involved groups exhibiting motor hysteria, where pent-up stress accumulates over weeks or months. That is, hysterical fits, emotional agitation, shaking, screaming, twitching, hallucinations, and trance states affected members of a tightly knit, enclosed group exposed to long-standing religious, academic, or capitalist discipline.

Between the fifteenth and nineteenth centuries, exceedingly strict Christian religious orders appeared in various European convents. Coupled with a popular belief in witches and demons, this turn of events triggered dozens of episodes of epidemic motor hysteria among nuns, who were widely believed to be demonically possessed. Outbreaks typically lasted months and in several instances, endured in a waxing, waning fashion for years. Prominent incidents occurred at Yvertet (1550), Kintorp (1552), Cologne and Flanders (1560), Aix (1609), Madrid (1628), Loudun (1632), and Louviers (1642). Histrionics and role playing were also a significant part of the syndrome. Elders typically coerced young girls into joining these socially isolated religious orders, where they practiced rigid discipline in confined, all-female living quarters. Their plight was often pitiful. Forced to take vows of chastity and poverty, many endured bland

and near-starvation diets, repetitious prayer rituals, and intervals of fast-ing. Punishment for even minor transgressions included flogging and incarceration. Male associations were forbidden. Not surprisingly, the hys-terical fits appeared under the strictest administrations. Priests were sum-moned to exorcise the demons. Disliked individuals were often accused of casting spells and were banished, imprisoned, or — in many instances — burned at the stake. In this regard, witchcraft accusations were often a way to settle scores under the guise of religion and justice. These rebellious nuns released frustrations by using foul, often blasphemous language, by engag-ing in crude sexual behavior such as rubbing private parts or thrusting their hips to denote mock intercourse.[2] Often, community members would come to watch these spectacles, while priests would try to exorcise the demons in a continuing drama to rival any modern-day soap opera.

The number and descriptions of these complex episodes of "demonic possession" in nunneries is remarkable. Over one hundred books alone have been written on the outbreaks at Loudun, France, between 1632 and 1634, where Father Urbain Grandier was accused of bewitching a convent into hysterical fits and was burned alive. The Loudun nuns were presum-ably possessed by Grandier's demons, and they used the public exorcisms to draw attention to his immoral overtures and their pious sufferings. Their histrionic displays included the use of ventriloquism and vomiting objects such as hair, worms, straw, and even what was purported to have been a piece of heart from a child sacrificed by witches.[3] On rare occa-sions, nuns were even put to death for bewitching other members of their religious order. In 1749, in one of the last recorded cases of its kind, an epidemic of coughing, screaming, twisting, squirming, feelings of suffoca-tion, and trance states swept through the Unterzell convent near Wuzburg, Germany. Suspicion of witchcraft fell on a young nun named Maria Renata von Mossau, who was beheaded in the market place to the cheers of an enthralled crowd. Her body was burned.[4]

Major outbreaks were also recorded at a convent in Lyons in 1526, Wertet (1550), Oderheim (1577), Mons (1585), Milan (1590), Aix-en-Provence (1611), Lille (1613), Chinon (1640), Auxonne (1662), and Toulouse (1681). At Cambrai, France, in 1491, a group of nuns exhibited fits, yelped like dogs, and foretold the future. In Xante, Spain in 1560, nuns "bleated like sheep, tore off their veils, [and] had convulsions in church."[5]

At one French convent, "the nuns meowed together every day at a cer-tain time for several hours together."[6] During this period, it was widely believed that humans could be possessed by many animals who were con-sidered to be potential friends with the devil. In France, cats were espe-cially despised for this very reason.[7] This may help to explain the "meowing

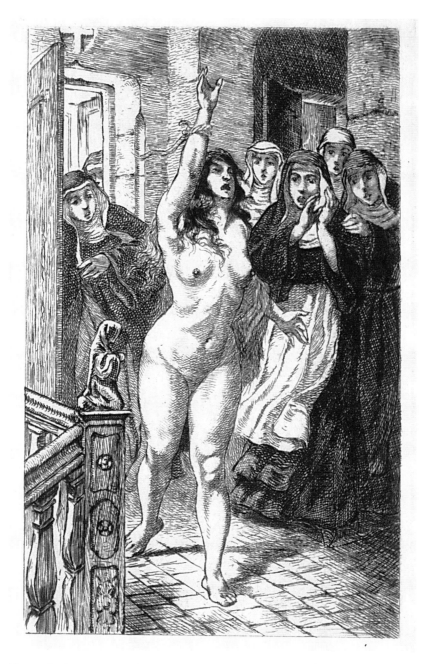

Figure 15.1: At a seventeenth-century European convent, a nun believed to have been possessed by demons strips naked during a fit of hysterics. (Etching by Martib van Maele. Courtesy of the Mary Evans Picture Library.)

nuns." The recipe for these outbreaks seems to have been extreme stress brought on by an inhuman lifestyle that triggered hysterical fits and hyper-suggestibility — with the content of their delusions reflecting the beliefs of the times.

During the eighteenth, nineteenth and early twentieth centuries, harsh working conditions and weak or nonexistent labor unions led to a flurry of mass motor hysteria outbreaks in oppressive Western job settings, most typically factories. Episodes were recorded in England, France, Germany, Italy, and Russia. They included convulsions, abnormal movements, and neurological complaints. During this same period, strict academic discipline in many European schools — especially in Germany, Switzerland, and France — triggered outbreaks of motor hysteria involving convulsions, contractures, shaking, and laughing.

During the twentieth century, epidemic hysteria episodes are dominated by environmental concerns, especially exaggerated or imaginary fears involving mysterious odors. They have a rapid onset and recovery and involve anxiety hysteria. Unsubstantiated claims of strange odors and gassings are a common contemporary trigger of epidemic hysteria outbreaks in schools.[8] A typical incident occurred in Southeast Asia in August 1985, when sixty-five students and a teacher at a Singapore secondary school were suddenly stricken with chills, headaches, nausea, and breathlessness. Doctors could find no cause for the symptoms. The episode began when several pupils detected an unusual smell. A rumor existed that gas had infiltrated the school, apparently from a nearby construction site. Investigators found "that those who accepted the idea succumbed, and those who were indifferent to it were immune."[9] This report is similar to a mystery gas at a Hong Kong school a few years earlier that affected over 355 students ages six to fourteen. Before the outbreak, there were rumors of a recent toxic-gas scare at a nearby school. Several teachers had even discussed the incident with their pupils — some to the point of advising them as to what action to take if it should hit their school.[10]

On the afternoon of July 8, 1972, in Hazlerigg, England, stench from a pigsty may have triggered an outbreak of stomach pain, nausea, faintness, and headache at a schoolchildren's gala.[11] That same year, an epidemic of headache and overbreathing affecting sixteen pupils at a junior high school in Tokyo, Japan, was traced to a pungent smog.[12] A 1994 episode of breathing problems among twenty-three students in a female dormitory at an Arab school in the United Arab Emirates was triggered by a "toxic fire" that turned out to be the harmless smell of burning incense.[13]

The perceived threatening agent must be seen as credible to the affected group. For instance, on any given school day, a fainting student would not be expected to trigger mass hysteria. Yet if the student fainted during the 1991 Persian Gulf War, and it coincided with the detection of a strange smell in the building, many of the naive schoolchildren might exhibit sudden, extreme anxiety after assuming that it was an Iraqi poison-gas attack. A similar episode was reported at a Rhode Island elementary school during the Gulf War, when there was intense publicity about chemical-weapons attacks on Israel and the possibility of terrorist attacks on the United States. In all, seventeen seventh- and eighth-graders were rushed to a nearby hospital before quickly recovering.[14]

Strange odors are also a common twentieth-century trigger of epidemic anxiety hysteria in job settings,[15] with gas-poisoning fears leading to lost productivity time in data processing centers,[16] telephone offices,[17] and electronic-assembly plants.[18] On the morning of February 19, 1986, nineteen workers were suddenly stricken with headaches, nausea, and light-headedness at a compressor-manufacturing factory in the United States. Investigators found that a previous chemical exposure, combined with press speculation questioning plant safety, resulted in epidemic hysteria after several employees smelled a harmless odor.[19]

Strange odors are also commonly blamed in rare episodes of mass hysteria that spread to communities.[20] For instance, in Soviet Georgia during political unrest in 1989, epidemic hysteria spread among four hundred adolescent females at several nearby schools. The incident transpired following rumors that students were exposed to poison gas by Russian authorities, who had recently used chemical weapons such as chloropicrin to disperse a large rally.[21] Intense media publicity surrounding the confirmed use of poison gases and rumors that the students had been gassed triggered the rapid spread of anxiety reactions. The transient complaints mimicked the poison gas symptoms: stomachache, burning eyes, skin irritation, and dry throat. Media coverage of this and the previous case were instrumental in spreading both episodes to the wider community.

Social Delusions: Rational, Irrational, or Nonrational?

Social delusions involving mass adherence to a false belief, sometimes triggering hysterical epidemics, have often been viewed as irrational. In the preface to this book, sociologist Erich Goode sagely observes that social delusions are inadequately explained by either rational-choice or irrationality models of behavior. He also comments on the remarkably faddish nature with which such theories have risen or fallen from favor over the decades. As Goode suggests, we need not "buy into" this polemic.

Rationalists typify pre–Renaissance history as replete with superstition and irrationalism, whereby erroneous thoughts appear mainly in the minds of the mentally disturbed or among the masses seized in the turmoil of dysfunctioning societies during periods of extreme stress and social change. These occasional transgressions are believed to be principally confined to underdeveloped or unenlightened societies. The relative immunity of the West to episodes of irrationalism is attributed to following scientific principles and rationalistic philosophy. This enlightenment framework produced a scientific model from which to interpret claims and public discourse about social delusions, reducing them to examples of social disorganization, anomie, or system disturbance.

Rational-choice model proponents typify behavior as involving deliberate and calculated decisions, whereby participants choose certain actions after weighing costs and benefits. Early theorists, such as British philosopher Jeremy Bentham,[22] viewed behavioral outcomes as motivated by the inherent desire to maximize pleasure and minimize pain. Many of the world's criminal-justice systems are based on a form of the rational-choice model. They assume that people defined as criminals or deviants possess a free will and choose their actions. While some actions may appear "irrational" to outsiders unfamiliar with the decision-making rationale, of central importance is the rational logic to the participant. Rational-choice theory overemphasizes the role of free will and devalues the conditions and meaning behind the decision to participate in collective actions.

Let us take as an example, the category of immediate community threats, under which the "mad gasser" is placed. These social delusions were not deliberate, calculated decisions. They were relatively spontaneous, anxiety-generating episodes driven by the presence of an exaggerated threat, an ambiguous situation, and rumors. Neither can we view the exaggerated threatening agent as exemplifying irrational thinking because in each of the episodes discussed in this book, the irrational belief appeared temporarily plausible to participants based on social and/or cultural reinforcements. In avoiding the rational-irrational dichotomy, there is a third alternative. Delusions can be considered what anthropologist Richard Shweder calls "non-rational" or what psychiatrist Wolfgang Jilek terms "arational." Jilek describes as a Eurocentric fallacy the pathology-labeling, by Western or Western-trained "experts" of people holding beliefs or manifesting behavior accepted as normal in a culture-specific non–Western context.

The Western notion of rationality is a European-centered social and cultural construct that is typically assumed to be a universal process. However, what is logical and rational in one culture may be the opposite in another. The same is true for subcultures and within regional enclaves. Anthropologist Richard Shweder questioned the validity of a universal social law and the view of history as a battleground between reason and science (rationality) versus unreason and superstition (irrationality):

> A central tenet of the romanticist [nonuniversalist] view holds that ideas and practices have their foundation in neither logic nor empirical science, that ideas and practices fall beyond the scope of deductive and inductive reason, that ideas and practices are neither rational nor irrational but rather *non*rational. ... [T]hus, to ask which is superior, Islam or Christianity, an animistic world view or a mechanistic world view, a social order premised on individualism, equality, and monogamy or one premised on holism, hierarchy, and polygamy is like asking, "Which is the more valid mode of artistic expression, cubism or impressionism?"[23]

It cannot be overemphasized that the use of the word "delusion" in the term "collective delusion" does not connote a pathological loss of contact with material reality, as it does in the psychiatric sense, but simply the presence of an erroneous belief. Classic studies on human perception and conformity are noteworthy.[24] False convictions and perceptions during social delusions is consistent with perceptual psychology research, which supports the tendency of observers to interpret information patterns in ways that reflect their mental state and broad social and cultural reference system at any given time.

Human perception is a selective and organizational process that is based more on inference than reality, allowing for interpretations that may differ substantially from material reality. This is especially pronounced when the perception of indistinct stimuli or conflicting information patterns are involved within groups. Such situations may result in members both developing an increased need to define the situation and depending more on the judgment of others to validate reality. Thus, as Leon Festinger remarked, an opinion or conviction "is 'correct,' 'valid,' and 'proper' to the extent that it is anchored in a group of people with similar beliefs, opinions, and attitudes."[25] People continually test reality by comparing their perceptions with those of others. It should come as no surprise that human perception often results in observations that do not reflect the real world but reflect the socially constructed world of the observers.

What constitutes reality for any person, group, or culture, is socially constructed,[26] a process that helps to maintain social continuity and meaning. Humans arbitrarily create their own social order and meanings based mostly on faith. A key part of ordering social reality is the formation of perceptual frames of meaning, which are orientations toward viewing the world. As anthropologist John Connor observed, culture is a collection of similar perceptual sets through which a particular people impose order by defining "reality."[27] Similarly, the possibility that certain people could erroneously believe in the presence of mad gassers or other folk beliefs has typically and wrongly received a label of irrationality based on the evaluations of scientists, who find such realities to be implausible and, hence, reflecting nonsense and pseudoscience.

Indeed, scientists are always trying to find something wrong with the affected people. Yet their findings are conflicting and inconclusive. This is not surprising because we are dealing with social realities and the consequences of beliefs. Investigators of modern-day epidemic hysteria outbreaks in school and job settings have used standardized personality tests to identify social, psychological, even physical characteristics—such as gender—to try to tell why some members of the same group are affected while others are not. There is no consistent pattern. Thirty-five affected workers at a fish-packaging plant scored higher than controls on the Eysenck Personality Inventory scale for extraversion,[28] while ninety affected electronics-assembly workers scored lower than those who were not affected.[29] Goldberg associated absenteeism and being affected;[30] Cole did not.[31] Some results suggest that those affected score higher on scales for paranoia,[32] neuroticism,[33] and hysterical traits;[34] others found no correlations.[35] Gary Small and his colleagues link academic performance and becoming ill;[36] Goh found no association.[37] Small also correlated the death of a significant other during early childhood and being stricken with epidemic hysteria.[38] Yet this observation was not confirmed in another study by the same researcher.[39] Some investigators report that those affected have below-average IQs;[40] opposite impressions were given by others.[41]

However, no one is immune from social delusions because humans continually construct reality. The perceived danger needs only to be plausible to gain acceptance within a particular group. Collective delusions can occur at any time and any place to any group. Scientists must become more aware of the diversity of social realities across different historical periods, cultures, and subcultures. Humans interpret their world within specific social and cultural contexts that need to be appreciated before reductive or value-laden judgments are imposed. Failure to understand this key point too often results in distorting the ethnographic record by reducing foreign, unfamiliar, unpopular, or implausible folk realities and the consequences of these beliefs to grandiose categories of the irrational.

A Challenge for Health Professionals

The description of epidemic hysteria poses a special challenge for scientists because it is often met with negative emotional responses by victims and community members. Also, health authorities can only indicate negative findings, and rumors about the illness are likely to be viewed by the community as reinforcing the existence of the imaginary triggering agent. It is important for physicians to confirm rumors and make assessments based on the facts available. This is not an easy task because the emotionality surrounding episodes can be distracting. Physicians should describe these phenomena by dispassionately adhering to the following criteria: transient, benign symptoms in a cohesive social unit with no plausible organic basis that are characterized by rapid onset and recovery among a preponderance of female participants. Extraordinary anxiety among the affected group is usually discernible, and symptoms typically spread down the age scale due to social status.

Epidemic hysteria is a fascinating, often misunderstood phenomenon that will gain more interest and respectability once ambiguous, confusing issues are clarified in a manner that will satisfy the interdisciplinary professionals who encounter this subject. To achieve this, we need unambiguous, nonpejorative, universal definitions that are politically sensitive and acceptable to all disciplines. We also need to emphasize the importance of providing detailed knowledge of the context and meaning of the situation to ensure that the behavior under scrutiny meets any preset criteria — and only that criteria. In following this course, we minimize the risk of unconsciously imposing psychiatric rubrics that reflect the biases of contemporary, Western-trained social scientists onto collective episodes that are governed by unfamiliar conduct codes and "exotic" social realities. An example of such a misdiagnosis may be the medieval dance mania.

Western-trained scientists have a history of labeling seemingly strange collective behaviors and beliefs under the stigmatizing rubric of "epidemic hysteria" when the participants were clearly not suffering from hysteria.[42] Examples include mass suicide,[43] riots,[44] and "masturbatory insanity."[45] Political movements during World War II, such as Japanese imperialism, have been interpreted as mass mental disturbance,[46] as has Nazism.[47] For instance, Cartwright and Biddiss typify those following Hitler as "mentally sick."[48] Boling and Brotman have labeled clusters of pyromania as epidemic hysteria.[49] Mass behaviors labeled as fads, fashions, crazes, and booms have also been defined as epidemic hysteria.[50]

Final Thoughts

At the dawn of the twenty-first century, there are heightening environmental concerns over the depletion of the ozone layer, acid rain, chemical and biological weapons, and the fear of contaminants in our food, air, and drinking water. This situation should continue to incubate hysterical outbreaks in schools and job settings, mostly in the form of mass anxiety hysteria following exposure to a strange but harmless odor.

Communitywide episodes such as the mad gasser of Mattoon and Botetourt may recur, as we can expect more outbreaks of epidemic hysteria in public places.[51] Domestic or foreign terrorist threats and the increasing reach of mass communications suggest that more widespread manifestations of illness fears are likely. Perhaps contemporary delusions involving mad gassers are a relatively new variation on an old theme reflecting the fears of our age. They may be a sign of the times where chemical, biological, and nuclear weapons are a constant threat to the survival of humanity itself. Like a chameleon, epidemic hysteria will mirror the times, thriving on fear and uncertainty.

Social delusions and epidemics of hysteria contain powerful symbolic messages that mirror prevailing beliefs, attitudes, and stereotypes that we should carefully heed. Why? Because they will continue to occur. They are part of the human psyche. We should not treat them as irrational or examples of human folly. They are part of the remarkable ethnographic record of humanity. They are demons and angels from within. We should accept them as part of ourselves and strive to understand them. In doing so, we will better understand ourselves, for they are our own creations. They are mysterious, chilling, and far more real than any science-fiction author or movie scriptwriter could envisage.

Notes

Foreword

1. Rabinow, P. (1984) (editor). "Introduction." *The Foucault Reader.* New York: Pantheon, p. 15.

Preface

1. Evans, H. (1983). "Falling into Place," *Fortean Times* 41:22 (Winter).
2. Jones, T.F., A.S. Craing, D. Hoy, E.W. Gunter, D.L. Ashley, D.B. Barr, J.W. Brock, and W. Schaffner (2000). "Mass Psychogenic Illness Attributed to Toxic Exposure at a High School." *The New England Journal of Medicine* 342 (2):96–100.

Chapter 1

1. Cited in Tripp, R.T. (compiler) (1970). *The International Thesaurus of Quotations.* New York: Thomas Y. Crowell, p. 303.
2. Alloy, L.B., J. Acocella, and R. Bootzin (1996). *Abnormal Psychology: Current Perspectives* (seventh edition). New York: McGraw-Hill, p. 584.
3. My thanks to psychiatrists Wolfgang G. Jilek and Louise Jilek-Aall for their assistance in composing this definition.
4. American Psychiatric Association. (1987). *Diagnostic and Statistical Manual of Mental Disorders* (third edition, revised). Washington, DC: American Psychiatric Association, p. 257.
5. Psychiatrists Wolfgang Jilek and Louise Jilek-Aall assisted in composing this definition.
6. Wessely, S. (1987). "Mass Hysteria: Two Syndromes?" *Psychological Medicine* 17: 109–20.
7. Modan, B., M. Tirosh, E. Weissenberg, C. Acker, T. Swartz, C. Coston, A. Donagi, M. Revach, and G. Vettorazzi (1983). "The Arjenyattah Epidemic." *Lancet* ii:1472–76.
8. Goldsmith, M.F. (1989). "Physicians with Georgia on Their Minds." *Journal of the American Medical Association* 262:603–04.
9. Radovanovic, Z. (1995). "On the Origin of Mass Casualty Incidents in Kosovo, Yugoslavia, in 1990." *European Journal of Epidemiology* 11:1–13.
10. McLeod, W.R. (1975). "Merphos Poisoning or Mass Panic?" *Australian and New Zealand Journal of Psychiatry* 9:225–229; Christophers, A.J. (1982). "Civil Emergency: Butyl

Mercaptan Poisoning in the Parnell Civil Defense Emergency: Fact or Fiction?" *New Zealand Medical Journal* (April 28):277–278.

11. David, A.S., and S.C. Wessely (1995). "The Legend of Camelford: Medical Consequences of a Water Pollution Accident." *Journal of Psychosomatic Research* 39:1–9.

12. Calmeil, L.F. (1845). *De la Folie, Consideree Sous le Point de vue Pathologique, Philosophique, Historique et Judiciaire* [On the Crowd, Considerations on the Point of Pathology, Philosophy, History, and Justice]. Paris: Baillere.

13. Notably absent from this chapter is a discussion of perhaps the most widely studied outbreaks of so-called epidemic hysteria in history — the dancing mania that swept across Europe during the Middle Ages. Episodes were typified by wild orgies, fasting, dancing, singing, screaming, hallucinations, shaking, twitching, and general bizarre behavior. The Italian variant, tarantism, was commonly attributed to tarantula spider bites, and the cure was held to be dancing to music, during which the "venom" was sweated from the body. While tarantism and dance mania episodes continue to be widely viewed as epidemic hysteria, recent evidence suggests otherwise. Based on an examination of a representative sample of medieval chronicles, these "outbreaks" are best explained as deviant religious sects that gained followers during pilgrimages through Europe in years of turmoil. This helps to explain some of their "strange" customs. Their symptoms (visions, fainting, tremor) are predictable for any group engaging in sporadic dancing, emotional worship, fasting, and alcohol consumption — often enduring for weeks. Their actions have been mistranslated by contemporary scholars evaluating these behaviors removed from their regional context and meaning. These episodes will be discussed separately in Chapter 7. See Bartholomew, R.E. (1998). "Dancing with Myths: The Misogynist Construction of Dancing Mania." *Feminism & Psychology* 8 (2):173–83; Bartholomew, R.E. (1997). "Epidemic Hysteria: A Dialogue with François Sirois." *Medical Principles and Practice* 6:38–44; Bartholomew, R.E. (1994). "Tarantism, Dancing Mania and Demonopathy: The Anthro-Political Aspects of Mass Psychogenic Illness. *Psychological Medicine* 24:281–306; Bartholomew, R.E. (1994). "When the Consequences of Beliefs are Defined as Psychiatric Entities." *Journal of Developmental and Behavioral Pediatrics* 15 (1):62–65.

14. Frankel, S. (1976). "Mass Hysteria in the New Guinea Highlands: A Telefomin Outbreak and Its Relationship to other New Guinea Hysterical Reactions." *Oceania* 47:105–33.

15. Armstrong, H., and P. Patterson (1975). "Seizures in Canadian Indian Children." *Canadian Psychiatric Association Journal* 20:247–55.

16. Weintraub, M. I. (1983). *Hysterical Conversion Reactions: A Clinical Guide to Diagnosis and Treatment.* Lancaster, England: MTP Press, p. 5.

17. Hirsch, A. (1883). *Handbook of Geographical and Historical Pathology.* London: New Sydenham Society; Markush, R.E. (1973). "Mental Epidemics: A Review of the Old to Prepare for the New." *Public Health Reviews* 4 (2):353–442; Sirois, F. (1982). "Perspectives on Epidemic Hysteria." In *Mass Psychogenic Illness: A Social Psychological Analysis.* Colligan M., J. Pennebaker, and L. Murphy pp. 217– 36. Hillsdale: New Jersey: Lawrence Erlbaum; Olkinuora, M. (1984). "Psychogenic Epidemics and Work." *Scandinavian Journal of Work, Environment and Health* 10 (6):501–15; Bartholomew, R.E., and F. Sirois (1996) "Epidemic Hysteria in Schools: An International and Historical Overview." *Educational Studies* 22:285–311.

18. Bartholomew, R.E. (1998). "The Medicalization of Exotic Deviance: A Sociological Perspective on Epidemic *Koro*." *Transcultural Psychiatry* 35 (1):5–38; Bartholomew, R.E. (1997). "Collective Delusions: A Skeptic's Guide." *The Skeptical Inquirer* 21 (3):29–33; Bartholomew, R.E. (1993). "Redefining Epidemic Hysteria: An Example from Sweden." *Acta Psychiatrica Scandinavica* 88:178–82.

19. My conceptualization of what constitutes a social delusion is also problematic in that it is a social construct of Robert E. Bartholomew. For instance, I have chosen for convenience and manageability to exclude collective episodes that originated in an organized, ritualized, or institutionalized manner. This conveniently eliminates a voluminous body of literature on various ecstatic religious groups that employ techniques that precipitate such conditions as mass glossolalia ("speaking in tongues"), shaking, twitching, ecstasies, altered consciousness and/or possession states. Technically all religious movements could

be considered social delusions— even institutionalized political ideologies such as communism and its emphasis on the "cult" of the collective or Western democracies and their exaggerated focus on the "cult" of the individual.

20. Sullivan, J., and J. McCloy (1974). "The Jersey Devil's Finest Hour." *New York Folklore Quarterly* 30 (3):233–39.

21. McCloy, J.F., and R. Miller (1976). *The Jersey Devil.* Wallingford, Pennsylvania: Middle Atlantic Press, p. 39.

22. *Ibid.*, pp. 40–41.

23. Clark, J.S. (1999). *Unexplained.* Detroit. Visible Ink, p. 562.

24. Bartholomew, R. E. (1993). "Redefining Epidemic Hysteria: An Example from Sweden." *Acta Psychiatrica Scandinavica* 88:178–82.

25. Jacobs, N. (1965). "The Phantom Slasher of Taipei: Mass Hysteria in a Non-Western Society." *Social Problems* 12:318–28.

26. Burnham, W.H. (1924). *The Normal Mind.* New York: D. Appleton-Century.

27. Goss, M. (1987). *The Halifax Slasher: An Urban Terror in the North of England.* London: Fortean Times.

28. *Ibid.*, p. 27.

29. *Ibid.*, p. 44.

30. *Ibid.*, p. 27.

31. *Ibid.*, pp. 16–19.

32. Barnes, R.H. (1993). "Construction Sacrifice, Kidnapping and Head-Hunting Rumours on Flores and Elsewhere on Indonesia." *Oceania* 64: 146–58; Erb, M. (1991). "Construction Sacrifice, Rumors and Kidnapping Scares in Manggarai: Further Comparative Notes from Flores." *Oceania* 62:114–126; Forth, G. (1991). "Construction Sacrifice and Head-Hunting Rumours in Central Flores (Eastern Indonesia): A Comparative Note." *Oceania* 61:257–66; Bhar, S. (1980). "A Headhunter Scare in a Simunul Bajau Village in Sandakan, 1979." *Borneo Research Bulletin* 12:26–29.

33. Drake, R.A. (1989). "Construction Sacrifice and Kidnapping: Rumor Panics in Borneo." *Oceania* 59:269–78. See p. 275.

34. Sjahrir, S. (1949). *Out of Exile* (translated by Charles Wolf). New York: Greenwood Press.

35. *Ibid.*, p. 162.

36. *Ibid.*, p. 164.

37. Drake (1989).

38. Barnes (1993). Forth (1991).

39. Ellis, B. (1996). "Chupacabras Mania Spreads." *Foaftale News* 39:2–3.

40. Pronounced CHUP-ah-ca-bra.

41. Sylvia R. Gallagher of Huntington Beach, California, kindly pointed out helpful information on the origin of the term "goatsucker."

42. Preston, J. (1996). "In the Tradition of Bigfoot and Elvis, the Goatsucker." *New York Times*, June 2, p. 2E.

43. Navarro, M. "A Monster on Loose? Or Is It Fantasy?" *New York Times*, January 26, 1996, p. A10.

44. Ellis (1996). p. 2.

45. Erich Goode kindly provided sources for the chupacabra outbreaks.

46. Mackay, C. (1852). *Memoirs of Extraordinary Popular Delusions and the Madness of Crowds* (volume 2). London: Office of the National Illustrated Library.

47. Mackay (1852). p. 259.

48. Bartholomew, R.E. (1992). "A Brief History of Mass Hysteria in Australia." *The Skeptic* (Australia) 12:23–26.

49. Bainbridge, W.S. (1987). "Collective Behavior and Social Movements." Pp. 544–76. In R. Stark (ed.), *Sociology.* Belmont, California: Wadsworth; Cantril, H. (1940). *The Invasion from Mars: A Study in the Psychology of Panic.* Princeton, New Jersey: Princeton University Press; Miller, D. (1985). *Introduction to Collective Behavior.* Belmont, California: Wadsworth.

50. Goode (1992).

51. Victor, J.S. (1990). "The Spread of Satanic-Cult Rumors." *The Skeptical Inquirer* 14(3):287–291. See p. 290.

52. Hicks, R. (1990). "Police Pursuit of Satanic Crime Part II: The Satanic Conspiracy and Urban Legends." *The Skeptical Inquirer* 14:378–89.

53. Victor, J.S. (1989). "A Rumor-Panic about a Dangerous Satanic Cult in Western New York." *New York Folklore* 15:23–49; Bromley, D.G. (1989). "Folk Narratives and Deviance Construction: Cautionary Tales as a Response to Structural Tensions in the Social Order." In *Deviance and Popular Culture*. Edited. by C. Sanders.

54. Cockburn, A. (1990). "Abused Imaginings." *New Statesman and Society* 85:19–20.

55. Mackay (1852). pp. 261–65.

56. *Ibid.*, p. 264.

57. Nevins, W.S. (1916). *Witchcraft in Salem Village.* New York: Franklin; Caporael, L. (1976). "Ergotism: The Satan Loosed in Salem?" *Science* 192:21–26; Karlsen, C.F. (1989). *The Devil in the Shape of a Woman: Witchcraft in Colonial New England.* New York: Vintage.

58. Persinger, M., and J. Derr (1989). "Geophysical Variables and Behavior: LIV. Zeitoun (Egypt) Apparitions of the Virgin Mary as Tectonic Strain-Induced Luminosities." *Perceptual and Motor Skills* 68:123–28; Yassa, R. (1980). "A Sociopsychiatric Study of an Egyptian Phenomenon." *American Journal of Psychotherapy* 34:246–51.

59. Toibin, C. (1985). *Moving Statues in Ireland: Seeing Is Believing.* County Laois, Ireland: Pilgram Press.

60. Kirk, R. (1812) *The Secret Commonwealth of Elves, Funs and Fairies.* London: Longman; Evans-Wentz, W.Y. (1909) *The Fairy Faith in Celtic Countries.* Rennes, France: Oberthur.

61. Sheaffer, R. (1981) *The UFO Verdict.* Buffalo, New York: Prometheus.

62. Jung, C. (1959) *Flying Saucers: A Modern Myth of Things Seen in the Sky.* New York: Harcourt Brace and World.

63. Bullard, T. E. (1989). "UFO Abduction Reports: The Supernatural Kidnap Narrative Returns in Technological Guise." *Journal of American Folklore* 102 (404):147–70.

64. Kurtz, P. (1991). *The Transcendental Temptation: A Critique of Religion and the Paranormal.* Buffalo, New York: Prometheus.

65. Healy, T., and P. Cropper (1994). *Out of the Shadows: Mystery Animals of Australia.* Chippendale, Australia: Ironbark; Clark, J, and L. Coleman (1978). *Creatures of the Outer Edge.* New York: Warner.

66. Jilek-Aall, L. (1972). "What is a Sasquatch — Or, the Problematics of Reality Testing." *Canadian Psychiatric Association Journal* 17 (3):243–47.

67. Tumin, M.M., and A.S. Feldman (1955). "The Miracle at Sabana Grande." *Public Opinion Quarterly* 19:124–39.

68. Arnold, K. (1950). *The Flying Saucer As I Saw It.* Boise, Idaho: pamphlet; Arnold, K., and R.A. Palmer (1952). *The Coming of the Saucers: A Documentary Report on Sky Objects That Have Mystified the World.* Amherst, Wisconsin: Self-published; Clark, J. (1998). *The UFO Encyclopedia: The Phenomenon from the Beginning, Volume One: A–K* (second edition). Detroit: Omnigraphics, Incorporated, pp. 139–43; Gardner, M. (1988). *The New Age: Notes of a Fringe Watcher.* Buffalo, New York: Prometheus Books.

69. Gardner, M. (1957). *Fads and Fallacies in the Name of Science.* New York: Dover, p. 56; Story, R.D. (1980). *The Encyclopedia of UFOs.* New York: Doubleday, p. 25; Sachs, M. (1980). *The UFO Encyclopedia.* New York: Perigee, pp. 207–8.

70. Strentz, Herbert J. (1970). "A Survey of Press Coverage of Unidentified Flying Objects, 1947–1966." Ph.D. dissertation, Northwestern University, department of journalism.

71. Johnston, F. (1980). *When Millions Saw Mary.* Chulmleigh, England: Augustine Publishing.

72. Persinger, M., and J. Derr (1989). pp. 123–28.

Chapter 2

1. Cited in Tripp, R.T. (compiler) (1970). *The International Thesaurus of Quotations.* New York: Thomas Y. Crowell, p. 404.

2. Sirois, F. (1975). "A Propos de la Frequence des Epidemies d'hysterie" [On the Frequency of Epidemic Hysteria]. *Union Medicale du Canada* (Montreal) 104:121–23.

3. Sirois, F. (1982). "Perspectives on Epidemic Hysteria." In *Mass Psychogenic Illness: A Social Psychological Analysis.* Edited by M. Colligan, J. Pennebaker and L. Murphy. (Hillsdale, New Jersey: Lawrence Erlbaum), pp. 217–36.

4. Faust, H.S., and L.B. Brilliant (1981). "Is the Diagnosis of 'Mass Hysteria' an Excuse for Incomplete Investigation of Low-Level Environmental Contamination?" *Journal of Occupational Medicine* 23:22–26; Bartholomew, R.E. (1990). "Ethnocentricity and the Social Construction of 'Mass Hysteria.'" *Culture, Medicine and Psychiatry* 14:455–94; Brabant, C., D. Mergler, and K. Messing (1990). "Va te Faire Soigner, ton usine est Malade; La Place de l'hysterie de Mass and la Problematique de la sante des Femmes au Travail." [Go Take Care of Yourself, Your Factory Is Sick: The Place of Mass Hysteria in the Problem of Women's Health at Work]. *Sante Mentale au Quebec* 15:181–204.

5. Sirois, F. (1974). "Epidemic Hysteria." *Acta Psychiatrica Scandinavica Supplementum* 252:7–46; Sirois, F. (1982). Wessely, S. (1987). "Mass Hysteria: Two Syndromes?" *Psychological Medicine* 17:109–20.

6. Kendell, R.E., and A.K. Zealley (eds). (1993). *Companion to Psychiatric Studies* (fifth edition). London: Churchill Livingstone.

7. Mackay, C. (1852). *Memoirs of Extraordinary Popular Delusions and the Madness of Crowds* (volume II). London, Office of the National Illustrated Library, pp. 539–40.

8. Mohr, P.D., and M.J. Bond (1982). "Epidemic Blindness." *British Medical Journal* 284:961–62.

9. Schuler, E.A., and V.J. Parenton (1943). "A Recent Epidemic of Hysteria in a Louisiana High School." *Journal of Social Psychology* 17:221–35.

10. Benaim, S.M., J. Horder, J. Anderson (1973). "Hysterical Epidemic in a Classroom." *Psychological Medicine* 3:66–73.

11. American Psychiatric Association (1994). *Diagnostic and Statistical Manual of Mental Disorders* (fourth edition). Washington, DC: American Psychiatric Association, p. 457.

12. Smelser, N.J. (1962). *Social Change in the Industrial Revolution.* London: Routledge and Kegan Paul.

13. Smelser, N.J. (1971). "Theoretical Issues of Scope and Problems." In *Readings in Collective Behavior.* Edited by Robert R. Evans. Chicago: Rand McNally. pp. 89–94. See p. 92.

14. (1988). "Hysteria at School During Blackout." *The Star*, April 30.

15. Wong, S.W., B. Kwong, Y.K. Tam, and M.M. Tsoi (1982). "Psychological Epidemic in Hong Kong." *Acta Psychiatrica Scandinavica* 65:421–36. See p. 430.

16. Goldberg, E.L. (1973). "Crowd Hysteria in a Junior High School." *Journal of School Health* 43:362–66.

17. McEvedy, C.P., A. Griffith, and T. Hall (1966). "Two School Epidemics." *British Medical Journal* ii:1300–02; Moss and McEvedy (1966). op cit.

18. Knight, J.A., T.I. Friedman, and J. Sulianti (1965). "Epidemic Hysteria: A Field Study." *American Journal of Public Health* 55:858–65.

19. Olson, W.C. (1928). "Account of a Fainting Epidemic in a High School." *Psychology Clinic* 18:34–38; Olczak, P., E. Donnerstein, T. Hershberger, and I. Kahn (1971). "Group Hysteria and the MMPI." *Psychological Reports* 28:413–14; Teoh, J., and K. Yeoh (1973). "Cultural Conflict in Transition: Epidemic Hysteria and Social Sanction." *Australian and New Zealand Journal of Psychiatry* 7:283–95; Tam, Y.K., M.M. Tsoi, G.B. Kwong, and S.W. Wong (1982). "Psychological Epidemic in Hong Kong, Part 2, Psychological and Physiological Characteristics of Children Who Were Affected." *Acta Psychiatrica Scandinavica* 65:437–49; Wong, S.W., et al. (1982). op cit.

20. Goldberg (1973). op cit.

21. Cole, T.B. (1990). "Pattern of Transmission of Epidemic Hysteria in a School." *Epidemiology* 1:212–18.

22. Small, G.W., M.W. Propper, E.T. Randolph, and S. Eth (1991). "Mass Hysteria Among Student Performers: Social Relationship as a Symptom Predictor." *American Journal of Psychiatry* 148:1200–05.

23. Goh, K.T. (1987). "Epidemiological Enquiries into a School Outbreak of an Unusual Illness." *International Journal of Epidemiology* 16 (2):265–70.

24. Small, et al. (1991). op cit.; Small, G.W., and A.M. Nicholi (1982). "Mass Hysteria Among Student Performers: Early Loss as a Predisposing Factor." *Archives of General Psychiatry* 39:721–24.

25. Small, G., and J. Borus (1983). "Outbreak of Illness in a School Chorus. Toxic Poisoning or Mass Hysteria?" *New England Journal of Medicine* 308:632–35.

26. Knight, J.A., et al. (1965). "Epidemic Hysteria: A Field Study." *American Journal of Public Health* 55:858–65; Michaux, L., T. Lemperiere, and C. Juredieu (1952). "Considerations Psychpathologiques sur une Epidemie d'hysterie Convulsive dans un Internat Professionnel" [Considerations of an Epidemic of Convulsive Hysteria in a Boarding School]. *Archives Francaises Pediatrie* 9:987–90.

27. Olson, W.C. (1928). "Account of a Fainting Epidemic in a High School." *Psychology Clinic* 18:34–38; Schuler, E.A., and V.J. Parenton (1943). op cit.; Theopold (1955). "Induzierter Amplexus neuralis bei Madchen einer Schulklasse" [Induced Neural Amplexus in Girls in a School Class]. *Monatsschrift fur Kinderheilkunde* 103.

28. Kerckhoff, A.C. (1982). "A Social Psychological View of Mass Psychogenic Illness." In *Mass Psychogenic Illness: A Social Psychological Analysis*. Edited by M. Colligan, J. Pennebaker, and L. Murphy (eds.), Hillsdale, New Jersey: Lawrence Erlbaum; pp. 199–215. Lee, R.L. (1979). "The Social Meaning of Mass Hysteria in West Malaysia and Singapore." Ph.D diss., University of Massachusetts.

29. Thomas, W.I. (1923). *The Unadjusted Girl*. Boston: Little, Brown & Co.

30. Lee, R.L., and S.E. Ackerman (1980). "The Socio-Cultural Dynamics of Mass Hysteria: A Case Study of Social Conflict in West Malaysia." *Psychiatry* 43:78–88. See p. 79.

31. Lee and Ackerman (1980). p. 79.

32. Kerckhoff (1982). op cit.

33. Rockney, R.M., and T. Lemke (1992). "Casualties from a Junior High School During the Persian Gulf War: Toxic Poisoning or Mass Hysteria?" *Journal of Developmental and Behavioral Pediatrics* 13:339–42.

34. Modan, B., M. Tirosh, E. Weissenberg, C. Acker, T. Swartz, C. Coston, A. Donagi, M. Revach, and G. Vettorazzi (1983). "The Arjenyattah Epidemic." *Lancet* ii:1472–76.

35. Goldsmith, M.F. (1989). "Physicians with Georgia on Their Minds." *Journal of the American Medical Association* 262:603–4.

36. Legendre, J. (1936). "A Propos du Koro: Une Curieuse Epidemie" [On *Koro*: A Curious Epidemic]. *La Presse Medicale*: 1534.

37. Tseng, W.S., K.M. Mo, L.S. Li, G.Q. Chen, L.W. Ou, and H.B. Zheng (1992). "*Koro* Epidemics in Guangdong, China: A Questionnaire Survey." *The Journal of Nervous and Mental Disease* 180 (2):117–23.

38. Mun, C.I. (1968). "Epidemic *Koro* in Singapore." *British Medical Journal* i:640–41.

39. Jilek, W.G. (1986). "Epidemics of 'Genital Shrinking' (*Koro*): Historical Review and Report of a Recent Outbreak in Southern China." *Curare* 9:269–82. See p. 273.

40. Dutta, H., R. Phookan, and P.D. Das (1982). "The *Koro* Epidemic in Lower Assam." *Indian Journal of Psychiatry* 24:370–74.

41. Parsons, T. (1955). "Family Structures and the Socialization of the Child." In *Family, Socialization, and the Interaction Process*. Edited by T. Parsons and R. Bales. New York: The Free Press, 35–131; Colligan, M.J., and L.R. Murphy (1979). "Mass Psychogenic Illness in Organizations: An Overview." *Journal of Occupational Psychology* 52:77–90.

42. Klein, D.F. (1993). "False Suffocation Alarms, Spontaneous Panics, and Related Conditions: An Integrative Hypothesis." *Archives of General Psychiatry* 50:306–17.

43. Aro, H., and V. Taipale (1987). "The Impact of Timing of Puberty on Psycho-

somatic Symptoms Among Fourteen to Sixteen-Year-Old Finnish Girls." *Child Development* 58:261–68.

44. American Psychiatric Association (1994). op cit.
45. American Psychiatric Association (1994). p. 455.
46. Lewis, I.M. (1971). *Ecstatic Religion*. Harmondsworth, England: Penguin.
47. Lee and Ackerman (1980). op cit.
48. Wessely (1987). op cit.
49. Schuler and Parenton (1943). op cit.
50. Benaim et al. (1973). op cit.
51. Teoh et al. (1975). op cit
52. Moss, P.D., and C.P. McEvedy (1966). "An Epidemic of Overbreathing Among Schoolgirls." *British Medical Journal* ii:1295–1300.
53. *Ibid.*, p. 1299.
54. Johnson, H. (1908). "Moral Instruction and Training in France." Pp. 1–50. In *Moral Instruction and Training in Schools: Report of an International Inquiry* (volume 2). Edited by M.E. Sadler. London: Longmans, Green and Company, see p. 26.
55. Johnson (1908), p. 26.
56. Johnson (1908), p. 27.
57. Dumville, B. (1908). "Should the French System of Moral Instruction Be Introduced into England." In *Moral Instruction and Training in Schools: Report of an International Inquiry, Volume 2*. Edited by M.E. Sadler. London: Longmans, Green, and Company. pp. 116–17.
58. Spiller, G. (1908a). "Moral Education in the Boys' Schools of Germany." In *Moral Instruction and Training in Schools: Report of an International Inquiry*, (volume 2). Edited by M. E. Sadler. pp. 213–30. London: Longmans, Green and Company, p. 215.
59. Montgomery, J.D. (1908). "The Education of Girls in Germany: Its Methods of Moral Instruction and Training." pp. 231–41. In *Moral Instruction and Training in Schools: Report of an International Inquiry*, (volume 2). Edited by M.E. Sadler. London: Longmans, Green and Company, pp. 237–38.
60. Spiller, G. (1908b). "An Educational Democracy: Moral Instruction and Training in the Schools of Switzerland." pp. 196–206. In *Moral Instruction and Training in Schools: Report of an International Inquiry* (volume 2). Edited by M.E. Sadler. London: Longmans, Green and Company, p. 196.
61. Ibid., pp. 199, 203.
62. Aemmer, F. (1893). *Eine Schulepidemie von Tremor Hystericus* [A School Epidemic of Hysterical Tremor]. Inaugural diss., Basel, Switzerland.
63. Zollinger, E. (1906). "Uber die Padagogische Behandlung des Nervosen Zitterns der Schulkinder" [On the Educational Treatment of Nervous Trembling in School Children]. *Jahrbuch der Schweiz Gesellschaft fur Schulgesundheitspflege* 7:20–47.
64. Hirt, L. (1893). "Eine Epidemie von Hysterischen Krampfen in einer Schleisischen Dorfschule" [An Epidemic of Hysterical Cramp in a Village School in Schleisischen]. *Zeitschrift fur Schulgesundheitspflege* 6:225–29. (Summary of an article by L. Hirt in the *Berliner Klinische Wochenschrift*).
65. Schoedel, J. (1906). "Uber Induzierte Krankheiten" [On Induced Illness]. *Jahrbuch fur Kinderheilkunde* 14:521–28.
66. Burnham, W.H. (1924). *The Normal Mind*. New York: D. Appleton-Century, p. 327.
67. Small, M. H. (1896). "The Suggestibility of Children." *Pedigogical Seminary* 4:176–220.
68. Kerr, J. (1907). *Report of the London Medical Officer* (Education). London: London County Council, p. 32.
69. Muhangi, J.R. (1973). "Mass Hysteria in an Ankole School." *East African Medical Journal* 50:304–9; Ebrahim, G.J. (1968). "Mass Hysteria in School Children, Notes on Three Outbreaks in East Africa." *Clinical Pediatrics* 7:437–38; Kagwa, B.H. (1964). "The Problem of Mass Hysteria in East Africa." *East African Medical Journal* 41:560–66; Rankin, A.M., and P.J. Philip (1963). "An Epidemic of Laughing in the Buboka District of Tanganyika." *Central African Journal of Medicine* 9:167–70.

70. Dhadphale, M., and S.P. Shaikh (1983). "Epidemic Hysteria in a Zambian School: 'The Mysterious Madness of Mwinilunga.'" *British Journal of Psychiatry* 142:85–88.

71. *Ibid.*, p. 87.

72. Ebrahim (1968). op cit., p. 438.

73. Teoh, J.I., and E.S. Tan (1976). "An Outbreak of Epidemic Hysteria in West Malaysia." In *Culture-Bound Syndromes, Ethnopsychiatry, and Alternate Therapies, Volume IV of Mental Health Research in Asia and the Pacific*. Edited by W.P. Lebra. Honolulu: University Press of Hawaii, pp. 32–43.; Teoh and Yeoh (1973). op cit.

74. Tan, E.S. (1963). "Epidemic Hysteria." *Medical Journal of Malaya* 18:72–76.

75. Selvadurai, S. (1985). "Problems of Residential Students in a Secondary Technical School." master's diss., University of Malaya, Kuala Lumpur.

76. Deva, M.P. (1990). *Psychiatry: A Brief Outline of Clinical Psychological Medicine*. Selangor, Malaysia: Ophir Medical Specialists.

77. Ackerman, S.E. (1980). "Cultural Process in Malaysian Industrialization: A Study of Malay Women Factory Workers." Ph.D thesis, University of California at San Diego. Ann Arbor, Michigan: University Microfilms.

78. Teoh, J., S. Soewondo, and M. Sidharta (1975). "Epidemic Hysteria in Malaysia: An Illustrative Episode." *Psychiatry* 8 (3):258–68. See p. 260.

79. Skeat, W.W. (1900). *Malay Magic*. London: Macmillan; Gimlette, J.D. (1915). *Malay Poisons and Charm Cures*. London: Oxford University Press; Chen, P.C.Y. (1970). "Indigenous Malay Psychotherapy." *Tropical and Geographical Medicine* 22:409; Endicott, K. (1970). *An Analysis of Malay Magic*. Oxford: Clarendon.

80. Benaim et al. (1973). op cit.

81. Hecker, J.F.C. (1837). *The Dancing Mania of the Middle Ages* (translated by B. Babington). New York: B. Franklin; Calmeil, L.F. (1845). *De la Folie, Consideree Sous le Point de vue Pathologique, Philosophique, Historique et Judiciaire* [On the Crowd, Considerations on the Point of Pathology, Philosophy, History, and Justice]. Paris: Baillere; Madden, R.R. (1857). *Phantasmata or Illusions and Fanaticisms of Protean Forms Productive of Great Evils*. London: T.C. Newby; Davy, R.B. (1880). "St. Vitus' Dance and Kindred Affection; The Recent Epidemic at the Ursulin Convent in Brown County, Ohio; A Sketch of the Historic Disease." *Cincinnati Lancet and Clinic* 4:440–45, 467–73; Garnier, S. (1895). *Barbe Buvee, en Religion, Soeur Sainte-Colombe et la Pretendue Possession des Ursulines d'Auxonne* [Barbara Buvee, and Religion, Sister Columbe, and the Feigned Possession of the Ursulines at Auxonne]. Paris: Felix Alcan; Loredan, J. (1912). *Un Grand Proces de Sorcellerie au XVIIe siecle, L'Abbe Gaufridy et Madeleine de Demandolx (1600–1670)* [The Grand Process of Witchcraft in the Seventeenth Century, L'Abbe Gaufridy and Madeleine de Demandolx (1600–1670)]. Paris: Perrin et Cie; Huxley, A. (1952). *The Devils of Loudun*. New York: Harper & Brothers; Rosen, G. (1968). *Madness in Society*. London: Routledge and Kegan Paul; Thomas, K. (1971). *Religion and the Decline of Magic*. London: Weidenfeld and Nicolson; Bartholomew, R.E. (1994). "Tarantism, Dancing Mania and Demonopathy: The Anthro–Political Aspects of 'Mass Psychogenic Illness.'" *Psychological Medicine* 24:281–306.

82. Philen, R.M., E.M. Kilbourn, and T.W. McKinley (1989). "Mass Sociogenic Illness by Proxy: Parentally Reported in an Elementary School." *Lancet* ii:1372–76. See p. 1376.

83. Wessely (1987). op cit.

84. Aldous, J.C., G.A. Ellam, V. Murray, and G. Pike (1994). "An Outbreak of Illness Among Schoolchildren in London: Toxic Poisoning Not Mass Hysteria." *Journal of Epidemiology and Community Health* 48:41–45.

85. Roueche, B. (1978). "Annals of Medicine." *The New Yorker* 21:63–70.; Nitzkin, J.L. (1976). "Epidemic Transient Situational Disturbance in an Elementary School." *Journal of the Florida Medical Association* 63:357–59.

86. Wong et al. (1982). op cit.

87. Cartter, M.L., P. MsHar, and H. Burdo (1989). "The Epidemic Hysteria Dilemma." *American Journal of Diseases in Childhood* 143:89.

88. Wessely (1987). op cit., p. 188.

89. References for Table 2.1 are listed in chronological order of appearance in the table and appear as follows: Bokai, cited in Szego, K. (1896). "Uber die Imitationskrankheiten

der Kinder" [About the Imitative Illnesses of Children]. *Jahrbuch fur Kinderheilkunde* 41:133–45; Legendre (1908). op cit.; Olson (1928). op cit.; Pfeiffer, P.H. (1964). "Mass Hysteria Masquerading as Food Poisoning." *Journal of the Maine Medical Association* 55:27. Moss et al. (1966). op cit.; McEvedy and Moss (1966). op cit.; "Four-Man Medical Team Visits School: Student Describes Mystery Ghost." *Straits Times,* November 21, 1966, p. 11; Mausner, J. S., and H.M. Gezon (1967). "Report on a Phantom Epidemic of Gonorrhea." *American Journal of Epidemiology* 85:320–331; Lyons, H.A., and P.E. Potter (1970). "Communicated Hysteria — An Episode in a Secondary School." *Journal of the Irish Medical Association* 63:377–79; "Hysteria Breaks Out in Another School in Pahang." *Straits Times,* April 30, 1971, p. 10; "Peace Offering Brings School 'in Hysterics' back to Normal." *Straits Times,* May 1, 1971, p. 20; "'Hysteria' Pupils Out of Hospital." *Straits Times,* May 7, 1971, p. 21; "A Mass Hysteria Puts an End to First Aid Course." *Straits Times,* April 5, 1972, p. 17; "Two Girls Warded for Hysteria Leave Hospital." *Straits Times,* April 6, 1972, p. 4; Goldberg (1973). op cit.; Smith, H.C.T., and E.J. Eastham (1973). "Outbreak of Abdominal Pain." *Lancet* ii:956–59; Levine, R.J., D.J. Sexton, F.J. Romm, B.T. Wood, and J. Kaiser (1974). "An Outbreak of Psychosomatic Illness at a Rural Elementary School." *Lancet* ii:l500–03; Polk, L.D. (1974). "Mass Hysteria in an Elementary School." *Clinical Pediatrics* 13:1013–14; Sirois (1974). op cit.; Sirois (1975). op cit.; Nitzkin (1975). op cit.; Levine, R.J. (1977). "Epidemic Faintness and Syncope in a School Marching Band." *Journal of the American Medical Association* 238 (22):2373–76; Figueroa, M. (1979). "(Related) in Epidemic Hysteria (Editorial)." *British Medical Journal* ii:409; "Mass Hysteria Hits School Kuah." *The Star,* March 27, 1978; Forrester, R.M. (1979). "Epidemic Hysteria — Divide and Conquer." *British Medical Journal* 2:669; Bebbington, E., C. Hopton, H.I. Lockett, and R.J. Madeley (1980). "From Experience: Epidemic Syncope in Jazz Bands." *Community Medicine* 2:302–7; O'Donnell, B., T.J. Elliot, and C. Huibonhoa (1980). "An Outbreak of Illness in a Rural School." *Journal of the Irish Medical Association* 73:300–302; Lee and Ackerman (1980). op cit.; Moffat, M.E. (1982). "Epidemic Hysteria in a Montreal Train Station." *Pediatrics* 70:308–10; Small and Nicholi (1982). op cit.; Wong et al. (1982). op cit.; Tam et al. (1982). op cit.; "Hysteria at Girls' School." *New Straits Times,* May 18, 1982; "School Hit by Mass Hysteria." *New Straits Times,* September 9, 1982; "Hysterical Schoolgirls Cause Panic." *The Echo,* September 9, 1982; "Hysteria Probe." *Bernama,* September 10, 1982; Omar, A. "Mass Hysteria in Two Johore Schools." *New Straits Times,* September 21, 1982; Modan et al. (1983). op cit.; Small and Borus (1983). op cit.; Wason, S., and J. Bausher (1983). "Epidemic Mass Hysteria." *The Lancet* ii:731–32; Roback, H.B., E. Roback, and J.D. LaBarbera (1984). "Epidemic Grieving at a Birthday Party: A Case of Mass Hysteria." *Journal of Developmental and Behavioral Pediatrics* 5:86–89; "'Pontianak' Hysteria." *New Straits Times,* September 21 1983; Veera, R. V. "Soccer Women Fall Foul to Hysterical Fits." *New Straits Times,* August 10, 1983; "School Closes after 13 Become Hysterical." *Bernama,* August 22, 1983; "School Hit by Hysteria." *Bernama,* August 26, 1983; "Sekolah Ditutup Kerana 15 Murid Sakit Histeria" [School closed because 15 students had hysteria disease]. *Berita Harian,* August 29, 1983; Robinson, P., M. Szewczyk, L. Haddy, P. Jones, and W. Harvey (1984). "Outbreak of Itching and Rash." *Archives of Internal Medicine* 144:159–62; Araki, S., and T. Honma (1986). "Mass Psychogenic Systemic Illness in School Children in Relation to the Tokyo Photochemical Smog." *Archives of Environmental Health* 41:159–62; "15 Pupils Hit by Mystery Itch." *New Straits Times,* June 6, 1984; "Bomoh to the Aid of Hysteria-stricken Pupils." *New Straits Times,* May 22, 1984; Goh, K.T. (1987). "Epidemiological Enquiries into a School Outbreak of an Unusual Illness." *International Journal of Epidemiology* 16 (2):265–70; "Three in Hospital After Bouts of Hysteria." *New Straits Times,* February 22, 1986; "9 Pelajar Diserang Histeria" [9 students were stricken with hysteria]. *Utusan,* February 22, 1986; "Sembilan Pelajar Diserang Histeria" [Nine students were stricken with hysteria]. *Berita Harian,* February 22, 1986; Elkins, G.E., L.A. Gamino, and R.R. Rynearson (1988). "Mass Psychogenic Illness, Trance States and Suggestion." *American Journal of Clinical Hypnosis* 30:267–75; "Department Probes Hysteria Outbreak." *New Straits Times,* September 4, 1987; "11 hit by hysteria." *The Malay Mail,* September 23, 1987; "Hysteria Hits 23 Students." *Bernama,* October 1, 1987; Ruiz, M.T., and J.M. Lopez (1988). "Mass Hysteria in a Secondary School." *International Journal of Epidemiology* 17:475–76; Cartter et al. (1989). op cit; "Hysteria at School During

Blackout." *The Star*, April 30, 1988; Gamino, L. A., G.R. Elkins, and K.U. Hackney (1989). "Emergency Management of Mass Psychogenic Illness." *Psychosomatics* 3 (4):446–49; Goldsmith (1989). op cit.; Philen et al. (1989). op cit.; Selden, B.S. (1989). "Adolescent Epidemic Hysteria Presenting as a Mass Casualty, Toxic Exposure Incident." *Annals of Emergency Medicine* 18 (8):892–895; Cole (1990). op cit.; Small et al. (1991). op cit.; Baker, P., and D. Selvey (1992). "Malathio-Induced Epidemic Hysteria in an Elementary School." *Veterinary and Human Toxicology* 34:156–60; Desenclos, J.C., H. Gardner, and M. Horan (1992). "Mass Sociogenic Illness in a Youth Center." *Revue d'Epidemiologie et de Sante Publique* 40:201–8; Krug, S. (1992). "Mass Illness at an Intermediate School: Toxic Fumes or Epidemic Hysteria?" *Pediatric Emergency Care* 8:280–82; Rockney and Lemke (1992). op cit.; Taylor, B.W., and J.E. Werbicki (1993). "A Case of Mass Hysteria involving 19 Schoolchildren." *Pediatric Emergency Care* 9:216–17.

     90. References for Table 2.2: Hirsch, A. (1883). *Handbook of Geographical and Historical Pathology*. London: New Sydenham Society; Regnard, M., and J. Simon (1877). "Sur une Epidemie de Contracture des Extremites Observee a Gentilly" [On an Epidemic of Limb Contracture Observed in Gentilly]. *Comptes Rendus des Seances de la Societe de Biologie* (Paris) 3:344–47, 350–53; Armainguad, M. (1879). "Recherches Cliniques sur l'hysterie; Relation d'une Petite Epidemie d'hysterie Observee a Bordeaux" [Clinical Research on Hysteria and its Relation to a Small Epidemic of Hysteria Observed in Bordeaux] *Memoire et Bulletin de la Societe de Medecine et Chirurgie de Bordeaux*:551–79; Laquer, L. (1888). "Uber eine chorea-epidemie" [An Epidemic of Chorea]. *Deutsche Medizinische Wochenschrift* 14:1045–46; Wichmann, R. (1890). "Eine sogenannte veitstanzepidemie in Wildbad" [A So-called Epidemic of St. Vitus Dance in Wildbad]. *Deutsche Medizinische Wochenschrift* 16:632–36, 659–63; Schatalow, N. (1891). "Zur Frage von der Epidemischen Hysterie" [On the Question of Epidemic Hysteria]. *Neurologische Centralblatt* 10:405; Palmer (1892). "Psychische seuche in der Sbersten Slasse einer Sadchenschule" [A Psychic Epidemic in the Highest Grade of a Girls School]. *Zentralblatt fur Nervenheilkunde und Psychiatrie* 3:301–8; Rembold, S. (1893). "Acute Psychiche Contagion in Einer Madchenschule" [Acute Psychic Contagion in a Girls School]. *Berliner Klinische Wochenschrift* 30:662–63; Hagenbach, E. (1893). Chorea-epidemie [Epidemic Chorea]. *Korrespondenz-Blatt f Schweizer Aerzte* (Basel) 23:631–32; Sirois (1974). op cit.; Leuch (1896). "Eine Sogenannte Chorea-Epidemie in der Schule" [A So-called Chorea Epidemic in the School]. *Korrespondenz-Blatt f Schweizer Aerzte* (Basel) 26:465–76; Von Holwede (1898). "Eine Epidemie von Hysterischen Anfallen in einer Burgerschule zu Braunschweig" [Hysterical Attacks in a Middle School in Brunswick]. *Jahrbuch fur Kinderheilkunde* 48:229–34; Zollinger, E. (1906). op cit.; Schutte, P. (1906). "Eine neue form Hysterischer Zustande bei Schulkindern" [A New Form of Hysterical Conditions in School Children]. *Muenchener Medizinsche Wochenschrift* 53:1763–64; Schoedel (1906). op cit.; Sterling, W. (1936). "Epidemia dzieciecej histeri religijnej" [Epidemic of Infantile Religious Hysteria]. *Warsz Czas Lek* 13:728–31, 749–52; Schuler and Parenton (1943). op cit.; Michaux et al. (1952). op cit.; Theopold (1955). op cit.; Rankin and Philip (1963). op cit.; Tan (1962). op cit.; Kagwa (1964). op cit.; Knight et al. (1965). op cit.; Helvie, C. (1968). "An Epidemic of Hysteria in a High School." *Journal of School Health* 38:505–9; Olczak et al. (1971). op cit.; Tan S. "50 Girls in School Hit by Strange Hysteria." *Straits Times*, March 26, 1971, pp. 1, 24; Tan, S. "Girls Hit Again by Hysteria." *Straits Times*, March 27, 1971, p. 15; Muhangi (1973). op cit.; Teoh and Yeoh (1973). op cit.; Tan, S. "Hostel Hysterics: 250 Pupils Boycott Classes." *The New Straits Times*, March 13 1973, p. 18; "Hysteria Attacks Shut Down Trade School." *New Straits Times*, March 16, 1973, p. 6; Adomakoh, C.C. (1973). "The Pattern of Epidemic Hysteria in a Girls' School in Ghana." *Ghana Medical Journal* 12:407–11; Benaim et al. (1973). op cit.; Teoh et al. (1975). op cit.; Ackerman, S.E., and R.L. Lee (1978). "Mass Hysteria and Spirit Possession in Urban Malaysia: A Case Study." *Journal of Sociology and Psychology* 1:24–35; "Hysteria Attacks Shut Down Trade School." *New Straits Times*, March 16, 1973, p. 6; Mohr and Bond (1982). op cit.; Dhadphale and Shaikh (1983). op cit.; "New Hostel for Al-Ulum Girls." *Malay Mail*, July 21 1981; Vijian, K. "Hysteria Hits Estate Classes." *New Straits Times*, June 26, 1982; "Estate School Spirit on the Prowl Again." *New Straits Times*, August 17, 1982; "More Pupils Affected by Hysteria." *Bernama*, October 26, 1986; "12 lagi Murid Perempuan Diserang Histeria" [12 more

female students stricken with hysteria], *Utusan*, October 26, 1986; 17 Bahu Pupils Hit by Hysteria. *Bernama*, October 22, 1986; Rachel, A. "Probing Hysteria Cases in Two Schools." *New Straits Times*, July 4, 1986; Rachel A. (1986). op cit. (separate episode from the previous citation); "12 Lagi Murid Perempaun Diserang Histeria" [12 more female students stricken with hysteria], *Utusan*, October 26, 1986; "More Pupils Affected by Hysteria." *Bernama*, October 26, 1986; "Hysteria Students 'Cured.'" *New Straits Times*, July 21, 1987; "Hysteria Hits 16 Pupils of Residential School." *New Straits Times*, August 25, 1987; "Hysteria Hit School Closed for Two Days." *New Straits Times*, July 8, 1987; "Outbreak of Hysteria Caused by a Bomoh." *New Straits Times*, July 9, 1987; "Students Still Hysterical." *New Straits Times*, July 10. 1987; "100 pupils and Two Teachers Yet to Return." *New Straits Times*, July 10, 1987; "Hysteria Students to Be Transferred." *Bernama*, May 20, 1985; "Hysterical Pupils Take Schoolmates Hostage." *New Straits Times*, May 19, 1987, p. 1; "Hysteria: Schoolgirls 'Confess.'" *New Straits Times*, May 21, 1987, p. 3; "Hysteria Blamed on 'Evil Spirits': School Head Wants the Ghosts to Go." *New Straits Times*, May 23, 1987, p. 7; "Council to Meet Over Hysteria Stricken Girls." *New Straits Times*, May 24, 1987, p. 4; "Seven Girls Scream for Blood: Hysterical Outbursts Continue." *New Straits Times*, May 25, 1987, p. 4; 55. "Interview: Fatimah, "'I Only Fulfilled My Parents' Wishes.'" *New Straits Times*, May 31, 1987, p. 7; "I Can't Believe It, Says Pupil." *New Straits Times*, May 31, 1987, p. 7; "Transfer Plan for Girls Hit by Hysteria." *New Straits Times*, July 21, 1987; "First Group of Hysteria Girls Sees Psychiatrist." *New Straits Times*, August 11, 1987; "Hysteria: Second Batch Visits 'Shrink.'" *New Straits Times*, August 13, 1987; "Parents of 'Hysteria' Girls Agree to Transfer." *New Straits Times*, July 24, 1987; "Girls Turn Hysterical After Forest Outing." *New Straits Times*, June 12, 1989; "Hysterics Over 'Spirit of the Coin.'"*New Straits Times*, June 17, 1989; Wittstock, B., L. Rozental, and C. Henn (1991). "Mass Phenomena at a Black South African Primary School." *Hospital and Community Psychiatry* 42:851–53; "Students Hit by Hysteria." *New Straits Times*, February 24, 1989; "100 Factory and College Girls in Hysterical Drama." *New Straits Times*, September 18, 1991; Wahab, A., and F. Jamaludin. "Hysterical 15 Get More Time." *New Straits Times*, September 27, 1991; "Hysteria in Three Schools Under Control." *New Straits Times*, September 29, 1991; "Hysteria Hits 30 More Students." *New Straits Times*, October 1, 1991; Jamaludin, F. "'Haunted' School Ban Newsmen." *New Straits Times*, October 3, 1991; "Klang Pupils in a Frenzy: Hysteria Hits School." *Malay Mail*, July 20, 1993; De Paul, V. "Mass Hysteria in Sentul Girls' School." *Malay Mail*, January 28, 1994, p. 12; Spitlers C., et al. (1996). "Outbreak of Unexplained Illness in a Middle School — Washington, April 1994." *MMWR* 45:6–9.

Chapter 3

1. Cited in Tripp, R.T. (compiler) (1970). *The International Thesaurus of Quotations*. New York: Thomas Y. Crowell, p. 660.

2. Clark, R. (1984). *The Survival of Charles Darwin*. New York: Random House, p. 23.

3. Kleinman, A. (1988*). Rethinking Psychiatry: From Cultural Category to Personal Experience*. New York: The Free Press, p. 12.

4. One important information source that we have excluded is newspaper reports of OMPI. While most major newspapers keep electronic copies and some are relatively easy to search, presently most do not date back more than a few years, and many can be extremely tedious and time consuming to search. This will be an important database to search in five or ten years time, when more newspapers dating back much further are available.

5. Indeed, it is difficult to differentiate between a conversion subject and a malingerer deliberately producing symptoms. Studies indicate that a majority of those diagnosed with conversion are actually suffering from neurological disorders that are most difficult to detect in their early stages See Alloy, L.B., J. Acocella, and R.R. Bootzin (1996). *Abnormal Psychology: Current Perspectives* (seventh edition). New York: McGraw-Hill.

6. Szasz, T.S. (1974). *The Myth of Mental Illness*. New York: Harper & Row.

7. Slater, E. (1965). "Diagnosis of 'hysteria.'" *British Medical Journal* i:1395–99. Slater

followed the course of 112 subjects who had been previously diagnosed with hysterical symptoms. After approximately a decade, he noted that 60 percent had organic illness, 8 percent had depression or schizophrenia, and the remainder exhibited symptoms of Briquet's syndrome or ambiguous signs and symptoms that were labeled under the hysteria rubric. According to Slater (1965, p. 1399): "The diagnosis of 'hysteria' is a disguise for ignorance and a fertile source of clinical error." He concludes that "[n]o evidence has yet been offered that patients suffering from 'hysteria' are in medically significant terms anything more than a random selection. ... The only thing that 'hysterical' patients can be shown to have in common is that they are all patients."

   8. Micale, M.S. (1995) *Approaching Hysteria: Disease and Its Interpretations.* Princeton, New Jersey: Princeton University Press. This reference aptly summarizes these approaches, noting that its disease history has been viewed

> as a scientific, clinical, social, economic, political, sexual, cultural, and aesthetic construction. It has been interpreted as a chapter in the history of medical thought, an episode in the discovery of the unconscious, a study in mind/body relations, and an example of the misdiagnosis of organic disease. It has been written about as a repressed cry for sexual release, an exhibitionistic erotic performance, and a passive, pathological escape from social oppression; as a caricature of femininity, an exploration of masculinity, and a codification of misogynistic male science; as an exercise in scientific pornography and a program for gender normalization. It has been studied as a social metaphor, a literary typos, a visual icon, and a surrogate form of religious experience; as a morbid manifestation of Victorian civilization, a secret strategy for professional expansion ... (and) discussed as an actual psychiatric disorder.

   9. Smith-Rosenberg, C. (1972). "The Hysterical Woman: Sex Roles and Role Conflict in Nineteenth-Century America. "Social Research" 39 (4): 652–678; Ehrenreich, B., and D. English (1978). *For Her Own Good: 150 Years of the Experts' Advice to Women.* Garden City, New York: Anchor Press; Showalter, E. (1991). *The Female Malady: Women, Madness and English Culture 1830–1980.* London: Virago Press; Ussher, J. (1991). *Women's Madness: Misogyny or Mental Illness?* Hemel Hempstead, U.K.: Harvester Wheatsheaf; Russell, D. (1995). *Women, Madness and Medicine.* Cambridge, U.K.: Polity Press; Micale, M.S. (1995). *Approaching Hysteria: Disease and Its Interpretations.* Princeton, New Jersey: Princeton University Press, pp. 66–88.

   10. Rack, P. (1982). *Race, Culture, and Mental Disorder.* London: Tavistock Publications, p. 141; Weintraub, M.I. (1983). *Hysterical Conversion Reactions: A Clinical Guide to Diagnosis and Treatment.* Lancaster, United Kingdom: MTP Press, p. 5.

   11. Kleinman (1988). p. 41.

   12. Miller, E. (1988). "Hysteria." In *Adult Abnormal Psychology.* London: Churchill Livingstone. Edited by E. Miller and P.J. Cooper, pp. 245–67.; Miller, E. (1987). "Hysteria: Its Nature and Explanation." *British Journal of Clinical Psychology* 26:163–73.

   13. Miller (1987). p. 171.

   14. Faust, H.S., and L.B. Brilliant (1981). "Is the Diagnosis of 'Mass Hysteria' an Excuse for Incomplete Investigation of Low-level Environmental Contamination?" *Journal of Occupational Medicine* 23:22–26; Brabant, C., D. Mergler, and K. Messing (1990). "Va te faire soigner, ton usine est malade: la place de l'hysterie de mass et la problematique de la sante des femmes au travail." *Sante Mentale au Quebec* 15:181–204.

   15. Sirois, F. (1982a). "Perspectives on Epidemic Hysteria." *In Mass Psychogenic Illness: A Social Psychological Analysis.* Edited by M. Colligan, J. Pennebaker and L. Murphy. Hillsdale, New Jersey: Lawrence Erlbaum, pp. 217–36; Sirois, F. (1974). "Epidemic Hysteria." *Acta Psychiatrica Scandinavica Supplementum* 252: 7–46; McGrath, J.E. (1982). Complexities, Cautions and Concepts in Research on Mass Psychogenic Illness. In *Mass Psychogenic Illness: A Social Psychological Analysis.* Edited by M. Colligan, J. Pennebaker and L. Murphy. Hillsdale, New Jersey: Lawrence Erlbaum, pp. 57–85; Wessely, S. (1987). "Mass Hysteria: Two Syndromes?" *Psychological Medicine* 17:109–120.

   16. Colligan, M.J., and L.R. Murphy (1979). "Mass Psychogenic Illness in Organizations: An Overview." *Journal of Occupational Psychology* 52:77–90.

17. Schutte, P. (1906). "Eine neue form Hysterischer Zustanden bei Schulkindern" [A new form of hysterical condition in school children]. *Muenchener Medizinsche Wochenschrift* 53:1763–64; Olson, W.C. (1928). "Account of a Fainting Epidemic in a High School." *Psychology Clinic* 18:34–38; Sterling, W. (1936). "Epidemia dzieciecej histeri religijnej" [Epidemic of infantile religious hysteria]. *Warsz Czas Lek* 13:728–31; 749–52; Schuler, E.A., and V.J. Parenton (1943). "A Recent Epidemic of Hysteria in a Louisiana High School." *Journal of Social Psychology* 17:221–35; Smith, H.C.T., and E.J. Eastman (1973). "Outbreak of Abdominal Pain." *Lancet* 11:956–59; Rockney, R., and T. Lemke (1992). "Causalities from a Junior-Senior High School During the Persian Gulf War: Toxic Poisoning or Mass Hysteria?" *Journal of Developmental and Behavioral Pediatrics* 13:339–42.

18. Williams, F.E. (1923). "The Vailala Madness and the Destruction of Native Ceremonies in the Gulf Division." *Papuan Anthropology Reports No. 4*. Port Moresby, New Guinea: Government Printer; Johnson, D.M. (1945). "The 'Phantom Anesthetist' of Mattoon: A Field Study of Mass Hysteria." *Journal of Abnormal and Social Psychology* 40:175–86; Monberg T. (1962). "Crisis and Mass Conversion on Rennell Island in 1938." *Journal of the Polynesian Society* 71:145–50; Yassa, R. (1980). "A Sociopsychiatric Study of an Egyptian Phenomenon." *American Journal of Psychotherapy* 34:246–51.

19. Champion, F.P., et al. (1963). "Mass Hysteria Associated with Insect Bites." *Journal of the South Carolina Medical Association* 59:351–53; Kerckhoff, A.C., and K.W. Back (1965). "Sociometric Patterns in Hysterical Contagion." *Sociometry* 28:2–15; Kerckhoff, A.C., and K.W. Back (1968). *The June Bug: A Study of Hysterical Contagion*. Englewood Cliffs, NJ: Prentice-Hall.

20. Stahl, S.M., and M. Lebedun (1974). "Mystery Gas: An Analysis of Mass Hysteria." *Journal of Health and Social Behavior* 15:44–50.

21. Wessely (1987). op cit.

22. Kerckhoff and Back (1965). op cit.; Wessely (1987). op cit.; Shepard, R.D., and W.H. Kroes (1975). "Report of an Investigation at the James Plant." Internal report prepared for the National Institute for Occupational Safety and Health, Cincinnati, Ohio. In *Mass Psychogenic Illness: A Social Psychological Analysis*. Edited by M. Colligan, J. Pennebaker and L. Murphy. Hillsdale, New Jersey: Lawrence Erlbaum; Colligan M.J., and L.R. Murphy (1982). "A Review of Mass Psychogenic Illness in Work Settings." In *Mass Psychogenic Illness: A Social Psychological Analysis*. Edited by M. Colligan, J. Pennebaker and L. Murphy. Hillsdale, New Jersey: Lawrence Erlbaum, pp.33–52; Sparks, P.J., P.G. Simon, W.J. Katon, L.C. Altman, G.H. Ayars, and R.L. Johnson (1990). "An Outbreak of Illness Among Aerospace Workers." *Western Journal of Medicine* 153:28–33.

23. St. Clare, W. (1787). *Gentleman's Magazine* 57:268.

24. Smelser, N.J. (1962). *Social Change in the Industrial Revolution*. London: Routledge and Kegan Paul.

25. Ackerman, S.E. (1980). *Cultural Process in Malaysian Industrialization: A Study of Malay Women Factory Workers*. Ph.D diss., University of California at San Diego. Ann Arbor, MI: University Microfilms.

26. Skeat, W.W. (1900). *Malay Magic*. London: MacMillan; Endicott, K. (1970). *An Analysis of Malay Magic*. Oxford: Clarendon.

27. Daikos, G.K., S. Garzonis, and A. Paleologue (1959). "Benign Myalgic Encephalomyelitis: An Outbreak in a Nurses' School in Athens." *Lancet* i:693–96; Pool, J.H., J.N. Walton, E.G. Brewis, P.R. Uldall, A.E. Wright, and P.S. Gardner (1961). "Benign Myalgic Encephalomyelitis in Newcastle Upon Tyne." *Lancet* i:733–37.

28. Shelokov, A., K. Habel, E. Verder, and W. Welsh (1957). "Epidemic Neuromyasthenia: An Outbreak of Poliomyelitis-like Illness in Student Nurses." *New England Journal of Medicine* 257:345–55; Poskanzer, D.C., D.A. Henderson, E.C. Kunkle, S.S. Kalter, W.B. Clement, and J.D. Bond (1957). "Epidemic Neuromyasthenia: An Outbreak in Punta Gorda, Florida." *New England Journal of Medicine* 257:356–64; Albrecht, R.M., V. Oliver, and D. Poskanzer (1964). "Epidemic Neuromyasthenia: Outbreak in a Convent in New York State." *Journal of the American Medical Association* 187:904–7.

29. White, D.N., and R.B. Burtch (1954). "Iceland Disease: A New Infection Simulating Acute Anterior Poliomyelitis. *Neurology* 4:506–16; Deisher, J.B. (1957). "Benign Myalgic Encephalomyelitis (Iceland Disease) in Alaska." *Northwest Medicine* 56:1451–56.

30. Gilliam, A.G. (1938). "Epidemiologic Study of an Epidemic, Diagnosed as Poliomyelitis, Occurring Among the Personnel of the Los Angeles County General Hospital During the Summer of 1934." *Bulletin* (U.S. Public Health Service Division of Infectious Diseases, National Institutes of Health), 240:1–90; Sigurdsson, B.J., J. Sigurjonsson, J. Sigurdsson, J. Thorkelsson, and K. Gudmundsson (1950). "Disease Epidemic in Iceland Simulating Poliomyelitis." *American Journal of Hygiene* 52:222–38.

31. Acheson, E. (1959). "The Clinical Syndrome Variously Called Benign Myalgic Encephalomyelitis, Iceland Disease and Epidemic Neuromyasthenia." *American Journal of Medicine* 26:569–95; Briggs, M.C., and Levine, P.H. (1994). "A Comparative Review of Systemic and Neurological Symptomatology in 12 Outbreaks Collectively Described as Chronic Fatigue Syndrome, Epidemic Neuromyasthenia and Myalgic Encephalomyelitis." *Clinical and Infectious Diseases* 18 (1): pp. S32–42; Chester, A.C., and P.H. Levine (1994). "Concurrent Sick Building Syndrome and Chronic Fatigue Syndrome: Epidemic Neuromyasthenia Revisited." *Clinical and Infectious Diseases* 18 (1): pp. S43–48.

32. Shelokov et al., (1957). op cit.; Poskanzer et al., (1957). op cit.; 1957; Albrecht et al., (1964). op cit.

33. Merskey, H. (1979). *The Analysis of Hysteria.* London: Bailliere Tindall.

34. Gilliam (1938). op cit.; Ramsay, A.M. (1957). "Encephalomyelitis in North-west London. An Endemic Infection Simulating Poliomyelitis and Hysteria." *Lancet* ii:1196–2200.

35. McEvedy, C.P., and A.W. Beard (1973). "A Controlled Follow-up of Cases Involved in an Epidemic of 'Benign Myalgic Encephalomyelitis.'" *British Journal of Psychiatry* 122:141–50. See p. 147.

36. Lucire Y. (1986). "Neurosis in the Workplace." *Medical Journal of Australia* 145:323–327; Ferguson, D. (1987). "RSI: Putting the Epidemic to Rest." *Medical Journal of Australia* 147:213; Hall, W., and L. Morrow (1988). "Repetition Strain Injury: An Australian Epidemic of Upper Limb Pain." *Social Science and Medicine* 27:645–49.

37. Bell, D.S. (1989a). "'Repetitive Strain Injury': An Iatrogenic Epidemic of Simulated Injury." *Medical Journal of Australia* 151:280–84; Bell, D.S. (1989b). "'Repetitive Strain Injury': An Iatrogenic Epidemic. In Reply." *Medical Journal of Australia* 151:599–600.

38. Beard, G.M. (1879). "Conclusions from the Study of 125 Cases of Writer's Cramp and Allied Affectations." *Medical Record*: 224–47.

39. Smith, H., H. Culpin, E. Farmer (1927). *A Study of Telegraphists' Cramp.* Medical Research Council, Industrial Fatigue Research Board. London, U.K.

40. Anonymous (1911). *Great Britain and Ireland Post Office, Department Committee on Telegraphist's Cramp Report.* London: His Majesty's Stationary Office; Lucire (1986). op cit.

41. Lucire (1986). op cit.

42. Leino, P., and V. Hanninen (1995). "Psychosocial Factors at Work in Relation to Back and Limb Disorders." *Scandinavian Journal of Work, Environment and Health* 21:134–42. See p. 134.

43. Wessely, S. (1997). "Psychological, Social and Media Influences on the Experience of Somatic Symptoms." Paper prepared for ESF workshop on "Cognitive Functions as Mediators of Environmental Effects on Health," September 15–17, 1997, p. 9.

44. Sirois, F. (1997). "Epidemic Hysteria: A Dialogue with Robert E. Bartholomew." *Medical Principles and Practice* 6:45–50.

45. Sirois, F. (1994). "Epidemic Hysteria: School Outbreaks 1973–1993." unpublished.

46. Sirois (1997). op cit.; Sirois (1994). op cit.

47. Klein, D.F. (1993). "False Suffocation Alarms, Spontaneous Panics, and Related Conditions: An Integrative Hypothesis." *Archives of General Psychiatry* 50:306–17.

48. Golding, J., R. Smith, and M. Kashner (1991). "Does Somatization Disorder Exist in Men?" *Archives of General Psychiatry* 48:231–35; American Psychiatric Association (1994). *Diagnostic and Statistical Manual of Mental Disorders* (fourth edition). Washington, DC: American Psychiatric Association.

49. American Psychiatric Association (1994). op cit.; Guggenheim, F.G. (1995). "Somatoform Disorders." pp. 1251–70. In *Comprehensive Textbook of Psychiatry VI*, (Volume 1, sixth edition). Edited by Harold I. Kaplan and Benjamin J. Sadock. Baltimore: Williams and Wilkins, see p. 1253.

50. Struewing J.P., and G. C. Gray (1990). "Epidemic of Respiratory Complaints Exacerbated by Mass Psychogenic Illness in a Military Recruit Population." *American Journal of Epidemiology* 132:1120–29.

51. Here we exclude as epidemic hysteria an episode of perceived genital shrinking among fifty male workers at a Thailand tapioca plantation that was recorded by Harrington (Harrington, J.A. [1982]. "Epidemic psychosis." *British Journal of Psychiatry* 141:98–99). This episode is more appropriately described as a collective delusion. See Bartholomew, R.E. (1994). "The Social Psychology of 'Epidemic' *Koro*." *The International Journal of Social Psychiatry* 40:44–60; Bartholomew, R.E. (1998). "The Medicalization of Exotic Deviance: A Sociological Perspective on Epidemic *Koro*." *Transcultural Psychiatry* 35:5–38.

52. Martin, K.A. (1996). *Puberty, Sexuality, and the Self: Boys and Girls at Adolescence.* New York: Routledge.

53. Parsons T. (1955). "Family Structures and the Socialization of the Child." In *Family, Socialization, and the Interaction Process.* Edited by T. Parsons and R. Bales. New York: The Free Press, pp. 35–131; Colligan and Murphy (1979). op cit.

54. Bourguignon, E. (1979). *Psychological Anthropology: An Introduction to Human Nature and Cultural Differences.* New York: Holt, Rinehart and Wilson, pp. 149–50.

55. Wool, C.A., and A.J. Barsky (1994). "Do Women Somatize More Than Men? Gender Differences in Somatization." *Psychosomatics* 35(5):445–52.

56. Jenkins, R. (1985). "Sex Differences in Minor Psychiatric Morbidity." *Psychological Medicine Monograph Supplement* 7:1–53.

57. Busfield, J. (1996*). Men Women and Madness: Understanding Gender and Mental Disorder.* London: Macmillan Press Ltd., p. 30.

58. Kerckhoff, A.C. (1982). "A Social Psychological View of Mass Psychogenic Illness." In *Mass Psychogenic Illness: A Social Psychological Analysis.* Edited by M. Colligan, J. Pennebaker and L. Murphy. Hillsdale, New Jersey: Lawrence Erlbaum, pp. 199–215. p. 211.

59. Colligan and Murphy (1980), p. 42.

60. Kapferer, B. (1983*). A Celebration of Demons: Exorcism and the Aesthetics of Healing in Sri Lanka.* Bloomington, Indiana: Indiana University Press; Bourguignon, E. (1979) pp. 149–50; Lewis, I.M. (1971). *Ecstatic Religion.* Harmondsworth, England: Penguin.

61. Siskind, J. (1973). *To Hunt in the Morning.* New York: Oxford.

62. Lewis, I.M. (1971). op cit.

63. Ong, A. (1988). "The Production of Possession: Spirits and the Multinational Corporation in Malaysia." *American Ethnologist* 15:28–42; Ong, A. (1987). *Spirits of Resistance and Capitalist Discipline: Factory Women in Malaysia.* Albany, New York: State University of New York Press.

64. Bartholomew, R.E. (1997). "Epidemic Hysteria: A Dialogue with Francois Sirois." *Medical Principles and Practice* 6:38–44.

65. Kapferer, B. (1983). op cit., p. 96.

66. Of course, it could also be argued that the young are subordinate to the old. Among youth, female participation in MPI episodes is overwhelmingly high.

67. Abdul Rahman, T. (1987). "As I See It... Will the Hysteria Return?" *New Straits Times* (Malaysia), July 6.

68. Lee, R.L., and S.E. Ackerman (1980). "The Sociocultural Dynamics of Mass Hysteria: A Case Study of Social Conflict in West Malaysia." *Psychiatry* 43:78–88. p. 85.

69. Bourguignon, E. (1978). "Spirit Possession and Altered States of Consciousness: The Evolution of an Inquiry." In *The Making of Psychological Anthropology.* Edited by G.D. Spindler. Berkeley: University of California Press, pp. 477–515; Bourguignon (1979). pp. 258–61.

70. Bourguignon, E. (1974). *Culture and the Varieties of Consciousness.* Reading, Massachusetts: Addison-Wesley, p. 24.

71. Bourguignon (1979). p. 261. Italics in original.

72. Ackerman, S.E., and R.L. Lee (1981). "Communication and Cognitive Pluralism in a Spirit Possession Event in Malaysia." *American Ethnologist* 8:789–99.

73. Bell, A., and A.T. Jones (1958). "Fumigation with Dichlorethyl Ether and Chlordane: Hysterical Sequelae." *Medical Journal of Australia* 5:258–63.

74. Boulougouris, J.C., A.D. Rabavilas, C.N. Stefanis, N. Vaidakis, and D.G. Tabouratzis (1981). "Epidemic Faintness: A Psychophysiological Investigation." *Psychiatria Clinica* 14:215–25.

75. Sinks, T., P.R. Kerndt, and K.M. Wallingford (1989). "Two Episodes of Acute Illness in a Machine Shop." *American Journal of Public Health* 79:1024–28.

76. Yassi, A., J.L. Weeks, K. Samson, and M.B. Raber (1989). "Epidemic of 'Shocks' in Telephone Operators: Lessons for the Medical Community." *Canadian Medical Association Journal* 140:816–20.

77. Donnell, H.D., J.R. Bagby, R.G. Harmon, J.R. Crellin, H.C. Chaski, M.F. Bright, M. Van Tuinen, and R.W. Metzger (1989). "Report of an Illness Outbreak at the Harry S Truman State Office Building." *American Journal of Epidemiology* 129:550–58.

78. Sparks et al. (1990). op cit.

79. Colligan and Murphy (1979). op cit.

80. Markush, R.E. (1973). "Mental Epidemics: A Review of the Old to Prepare for the New." *Public Health Reviews* 4:353–442.

81. Bauer, R.M., K.W. Greve, E.L. Besch, C.J. Schramke, J. Crouch, A. Hicks, M.R. Ware, and W.B. Lyles (1992). "The Role of Psychological Factors in the Report of Building-Related Symptoms in Sick Building Syndrome." *Journal of Consulting and Clinical Psychology* 60 (2) 213–19; Ryan, C.M., and L.A. Morrow (1992). "Dysfunctional Buildings or Dysfunctional People: An Examination of the Sick Building Syndrome and Allied Disorders." *Journal of Consulting and Clinical Psychology* 60 (2) 220–24.

82. Brodsky, C.M. (1983). "Allergic to Everything: A Medical Subculture." *Psychosomatics* 24:731–42; Bardana, E.J., and A. Montanaro (1986). "Tight Building Syndrome." *Immunology and Allergy Practice* 8:74–88.

83. Bartholomew, R.E. (1990). "Ethnocentricity and the Social Construction of 'Mass Hysteria.'" *Culture, Medicine and Psychiatry* 14:455–94.

84. Sirois F. (1982b). "Epidemic Hysteria." In A. Roy (ed.), *Hysteria* (101–15). New York: John Wiley; Sirois, F. (1977). Remarques sur l'hysterie collective [Remarks on epidemic hysteria]. *Evolution Psychiatrique* 42:111–24.

85. Inglis, B. (1990). *Trance: A Natural History of Altered States of Consciousness.* London: Paladin, p. 217.

86. Teoh, J. (1972). "Epidemic hysteria in Malaysia." In *Proceedings of the 7th Malaysia-Singapore Congress of Medicine* (August 14–16). The Academy of Medicine of Malaysia, General Hospital, Kuala Lumpur, Malaysia, 73–78.

87. Cruz, C.M. (1990). "Health and Work: The Case of the Gas Emissions at the Industrial Complex of Mayaguez." *Puerto Rican Health Sciences Journal* 9:123–125.

88. For complicated reasons, I (RB) was unable to study these outbreaks, but they were numerous between 1993 and 1995, and none to my knowledge were ever recorded in scientific studies, and only very occasionally did they appear in Malaysian newspaper reports.

89. Notes and References for Table 3.1: All outbreaks involve factories unless otherwise specified. In cases discussed in multiple reports, or the same author(s) in separate articles, we have relied on figures provided in the most recent publication when there are any minor discrepancies between reports. * = approximately; - = not specified; ^ - although not stated explicitly, it appears clearly implied that all of those affected are female; "Liability" refers to emotional mood swings.

References are listed in chronological order of appearance in the table. Parigi, S., and F. Giagiotti (1956). "Su di una epidemica di isterismo" [On an epidemic of hysteria]. *Rassegna di Studi Psichiatri* (Siena), 45:1112–14; Bell and Jones 1956). op cit.; Champion et al. (1963). op cit.; McEvedy, C.P., A. Griffith, T. Hall (1966). "Two School Epidemics. *British Medical Journal* ii:1300–2; Markush (1973). op cit.; Stahl, S.M. (1982). "Illness As an Emergent Norm or Doing What Comes Naturally." In *Mass Psychogenic Illness: A Social Psychological Analysis.* Edited by M. Colligan, J. Pennebaker and L. Murphy. Hillsdale, New Jersey: Lawrence Erlbaum, pp. 183–98; Phillips, P.E. (1974). "Internal Report Prepared for the Division of Health, the State of Missouri." In M.J. Colligan and L.R. Murphy. "A Review of Mass Psychogenic Illness in Work Settings." In *Mass Psychogenic Illness: A Social Psychological Analysis.* Edited by M.J. Colligan, J. Pennebaker and L. Murphy. Hillsdale, New Jersey:

Lawrence Erlbaum, pp. 33–52; Folland, D.S. (1975). "Suspect Toluene Exposure at a Boot Factory: Internal Report from the Tennessee Department of Health: Tennessee. In M.J. Colligan and L.R. Murphy. "A Review of Mass Psychogenic Illness in Work Settings." Edited by M.J. Colligan, J. Pennebaker and L. Murphy. Hillsdale, New Jersey: Lawrence Erlbaum, pp. 33–52; "National Institute of Occupational Safety and Health study TA-76-102." In Colligan and Murphy (1982); "National Institute of Occupational Safety and Health study HHE-77-27-437." In Colligan and Murphy (1982); "National Institute of Occupational Safety and Health study TA-77-35." In Colligan and Murphy (1982); "National Institute of Occupational Safety and Health study TA-78-58." In Colligan and Murphy (1982); "National Institute of Occupational Safety and Health study TA-78-10. In Colligan and Murphy (1982); "National Institute of Occupational Safety and Health study HHE-78-116-557." In Colligan and Murphy (1982); "National Institute of Occupational Safety and Health Report. In Colligan and Murphy (1982); "National Institute of Occupational Safety and Health Report." In Colligan and Murphy (1982); Maguire, A. (1978). "Psychic Possession Among Industrial Workers." *Lancet* i:376–78; Cunliffe, W.J. (1978). "Psychic Possession Among Industrial Workers." *Lancet* ii:44; Cohen, B. M. Colligan, W. Wester, and M. Smith (1978). "An Investigation of Job Satisfaction Factors in an Incident of Mass Psychogenic Illness at the Worksplace." *Occupational Health Nursing* 26:10–16; Murphy, L.R., and M.J. Colligan (1979). "Mass Psychogenic Illness in a Shoe Factory: A Case Report." *International Archives of Occupational and Environmental Health* 44:133–38; Boulougouris et al. (1981); Phoon, W.H. (1982). "Outbreaks of Mass Hysteria at Workplaces in Singapore: Some Patterns and Modes of Presentation." In *Mass Psychogenic Illness: A Social Psychological Analysis*. Edited by M. Colligan, J. Pennebaker and L. Murphy. Hillsdale, New Jersey: Lawrence Erlbaum, pp. 21–32; Boxer, P.A. (1985). "Occupational Mass Psychogenic Illness: History, Prevention, Management." *Journal of Occupational Medicine* 27:867–72; Ilchyshyn, A., and A.G. Smith (1985). "Gum Arabic Sensitivity with Epidemic Hysteria Dermatologica." *Contact Dermatitis* 13:282–83; Alexander, R.W., and M.J. Fedoruk (1986). "Epidemic Psychogenic Illness in a Telephone Operator's Building." *Journal of Occupational Medicine* 28:42–45; Donnell et al. (1989). op cit.; Hall, E.M., and J.V. Johnson (1989). "A Case of Stress and Mass Psychogenic Illness in Industrial Workers." *Journal of Occupational Medicine* 31:243–50; Sinks et al. (1989). op cit.; Yassi et al. (1989). op cit.; Sparks et al. (1990). op cit.; Struewing and Gray (1990). op cit.

90. References for Table 3.2: St. Clare (1787). op cit; Seeligmuller, A. (1876). "Uber epidemisches auftreten von hysterischen zustanden." *Allgemeine Zeitschift fur Psychiatrie* (Berlin), 33:510–28; Bouzol, M. (1884). "Relation d'une epidemie a phenomene Hysterico-choreique observee a Algon (Ardeche) en 1882." *Lyon Medical* 47:¢42–48, 174–84, 211–17; Schatalow, N. (1891). "Zur frage von der epidemischen hysterie." *Neurologisches Central-blatt* 10:405; Bechtereff, V. (1914). "Donnees sur l'epidemie neuro-psychique observee chez les travailleurs d'usine de riga et de petro-grad en mars 1914." *Obozrienie Psikhiatrii Nevrologii (Review of Psychiatry and Neurology* 19:585–613; Franchini, A. (1947). "Manifestazioni isteriche collettive interpretate come sintomi di intossicazione da gas ignoto." *Medicina di Lavoro* 38:57–60; Parin, P. (1948). "Die kriegneurose der Jogislawen." *Schweizer Arch f Neurol u Psychiat* 61:303–24; Chew, P.K. (1978). "How to Handle Hysterical Factory Workers." *Occupational Health and Safety* 47 (2): 50–54; Ackerman and Lee (1981). op cit.; Phoon (1982). op cit.; Chan, M., and W.C. Kee (1983). "Epidemic Hysteria: A Study of High Risk Factors." *Occupational Health and Safety* 52:55–64; Ong (1987). op cit.

91. References for Table 3.3: Beard (1879). op cit.; Smith et al. (1927). op cit.; Gilliam (1938). op cit.; Acheson, E. (1954). "Encephalomyelitis Associated with Poliomyelitis Virus. An Outbreak in a Nurses' Home." *Lancet* ii:1044–48; Acheson (1959). op cit.; Acheson, E. (1955). "Letter." *Lancet* ii:350–52; Shelokov et al., 1957; Anonymous (1955). "Clinical Meeting of the Natal Coastal Branch. The Durban Mystery Disease." *South African Medical Journal* 29:997; Hill, R.C. (1955). "Memorandum on the Outbreak Amongst the Nurses at Addington, Durban." *South African Medical Journal* 29:344; Hill, R.C., R.W. Cheetham, H.L. Wallace (1955). "Epidemic Myalgic Encephalopathy." *Lancet* 1:689–93; McEvedy, C. and A. Beard (1970a). "Royal Free Hospital Epidemic of 1955: A Reconsideration." *British Medical Journal* i:7–10; McEvedy, C., and A. Beard (1970b). "Concept of Benign Myalgic

Encephalomyelitis." *British Medical Journal* i:11–15; Poskanzer et al. (1957). op cit.; Geffen, D., and S. Tracy (1957). "Outbreak of Acute Infective Encephalomyelitis in a Residential Home for Nurses in 1956." *British Medical Journal* ii:904; Daikos et al. (1959). op cit.; Ikeda, Y. (1966). "An Epidemic of Emotional Disturbance Among Leprosarium Nurses in a Setting of Low Morale and Social Change." *Psychiatry* 29:152–64; Albrecht (1964). op cit.; Dillon, M.J., W.C. Marshall, and J.A. Dudgeon (1974). "Epidemic Neuromyasthenia: Outbreak Among Nurses at a Children's Hospital." *British Medical Journal* 1:301–305; Lucire (1986). op cit.

Chapter 4

1. Cited in Tripp, R.T. (compiler) (1970). *The International Thesaurus of Quotations.* New York: Thomas Y. Crowell, p. 529.
2. Pronounced "BOT-uh-tot," and often mispronounced "BOT-uh-tort."
3. Stoner, R.D. (1962). *A Seed-Bed of the Republic.* Tennessee: Kingsport Press.
4. Cohen, I.B. (1942). *An Economic and Social Survey of Botetourt County.* Charlottesville, Virginia: University of Virginia.
5. At the time it was never referred to as "the mad gasser." The press used such terms as "the phantom gas tosser," "the Botetourt Bogey," and most commonly, "the gasser" or "the gas man."
6. "Gas 'Attack' on Family Is Probed. Fumes at Night Fell Girl and Make Others Ill at Haymakertown Home." *Roanoke Times*, December 24, 1933, p. 13.
7. *Ibid.*
8. The property in question had been the home of an earlier settler named Bryan McDonald, Jr., part of which was built in 1766.
9. "Expects to Resign. ...Botetourt Investigator to Go Through with Kent Case and Retire." *Roanoke Times*, August 25, 1934.
10. "One Gas Victim Seriously Ill. Officers Seek Clues Here with Little Success." *Roanoke Times*, December 30, 1933, p. 2; "Girl Still Ill." *Roanoke Times*, January 2, 1933, p. 10.
11. "Gas 'Attack' on Family Is Probed. Fumes at Night Fell Girl and Make Others Ill at Haymakertown Home." *Roanoke Times*, December 24, 1933, p. 13.
12. "Third Attack Overcomes Girl." *Roanoke Times*, December 24, 1933, p. 13.
13. A 1998 interview between Robert Willis and Mr. Hall's daughter, Catherine Hall Jenks, who witnessed the incident.
14. "Police Seek Clue to 'Gas Attacks' on Two Families." *Lynchburg News*, December 27, 1933, p. 1; "Gas Attacks on Homes Continue. Second Reported from Cloverdale. Physicians Not Sure of Vapor's Nature." *Roanoke Times*, December 27, 1933, p. 2.
15. *Ibid.*
16. "Gas Attacks ... Second Reported from Cloverdale." *Roanoke Times*, December 27, 1933, p. 2.
17. "...Seek Motive." *Roanoke Times*, December 27, 1933, p. 2.
18. "Stealthy Gasser Is Active Again. Troutville Man Is Latest Victim." *Roanoke Times*, December 29, 1933, p. 2.
19. "Gas Attacks Appear to Have Ceased in Botetourt County." *Roanoke Times*, January 2, 1934, p. 10.
20. "...Effective Technique." *Roanoke Times*, December 29, 1933, p. 2.
21. *Ibid.*
22. "...Finds Woman's Track." *Roanoke Times*, December 29, 1933, p. 2.
23. "One Gas Victim." *Roanoke Times*, December 30, 1933, p. 2.
24. "Gasser Busy in West Botetourt. Fourth Attack Is Reported..." *Roanoke Times*, January 12, 1934, p. 2.
25. *Ibid.*, p. 2.
26. A 1998 telephone interview between Ruth Harris Morris of Salem, Virginia, and Robert Willis.

27. "Woman and Babe Flee." *Roanoke Times*, January 12, 1934, p. 2.

28. "...Suspect None." *Roanoke Times*, January 12, 1934, p. 2.

29. A 1998 telephone interview between Roy Harris and Robert Willis.

30. A 1998 telephone interview between Thelma Lee Kyle and Robert Willis.

31. "...Reports Chlorine Used." *Roanoke Times*, January 21, 1934, p. 15; "Nauseating Gas Released in at Least Six Homes." *Roanoke World-News*, January 22, 1934.

32. "...Sees Man Run." *Roanoke Times*, January 22, 1934, p. 2.

33. "No Motive Known." *Roanoke Times*, January 22, 1934, p. 2.

34. *Ibid.*

35. "Attacks with Gas Puzzle Fincastle." *Lynchburg News*, January 23, 1934, p. 11.

36. *Ibid.*

37. "Four More Homes in Botetourt Visited by Gasser. Shots Fired at Fleeing Suspect." *Roanoke Times*, January 23, 1934, p. 2.

38. "Botetourt Bogey Baffles Officers. Gas Man Elusive After Terrorizing Residents for a Month." *Roanoke Times*, January 22, 1934, p. 2.

39. "Gasser Reported in Action. Family, Fearing to Stay in House at Night, Finds Fumes on Return." *Roanoke Times*, January 25, 1934, p. 2.

40. "...Fears Injury to Innocent." *Roanoke Times*, January 31, 1934, p. 2.

41. *Ibid.*, p. 2; "Gasser Again Active in Fincastle County." *Lynchburg News*, January 25, 1934, p. 1.

42. *Ibid.*, p. 2.

43. "...Occurs at Customary Hour." *Roanoke Times*, January 24, 1934, p. 2.

44. "Continue Search for 'Gas' Clues. Officers' Test Eliminates Chlorine — Inhabitants Are Highly Keyed." *Roanoke Times*, January 31, 1934, p. 2.

45. "Another Home in Botetourt Attacked with Nauseating Fumes at Usual Hour." *Lynchburg News*, January 30, 1934, pp. 1–2.

46. "...Fears Injury to Innocent." *Roanoke Times*, January 31, 1934, p. 2.

47. "Gas Throwers Make New Foray ... Reward of $500 Authorized." *Roanoke Times*, January 30, 1934, p. 2; "Reward Offered by County Board to Catch Gasser." *Lynchburg News*, January 30, 1934, p. 1.

48. The bill was introduced at the prompting of Justice Benjamin Haden.

49. "Gas Throwing Prompts Bill for Rigorous Penalties. Sponsors Propose Prison Sentence." *Roanoke Times*, January 24, 1934, p. 2.

50. "...Fears Injury to Innocent." *Roanoke Times*, January 31, 1934, p. 2; "Noxious Gas Bill Passed by House." *Roanoke World-News*, January 31, 1934, pp. 1, 8.

51. "This Gas Attack Less Diabolical Than Real Thing." *Roanoke Times*, January 25, 1934, p. 2; "...Noticed Car Passing." *Roanoke Times*, February 12, 1934, p. 1.

52. *Ibid.*

53. "Gasser Suspect Greeted with Buckshot Barrage." *Roanoke Times*, January 27, 1934, p. 2.

54. "Spirited Pup Is Gas Thrower Foe." *Roanoke Times*, January 28, 1934, p. 2.

55. "Hoax Angle Taken Up." *Roanoke Times*, January 30, 1934.

56. "...Sheriff 'From Missouri,'" *Roanoke Times*, February 6, 1934, p. 2.

57. "Mysterious Gas Thrower Visits Home at Vinton." *Roanoke Times*, February 6, 1934, p. 3.

58. New 'Gassings' Puzzle to Police." *Lynchburg News*, February 7, 1934, p. 3.

59. "Dog Acts Queerly." *Roanoke Times*, February 6, 1934, p. 7.

60. *Ibid.*, p. 7; "Troutville Home Gas Attack ... Officers Again Find No Clues." *Roanoke Times*, February 5, 1934, p. 2.

61. "Not to Hesitate to Nab Gasser." *Roanoke Times*, February 6, 1934, pp. 2, 7.

62. "Latest Call Investigated." *Roanoke Times*, February 6, 1934, p. 2.

63. "Rorer Avenue Home Target of Mysterious Gas Attack." *Roanoke Times*, February 8, 1934, pp. 1, 4; "Gas Attack Is Made on Local Home." *Roanoke World-News*, February 8, 1934, pp. 1, 17; "'Gasser' Active in Roanoke Home." *Lynchburg News*, February 9, 1934, p. 8.

64. "Gas Not Identified." *Roanoke Times*, February 8, 1934, p. 4.

65. "Six Victims of Gas Tell of Attacks." *Roanoke World-News*, February 9, 1934, p. 1.

66. Attacks by Mystery Gasser Keep Police Busy. Reports of Nocturnal Visits Come from Widely Separated Spots." *Roanoke Times*, February 9, 1934, pp. 1, 4.

67. "Seven Suspected Visits of 'Gasser' Reported to Police." *Roanoke Times*, February 10, 1934, p. 3.

68. *Ibid.*, p. 3.

69. "Victim Recovering." *Roanoke Times*, February 10, 1934, p. 3.

70. "...Second Occurrence." *Roanoke Times*, February 11, 1934, pp. 1–2.

71. "...Second Occurrence." *Roanoke Times*, February 11, 1934, pp. 1, 2; "Gas May Be Insecticide, Chemist Tells Police; Report 8 More Gassings." *Roanoke World-News*, February 12, 1934.

72. *Ibid.*

73. *Ibid.*

74. *Ibid.*

75. "Bottle of Old Liquid Seen as Clue to Mysterious 'Gassings.' Authorities Investigating Reported Attacks." *Roanoke Times*, February 11, 1934, pp. 1, 2.

76. "Sample of 'Gas' Is Found to Be Harmless to Humans." *Roanoke Times*, February 12, 1934, p. 1.

77. "'Gas Man' Takes Full Night Off. Skeptical Police Get but One Call and Find Burning Rubber to Blame." *Roanoke Times*, February 12, 1934, p. 1.

78. "Roanoke Has No Gasser." *Roanoke Times*, February 14, 1934, p. 6.

79. "Botetourt's Mysterious 'Gassers,'" *Roanoke Times*, February 24, 1934, p. 6.

80. Interview between Robert Willis and Lomax Breckinridge in 1998.

Chapter 5

1. Pronounced "MAT-tune" and often mispronounced as "Mah-TUNE."

2. Johnson, D.M. (1945). "The 'Phantom Anesthetist' of Mattoon: A Field Study of Mass Hysteria. *Journal of Abnormal and Social Psychology* 40:175–86.

3. One could cite dozens of examples. For a few, see Goode, E. (1992). *Collective Behavior*. New York: Harcourt Brace Jovanovich; Miller, D.L. (1985). *Introduction to Collective Behavior*. Belmont, California: Wadsworth; Klapp, O.E. (1972). *Currents of Unrest*. New York: Holt, Rinehart and Winston; Smelser, N.J. (1962). *Theory of Collective Behavior*. New Jersey: Prentice-Hall.

4. Clark, J. (1999). *Unexplained!* Farmington Hills, Michigan: Visible Ink Press; Smith, W. (1994). "The Mattoon Phantom Gasser." *The Skeptic* 3 (1):33–39; Clark, J. (1993). *Encyclopedia of Strange and Unexplained Physical Phenomena*. Detroit: Gale Research, pp. 202–205; Shoemaker, M.T. (1985). "The Mad Gasser of Botetourt." *Fate* 38 (6):62–68; Coleman, L. (1983). *Mysterious America*. Winchester, Massachusetts: Faber & Faber; Smith, W. (1984). "The Mattoon Gasser: A Modern Myth." *The International UFO Reporter* 9 (6):7, 9, 14; Vyner, J. (1961). "The Mystery of Springheel Jack." *Flying Saucer Review* 7 (3):3–6.

5. At the time of the episode, *Newsweek* estimated its population at 17,000, while *Time* placed it at 17,500. These figures are near its present-day population of 18,441, according to 1999 estimates from the Illinois Transportation Department.

6. Johnson, D.M. (1945). p. 176.

7. This reconstruction of the "attack" on Mrs. Kearney is taken from the following sources, which include separate firsthand interviews by Mattoon police and Chicago psychiatrist Harold S. Hulbert. "Anesthetic Prowler on Loose." *Daily Journal-Gazette*, September 2, 1944, p. 1; "Show How They Were Gassed." *Chicago Herald-American*, September 10, 1944, p. 10; Alley, E. "Illness of First Gas 'Victim' Blamed for Wave of Hysteria in Mattoon." *Chicago Herald-American*, September 17, 1944, p. 3; "Chicago Psychiatrist Analyzes Mattoon Gas Hysteria." *Chicago Herald-American*, September 17, 1944, p. 3.

8. "...Seen by Kearney." *Daily Journal-Gazette*, September 2, 1944, p. 1.

9. *Ibid.*

10. The *Daily Journal-Gazette,* hereafter referred to in the main text as the *Journal-Gazette* is the paper's popular name and appears on the banner. Its official full title is the *Daily Journal-Gazette and Commercial-Star.* In 1944, it was an independent newspaper published every evening except Sunday and holidays in the Journal-Gazette Building, 1711 Charleston Avenue, Mattoon.

11. Johnson, D.M. (1945). p. 180.

12. "Mattoon's Phantom 'Suggestive' Fear." *Chicago Herald-American,* September 21, 1944, p. 2.

13. *Ibid.*

14. *Ibid.*

15. *Ibid.*

16. "Anesthetic Prowler on Loose," p. 6.

17. *Ibid.*

18. *Ibid.*

19. Anonymous (1944). "The Madman of Mattoon." *Newsweek,* p. 47.

20. "Anesthetic Prowler Adds Victim." *Daily Journal-Gazette,* September 6, 1944, p. 1; "Intensify Hunt for Paralysis Gas Prowler." *Chicago Tribune,* September 7, 1944, p. 15.

21. "'Mad Gasser' Adds Six Victims! 5 Women and Boy Latest Overcome." *Daily Journal-Gazette,* September 9, 1944, p. 1.

22. "Safety Agent to Aid Police in 'Gas' Case." *Daily Journal-Gazette,* September 6, 1944, p. 6.

23. Johnson, D.M. (1945). p. 181.

24. *Ibid.*

25. *Ibid.*

26. "Mattoon Gets Jitters from Gas Attacks." *Chicago Herald-American,* September 10, 1944, p. 1.

27. Ballenger, C. "Mattoon's Gas Fiend Attacks Girl, 11, in Home." *Chicago Daily Tribune,* September 9, 1944, p. 10.

28. "'Mad Anesthetist' Strikes Again!" *Daily Journal-Gazette,* September 7, 1944, p. 1.

29. "...Additional Victims." *Daily Journal-Gazette,* September 8, 1944, p. 1.

30. *Ibid.*

31. *Ibid.*

32. *Ibid.*

33. *Ibid.* "...Appears Near Midnight." *Chicago Daily Tribune,* September 8, 1944, p. 6.

34. "Letter to the Editor," *Daily Journal-Gazette,* September 8, 1944, p. 2.

35. "Hurt in Search for Prowler." *Daily Journal-Gazette,* September 8, 1944, p. 6.

36. "Mad Prowler Takes It Easy for Night." *Daily Journal-Gazette,* September 8, 1944, p. 1.

37. "Sidelights of 'Mad Gasser's' Strange Case." *Daily Journal-Gazette,* September 12, 1944, p. 4.

38. My thanks to Keay Davidson for pointing out this association.

39. "State Men Here to Aid in Gas Case." *Daily Journal-Gazette,* September 7, 1944, p. 12.

40. *Ibid.*

41. "Mattoon Fiend Fells Two More with Poison Gas." *Chicago Daily Tribune,* September 8, 1944, p . 6; p. 12.

42. "...Same Sensations." *Daily Journal-Gazette,* September 7, 1944, p. 1.

43. "Mattoon's Mad Anesthetist." *Daily Journal-Gazette,* September 8, 1944, p. 2.

44. "Mattoon Gets Jitters from Gas Attacks." *Chicago Herald-American,* September 10, 1944, p. 1.

45. "Many Prowler Reports; Few Real. City Calmer After Wild Week-End." *Daily Journal-Gazette,* September 11, 1944, p. 1.

46. "'Chasers' to Be Arrested." *Daily Journal-Gazette,* September 11, 1944, p. 1.

47. "Two Girls Gassed." *Chicago Daily Tribune,* September 11, 1944, p. 12.

48. "State Police Join Gas Maniac Hunt." *Chicago Herald-American,* September 12, 1944, p. 4.

49. "To All Citizens of Mattoon." *Daily Journal-Gazette*, September 11, 1944, p. 1.
50. Anonymous. (1944). "At Night in Mattoon." *Time*, Volume 44(12), pp. 23–24.
51. "Sidelights of 'Mad Gasser's' Strange Case." *Daily Journal-Gazette*, September 12, 1944, p. 4.
52. "'Mad Gasser' Adds Six Victims! 5 Women and Boy Latest Overcome." *Daily Journal-Gazette*, September 9, 1944, p. 1.
53. *Ibid.*
54. "Gas Outside House. " *Daily Journal-Gazette*, September 9, 1944, p. 1.
55. "Gas Terror Grows." *Chicago Herald-American*, September 12, 1944, p. 1.
56. "Two Women Believed Victims Examined at Hospital." *Daily Journal-Gazette*, September 11, 1944, p. 1.
57. Erickson, G. "Gas Terror Grows." *Chicago Herald-American*, September 12, 1944, p. 1.
58. *Ibid.*, p. 1.
59. *Ibid.*
60. Ballenger, C. "Gas Spraying Phantom Hits 2 More Homes." *Chicago Daily Tribune*, September 11, 1944, p. 12.
61. "State Police Join Gas Maniac Hunt," op cit., p. 4.
62. *Ibid.*, p. 12.
63. *Ibid.*, p. 4.
64. "Mad Marauder of Mattoon is 5 Day a Week Man." *Illinois State Journal*, September 11, 1944, p. 7.
65. Anonymous (1944). "The Madman of Mattoon." *Newsweek*, p. 47.
66. M'Hugh, L. "Ape Man Clue at Mattoon." *Chicago Herald-American*, September 16, 1944, p. 3.
67. *Ibid.*
68. I am grateful to Bob Ladendorf for uncovering this information.
69. *Ibid.*, p. 1.
70. Ballenger, C. "FBI at Mattoon as Gas Prowler Attacks 5 More." *Chicago Daily Tribune*, September 10, 1944, p. 15; *Ibid.*, p. 1.
71. "'Mad Gasser' Case Limited to 4 Suspects." *Daily Journal-Gazette*, September 12, 1944, p. 1.
72. Johnson, D. (1945). p. 177.
73. Erickson, G. "Mad Gasser Called Myth." *Chicago Herald-American*, September 13, 1944, p. 1.
74. "'Gasser' Case 'Mistake,'" *Daily Journal-Gazette*, September 12, 1944, p. 4; "Police Chief Says Sprayer Tales Hoax." *Illinois State Journal*, September 13, 1944, p. 1.
75. *Ibid.*
76. Ballenger, C. "Assail Police for Calling Gas Scare a Hoax." *Chicago Daily Tribune*, September 14, 1944, p. 18.
77. *Ibid.*
78. *Ibid.*
79. "Atlas Statement.", *Daily Journal-Gazette*, September 13, 1944, p. 1.
80. *Ibid.*
81. "Suspect Woman Gas Terrorist. Find Prints of High-Heeled Shoes." *Chicago Herald-American*, September 15, 1944, p. 3.
82. "'Mad Gasser' Case Limited to 4 Suspects." *Daily Journal-Gazette*, September 12, 1944, p. 1.
83. "Debunk Mattoon Gas Scare." *Chicago Herald-American*, September 13, 1944, p. 4.
84. *Ibid.*
85. Schiff, S.D. (1980). *Mad Scientists: An Anthology of Fantasy and Horror*. Garden City, New York: Doubleday, p. ix.
86. *Ibid.*, p. 1.
87. "Press Search for Mattoon Prowler." *Illinois State Journal*, September 12, 1944, p. 5.
88. "Mattoon Will-o'-the-Wisp." *Daily Journal-Gazette*, September 14, 1944, p. 1.

89. "Police Get Two False Alarms During Night." *Daily Journal-Gazette*, September 13, 1944, p. 1.

90. *Ibid.*

91. "Cole Amplifies Statement." *Daily Journal-Gazette*, September 13, 1944, p. 1.

92. Alley, E. "Credulity Seat of Mattoon's Terror." *Chicago Herald-American*, September 20, 1944, p. 4.

93. Johnson, D. (1945). pp. 177–78.

94. Anonymous (1944). *Time*, pp. 23–24.

95. "Study Terror in Mattoon." *Chicago Herald-American*, September 18, 1944, p. 1.

96. Anonymous (1931). "United States Army Extension Courses, Special Text No. 17." *Medical Aspects of Chemical Warfare*, section I, p. 2.

97. "No Gas, Not Even Madman Seen During Night." *Daily Journal-Gazette*, September 15, 1944, p. 6.

98. "Death Toll at 25; At Least 65 Injured." *Daily Journal-Gazette*, September 14, 1944, p. 1; "Toll of Train Crash at 29." *Daily Journal-Gazette*, September 14, 1944, p. 10.

99. *Ibid.*, p. 6.

100. "The 'Perfumed City' Speaks,'" *Daily Journal-Gazette*, September 20, 1944, p. 2.

101. *Ibid.*

102. Anonymous (1944). *Time*, p. 23.

103. "Letter to the Editor,'" *Daily Journal-Gazette*, September 26, 1944, p. 2.

104. "Letter to the Editor,'" *Daily Journal-Gazette*, September 29, 1944, p. 2.

105. "All Quiet on Mattoon's 'Gas Front,'" *Daily Journal-Gazette*, September 14, 1944, p. 1.

106. Baynes, H. G. (1941). *Germany Possessed*. London: Jonathan Cape.

107. Norman, E. H. (1945). "Mass Hysteria in Japan." *Far Eastern Survey* 14 (6):65–70.

108. Brown, W. (1944). "The Psychology of Modern Germany." *British Journal of Psychology* 34:43–59. See p. 59.

109. Cartwright, F.F., and M.D. Biddiss (1972). *Disease and History*. New York: Thomas Y. Crowell, pp. 208–10.

110. Asch, S.E. (1955). "Opinions and Social Pressure." *Scientific American* 193:31–35; Zimbardo, P.G. (1972). "Pathology of Imprisonment." *Society* 9:4–8; Sherif, M., and O.J. Harvey (1952). "A Study in Ego-Functioning: Elimination of Stable Anchorages in Individual and Group Situations." *Sociometry* 15:272–305.

111. Kren, G. (1978–1979). "Psychohistory and the Holocaust." *Journal of Psychohistory* 6:409–417; Asher, H. (1979). "Non-Psychoanalytic Approaches to National Socialism." *The Psychohistory Review* 7 (3):13–21.

112. Neugebauer, R. (1978). "Treatment of the Mentally Ill in Medieval and Early Modern England: A Reappraisal." *Journal of the History of the Behavioral Sciences* 14:158–69; Schoeneman, T. J. (1984). "The Mentally Ill Witch in Textbooks of Abnormal Psychology: Current Status and Implications of a Fallacy." *Professional Psychology Research and Practice* 15 (3):299–314; Spanos, N. P. (1978). "Witchcraft in Histories of Psychiatry: A Critical Analysis and an Alternative Conceptualization." *Psychological Bulletin* 85:417–39.

113. Boyer, S., and S. Nissenbaum (1974). *Salem Possessed*. Cambridge, Massachusetts: Harvard University Press, pp. xii–xiii.

114. Wolf, M.S. (1976). "Witchcraft and Mass Hysteria in Terms of Current Psychological Theories." *Journal of Practical Nursing and Mental Health Services* 14 (3):23–28.

115. Schoeneman, T.J. (1982). "Criticisms of the Psychopathological Interpretation of Witch Hunts: A Review." *American Journal of Psychiatry* 139 (8):1028–32. See p. 1030.

116. Letter from Wolfgang Jilek and Louise Jilek-Aall to Robert Bartholomew dated June 7, 2000.

117. *Ibid.*

118. "Hunt Escaped Nazi Here." *Daily Journal-Gazette*, August 31, 1944, p. 12. Wilhelm Zeigler was not taken into custody until the night of the first "gassing." He was arrested by police at a Peotoria, Illinois, tavern ("Nazi Prisoner Caught." *Daily Journal-Gazette*, September 2, 1944, p. 1).

119. "Two Homes Entered." *Daily Journal-Gazette*, August 31, 1944, p. 12.

120. "Robbery Wave Continues." *Daily Journal-Gazette*, September 1, 1944, p. 6.
121. *Ibid.*, p. 2.
122. *Ibid.*
123. Klass, P.J. (1974). *UFOs Explained*. New York: Vintage, pp. 283–84.
124. Loftus, E., and K. Ketcham (1991). *Witness for the Defense: The Accused, the Eyewitness, and the Expert Who Puts Memory on Trial*. New York: St. Martin's Press.
125. "Chemists Trace Mattoon Mad Man's 'Gardenia Gas,'" *Champaign News-Gazette*, September 9, 1944, p. 3.
126. "Letter," *Daily Journal-Gazette*, September 8, 1944, p. 2.
127. *Ibid.*
128. Anonymous (1944). *Newsweek*, p. 47.
129. Miller, D.L. (1985). p. 100.
130. Miller, D.L. (1985). p. 110.
131. My thanks to Keay Davidson for noting this association.
132. For an excellent discussion of paranormal phenomena from the standpoint of mainstream science, see Goode, E. (2000). *Paranormal Beliefs: A Sociological Introduction*. Prospect Heights, Illinois: Waveland Press; Zusne, L., and W.H. Jones (1982). *Anomalistic Psychology*. New Jersey: Lawrence Erlbaum Associates; Alcock, J.E. (1981). *Parapsychology: Science or Magic? A Psychological Perspective*. Toronto: Pergamon Press. Both books are reader-friendly and require no prior knowledge on the subject.
133. United States War Department (1919). *Final Report of General John J. Pershing. Volume 1*, part 1, p. 623.
134. Brown, F.J. (1968). *Chemical Warfare: A Study in Restraints*. Princeton, New Jersey: Princeton University Press.
135. *Ibid.*
136. *Ibid.*, citing the U.S. Congressional Record of 1927.
137. Ewing, R. (1927). "The Legality of Chemical Warfare." *American Law Review* 65:58–76; Fuller, J.F.C. (1928). *On Future Warfare*. London: Sifton Praed and Company Limited; De Madariaga, S. (1929). *Disarmament*. New York: Coward-McCann; Fradkin, E.K. (1929). "Chemical Warfare, Its Possibilities and Probabilities." *International Conciliation* 248:113; Brown, P. (1929). "Newest Weapon." *Commonweal* 9:538–39; Scammell, J. (1929). "Outlawry of Poison Gases in Warfare." *Current History* 30:396–403; Anonymous (1929). "War Gas Calamity in a Healing Clinic." *Literary Digest* 101:32–42; Allen D. (1929). "Our Mobilized War Machine: The Mobilization of Science." *World Tomorrow* 12: 512–14.
138. Kenworthy, J.M. (1930). *New Wars: New Weapons*. London: E. Matthews & Marrot; Hart, L. (1933). *The British Way of War*. New York: Macmillan Company; Lefebure, V. (1931). *Scientific Disarmament*. London: Mundamus; Duffield, M. (1931). *King Legion*. New York: Jonathan Cape and Harrison Smith.
139. Fradkin, E.K. (1934). *The Air Menace and the Answer*. New York: Macmillan Company, p. 1.
140. *Ibid.*
141. For a partial bibliography, see Fradkin (1934). pp. 321–322.
142. Anonymous (1933). *New York Times Index*. New York: R.R. Bowker.
143. *Ibid.*
144. "Gas in the Next War." *New York Times*, January 3, 1933, p. 22.
145. See, for example, Gesner, G.D. (1931). "Morning After." *Forum and Century* 86:240–46; Gilchrist, H.L. (1931). "Effects of Chemical Cases: Research Work of Chemical Warfare Service, U.S. Army." *U.S. Bureau of Labor Statistics Bulletin* 536:293–306; McDarment, C. (1931). "Clouds of Death." *Popular Mechanics* 55:177–79; Mills, J.E. (1932). "Chemical Warfare." *Foreign Affairs* 10:444–52; Anonymous (1932). "False Faces [Gas Masks] for Everyone." *Popular Mechanics* 57:970–71; Anonymous (1932). "New Shelter from Poison Gas Tested in France." *Popular Science Monthly* 121:38; Anonymous (1932). "Chemicals in Warfare." *Literary Digest* 114:32; Anonymous (1932). "Poison Gas." *Review of Reviews* 86:56. Anonymous (1933). "First Aid for Ghouls." *World Tomorrow* 14:55; Moore, J.M. (1933). "War We Intend to Avoid." *Forum* 89:218–23; Phillips, T.R. (1933). "Debunking Mars'

Newest Toys." *Saturday Review of Literature* 205:23; St. John, A. (1934). "Will Gas Destroy Populations in the Next War?" *Literary Digest* 117:17.

146. Cantril, H. (1940 [1947]). *The Invasion from Mars: A Study in the Psychology of Panic.* New Jersey: Princeton University Press, p. 160.

147. Harris, R., and J. Paxman (1991). *A Higher Form of Killing: The Secret Story of Chemical and Biological Warfare.* New York: The Noonday Press, p. 108.

148. *Ibid.*, p. 118.

149. Anonymous (1934). *New York Times Index.*, op cit.

150. Roosevelt, F.D. (1943). "Statement on Poison Gas." *Current History* 4:405; Lindley, E.K. (1943). "Thoughts on the Use of Gas in Warfare." *Newsweek* 22:24; Marshall, J. (1943). "We Are Ready with Gas If the Axis Turns on the Gas." *Collier's* 112:21; Scott, E.W. (1944). "Role of the Public Health Laboratory in Gas Defense." *American Journal of Public Health* 34:275–78; Wood, J.R. (1944). "Chemical Warfare: A Chemical and Toxicological Review." *American Journal of Public Health* 34:455–60; Sanders, V. (1945). "Our Army's Defense Against Poison Gas." *Popular Science* 146:106–11.

151. Brown, F.J. (1968). p. 244.

152. Anonymous (1944). "Should the US Use Gas?" *Time* 42:15.

153. Cousins, N. (1944). "The Poison Gas Boys." *Saturday Review of Literature*, 12.

154. Taylor, L.B., and C.L. Taylor (1985). *Chemical and Biological Warfare.* New York: Franklin Watts, pp. 23–38.

155. "Reports Chlorine Used." *Roanoke Times*, January 21, 1934, p. 15.

156. "Continue Search for 'Gas' Clues. Officers' Test Eliminates Chlorine — Inhabitants Are Highly Keyed." *Roanoke Times*, January 31, 1934, p. 2.

157. Harris, R., and J. Paxman (1991). p. 51.

Chapter 6

1. Cited in Jones, A. (ed.). *Chambers Dictionary of Quotations.* New York: Harper & Row, p. 635.

2. "'Pocket Monsters' Shock TV Viewers into Convulsions." *Japan Times*, December 17, 1997.

3. "Psychiatrists Seek Animation Probe." *Yomiuri Shimbun*, December 19, 1997.

4. Snyder, Janet. "Cartoon Sickens Children." American Broadcasting Corporation News, December 17, 1997; Snyder, Janet. "'Monster' TV cartoon Illness Mystifies Japan." Reuters report, December 17, 1997; "Govt. Launches Probe of 'Monster' cartoon." *Yomiuri Shimbun*, December 18, 1997.

5. Sullivan, K. "Japan's Cartoon Violence; TV Networks Criticized after Children's Seizures." *Washington Post Foreign Service*, December 19, 1997, p. D1.

6. Hayashi, T., T. Ichiyama, M. Nishikawa, H. Isumi, and S Furukawa (1998). "Pocket Monsters, a Popular Television Cartoon, Attacks Japanese Children." *Annals of Neurology* 44 (3):427.

7. Hayashi, et al. (1998). op cit.

8. Quirk, J.A., D.R. Fish, S.J.M. Smith, J. Sander, S.D. Shorvon, and P.J. Allen (1995). "First Seizures Associated with Playing Electronic Screen Games: A Community-based Study in Great Britain." *Annals of Neurology* 37 (6):733.

9. Yamashita, Y., T. Matsuishi, S. Ishida, T. Nishimi, and H. Kato (1998). "Pocket Monsters Attacks Japanese Children via Media." *Annals of Neurology* 44 (3):428.

10. Tobimatsu, S., Y.M. Zhang, Y. Tomoda, A. Mitsudome, and M. Kato (1999). "Chromatic Sensitive Epilepsy: A Variant of Photosensitive Epilepsy." *Annals of Neurology* 45 (6):790.

11. Furusho, J., et al. (1998). "Patient Background of the Pokémon Phenomenon: Questionnaire Studies in Multiple Pediatric Clinics." *Acta Paediatr Jpn* (6) 550–4.

12. Alloy, L.B., J. Acocella, and R. Bootzin (1996). *Abnormal Psychology: Current Perspectives* (seventh edition). New York: McGraw-Hill, p. 584.

13. Wessely, S. (1987). "Mass Hysteria: Two Syndromes?" *Psychological Medicine* 17: 109–120.

14. Smith, H.C.T., and E.J. Eastman (1973). "Outbreak of Abdominal Pain." *Lancet* 11:956–59; Small, G., and J. Borus (1983). "Outbreak of Illness in a School Chorus. Toxic Poisoning or Mass Hysteria?" *New England Journal of Medicine* 308:632–35.

15. Krug, S. (1992). "Mass Illness at an Intermediate School: Toxic Fumes or Epidemic Hysteria?" *Pediatric Emergency Care* 8:280–82; Rockney, R. M., and T. Lemke (1992). "Casualties from a Junior High School During the Persian Gulf War: Toxic Poisoning or Mass Hysteria?" *Journal of Developmental and Behavioral Pediatrics* 13:339–42.

16. Sirois, F. (1982). "Perspectives on Epidemic Hysteria." In *Mass Psychogenic Illness: A Social Psychological Analysis*. Edited by M. Colligan, J. Pennebaker and L. Murphy. Hillsdale, New Jersey: Lawrence Erlbaum, pp. 217–36.

17. Garnier, S. (1895). *Barbe Buvee, en Religion, Soeur Sainte-Colombe et la Pretendue Possession des Ursulines d'Auxonne* [Barbe Buvee, and Religion, Sister Columbe and the Feigned Possession of the Ursulines at Auxonne]. Paris: Felix Alcan; Calmeil, L.F. (1845). *De la Folie, Consideree Sous le Point de vue Pathologique, Philosophique, Historique et Judiciaire* [On the Crowd, Considerations on the Point of Pathology, Philosophy, History and Justice]. Paris: Baillere.

18. Norman, E.H. (1945). "Mass Hysteria in Japan." *Far Eastern Survey* 14 (6):65–70.

19. Norinaga cited in Norman (1945), p. 68.

20. Hecker, J.F.C. (1970[1837]). *The Dancing Mania of the Middle Ages*, translated by B. Babington. New York: B. Franklin.

21. Mora, G. (1963). "A Historical and Socio-Psychiatric Appraisal of Tarantism." *Bulletin of the History of Medicine* 37:417–39.

22. Rosen, G. (1968). *Madness in Society*. London: Routledge and Kegan Paul; Rosen, G. (1962). "Psychopathology in the Social Process: Dance Frenzies, Demonic Possession, Revival Movements and Similar so-called Psychic Epidemics. An Interpretation." *Bulletin of the History of Medicine* 36:13–44.

23. Mora, G. (1963). pp. 436–38.

24. Araki, S., and T. Honma (1986). "Mass Psychogenic Systemic Illness in School Children in Relation to the Tokyo Photochemical Smog." *Archives of Environmental Health* 41:159–162; Araki, S., T. Aman, K. Ushio, and T. Honma (1974). "Respiratory Alkalosis Associated with 'Photochemical Air Pollution in Tokyo (Tokyo Smog).'" *Japanese Journal of Public Health* 21:75–80; Daido, Shozo (1969). "Epidemic Hysteria with Hyperventilation Syndrome." *Journal of the Japanese Psychosomatic Society* 9:42.

25. Ikeda, Y. (1966). "An Epidemic of Emotional Disturbance Among Leprosarium Nurses in a Setting of Low Morale and Social Change." *Psychiatry* 29:152–64.

26. Wessely, S. (1995). "Hysteria After Gas Attacks." *The Times* (London), July 4, p. 14a.

27. Massey, E.W., W.L. Brannon, Jr., and T.L. Riley (1981). "The 'Jerks': Mass Hysteria or Epilepsy?" *Southern Medical Journal* 74 (5):607–9. See p. 609.

28. Pollock, G., and T.M. Clayton (1964). "Epidemic Collapse: A Mysterious Outbreak in 3 Coventry Schools." *British Medical Journal* ii:1625–27.

29. Radovanovic, Z. (1995). "On the Origin of Mass Casualty Incidents in Kosovo, Yugoslavia, in 1990." *European Journal of Epidemiology* 11:1–13.

30. Moore, S., and M. Ramirez (1998). "3 Sickened Pacoima Students Ingested LSD, 11 Other Hospitalized 4th Graders Had No Drugs in System." *Los Angeles Times*, September 25, 1998; telephone conversation between Robert Bartholomew and Solomon Moore, March 14, 2000.

31. Sinks, T., P.R. Kerndt, and K.M. Wallingford (1989). "Two Episodes of Acute Illness in a Machine Shop." *American Journal of Public Health* 79:1024–28.

32. Cartter, M.L., P. MsHar, and H. Burdo (1989). "The Epidemic Hysteria Dilemma." *American Journal of Diseases in Childhood* 143:89; Nitzkin, J.L. (1976). "Epidemic Transient Situational Disturbance in an Elementary School." *Journal of the Florida Medical Association* 63:357–59; Roueche, B. (1978). "Annals of Medicine." *The New Yorker* 21:63–70.

33. Hocking, B. (1990). "An Epidemic of Illness in an Indian Telephone Exchange." *Journal of the Indian Medical Association* 88(10):281–85.

34. Philen, R.M., E.M. Kilbourn, and T.W. McKinley (1989). "Mass Sociogenic Illness by Proxy: Parentally Reported in an Elementary School." *Lancet* ii:1372–76.

35. "Govt. Launches Probe of 'Monster' Cartoon." *Yomiuri Shimbun*, December 18, 1997.

36. Millett, C.J., D.R. Fish, and P.J. Thompson (1997). "A Survey of Epilepsy-Patient Perceptions of Video-Game Material/Electronic Screens and Other Factors as Seizure Precipitants." *Seizure* 6 (6):457–59.

37. McLuhan, M. (1962). *The Gutenberg Galaxy: The Making of Typographic Man.* Toronto: University of Toronto Press.

38. Bartholomew, Robert E. (1998). "The Martian Panic Sixty Years Later: What Have We Learned?" *Skeptical Inquirer* 22 (6):40–43.

39. Bartholomew, Robert E. (2000). "Re: Epidemic Hysteria Versus Collective Delusions: A Crucial Distinction." *American Journal of Epidemiology* 151 (2):206–7.

40. Cohen, Jeffrey. Personal correspondence, December 7, 1999.

41. Barr, J. (1983). "A Survey of Ecstatic Phenomena and 'Holy Spirit Movements' in Melanesia." *Oceania* 54:109–32; Robin, R. (1981). "Revival Movement Hysteria in the Southern Highlands of Papua New Guinea." *Journal for the Scientific Study of Religion* 20 (2):150–63; Worsley, P. (1957). *The Trumpet Shall Sound: A Study of 'Cargo' Cults in Melanesia.* London: MacGibbon and Kee; Williams, F.E. (1923). "The Vailala Madness and the Destruction of Native Ceremonies in the Gulf Division." *Papuan Anthropology Reports No. 4,* Port Moresby, New Guinea: Government Printer.

42. Owino, W. "Mass Hysteria Causes School's Temporary Closure." *Panafrican News Agency,* March 8, 2000; Adomakoh, C.C. (1973). "The Pattern of Epidemic Hysteria in a Girls' School in Ghana." *Ghana Medical Journal* 12:407–11; Muhangi, J.R. (1973). "Mass Hysteria in an Ankole School." *East African Medical Journal* 50:304–9; Ebrahim, G.J. (1968). "Mass Hysteria in School Children, Notes on Three Outbreaks in East Africa." *Clinical Pediatrics* 7:437–38; Anonymous (1966). "Two Schools Close in Tanzania Till Siege of Hysteria Ends." *New York Times,* May 25, p. 36; Kagwa, B. H. (1964). "The Problem of Mass Hysteria in East Africa." *East African Medical Journal* 41:560–66; Anonymous (1963). "Laughing Malady a Puzzle in Africa. 1000 Along Lake Victoria Afflicted in 18 Months—Most Are Youngsters. Schools Close Down." *New York Times,* August 8, 1963, p. 29; Rankin, A.M., and P.J. Philip (1963). "An Epidemic of Laughing in the Buboka District of Tanganyika." *Central African Journal of Medicine* 9:167–70.

43. Ong, A. (1988). "The Production of Possession: Spirits and the Multinational Corporation in Malaysia." *American Ethnologist,* 15:28–42; Ong, A. (1987). *Spirits of Resistance and Capitalist Discipline: Factory Women in Malaysia.* Albany, New York: State University of New York Press; Lee, R.L., S.E. Ackerman (1980). "The Socio-Cultural Dynamics of Mass Hysteria: A Case Study of Social Conflict in West Malaysia." *Psychiatry* 43:78–88; Ackerman, S.E. (1980). "Cultural Process in Malaysian Industrialization: A Study of Malay Women Factory Workers." Ph.D diss., University of California at San Diego. Ann Arbor, Michigan: University Microfilms; Lee, R.L. (1979). "The Social Meaning of Mass Hysteria in West Malaysia and Singapore." Ph.D diss., University of Massachusetts; Ackerman, S.E., and R.L. Lee (1978). "Mass Hysteria and Spirit Possession in Urban Malaysia: A Case Study." *Journal of Sociology and Psychology* 1:24–35; Teoh, J.I., E.S. Tan (1976). "An Outbreak of Epidemic Hysteria in West Malaysia." In *Culture-bound Syndromes, Ethnopsychiatry, and Alternate Therapies, Volume IV of Mental Health Research in Asia and the Pacific.* Edited by W.P. Lebra. Honolulu: University Press of Hawaii, pp. 32–43; Teoh J., S. Soewondo, and M. Sidharta (1975). "Epidemic Hysteria in Malaysia: An Illustrative Episode." *Psychiatry* 8 (3):258–68; Teoh, J.I., and K. Yeoh (1973). "Cultural Conflict in Transition: Epidemic Hysteria and Social Sanction." *Australia and New Zealand Journal of Psychiatry* 7:283–95; Tan, E.S. (1963). "Epidemic Hysteria." *Medical Journal of Malaya* 18:72–76.

44. Kerckhoff, A.C., and K.W. Back (1968). *The June Bug: A Study of Hysterical Contagion.* Englewood Cliffs, New Jersey: Prentice-Hall; Champion, F.P., R. Taylor, P.R. Joseph, and J.C. Heddon (1963). "Mass Hysteria Associated with Insect Bites." *Journal of the South Carolina Medical Association* 59:351–53.

45. Eastwell, H.D. (1979). "A Pica Epidemic: A Price for Sedentarism Among Australian Ex-Hunter-Gatherers." *Psychiatry* 42:264–73.

46. McLuhan, M. (1964). *Understanding Media: The Extension of Man*. New York: McGraw-Hill.

Chapter 7

1. Gordon, B.L. (1959). *Medieval and Renaissance Medicine*. New York: Philosophical Library, p. 562.
2. Hecker, J.F.C. (1844). *Epidemics of the Middle Ages*, translated by B. Babington. London: The Sydenham Society; Rosen, G. (1968). *Madness in Society*. London: Routledge and Kegan Paul; Sirois, F. (1982). "Perspectives on Epidemic Hysteria." In *Mass Psychogenic Illness: A Social Psychological Analysis*. Edited by M. Colligan, J. Pennebaker and L. Murphy. Hillsdale, New Jersey: Lawrence Erlbaum, pp. 217–36.
3. Goldenson, R.M. (1973). *Mysteries of the Mind: The Drama of Human Behavior*. Garden City, New York: Doubleday, p. 146.
4. Gloyne, H.F. (1950). "Tarantism: Mass Hysterical Reaction to Spider Bite in the Middle Ages." *American Imago* 7:29–42. See p. 29.
5. Schadewaldt, H. (1971). "Musik und Medizin" (Music and Medicine). *Arztliche Praxis* 23:1846–51, 1894–97.
6. De Martino, E. (1966). *La Terre du Remords* (The Land of Self-Affliction), translated by Claude Poncet. Paris: Gallimard.
7. Gallini, C. (1988). *La Ballerina Variopinta: Une Festa Guarigione in Sardegna* (The Multicolored Dancer: A Healing Festival in Sardinia). Naples: Liguori.
8. Sigerist, H.E. (1943). *Civilization and Disease*. Ithaca, New York: Cornell University Press, pp. 218–19.
9. Sigerist, H.E. (1943). p. 218; Rosen, G. (1968). p. 204.
10. Gloyne, H.F. (1950). p. 35.
11. Lewis, I.M. (1991). "The Spider and the Pangolin." *Man* 12 (3):513–25. See p. 514; De Martino, E. (1966). op cit.
12. Russell, J.F. (1979). "Tarantism." *Medical History* 23:404–25. See p. 416.
13. Lewis, I.M. (1991) p. 517.
14. Sigerist, H.E. (1943) p. 221.
15. Hecker, J.F.C. (1844) p. 87.
16. Kaplan, H.I., and B.J. Sadock (eds.) (1985). *Comprehensive Textbook of Psychiatry*. Volume 2. Baltimore: Williams and Wilkins, p. 1227.
17. Carson, R.C., J.N. Butcher, and S. Mineka (1998). *Abnormal Psychology and Modern Life* (tenth edition). New York: HarperCollins, p. 37.
18. Comer, R.J. (1996). *Fundamentals of Abnormal Psychology*. New York: W.H. Freeman and Company, p. 9.
19. Mora, G. (1963). "A Historical and Socio-Psychiatric Appraisal of Tarantism." *Bulletin of the History of Medicine* 37:417–39.
20. Carson, R.C., et al. (1998) p. 37.
21. Rosen, G. (1968). op cit.
22. Rust, F. (1969). *Dance in Society: An Analysis of the Relationship Between the Social Dance and Society in England from the Middle Ages to the Present Day*. London: Routledge and Kegan Paul, p. 20.
23. Bartholomew, R.E. (1998). "Dancing with Myths: The Misogynist Construction of Dancing Mania." *Feminism & Psychology* 8 (2):173–83.
24. Backman, E.L. (1952) p. 331.
25. *Ibid.*, p. 290.
26. *Ibid.*, p. 210.
27. Russell, J.F. (1979) p. 413.
28. Hecker, J.F.C. (1970 [1837]). *The Dancing Mania of the Middle Ages*, translated by B. Babington. New York: B. Franklin, p. 4.
29. *Ibid.*, p. 6.

30. *Ibid.*, p. 6.
31. Haggard, H.W. (1934). *The Doctor in History*. New Haven, Connecticut: Yale University Press, p. 187.
32. Backman, E.L. (1952) p. 147.
33. Rust, F. (1969) p. 22.
34. Hecker, J.F.C. (1970 [1837]) pp. 3–4.
35. Gallini, C. (1988). op cit.
36. De Martino, E. (1966). op cit.
37. Donaldson, L.J., J. Cavanagh, and J. Rankin (1997). "The Dancing Plague: A Public Health Conundrum." *Public Health* 111:201–4.
38. Lidz, T. (1963). "Hysteria." Pp. 818–26. In *The Encyclopedia of Mental Health*. Volume 3. Edited by A. Deutsch and H. Fishman. New York: Franklin Watts, see p. 822; Millon, T., and R. Millon (1974). *Abnormal Behavior and Personality: A Biosocial Learning Approach*. Philadelphia: W.B. Saunders, p. 22.
39. McGrew, R.E., and M.P. McGrew (1985). *Encyclopedia of Medical History*. New York: McGraw-Hill, p. 84.
40. *Ibid.*
41. Weir, E. (2000). "Raves: A Review of the Culture, the Drugs and the Prevention of Harm." *Canadian Medical Association Journal* 162 (13):1843–48.
42. Sigerist, H. E.. (1943). op cit.
43. Hecker, J.F.C.. (1970[1837]) p. 4.
44. Russell, J.F. (1979). op cit.

Chapter 8

1. Jilek, W.G. (1986). "Epidemics of 'Genital Shrinking' (*Koro*): Historical Review and Report of a Recent Outbreak in Southern China." *Curare* 9:269–82. See p. 276.
2. Gwee, A.L. (1968). "*Koro*—Its Origin and Nature as a Disease Entity." *Singapore Medical Journal* 9 (1):3–6. See p. 3.
3. Van Wulfften-Palthe, P.M. (1936). "Psychiatry and Neurology in the Tropics." In *Clinical Textbook of Tropical Medicine*. Edited by C. de Langen and A. Lichtenstein. Batavia: G. Kolff and Company, pp. 525–36. See p. 536.
4. Van Wulfften-Palthe, P.M. (1936). op cit.
5. Rin, H. (1965). "A Study of the Aetiology of *Koro* in Respect to the Chinese Concept of Illness." *International Journal of Social Psychiatry* 11:7–13.
6. Yap, P.M. (1965). "*Koro*—A Culture-bound Depersonalization Syndrome." *British Journal of Psychiatry* 111:43–50.
7. El Fakharani, M. (1980). "*Koro*—Ein Syndrom im Kulturwandel: Beobachtungen auf der ost-Indonesischen Insel Flores" [*Koro*—A Culture-specific Syndrome Observed on the Indonesian Island of Flores] *Curare* 3:241–44.
8. Edwards, J.W. (1985). "Indigenous Koro, a Genital Retraction Syndrome of Insular Southeast Asia." In *The Culture-Bound Syndromes*. Edited by R. Simons and C. Hughes. Dordrecht: D. Reidel, pp. 169–191.
9. Legendre, J. (1908). "Une Curieuse Epidemie" [A Curious Epidemic]. *Annales de Medecine Coloniale* 2:280.
10. Gwee, A.H., et al. (1969). "The *Koro* 'Epidemic' in Singapore." *Singapore Medical Journal* 10 (4):234–42.
11. Murphy, H.B.M. (1982). *Comparitive Psychiatry*. Berlin/Heidelberg/New York: Springer.
12. Mun, C.I. (1968). "Epidemic *Koro* in Singapore." "Letter." *British Medical Journal* i:640–41.
13. Jilek, W.G. (1986). op cit.; Tseng, W.S., K.M. Mo, J. Hsu, L.S. Li, L.W. Ou, G.Q. Chen, and D.W. Jiang (1988). "A Sociocultural Study of *Koro* Epidemics in Guangdong, China." *American Journal of Psychiatry* 145 (12):1538–43; Tseng, W. S., K.M. Mo, L.S. Li,

G.Q. Chen, L.W. Ou, and H.B. Zheng (1992). "*Koro* Epidemics in Guangdong, China: A Questionnaire Survey." *The Journal of Nervous and Mental Disease* 180 (2):117–23.

14. Buber, M. (1946). "Introduction." Pp. 9–13. In *Chinese Ghost and Love Stories, a Selection from the Liao Chai Stories by Pu Sung-Ling.* Edited and translated by R. Quong. New York: Pantheon Books.

15. Tseng, W.S., et al. (1988) p. 1540.

16. *Ibid.*, p. 122.

17. Jilek, W.G., and L. Jilek-Aall (1977a). "A *Koro* Epidemic in Thailand." *Transcultural Psychiatric Research Review* 14:56–59. See p. 58; Jilek, W.G., and L. Jilek-Aall (1977b). "Massenhysterie mit *Koro*-Symptomatik in Thailand" (Mass Hysteria with *Koro* Symptoms in Thailand). *Schweizer Archiv Neurologie Neurochirurgie und Psychiatrie* 120 (2): 257–59.

18. Suwanlert, S., and D. Coates (1979). "Epidemic *Koro* in Thailand — Clinical and Social Aspects." Abstract of the report by F.R. Fenton appearing in *Transcultural Psychiatric Research Review* 16:64–66.

19. Andelman, D. "Thai Junta Re-Examines Relations with Neighbor Nations and U.S." *New York Times*, October 18, 1976; Andelman, D. "Vietnam Accuses Thai Regime and Demands That It Free 800." *New York Times*, October 28, 1976, p. 30.

20. Andelman, D. "Campaign Grows Against Vietnamese in Thailand Region." *New York Times*, December 12, 1976, p. 3.

21. Jilek, W.G., and L. Jilek-Aall (1977a) p. 58.

22. Suwanlert and Coats (1979) p. 65.

23. Dutta, H., R. Phookan, and P.D. Das (1982). "The *Koro* Epidemic in Lower Assam." *Indian Journal of Psychiatry* 24:370–74; Sachdev, P.S., and A. Shukla (1982). "Epidemic *Koro* Syndrome in India." *Lancet* ii:1161; Nandi, D.N., G. Banerjee, H. Saha, and G.C. Boral (1983). "Epidemic *Koro* in West Bengal, India." *International Journal of Social Psychiatry* 29:265–68; Chakraborty, A., S. Das, and A. Mukherji (1983). "*Koro* Epidemic in India." *Transcultural Psychiatric Research Review* 20:150–51; Chakraborty, A. (1984). "An Epidemic of Koro in West Berngal, India." *Transcultural Psychiatric Research Review* 21:59–61; Sachdev, P.S. (1985). "*Koro* Epidemic in Northeast India." *Australian and New Zealand Journal of Psychiatry* 19:433–38.

24. Chakraborty et al. (1983). op cit.

25. Chowdhury, A.N., P. Pal, A. Chatterjee, M. Roy, and B.B. Das-Chowdhury (1988). "Analysis of North Bengal *Koro* Epidemic with Three-Year Follow Up." *Indian Journal of Psychiatry* 30:69–72; Chowdhury, A.N. (1991). "Medico-Cultural Cognition of *Koro* Epidemic: An Ethnographic Study." *Journal of the Indian Anthropological Society* 26:155–70.

26. Chowdhury, A.N. (1994). "*Koro* in Females: An Analysis of 48 Cases." *Transcultural Psychiatric Research Review* 31:369–80.

27. Chakraborty, A. (1990). "Identity, Land and Sex." Pp. 222–226. In C.N. Stefanis, C.R Soldatos and A.D. Rabavilas (eds.). *Psychiatry: A World Perspective.* (Volume 4). Amsterdam: Elsevier.

28. Ilechukwu, S.T.C. (1988). "Letter from S.T.C. Ilechukwu, M.D. (Lagos, Nigeria) Which Describes Interesting *Koro*-like Syndromes in Nigeria." *Transcultural Psychiatric Research Review* 25:310–14.

29. Ilechukwu, S.T.C. (1992). "Magical Penis Loss in Nigeria: Report of a Recent Epidemic of a *Koro*-like Syndrome." *Transcultural Psychiatric Research Review* 29:91–108. See p. 95.

30. *Ibid.*, p. 95.

31. *Ibid.*, p. 313.

32. *Ibid.*, pp. 96–97.

33. *Ibid.*, pp. 101–2.

34. Kraepelin, E. (1909). *Psychiatrie — Ein Lehrbuch fur Studierende and Arzte* [Psychiatry — A Textbook for Students and Physicians] (eighth edition, volume 1, Section I.B). Leipzig: J.A. Barth.

35. Emsley, R.A. (1985). "*Koro* in Non-Chinese Subject." *British Journal of Psychiatry* 146:102.

36. Devan, G.S., and Hong, O.S. (1987). "*Koro* and Schizophrenia in Singapore."

British Journal of Psychiatry 150:106–7; Edwards, J.G. (1970). "The *Koro* Pattern of Depersonalization in an American Schizophrenic Patient." *American Journal of Psychiatry* 126 (8):1171–73; Gittelson, N.L., and S. Levine (1966). "Subjective Ideas of Sexual Change in Male Schizophrenics." *British Journal of Psychiatry* 112:1171–73.

37. Kendall, E.M., and P.L. Jenkins (1987). "*Koro* in an American Man." *American Journal of Psychiatry* 144 (12):1621.

38. Cremona, A. (1981). "Another Case of *Koro* in a Briton." *British Journal of Psychiatry* 138:180.

39. Berrois, G.E., and S.J. Morley (1984). "*Koro*-like Symptoms in a Non-Chinese Subject." *British Journal of Psychiatry* 145:331–34.

40. Bartholomew, R.E. (1998). "The Medicalization of Exotic Deviance: A Sociological Perspective on Epidemic *Koro*." *Transcultural Psychiatry* 35 (1):5–38; Bartholomew, R.E. (1994). "The Social Psychology of 'Epidemic' *Koro*." *International Journal of Social Psychiatry* 40:44–60.

41. Oyebode, F., M.J. Jamieson, and K. Davison (1986). "*Koro*—A Psychophysiological Dysfunction." *British Journal of Psychiatry* 148:212–14; Thase, M.E., C.F. Reynolds, and J.R. Jennings (1988). "Nocturnal Penile Tumescence Is Diminished in Depressed Men." *Biological Psychiatry* 24:33–46.

42. Ross, D.F., J.D. Read, and M.P. Toglia (1994). *Adult Eyewitness Testimony: Current Trends and Developments*. Cambridge: Cambridge University Press; Buckhout, R. (1980). "Nearly 2000 Witnesses Can Be Wrong." *Bulletin of the Psychonomic Society* 16:307–10; Loftus, E.F. (1979). *Eyewitness Testimony*. Cambridge, Massachusetts: Harvard University Press.

43. Sprenger, J, and H. Kramer (1951). *Malleus Maleficarum*, translated with an introduction, bibliography, and notes by Montague Summers. London: Pushkin Press, pp. 119, 136.

Chapter 9

1. Lippman, W. (1922). *Public Opinion*, cited in MacDonnell, F. (1995). *Insidious Foes*. New York: Oxford University Press, p. 2.

2. Creighton, D. (1958). *Dominion of the North: A History of Canada*. London: Macmillan & Company, p. 437.

3. Morton, D. (1974). "Sir William Otter and Internment Operations in Canada during the First World War." *Canadian Historical Review* 55 (1):32–58. See p. 36.

4. MacDonnell, F. (1995) p. 23.

5. *Ibid.*, pp. 25–26.

6. Morton (1974) op cit.

7. Morton (1974), p. 46.

8. Morton (1974), pp. 48–49.

9. Morton (1974), p. 33; Keyserlingk, R.H. (1985). "Agents Within the Gates: The Search for Nazi Subversives in Canada During World War II." *Canadian Historical Review* 66 (2):211–39.

10. MacDonnell (1995), p. 21.

11. Kitchen, M. (1985). "The German Invasion of Canada in the First World War." *International History Review* 7 (2):245–60.

12. Kitchen (1985), p. 246.

13. *Ibid.*

14. *Ibid.*

15. Mount, G.S. (1993). *Canada's Enemies: Spies and Spying in the Peaceable Kingdom*. Toronto: Dundurn Press, p. 40.

16. *Ibid.*

17. "Aeroplane" instead of the present spelling "airplane" was the standard usage at the time.

18. Gibbs-Smith, C.H. (1985). *Aviation: An Historical Survey from Its Origins to the End of World War II*. London: Her Majesty's Stationary Office, p. 152.

19. "Reports Aeroplanes Over Oxford Village, *London Free Press* (Ontario), August 13, 1914, p. 2.

20. "Airship in Western Ontario." *Toronto Star*, August 31, 1914, p. 5.

21. *Ibid.*

22. Presently spelled "Petrolia."

23. "Three Aeroplanes Scan Topography of the Province." *London Free Press*, September 5, 1914, p. 8.

24. *Ibid.*

25. *Ibid.*

26. "Petrolea Planes ... Military Men Say, 'We Shouldn't Worry,'" *London Free Press*, September 5, 1914, p. 2.

27. "Why Get Excited?" *London Free Press*, September 5, 1914, p. 16.

28. "Believe 'Aeroplane' Is an American One." *London Free Press*, September 5, 1914, p. 16.

29. "Mysterious Flyer Now at Hamilton." *London Free Press*, September 12, 1914, p. 5.

30. "Pipe Line Road Saw Rhree Aeroplanes. Mr. Fred Bridge ... and Other People Say They Saw Spies." *London Free Press*, September 11, 1914, p. 9.

31. *Ibid.*

32. "Airships Restricted in Flights in Canada." *Toronto Globe*, September 18, 1914, p. 7; "Asks Permission to Fly Over Ontario." *London Free Press*, September 28, 1914, p. 3.

33. *Niagara Falls Gazette*, September 17, 1914, p. 1.

34. "Had an Aeroplane Scare." *Toronto Star*, October 10, 1914, p. 10.

35. "Aeroplane Reported Hovering Over Soo Locks. Residents Claim to Have Seen Craft Rise from South of American Canal." *Toronto Globe*, October 20, 1914, p. 9.

36. "Soldiers Claim They Saw Airship Over Barracks... Flew Directly Over the Ordnance Stores Department. Men Are Emphatic There Was No Mistake." *London Evening Free Press* (Ontario), October 21, 1914, p. 1.

37. ."Many Reports." *London Evening Free Press*, October 21, 1914, p. 1.

38. "Still See Them, but Military Authorities Are Not Worrying." *London Free Press*, October 23, 1914, p. 2.

39. "Signal Across River?" *Buffalo Express* (Buffalo, New York), November 19, 1914, p. 7.

40. "Seeing Things in Air. Forestville Man Says Two Aeroplanes Went Over Town in Dark." *Buffalo Express*, November 21, 1914, p. 7.

41. "Aeroplane Raid." *Toronto Daily Star*, December 4, 1914, p. 6.

42. "Saw an Aeroplane." *Niagara Falls Gazette* , December 12, 1914, p. 9.

43. "Strange Aeroplane Appears Six Miles from Montreal. Ottawa Officials ... Will Investigate Matter Immediately." *London Evening Free Press*, January 11, 1915, p. 2.

44. "Brockville's Story of the Air craft. Dropped Fireballs as They Crossed River." *Toronto Globe*, February 15, 1915.

45. *Ibid.*

46. *Ibid.*

47. *Ibid.*

48. "Scare in Ottawa Over Air Raid. Parliament Buildings Darkened on Report That Three Aeroplanes Crossed the Border." *New York Times*, February 15, 1915, p. 1.

49. "Were Also Seen at Gananoque." *New York Times*, February 15, 1915, p. 1; "Brockville's Story of the Air Craft." *Toronto Globe*, February 15, 1915.

50. "Ogdensburg Heard of This Friday." *New York Times*, February 15, 1915, p. 1.

51. "Police Force Augmented." *London Evening Free Press*, February 15, 1915, p. 1.

52. "Ottawa Again Dark." *New York Times*, February 16, 1915, p. 4.

53. "Parliament Hill in Darkness." *Toronto Globe*, February 16, 1915, p. 2.

54. "Were Toy Balloons and Not Aeroplanes! Brockville's Latest on Sunday Night's Scare." *Toronto Globe*, February 16, 1915, p. 1.

55. Toy balloons were also referred to as "fire balloons" and were commonly avail-

able at shops selling fireworks. They were composed of paper with candles attached near the mouth, which made them buoyant through the generation of heat.

56. "Were Toy Balloons..." *Toronto Globe*, February 16, 1915, pp. 1–2.
57. *Ibid.*, pp. 1–2.
58. "Air Raid from the States Improbable." *Toronto Globe*, February 16, 1915, p. 7.
59. "Saw Aeroplane ... After Landing, Took Flight Towards Montreal." *London Free Press*, July 6, 1915, p. 1.
60. "Saw an Aeroplane ...Passed Over the Southern Part of City." *London Evening Free Press*, July 17, 1915, p. 3.
61. "People Near Massena, Ont., Spy Strange Lights in Heavens." *London Evening Free Press*, July 20, 1915, p. 9.
62. "Saw Aeroplanes Hovering Over City of Quebec. Fully Creditable Persons Reported to Have Noticed Mysterious Aircraft." *London Evening Free Press*, July 21, 1915, p. 1.
63. "Strange Airships Seen Hovering Near Montreal." *London Evening Free Press*, July 19, 1915, p. 7.
64. *Ibid.*
65. "Point Edward Guard Brings Sown Balloons. Were at First Thought to Be Aeroplanes." *London Evening Free Press*, July 21, 1915, p. 7.
66. "French Believe German Officer 'Flew the Loop.'" *London Evening Free Press*, July 22, 1915, p. 1.
67. "Mysterious Light Passes Tillsonburg." July 23, 1915, p. 2.
68. "Another Aeroplane Seen Over the City." *London Free Press*, August 9, 1915, p. 2.
69. "Two Aeroplanes ... Close to Montreal." *London Evening Free Press*, February 7, 1916, p. 1.
70. "Display in Sky Mistaken for an Aerial Invasion." *London Evening Free Press*, February 14, 1916, p. 12.
71. "Unknown Aviator Surveys Windsor." *London Evening Free Press*, July 7, 1916, p. 14.
72. The most widely cited study of mass delusions remains sociologist Neil J. Smelser's *Theory of Collective Behavior*. New York: The Free Press, 1961. In it, Smelser identifies these common elements as episodes of "mass hysteria."
73. Condon, E.U. and D.S. Gillmor (ed.). (1969). *Scientific Study of Unidentified Flying Objects*. New York: Bantam; Corliss, W.R. (ed.) (1977). *Handbook of Unusual Natural Phenomena*. Glen Arm, Maryland: The Sourcebook Project; Corliss, W.R. (ed.) (1979). *Mysterious Universe: A Handbook of Astronomical Anomalies*. Glen Arm, Maryland: The Sourcebook Project.
74. Sherif, M. (1936). *The Psychology of Social Norms*. New York: Harper & Row.
75. Sabini, J. (1992). *Social Psychology*. New York: W.W. Norton & Company, pp. 24–25.
76. Loftus, E. (1979). *Eyewitness Testimony*. Cambridge, Massachusetts: Harvard University Press; Buckhout, R. (1980). "Nearly 2000 Witnesses Can Be Wrong." *Bulletin of the Psychonomic Society* 16:307–10; Ross, D.F., J. Read, and M.P. (1994). *Adult Eyewitness Testimony: Current Trends and Developments*. Cambridge: Cambridge University Press.
77. Buckhout, R. (1974). "Eyewitness Testimony." *Scientific American*, 231:23–31.
78. For descriptions of other war scares involving phantom aerial objects, refer to the following social science journals. For an examination of an episode of imaginary German monoplanes sighted over British South Africa in 1914, see Bartholomew, R.E. (1989). "The South African Monoplane Hysteria of 1914: A Test of Smelser's Theory of Hysterical Beliefs." *Sociological Inquiry* 59:287–300. Another scare involved "ghost" zeppelins over New Zealand in 1909. See Bartholomew, R.E. (1992). "A Brief History of Mass Hysteria in Australia," *The Skeptic* 12:23–26. Finally, for discussion of a major scare involving phantom V-rockets over Scandinavia shortly after the close of World War II, consult Bartholomew, R.E. (1993). "Redefining Epidemic Hysteria: An Example from Sweden." *Acta Psychiatrica Scandinavica* [The Scandinavian Journal of Psychiatry] 88:178–82.
79. I wish to thank Professor Thomas Bullard, department of folklore, Indiana University at Bloomington, who supplied the press accounts used in this article.

Chapter 10

1. Cited in K.L. Roberts (compiler). (1940). *Hoyt's New Cyclopedia of Practical Quotations.* New York: Funk & Wagnalls, p. 120.

2. Anonymous (1954). "A New Look for Windshields. In Bellingham, Wash. 1,500 Cars Are Damaged by Ghostly Little Pellets." *Life* xxxx:34–35. See p. 34.

3. Medalia, N.Z., and O. Larsen (1958). "Diffusion and Belief in a Collective Delusion." *American Sociological Review* 23:180–86. See p. 183.

4. *Ibid.*

5. *Ibid.*, p. 186.

6. *Ibid.*

7. Edwards, F. (1959). "Britain's Mystery Mile." In *Stranger Than Science.* London: Pan Books, 122–24.

8. "'Bullet' Hit BBC Coach.'" *Evening Standard* (London), December 8, 1950, p.1; "Hell-Fire Pass? Curious Incidents on the Portsmouth Road at Esher." *Esher News and Advertiser*, January 12, 1951, p. 2.

9. *Ibid.*

10. *Ibid.*

11. *Ibid.*

12. "Stones or Bullets?" *Esher News and Advertiser*, January 26, 1951, p. 2.

13. "Shots Start Again on the Portsmouth Road." *Esher News and Advertiser*, December 21, 1951, p. 2.

14. "Mysterious Missiles. Seventh Incident on Portsmouth Road." *Esher News and Advertiser*, February 9, 1951, p. 2.

15. "Shots Start Again on the Portsmouth Road," op. cit., p. 2.

16. *Ibid.*

17. *Ibid.*

18. "Another Car Has Its Windscreen Shattered." *Esher News and Advertiser*, March 14, 1952, p. 2.

19. "'I Felt the Car Rock,' Says Bullet Victim." *Esher News and Advertiser*, March 21, 1952, p. 2.

20. *Ibid.*

21. "Shattered Windscreens." *Esher News and Advertiser*, April 18, 1952, p. 2.

22. "Car's Windscreen Frosted Over." *Esher News and Advertiser*, May 16, 1952, p. 2.

23. May 8 according to Edwards, F. (1959). op cit., but this is probably erroneous.

24. "Sniper Smashes Another Car Windscreen." *Esher News and Advertiser*, May 9, 1952, p. 6.

25. "Aircraft or Airguns?" *Esher News and Advertiser*, June 20, 1952, p. 2.

26. "Windscreen Hit at Esher." *Esher News and Advertiser*, June 6, 1952, p.3.

27. *Ibid.*

28. "Aircraft or Airguns?"

29. "Aircraft or Airguns?"

30. Edwards, F. (1959). pp. 122–24. "The Mystery Develops!" *Esher News and Advertiser*, June 27, 1952, p. 2.

31. "New Windscreen Mystery." *Evening Standard* (London), June 18, 1952, p. 6.

32. "Police Statement Urged." *Esher News and Advertiser*, July 4, 1952, p. 2.

33. "Missiles on Portsmouth Road." *Esher News and Advertiser*, August 1, 1952, p. 3.

34. *Ibid.*

35. "Or Catapults?" *Esher News and Advertiser*, July 11, 1952, p. 2.

36. *Ibid.*

37. "Portsmouth Road 'Missiles.'" *Esher News and Advertiser*, August 22, 1952, p. 2.

38. "Owner Says Car Was Hit by Stone." *Esher News and Advertiser*, December 5, 1952, p. 3.

39. "The Portsmouth Road Mystery." *Esher News and Advertiser*, January 30, 1953, p. 5.

40. "Four 'Missile' Incidents." *Esher News and Advertiser*, April 24, 1953, p. 4.

41. 'The Portsmouth Road Incidents." *Esher News and Advertiser*, February 20, 1953, p. 5.

42. 'Shattered Windscreens." *Esher News and Advertiser*, May 8, 1953, p. 4.

43. "More Windscreens Shattered." *Esher News and Advertiser*, May 15, 1953, p. 4.

44. "Windscreen Bogey Moves to Ealing." *Esher News and Advertiser*, December 11, 1953, p. 3.

45. *Ibid.*, p. 2.

46. *Ibid.*, p. 4.

47. "Supersonic Flight and Sonic 'Bangs.'" *Esher News and Advertiser*, December 5, 1952, p. 3.

48. *Ibid.*, p. 2.

49. *Ibid.*, p. 3.

50. *Ibid.*, p. 2.

51. "Mystery of a Shot." *Evening Standard*, May 4, 1927, p. 13; 55. "Bullet Through Open Window." *Evening Standard*, June 4, 1952, p. 1; "Bullet Breaks Windscreen." *Evening Standard*, June 12, 1952, p. 6.

52. Bowden, F.P., et al. (1964). "The Brittle Fracture of Solids by Liquid Impact, Solid Impact, and by Shock." *Proceedings of the Royal Society, Series A* 282:331–43; Knight, C.G. (1977). "Impact of Small Steel Spheres on Glass Surfaces." *Journal of Materials Science* 12:1573–86; Chaudhri, M.M., and C. Liangyi (1986). "The Catastrophic Failure of Thermally Tempered Glass Caused by Small-Particle Impact." *Nature* 320:48–50.

53. "More 'Missiles.'" *Esher News and Advertiser*, December 19, 1952, p. 4.

54. *Ibid.*, p. 2.

55. "More Windscreens Damaged." *Esher News and Advertiser*, January 4, 1952, p. 2.

56. *Ibid.*, p. 2; *Ibid.*, p. 2; *Ibid.*, p. 2; *Ibid.*, p. 3; "Owner Says Car Was Hit by Stone." *Esher News and Advertiser*, December 5, 1952, p. 3.

57. *Ibid.*, p. 3.

58. *Ibid.*, p. 3

59. "Increased Car Traffic Through Esher." *Esher News and Advertiser*, November 9, 1951, p. 3.

60. Survey carried out on behalf of Edgeguard International Limited., Castle Rock, Colorado, United States of America.

61. Ministry of Transportation and Highways. *Windshield Damage Study*. (1993). Victoria, Canada.

62. *Ibid.*, p. 3; "Taxi Windscreen Starred." *Esher News and Advertiser*, August 22, 1952, p. 2.

63. *Ibid.*, p. 2.

64. *Ibid.*, pp. 2, 28. "More "Missiles." *Esher News and Advertiser*, December 19, 1952, pp. 4, 29. "Missile Strikes Windscreen." January 9, 1953, p. 5.

65. *Ibid.*, p. 2.

66. *Ibid.*, p. 2.

67. Thanks to the staffs of the Esher Library, British Newspaper Library, D.M.S. Watson Science Library, British Automobile Association, *Esher News*, and *Fate Magazine*.

Chapter 11

1. Cited in K.L. Roberts (compiler). (1940). *Hoyt's New Cyclopedia of Practical Quotations*. New York: Funk & Wagnalls, p. 268.

2. Goode, E., and N. Ben-Yehuda (1994). *Moral Panics: The Social Construction of Deviance*. Oxford: Blackwell, p. 12.

3. Cohen, S. (1972). *Folk Devils and Moral Panics: The Creation of the Mods and Rockers*. London: MacGibbon and Key.

4. Victor, J.S. (1998). "Moral Panics and the Social Construction of Deviant Behavior:

A Theory and Application to the Case of Ritual Child Abuse." *Sociological Perspectives* 41 (3):541–65. See p. 542.

5. Rubington, E., and M.S. Weinberg (1973). *Deviance: The Interactionist Perspective* (second edition). New York: The Macmillan Company, vii.

6. Schur, E.M. (1971). *Labeling Deviant Behavior*. New York: Harper & Row, p. 27.

7. Cohen, S. (1972), p. 9.

8. Goode and Ben-Yehuda (1994). op cit.

9. Barlow, H.D. (1993). *Introduction to Criminology* (sixth edition). New York: HarperCollins, p. 258.

10. Goode and Ben-Yehuda (1994), pp. 34–35.

11. Victor (1998), p. 543.

12. Goode and Ben-Yehuda (1994), p. 36.

13. Goode and Ben-Yehuda (1994), pp. 144–84.

14. Victor (1998), p. 546.

15. Victor, J.S. (1993). *Satanic Panic: The Creation of a Contemporary Legend*. Chicago: Open Court; Victor, J.S. (1991). "The Dynamics of Rumor-Panics About Satanic Cults. In *The Satanism Scare*. Edited by James Richardson, J. Best and D. Bromley. New York: Aldine de Gruyter, pp. 221–36; Hicks, R. (1990). "Police Pursuit of Satanic Crime Part II: The Satanic Conspiracy and Urban Legends." *Skeptical Inquirer* 14:378–89.

16. Victor, J.S. (1989). "A Rumor-Panic About a Dangerous Satanic Cult in Western New York." *New York Folklore* 15:23–49.

17. Goode and Ben-Yehuda (1994), p. 144.

18. Victor (1998), p. 548.

19. Winkler, L. (1984). *Catalogue of UFO-like Data Before 1947*. Mt. Ranier, Maryland: Fund for UFO Research, p. 4.

20. Sundelius, B. (ed.) (1982). *Foreign Policies of Northern Europe*. Boulder, Colorado: Westview.

21. Moller, Y. (1986). *Osten Unden: A Biography*. Stockholm: Norstedts, p. 291.

22. Letter from Defense Staff archives from Alice Ahlsen, Fransborg, Barkarby, July 11, 1946.

23. *The Swedish Weather Bureau Yearbook* (1946).

24. *Borlange Tidning*, January 18, 19, 24, 26, and February 2, 1946; *Dala-Demokraten*, January 19, 1946; *Saters Tidning*, January 19, 1946.

25. Vallee, J. (1965). *Anatomy of a Phenomenon: UFOs in Space*. New York: Ballantine, p. 43.

26. "Mystery in the Sky in Skane: 'Wingless, cigar-shaped body' Amazes Landskrona Inhabitants." *Morgon-Tidningen*, May 28, 1946, p. 12. A sighting at about the same time by a Danish border guard near the parish of Rudbbl described a rapidly moving "bright light, followed by a tail." See "The Danes See a Mysterious Fireball Too." *Morgon-Tidningen*, May 29, 1946, p. 7.

27. "Night Workers Took Shelter from the Rocket Bomb in Landskrona." *Aftonbladet*, May 25, 1946; "Rocket Bomb or What?" Strange Aerial Body Over Landskrona." *Landskrona-Posten*, May 25, 1946.

28. "Remote-directed Bombs Haunt Both Here and There." *Morgon-Tidningen*, May 27, 1946; "Ghost Flier or Remote-controlled Bombs?" *Aftontidningen*, May 27, 1946.

29. "Fire-spewing 'Log'— Meteor or Projectile?" *Expressen*, May 25, 1946.

30. "The V-bomb over Landskrona: A Piece of Fireworks?" *Goteborgs-Tidningen*, May 25, 1946.

31. "The Wingless Airplane Could Be a V-bomb." *Dagens Nyheter*, May 26, 1946.

32. "The Ghost Bomb a Serious Threat. 'Monster in Miniature for the Next War,'" *Svenska Dagbladet*, August 7, 1946, p. 7.

33. *Ibid.*

34. Advertisement for *Se* magazine appearing in *Svenska Dagbladet*, August 16, 1946, p. 9.

35. "Around." *Svenska Dagbladet*, August 18, 1946, p. 4.

36. The following appeared in the *Morgon-Tidningen*, July 12, 1946, p. 8: "Trembling

people walk about wondering what will happen.... Limitless is our wonder, no one knows what it will bring, just now upon the sky, here the horned beast was seen.... Terrible is a summer's night, listen to the laughter of the ghosts, when on the wheels of the atom bombs, they play tag in the heavens." A poem in Copenhagen's *Berlingske Tidende*, July 31, 1946, last page, made reference to a recent sensational ghost rocket sighting over Byen, expressing relief that the "rocket" was actually a meteor: "People breathed a little scared in Hong.... It was like a great meteor in and arc over the region below. People thought at once of this rocket which travels so mysteriously.... But surely people can be at ease on Hong. It was not a great power on an expedition of war." On July 12, a poem titled "Anxiety on the Air" appeared in the *Vasterbottens Folkblad*, stating in part: "What is it that's flying here and there...That man can never rest in peace, of atoms and other troublesome things, in a calmer world some may believe—but I, I believe in nothing." Other poems on the ghost rockets include "The Great Riddle." *Stockholms-Tidningen*, August 18, 1946; "The Ghost Rocket in Denmark." *Dagens Nyheter*, August 19, 1946.

37. *Svenska Dagbladet*, September 4, 1946, p. 3; "Swedes Use Radar in Fight on Missiles." *New York Times*, August 13, 1946, p. 4.

38. "Russians Cry 'Slander' to Rocket-firing Charge." *New York Times*, September 4, 1946, p. 10.

39. "The Russians Talk About Lies and Panic." *Svenska Dagbladet*, September 4, 1946, p. 3.

40. "Sic Transit." *Ny Dag*, August 6, 1946.

41. "Sweden Used as a Shooting Range." *Halsingborgs Dagblad*, July 26, 1946.

42. "Rocket, Meteor or Phantom?" *Aftonbladet*, August 7, 1946.

43. "Around." *Morgon-Tidningen*, August 16, 1946, p. 11.

44. Memo titled "Headquarters, Defense Staff Department L (Air Defense) 7:49. June 12, 1946. Reports concerning light phenomena." The memo was issued "[o]n order of the Supreme Commander" and signed by T. Bonde (acting chief of the Swedish Defense Staff) and Nils Ahlgren (head of the Air Defense department of the Swedish Defense Staff).

45. "Enigmatical Paper Find from 'Ghost Bomb.' Dalarma-Varmland Also Has Had Visits." *Morgon-Tidningen*, July 11, 1946, p. 1; "The Military Has a Bomb Fragment," *Svenska Dagbladet*, July 11, 1946, p. 9.

46. For descriptions of "ghost bomb" crashes with "missile" fragments, refer to "The Space Projectile." *Sundsvalls Tidning*, July 13, 1946; "The Njurunda Findings Not Meteorite Stones Declares Research Institute." *Sundsvalls Tidning*, July 14, 1946, p. 1; "Distinct and Good Reports About Bomb and Light Phenomena." *Goteborgs Handels-och Sjofarts Tidning*, July 13, 1946, p. 22; "Space Projectile in Nederkalix." *Svenska Dagbladet*, July 19, 1946, p. 3; "Two Rockets Down in Lake Mjosa." *Aftenposten*, July 19, 1946; "Rocket Bomb Falls in Mjosa." *Svenska Dagbladet*, July 20, 1946, p. 9; "Ghost Rocket Down in Norrbotten Lake. 2-Meter Long Projectile—Huge Pillar of Water." *Norrbottens-Kuriren*, July 20, 1946; "Ghost Projectile Delved for in Norrland Lake." *Svenska Dagbladet*, July 21, 1946, p. 3; "Another Space Projectile Down in Norrbotten Lake." *Norrbottens-Kuriren*, July 22, 1946; "Projectile Crash Also in Njutanger." *Sundsvalls Tidning*, July 23, 1946; "Lake Bottom in the 'Bomb Lake' Searched Through." *Morgon-Tidningen*, July 23, 1946, p. 5; "The Bomb Disappeared into the Water and the Swedes Will Now Empty the Lake." *Arbeiderbladet*, July 30, 1946; "Mysterious Object Has Been Found in Bleklinge." *Sydostra Sveriges Dagblad*, August 5, 1946, p. 1; "Mysterious Fireball Over Stockholm, Crash Seen." *Dagens Nyheter*, August 10, 1946, p. 1; "Cyclist Nearly Struck by Fist-sized 'Ghost Rocket.'" *Morgon-Tidningen*, August 10, 1946, p. 10; "Danes Find Metal Piece of a Ghost Bomb." *Morgon-Tidningen*, August 22, 1946, p. 1.

47. "Sweden's Bomb." *Manchester Guardian*, August 13, 1946, p. 4.

48. "Around." *Svenska Dagbladet*, August 18, 1946, p. 4.

49. "Pit in the Ground a Ghost Bomb Mark?" *Svenska Dagbladet*, August 3, 1946, p. 3.

50. "Mysterious Projectile Falls from the Air." *Svenska Dagbladet*, August 9, 1946, p. 3.

51. "The 'Projectile' Is a Steam Valve Part. Experts Agree." *Svenska Dagbladet*, August 16, 1946, p. 3; "Ghost Bomb Screw a Steam Valve." *Morgon-Tidningen*, August 16, 1946, p. 7.

52. "Ghost Phenomenon Hidden in a Moss in a Blekinge Wood." *Dagens Nyheter*, August 4, 1946.

53. "Military Investigate Mysterious Space Find in Blekinge Islands." *Morgon-Tidningen*, August 5, 1946, last page.

54. "Airplane Antenna Taken for a Ghost Bomb." *Morgon-Tidningen*, August 6, 1946, p. 7; "The Mysterious Find Was an Airplane Antenna." *Sydostra Sveriges Dagblad*, August 6, 1946.

55. "Poisonous Material from Rocket Bombs?" *Morgon-Tidningen*, August 13, 1946, p. 7.

56. Tidningarnas Telegrambyra newswire of July 27, 1946; "Ghost Rocket in the Hen House?" *Stockholms-Tidningen*, July 28, 1946; "Space Projectile Causes a Fire?" *Svenska Dagbladet*, July 28, 1946, p. 5.

57. "MT Continues to Say There Have Been Many Fires ... in the Dry Weather, Some Probably Started by Arson. Sparks Not Ghost Bomb, the True Cause ... a Blasting Cap." *Morgon-Tidningen*, August 1, 1946, p. 3.

58. "Ghost Rocket Crashed a Barn in a Norrland Village." *Goteborgs-Tidningen*, August 12, 1946.

59. "A Tornado Demolished the Barn." *Stockholms-Tidningen*, August 13, 1946.

60. "Ghost Rocket Caused the Svartvik Fire?" *Sundsvalls Tidning*, July 31, 1946; "Ghost Bomb Was Not the Cause of the Svartvik Fire." *Svenska Dagbladet*, August 1, 1946, p. 1.

61. "Over-heating Thought to Have Caused the Svartvik Fire." *Sundsvalls Tidning*, August 16, 1946.

62. Letter from Defense Staff archives dated August 9, 1946.

63. "Did the Accident Plane Collide with a Returning Ghost Rocket?" *Expressen*, August 13, 1946.

64. "Space Rocket Not the Cause for the Valdshult Accident." *Jonkopings-Posten*, July 15, 1946; "Investigation of the B18 Accident: The Pilot Lost Control." *Expressen*, August 16, 1946; "Fatal Accident: The ... Crash Not Because of Space Rocket," *Morgon Tidningen*, August 16, 1946, p. 11.

65. Press release from the Swedish Defense Staff published by the Tidningaras Telegrambyra news agency, October 10, 1946.

66. Liljegren, A., and C. Svahn (1989). "Ghost Rockets and Phantom Aircraft." In *Phenomenon: Forty Years of Flying Saucers*. Edited by J. Spencer and H. Evans. New York: Avon, pp. 53–60.

67. Based on a large number of former secret documents from defense staff archives examined by Anders Liljegren and Clas Svahn. In numerous other cases, local police were ordered to conduct investigations.

68. Orvik, N. (1973). *Europe's Northern Cap and the Soviet Union*. New York: AM; Vayrynen, R. (1972). *Conflicts in Finnish-Soviet Relations: Three Comparative Case Studies*. Tampere: Tampere University.

69. *National Encyclopedia* [of Sweden] (volume 18). Bokforlaget Bra Bocker: Hoganas, p. 11.; "Saw Filers and Ghost Fliers." *Norrbottens-Kuriren*, January 20, 1934.

70. Scott, F. (1977). *Sweden: The Nation's History*. Minneapolis: University of Minnesota Press, p. 399.

71. Lindberg, F. (1958). *Den Svenska utrikespolitikens historia* [History of Swedish foreign policy]. Stockholm: P.A. Norstedt & Soner, pp. 117–19, 123–24, 282–83; Lindberg, F. (1953). *Var sagfilarna Ryska spioner?* [Were the Saw Filers Russian Spies?] *Horde* ni, 341–47.

72. *Ibid*.

73. *Ibid*.

74. "The 'Sawfilers' of the Air Guilty of the Disorder by Mountains and Coasts?" *Vasterbottens Folkblad*, January 10, 1934, p. 1; "The Ghost Fliers of Norrland Soviet-Russian Military Experts! " *Nya Dagligt Allehanda*, January 10, 1934, p. 1; "Soviet Machines That Haunt Us." *Umebladet*, January 11, 1934, p. 1; "Systematic Military Espionage Is the Mission of the Ghost Flier in Norrland." *Aftonbladet*, January 13, 1934, p. 1; "Soviet Machines That Cross Over Swedish Areas? The Boden Fort a Taboo for Strangers. Both Swedish and Norwegian Government Take on Special Measures." *Umebladet*, January 15, 1934, p. 1; "The

Flying X's Soviet-Russian Planes in Spite of Denials." *Norrbottens-Kuriren*, January 16, 1934, p. 4; "The Night Fliers Soviet-Russian." *Umebladet*, January 18, 1934, p. 1; "The Ghost Flier Over Kemi Was a Russian. Finnish Authorities Confirm." *Norrbottens-Kuriren*, January 27, 1934, p. 15; "The Ghost fliers... Base and Depot in the Vicinity of Boris Gleb. " *Aftonbladet*, January 27, 1934, p. 18; "Do Finnish Authorities Have a Solution? Mysterious Light on the Ice Outside Kemi. Is the Flier of Russian Nationality?" *Svenska Dagbladet*, January 28, 1934, pp. 3, 6; "Is Weapons Transport the Ghost Flier's Main Purpose... Russian Base, Thinks Finnish Expert." *Svenska Dagbladet*, January 30, 1934; "Do the Russians Want to Intimidate Scandinavia? The Ghost Raids Russian War Plans, Says Finnish Air Expert." *Aftonbladet*, January 30, 1934, p. 1; "Base of the Ghost Flier." *Nya Dagligt Allehanda*, February 12, 1934, p. 8; "The Secretary of Defense, 'the Ghost Fliers' and the Mysterious Radio Signals." *Nya Dagligt Allehanda*, April 17, 1934.

75. "The Fliers German Front Pilots." *Stockholms-Tidningen*, December 29, 1933, p. 20; "The Hauntings Arranged to Motivate the Demand for New Bombers. Has the Nazi Junker Works and Air Administration Arranged the Matter Together." *Ny Dag*, January 17, 1934, p. 1; "New Theory on the Ghost. German Rockets." *Hufvudstadsbladet*, February 9, 1934, p. 3; "Crossmarked Airplane Seen at Low Level Over Jokkmokk... Only German Machines Carry Crossmarks." *Social-Demokraten*, March 16, 1937.

76. "The Ghost Flier a Japanese Machine. " *Umebladet*, January 23, 1934, p. 3; "The Japanese Warship Near Lofoten?" *Umebladet*, January 24, 1934, p. 1; "The Ghost Flights Now Directed from the White Sea Coasts?" *Vasterbottens-Kuriren*, January 25, 1934; "Japanese Help Cruiser Confirmed Off the Coast of Northern Norway." *Norrbottens-Kuriren*, January 31, 1934, p. 7.

77. "The Mysterious Light Still Haunts. Airplanes Seen in Norway and in the North. What's the Truth? Liquor Traders Attend Their Customers in a Modern Way?" *Vasterbottens Folkblad*, December 27, 1933, p. 1; "The Giant Airplane Goes with Liquor Over Norrland. A Regular Smuggler's Line Between Vasa and Mo in Northern Norway." *Stockholm-Tidningen*, December 28, 1933, p. 1; "Liquor Smugglers Use the Air for Their Own Purposes." *Vasterbottens Folkblad*, December 28, 1933, p. 1; "Finnish Customs Convinced That Smugglers Fly the Atlantic — the Gulf of Bothnia. Transport Cost Would Be Almost Three Crowns Per Litre Through the Air." *Norrlandska Social-Demokraten*, December 28, 1933, p. 1.

78. "Weapons Smuggling by the Mysterious Flights? The Guverte Plateau a Possible Depot." *Nya Dagligt Allehanda*, December 31, 1933, p. 1.

79. *Statens offentliga utredningar* [official Swedish committee reports]. Forsvarsdepartementet [Ministry of Defense] (1995), p. 135; The Submarine Commission, *Ubatsfragan 1981–1994* [The submarine question, 1981–1994]. Published by the Swedish Government: Stockholm.

80. Von Hofsten, H. (1993). *I Kamp mot Overheten* [Struggle Against the Authorities]. Stockholm: T. Fischer & Co.; Agrell, Q. (1986). *Bakom Ubatskrisen. Militar Verksamhet, Krigsplanlaggning och Diplomati i Osterjoomradet* [Behind the Aubmarine Crisis: Military Activity, War Planning and Diplomacy in the Baltic Sea Area]. Stockholm: Liber; Hasselbohm, A. (1984). *Ubatshotet. En Kritisk Granskning av Harsfjardenincidenten och Ubatsskyddskommissionens Rapport* [The Submarine Threat: A Critical Survey of the Harsfjarden Incident and the Report from the Commission for Protection for Submarines]. Prisma: Stockholm; Leitenberg, M. (1987). *Soviet Submarine Operations in Swedish Waters 1980–1986.* Washington D.C.: The Center for Strategic and International Studies, New York: Praeger.

Chapter 12

1. Cited in K.L. Roberts (compiler) (1940). *Hoyt's New Cyclopedia of Practical Quotations.* New York: Funk & Wagnalls, p. 67.

2. Pick, D. (1989). *Faces of Degeneration.* Cambridge: Cambridge University Press; Fernando, S. (1991). *Mental Health, Race and Culture.* Hampshire, England: Macmillan Education Ltd; Fernando, S. (1988). *Race and Culture in Psychiatry.* London: Croom Helm.

3. Fingarette, H. (1988). *Heavy Drinking: The Myth of Alcoholism as a Disease.* Berkeley, California: University of California Press.

4. Rosecrance, J. (1985). "Compulsive Gambling and the Medicalization of Deviance." *Social Problems* 32 (3):275–84.

5. Greenberg, D.F. (1988). *The Construction of Homosexuality.* Chicago: University of Chicago Press; Bayer, R. (1981). *Homosexuality and American Psychiatry: The Politics of Diagnosis.* New York: Basic Books.

6. Cohen, S. (1972). *Folk Devils and Moral Panics: The Creation of the Mods and Rockers.* London: MacGibbon and Key, p. 9.

7. Victor, J.S. (1998). "Moral Panics and the Social Construction of Deviant Behavior: A Theory and Application to the Case of Ritual Child Abuse." *Sociological Perspectives* 41 (3):541–65. See p. 542.

8. Bromley, D.G. (1991). "Satanism: The New Cult Scare." In *The Satanism Scare.* Edited by J. Richardson, J. Best, and D. Bromley. New York: Aldine de Gruyter, pp. 49–72; Victor, J.S. (1991). "The Dynamics of Rumor — Panics about Satanic Cults." In *The Satanism Scare.* Edited by J. Richardson, J. Best, and D. Bromley. New York: Aldine de Gruyter, pp. 221–36.

9. Goode, E., and N. Ben-Yehuda (1994). *Moral Panics: The Social Construction of Deviance.* Oxford: Blackwell, p. 343.

10. Victor, J.S. (1990). "The Spread of Satanic-Cult Rumors." *Skeptical Inquirer* 14 (3):287–91. See p. 290.

11. Hicks, R. (1990). "Police Pursuit of Satanic Crime Part II: The Satanic Conspiracy and Urban Legends." *Skeptical Inquirer* 14:378–89. See p. 387.

12. Victor, J.S. (1989). "A Rumor-Panic about a Dangerous Satanic Cult in Western New York." *New York Folklore* 15:23–49.

13. Goode and Ben-Yehuda (1994). op cit.

14. Bartholomew, R.E. (1997a). "The American Airship Hysteria of 1896-97." In *The UFO Invasion.* Edited by K. Frazier, B. Karr, and J. Nickell. Buffalo, New York: Prometheus Books, pp. 15–28. Originally published in *Skeptical Inquirer* 14 (2):171–81 (1990).

15. Bullard, T.E. (1990). *The Airship File, Supplement II.* Bloomington, Indiana: Self-published; Bullard, T.E. (1983). *The Airship File Supplement I (Ohio, West Virginia, Indiana, Electric Balloons, Canadian and Norwegian Sightings from the World War I Period).* Bloomington, Indiana: Self-published; Bullard, T.E. (1982a). *The Airship File: A Collection of Texts Concerning Phantom Airships and Other UFOs Gathered from Newspapers and Periodicals Mostly During the Hundred Years Prior to Kenneth Arnold's Sighting.* Bloomington, Indiana: Self-published.

16. Bartholomew, R.E. (1991a). "The Quest for Transcendence: An Ethnography of UFOs in America." *Anthropology of Consciousness* 2 (1-2):1–12.

17. McCloy, J.F., and R. Miller (1976). *The Jersey Devil.* Wallingford, Pennsylvania: Middle Atlantic Press.

18. Johnson, D.M. (1945). "The 'Phantom Anesthetist' of Mattoon: A Field Study of Mass Hysteria." *Journal of Abnormal Psychology* 40: 175–86.

19. Jacobs, N. (1965). "The Phantom Slasher of Taipei: Mass Hysteria in a Non-Western Society." *Social Problems* 12:318–28; Goss, M. (1987). *Terror in the North of England.* London, Fortean Times Occasional Paper.

20. Bartholomew, R.E., and G.S. Howard (1998). *UFOs and Alien Contact: Two Centuries of Mystery.* Buffalo, New York: Prometheus Books.

21. Medalia, N.Z., and O. Larsen (1958). "Diffusion and Belief in a Collective Delusion." *Sociological Review* 23: 180–86.

22. Stewart, J.R. (1977). "Cattle Mutilations: An Episode of Collective Delusion." *Zetetic* (presently *Skeptical Inquirer*) 1–2, 55–66.

23. Bartholomew, R.E. (1993). "Redefining Epidemic Hysteria: An Example from Sweden." *Acta Psychiatrica Scandinavica* 88:178–82.

24. Victor, J.S. (1998). op cit.

25. Cohen, S. (1972). op cit.

26. Goode, E. (1992). *Collective Behavior.* New York: Harcourt Brace Jovanovich, p. 143.

27. Lever, J. (1983). *Soccer Madness.* Chicago: University of Chicago Press.

28. Massey, E.W., W.L. Brannon, Jr., and T.L. Riley (1981). "The 'Jerks:' Mass Hysteria or Epilepsy?" *Southern Medical Journal* 74 (5):607–9.
29. Robin, R. (1981). "Revival Movement Hysteria in the Southern Highlands of Papua New Guinea." *Journal for the Scientific Study of Religion* 20 (2):150–63.
30. Stephen, M. (1977). "Cargo Cult Hysteria: Symptoms of Despair or Technique of Ecstasy?" Occasional paper number 1. Research Centre for Southwest Pacific Studies, La Trobe University, Bundoora, Victoria, Australia; Samarin, W.J. (1972). *Tongues of Men and Angels*. New York: Macmillan.
31. Carr, W. (1978). *Hitler: A Study in Personality and Politics*. New York: St. Martin's Press.
32. DaMatta, R. (1984). "Carnival in Multiple Planes." In *Rite, Drama, Spectacle, Festival*. Edited by J.J. MacAloon. Philadelphia, Pennsylvania: ISHI, pp. 210–58.
33. Teoh, J., S. Soewondo, and M. Sidharta. (1975). "Epidemic Hysteria in Malaysia: An Illustrative Episode." *Psychiatry* 8(3):258–68.
34. Goode, E. (1992), p. 388.
35. Berger, P.L., and T. Luckmann (1966). *The Social Construction of Reality*. London: Allen Lane.
36. Goode and Ben-Yehuda (1994), p. 36.
37. Goode and Ben-Yehuda (1994), p. 36.
38. Tumin, M.M., and A.S. Feldman (1955). "The Miracle at Sabana Grande." *Public Opinion Quarterly* 19:124–39; Yassa, R. (1980). "A Sociopsychiatric Study of an Egyptian Phenomenon." *American Journal of Psychotherapy* 34:346–51; Persinger, M., and J. Derr (1989). "Geophysical Variables and Behavior: LIV. Zeitoun (Egypt) Apparitions of the Virgin Mary as Tectonic Strain-Induced Luminosities." *Perceptual and Motor Skills* 68:123–28.
39. Evans-Wentz, W.Y. (1909). *The Fairy Faith in Celtic Countries: Its Psychological Origin and Nature*. Rennes, France: Oberthur; Keightley, T. (1882). *The Fairy Mythology*. London: Longman; Kirk, R. (1815). *The Secret Commonwealth of Elves, Fauns and Fairies*. London: Longman; Bartholomew, R.E. (1989). *UFOlore: A Social Psychological Study of a Modern Myth in the Making*. Stone Mountain, Georgia: Arcturus.
40. Bartholomew (1989). op cit.
41. Bartholomew, R.E. (1991b). "The Symbolic Significance of Modern Myths." *Skeptical Inquirer* 15:430–31.
42. Bullard, T.E. (1989). "UFO Abduction Reports: The Supernatural Kidnap Narrative Returns in Technological Guise." *Journal of American Folklore* 102 (404): 147–70.
43. Bartholomew, R.E. (1997b). "Collective Delusions: A Skeptic's Guide." *Skeptical Inquirer* 21 (3):29–33; Bartholomew, R.E. (1991b). op cit.
44. Healy, T., and P. Cropper (1994). *Out of the Shadows: Mystery Animals of Australia*. Chippendale, New South Wales: Ironbark.
45. Tebbel, John (1952). *The Life and Good Times of William Randolph Hearst*. New York: E.P. Dutton; Hiebert, R., T. Bohn, and D. Ungurait (1974). *Mass Media: An Introduction to Modern Communication Media*. New York: David McKay Company, pp. 209–10.
46. Clarke, I.F. (1986). "American Anticipations: The First of the Futurists." *Futures* 18:584–96. See p. 589.
47. Bullard, T.E. (1982b). *Mysteries in the Eye of the Beholder*. Doctoral dissertation, Indiana University Folklore Department.
48. Bullard, T.E. (1982b), p. 203.
49. Gibbs-Smith, C.H. (1985). *Aviation: An Historical Survey from Its Origins to the End of World War II*. London: Her Majesty's Stationery Office, p. 221.
50. Lore, G., and H. Deneault (1968). *Mysteries of the Skies: UFOs in Perspective*. Englewood Cliffs, New Jersey: Prentice-Hall; Jacobs (1975). op cit.
51. Barlow, H.D. (1993). *Introduction to Criminology* (sixth edition). New York: HarperCollins, p. 258.
52. Umland, Rudolph (1938). "Phantom Airships of the Nineties." *Prairie Schooner* 12:247–60; Welsch, Roger L. (1979). "This Mysterious Light Called an Airship. Nebraska 'Saucer' Sightings, 1897." *Nebraska History* 60 (1):92–113; Jacobs (1975). op cit.; Bullard (1982c). op cit.; Bullard (1983). op cit.; Bullard (1990). op. cit.

53. Gibbs-Smith, C.H. (1985).

54. Jacobs, D.M. (1975). *The UFO Controversy in America*. Bloomington, Indiana: Indiana University Press, pp. 32–33.

55. Clark, J., and L. Coleman (1975). *The Unidentified: Notes Toward Solving the UFO Mystery*. New York: Warner, p. 133.

56. Bullard, T.E. (1998). "Waves." In *The UFO Encyclopedia: The Phenomenon from the Beginning, Volume One: A–K* (second edition). Edited by J. Clark. Detroit, Michigan: Omnigraphics, Incorporated, pp. 1004–23. See pp. 1011–12.

Chapter 13

1. Evans, B. (compiler) (1968). *Dictionary of Quotations*. New York: Delacorte, p. 339.

2. Friedman, S., and D. Berliner (1992). *Crash at Corona*. New York: Paragon House; Randle, K. (1995). *A History of UFO Crashes*. New York: Avon; McGhee, M., and B. Dickeson (1996). *The Gosford File: UFOs over the N.S.W. Central Coast*. Kogarah, New South Wales, Australia: INUFOR.

3. "An Airship Which Rode in a Wagon. Was Planted in a Gulch." *San Francisco Chronicle*, December 4, 1896, p. 5.

4. "Plunged from a Dizzy Height … It Landed Suddenly in a Ditch." *The Call* [San Francisco], December 4, 1896, p. 1; "An Airship in the Mud. Night of Weird Whirrings, Cries and Crashes Behind Twin Peaks." *San Francisco Examiner*, December 5, 1896, p. 1.

5. "An Inquest Now in Order. Air Ship Falls near Bethany and One Man Said to Be Killed," *St. Joseph Daily Herald*, April 6, 1897, p. 5.

6. "Stranger Than Fiction." *Iowa State Register*, April 13, 1897, p. 1.

7. "Is a Clever Fake. Airship Comes Down at Waterloo with One Passenger." *Cedar Rapids Evening Gazette*, April 16, 1897, p. 1.

8. "Hypothetical Fate of the Wonderful Airship," *Nashville Banner*, April 17, 1897, p. 1.

9. "A Windmill Demolishes It." *Dallas Morning News*, April 19, 1897, p. 5.

10. "Airships May Be Uncle Sam's." *The Galveston Daily News* of April 29, 1897, p. 10.

11. *Ibid*.

12. "Testimony by Schoolchildren. A Black Object." [Dunedin] *Evening Star*, July 31, 1909.

13. *Svenska Dagbladet*, February 7, 1934.

14. Good, T. (1997). *Beyond Top Secret*. London: Pan, p. 21.

15. Liljegren, A., and C. Svahn (1989). "Ghost Rockets and Phantom Aircraft." In *Phenomenon: Forty Years of Flying Saucers*. Edited by J. Spencer and H. Evans (eds.), New York: Avon, pp. 53–60.

16. Brunvand, J.H. (1981). *The Vanishing Hitchhiker*. New York: W.W. Norton.

17. I am indebted to Thomas E. Bullard for providing most of the press reports.

Chapter 14

1. Sagan, C. (1980). *Cosmos*. New York: Random House, p. 135.

2. Buckhout, R. (1974). "Eyewitness Testimony." *Scientific American* 231:23–31.

3. Ross, D.F., J.D. Read, and M.P. Toglia (1994). *Adult Eyewitness Testimony: Current Trends and Developments*. Cambridge: Cambridge University Press; Wells, G., and J. Turtle (1986). "Eyewitness Identification: The Importance of Lineup Models." *Psychological Bulletin* 99:320–29; Buckhout, R. (1980). "Nearly 2000 Witnesses Can Be Wrong." *Bulletin of the Psychonomic Society* 16:307–10; Loftus, E. (1979). *Eyewitness Testimony*. Cambridge, Massachusetts: Harvard University Press.

4. Turner, R., and L. Killian (1972). *Collective Behavior*. Englewood Cliffs, New Jersey: Prentice-Hall, p. 35; Krech, D., R.S. Crutchfield, and E.L. Ballschey (1962). *Individual and Society*. New York: McGraw-Hill; Asch, S.E. (1956). *Studies of Independence and Conformity: A Minority of One Against a Unanimous Majority*. Psychological Monographs 70; Sherif, M., and O.J. Harvey (1952). "A Study in Ego Functioning: Elimination of Stable Anchorages in Individual and Group Situations." *Sociometry* 15:272–305.

5. Cantril, H. (1947). *The Invasion from Mars: A Study in the Psychology of Panic*. Princeton, New Jersey: Princeton University Press, pp. 94–95.

6. Markush, R.E. (1973). "Mental Epidemics: A Review of the Old to Prepare for the New." *Public Health Reviews* 2:353–442. See p. 379.

7. Bulgatz, J. (1992). *Ponzi Schemes, Invaders from Mars & More Extraordinary Popular Delusions and the Madness of Crowds*. New York: Harmony Books, p. 129.

8. Loftus, E., and K. Ketcham (1991). *Witness for the Defense: The Accused, the Eyewitness, and the Expert Who Puts Memory on Trial*. New York: St. Martin's Press.

9. Cantril (1947), p. 181.

10. Goode, E. (1992). *Collective Behavior*. New York: Harcourt Brace Jovanovich; Bainbridge, W.S. (1987). "Collective Behavior and Social Movements." In *Sociology*. Edited by R. Stark. Belmont, California: Wadsworth, pp. 544–76.; Miller, D. (1985). *Introduction to Collective Behavior*. Belmont, California: Wadsworth.

11. Cantril (1947), p. 58.

12. *Ibid.*, p. xi.

13. Miller (1985), p. 100.

14. *Ibid.*, p. 106.

15. *Ibid.*, p. 107.

16. Goode (1992), p. 315.

17. Medalia, N.Z., and O. Larsen (1958). "Diffusion and Belief in a Collective Delusion." *Sociological Review* 23:180–86.

18. Bulgatz (1992), p. 137.

19. Anonymous. "'Mars Raiders' Cause Quito Panic; Mob Burns Radio Plant, Kills 15." *New York Times*, February 14, 1949, pp. 1, 7.

20. Bulgatz (1992), p. 139.

21. Noll, R. (ed) (1992). *Vampires, Werewolves, and Demons: Twentieth Century Reports in the Psychiatric Literature*. New York: Brunner/Mazel; Eisler, R. (1951). *Man into Wolf, an Anthropological Interpretation of Sadism, Masochism, and Lycanthropy; A Lecture Delivered at a Meeting of the Royal Society of Medicine*. London: Routledge & Paul.

22. Huxley, A. (1952). *The Devils of Loudun*. New York: Harper and Brothers; Garnier, S. (1895). *Barbe Buvee, en Religion, soeur Sainte-Colombe et la Pretendue Possession des Ursulines d'Auxonne* [Barbe Buvee and Religion, Sister Columbe and the Feigned Possession of the Ursulines at Auxonne]. Paris: Felix Alcan; Calmeil, L.F. (1845). *De la Folie, Consideree Sous le Point de vue Pathologique, Philosophique, Historique et Judiciaire* [On the Crowd, Considerations on the Point of Pathology, Philosophy, History and Justice]. Paris: Baillere.

23. Goode, E., and N. Ben-Yehuda (1994). *Moral Panics: The Social Construction of Deviance*. Oxford: Blackwell; Rosen, G. (1968). *Madness in Society*. London: Routledge and Kegan Paul.

24. Victor, J.S. (1990). "The Spread of Satanic-Cult Rumors." *Skeptical Inquirer* 14(3):287–91; Victor, J.S. (1989). "A Rumor-Panic About a Dangerous Satanic Cult in Western New York." *New York Folklore* 15:23–49.

Chapter 15

1. Cited in Tripp, R.T. (compiler) (1970). *The International Thesaurus of Quotations*. New York: Thomas Y. Crowell, p. 238.

2. For general descriptions of convent outbreaks during this period, see Calmeil, L.F. (1845). *De la Folie, Consideree Sous le Point de vue Pathologique, Philosophique, Historique et Judiciaire* [On the Crowd, Considerations on the Point of Pathology, Philosophy, History and Justice]. Paris: Baillere; Madden, R.R. (1857). *Phantasmata or Illusions and Fanaticisms of Protean Forms Productive of Great Evils.* London: T.C. Newby; Davy, R.B. (1880). "'St. Vitus' Dance and Kindred Affection; The Recent Epidemic at the Ursulin Convent in Brown County, Ohio; A Sketch of the Historic Disease." *Cincinnati Lancet and Clinic* 4:440–45, 467–73; Garnier, S. (1895). *Barbe Buvee, en Religion, Soeur Sainte-Colombe et la Pretendue Possession des Ursulines d'Auxonne* [Barbara Buvee and Religion, Sister Columbe and the Feigned Possession of the Ursulines at Auxonne]. Paris: Felix Alcan; Loredan, J. (1912). *Un Grand Proces de Sorcellerie au XVIIe siecle, L'Abbe Gaufridy et Madeleine de Demandolx (1600–1670)* [The Grand Process of Witchcraft in the Seventeenth Century, L'Abbe Gaufridy and Madeleine de Demandolx (1600-1670)]. Paris: Perrin et Cie; Rosen, G. (1968). *Madness in Society.* London: Routledge and Kegan Paul; Rosen, G. (1962). "Psychopathology in the Social Process: Dance Frenzies, Demonic Possession, Revival Movements and Similar So-called Psychic Epidemics. An Interpretation." *Bulletin of the History of Medicine* 36:13–44; Thomas, K. (1971). *Religion and the Decline of Magic.* London: Weidenfeld and Nicolson.

3. Huxley, A. (1952). *The Devils of Loudun.* New York: Harper and Brothers; De Certeau, M. (1970). *La Possession de Loudun* [The Possession of Loudun]. Julliard: Collection Archives.

4. Robbins, R.H. (1966). *The Encyclopedia of Witchcraft and Demonology.* New York: Crown, pp. 408–14.

5. Robbins, R.H. (1966), p. 393.

6. Hecker, J.F.C. (1844). *Epidemics of the Middle Ages*, translated by B. Babington. London: The Sydenham Society, p. 127.

7. Darnton, R. (1984). *The Great Cat Massacre and Other Episodes in French Cultural History.* New York: Basic Books.

8. Small, G.W., and A.M. Nicholi (1982). "Mass Hysteria Among Student Performers: Early Loss as a Predisposing Factor." *Archives of General Psychiatry* 39:721–24; Selden, B.S. (1989). "Adolescent Epidemic Hysteria Presenting as a Mass Casualty, Toxic Exposure Incident." *Annals of Emergency Medicine* 18(8):892–95; Taylor, B.W., and J.E. Werbicki (1993). "A Case of Mass Hysteria Involving 19 Schoolchildren." *Pediatric Emergency Care* 9:216–17; Krug, S. (1992). "Mass Illness at an Intermediate School: Toxic Fumes or Epidemic Hysteria?" *Pediatric Emergency Care* 8:280–82. Cole, T.B. (1990). "Pattern of Transmission of Epidemic Hysteria in a School." *Epidemiology* 1:212–18; Philen, R.M., E.M. Kilbourn, and T.W. McKinley (1989). "Mass Sociogenic Illness by Proxy: Parentally Reported in an Elementary School." *Lancet* ii:1372–76; Small, G.W., D.T. Feinberg, D. Steinberg, and M.T. Collins (1994). "A Sudden Outbreak of Illness Suggestive of Mass Hysteria in Schoolchildren." *Archives of Family Medicine* 3:711–16; Baker, P., and D. Selvey (1992). "Malathioinduced Epidemic Hysteria in an Elementary School." *Veterinary and Human Toxicology* 34:156–60.

9. Goh, K.T. (1987). "Epidemiological Enquiries into a School Outbreak of an Unusual Illness." *International Journal of Epidemiology* 16 (2):265–70. See p. 269.

10. Tam, Y.K., M.M. Tsoi, G.B. Kwong, and S.W. Wong (1982). "Psychological Epidemic in Hong Kong, Part 2, Psychological and Physiological Characteristics of Children Who Were Affected." *Acta Psychiatrica Scandinavica* 65:437–49.

11. Smith, H.C.T., and E.J. Eastham (1973). "Outbreak of Abdominal Pain." *Lancet* 2:956–58.

12. Araki, S., and T. Honma (1986). "Mass Psychogenic Systemic Illness in School Children in Relation to the Tokyo Photochemical Smog." *Archives of Environmental Health* 41:159–62.

13. Amin, Y., E. Hamdi, and V. Eapen (1997). "Mass Hysteria in an Arab Culture." *International Journal of Social Psychology* 43 (4):303–6.

14. Rockney, R.M., and T. Lemke (1992). "Casualties from a Junior High School During the Persian Gulf War: Toxic Poisoning or Mass Hysteria?" *Journal of Developmental and Behavioral Pediatrics* 13:339–42.

15. Sinks, T., P.R. Kerndt, and K.M. Wallingford (1989). "Two Episodes of Acute Illness in a Machine Shop." *American Journal of Public Health* 79:1024–28; Colligan, M.J., and L.R. Murphy (1979). "Mass Psychogenic Illness in Organizations: An Overview." *Journal of Occupational Psychology* 52:77–90; Boxer, P.A., M. Singal, and R.W. Hartle (1984). "An Epidemic of Psychogenic Illness in an Electronics Plant." *Journal of Occupational Medicine* 26:381–85; Boxer, P.A. (1985). "Occupational Mass Psychogenic Illness: History, Prevention, Management." *Journal of Occupational Medicine* 27:867–72.

16. Stahl, S., and M. Lebedun (1974). "Mystery Gas: An Analysis of Mass Hysteria." *Journal of Health and Social Behavior* 15:44–50; Stahl, S.M. (1982). "Illness as an Emergent Norm or Doing What Comes Naturally." In *Mass Psychogenic Illness: A Social Psychological Analysis*. Edited by M. Colligan, J. Pennebaker and L. Murphy. Hillsdale, New Jersey: Lawrence Erlbaum, pp. 183–98.

17. Alexander, R.W., and M.J. Fedoruk (1986). "Epidemic Psychogenic Illness in a Telephone Operator's Building." *Journal of Occupational Medicine* 28:42–45.

18. Colligan, M.J., and M.A. Urtes (1978). *An Investigation of Apparent Mass Psychogenic Illness in an Electronics Plant*. National Institute for Occupational Safety and Health; Colligan, M.J., M.A. Urtes, C. Wisseman, R.E. Rosensteel, T.L. Anania, and R. Hornung (1979). "An Investigation of Apparent Mass Psychogenic Illness in an Electronics Plant." *Journal of Behavioral Medicine* 2:297–309.

19. Sinks, T., P.R. Kerndt, and K.M. Wallingford (1989). "Two Episodes of Acute Illness in a Machine Shop." *American Journal of Public Health* 79:1024–28.

20. Johnson, D.M. (1945). "The 'Phantom Anesthetist' of Mattoon: A Field Study of Mass Hysteria." *Journal of Abnormal Psychology* 40:175–86; Radovanovic Z. (1995). "On the Origin of Mass Casualty Incidents in Kosovo, Yugoslavia, in 1990." *European Journal of Epidemiology* 11:1–13; McLeod, W.R. (1975). "Merphos Poisoning or Mass Panic?" *Australian and New Zealand Journal of Psychiatry* 9:225–29; David, A.S., and S.C. Wessely (1995). "The Legend of Camelford: Medical Consequences of a Water Pollution Accident." *Journal of Psychosomatic Research* 39:1–9, 67; Christophers, A.J. (1982). "Civil Emergency Butyl Mercaptan Poisoning in the Parnell Civil Defence Emergency: Fact or Fiction." *New Zealand Medical Journal* 95:277–78; Gamino, L.A., G.R. Elkins, and K.U. Hackney (1989). "Emergency Management of Mass Psychogenic Illness." *Psychosomatics* 3 (4): 446–49.

21. Goldsmith, M.F. (1989). "Physicians with Georgia on Their Minds." *Journal of the American Medical Association* 262:603–4;

22. Bentham, J. (1789). *An Introduction to the Principles of Morals and Legislation*. London: Pickering.

23. Shweder, Richard A. (1984). "Anthropology's Romantic Rebellion Against the Enlightenment, or There's More to Thinking Than Reason and Evidence." In *Culture Theory: Essays on Mind, Self and Emotion*. Edited by Richard Shweder and Robert LeVine. New York: Cambridge University Press, pp. 27–66. See p. 28.

24. Sherif, M., and O.J. Harvey (1952). "A Study of Ego Functioning: The Elimination of Stable Anchorages in Individual and Group Situations." *Sociometry* 15:272–305; Asch, S.E. (1955). "Opinions and Social Pressure." *Scientific American* 193:31–35.

25. Festinger, L. (1950). "Informal Social Communications." *Psychological Review* 57:271–80. See p. 272.

26. Berger, P.L., and T. Luckmann (1967). *The Social Construction of Reality*. London: Allen Lane.

27. Conner, J.W. (1975). "Social and Psychological Reality of European Witchcraft Beliefs." *Psychiatry* 38:366–80.

28. Smith, M., M. Colligan, and J. Hurrell (1978). "Three Incidents of Industrial Mass Psychogenic Illness." *Journal of Occupational Medicine* 20:339–400.

29. Colligan, M.J., et al. (1979). op cit.

30. Goldberg, E.L. (1973). "Crowd Hysteria in a Junior High School." *Journal of School Health* 43:362–66.

31. Cole, T.B. (1990). "Pattern of Transmission of Epidemic Hysteria in a School." *Epidemiology* 1:212-218.

32. Goldberg, E.L. (1973). op cit.

33. McEvedy, C. P., A. Griffith, and T. Hall (1966). "Two School Epidemics." *British Medical Journal* ii:1300–02; Moss, P.D., and C.P. McEvedy (1966). "An Epidemic of Overbreathing Among Schoolgirls." *British Medical Journal* ii:1295–1300.

34. Knight, J.A., T.I. Friedman, and J. Sulianti (1965). "Epidemic Hysteria: A Field Study." *American Journal of Public Health* 55:858–65; Colligan, M.J., et al. (1979). op cit.

35. Olson, W.C. (1928). "Account of a Fainting Epidemic in a High School." *Psychology Clinic* 18:34–38; Olczak, P., E. Donnerstein, T. Hershberger, and I. Kahn (1971). "Group Hysteria and the MMPI." *Psychological Reports* 28:413–14; Teoh, J., S. Soewondo, and M. Sidharta (1975). "Epidemic Hysteria in Malaysia: An Illustrative Episode." *Psychiatry* 8 (3):258–68; Tam, Y.K., M.M. Tsoi, G.B. Kwong, and S.W. Wong (1982). "Psychological Epidemic in Hong Kong, Part 2, Psychological and Physiological Characteristics of Children Who Were Affected." *Acta Psychiatrica Scandinavica* 65:437–49.

36. Small, G.W., M.W. Propper, E.T. Randolph, and S. Eth (1991). "Mass Hysteria Among Student Performers: Social Relationship as a Symptom Predictor." *American Journal of Psychiatry* 148:1200–5.

37. Goh, K. T. (1987). op cit.

38. Small, G.W., et al. (1991). op cit.; Small, G.W., and A.M. Nicholi (1982). "Mass Hysteria Among Student Performers: Early Loss as a Predisposing Factor." *Archives of General Psychiatry* 39:721–24.

39. Small, G., and J. Borus (1983). "Outbreak of Illness in a School Chorus. Toxic Poisoning or Mass Hysteria?" *New England Journal of Medicine* 308:632–35.

40. Knight, J.A., T.I. Friedman, and J. Sulianti (1965). op cit.; Michaux, L., Lemperiere, T., and Juredieu, C. (1952). "Considerations Psychpathologiquessur une Epidemie d'hysterie Convulsive dans un Internat Professionnel" [Considerations of an Epidemic of Convulsive Hysteria in a Boarding School]. *Archives Francaises Pediatrie* 9:987–90.

41. Olson, W.C. (1928). op cit.; Schuler, E.A., and V.J. Parenton (1943). "A Recent Epidemic of Hysteria in a Louisiana High School." *Journal of Social Psychology* 17:221–35; Theopold (1955). "Induzierte Amplexus neuralis bei Madchen einer Schulklasse" [Induced Neural Amplexus in Girls in a School Class]. *Monatsschrift fur Kinderheilkunde* 103.

42. Bartholomew, R.E. (1990b). "Ethnocentricity and the Social Construction of 'Mass Hysteria.'" *Culture, Medicine and Psychiatry* 14 (4):455–94; Bartholomew, R.E. (1993a). "Redefining Epidemic Hysteria: An Example from Sweden." *Acta Psychiatrica Scandinavica* 88:178–82; Bartholomew, R.E. (1994a). "Tarantism, Dancing Mania and Demonopathy: The Anthro-Political Aspects of "Mass Psychogenic Illness." *Psychological Medicine* 24:281–306; Bartholomew, R.E. (1994b). "The Social Psychology of 'Epidemic' *Koro*." *International Journal of Social Psychiatry* 40:44–60; Bartholomew, R.E. (1994d). "When the Consequences of Beliefs Are Defined as Psychiatric Entities." *Journal of Developmental and Behavioral Pediatrics* 15 (1):62–65; Bartholomew, R.E. (1997b). "Epidemic Hysteria: A Dialogue with Francois Sirois." *Medical Principles and Practice* 6:38–44.

43. Faguet, R.A., and K.F. Faguet (1982). "La Folie a Deux." In *Extraordinary Disorders of Human Behavior*. Edited by C.T.H. Friedmann and R. A. Faguet. New York: Plenum Press.

44. Smelser, N.J. (1962). *Theory of Collective Behavior*. New Jersey: Prentice-Hall.

45. Gilbert, A.N. (1975). "Doctor, Patient, and Onanist Diseases in the Nineteenth Century." *Journal of the History of Medicine and Allied Science* 30 (3):217–34.

46. Norman, E.H. (1945). "Mass Hysteria in Japan." *Far Eastern Survey* 14 (6):65–70. See p. 65.

47. Baynes, H.G. (1941). *Germany Possessed*. London: Jonathan Cape; Brown, W. (1944). "The Psychology of Modern Germany." *British Journal of Psychology* 34:43–59.

48. Cartwright, F.F., and M.D. Biddiss (1972). *Disease and History*. New York: Thomas Y. Crowell, p. 210.

49. Boling, L., and C. Brotman (1975). "A Fire Setting Epidemic in a State Mental Health Center." *American Journal of Psychiatry* 132:946–50.

50. Brown, R.W. (1954). "Mass Phenomena." In *Handbook of Social Psychology* (volume 2). Edited by G. Lindzey. Cambridge, Massachusetts: Addison-Wesley, pp. 833–73.

51. A case of an imaginary gasser predating the Botetourt and Mattoon episodes

occurred in 1910 and involved Halley's Comet. Newspaper reports, bolstered by an irresponsible astronomer, claimed that the comet might veil earth in a mist of poison gas. Some alarmed citizens went so far as to stuff rags in doorways. Davidson, K. (1999). Letter to Robert Bartholomew dated February 11; Sagan, C. (1980). *Cosmos*. New York: Random House, p. 80.

Index